HANDBOOK OF RESEARCH ON ENTREPRENEURSHIP POLICY

Handbook of Research on Entrepreneurship Policy

Edited by

David B. Audretsch

Director, Max Planck Institute of Economics, Jena, Germany and Ameritech Chair of Economic Development, Indiana University, Bloomington, USA

Isabel Grilo

Directorate-General for Enterprise and Industry, European Commission, CORE, Université catholique de Louvain, Belgium and GREMARS, Université de Lille 3, France

A. Roy Thurik

Professor of Economics and Entrepreneurship, Erasmus University Rotterdam, The Netherlands and Scientific Advisor of EIM Business and Policy Research (a member of Panteia), Zoetermeer, The Netherlands

PUBLISHED IN ASSOCIATION WITH THE MAX PLANCK INSTITUTE OF ECONOMICS AND EIM BUSINESS & POLICY RESEARCH

Max Planck Institute
of Economics

EIM Business & Policy Research

Edward Elgar
Cheltenham, UK • Northampton, MA, USA

Published by
Edward Elgar Publishing Limited
Glensanda House
Montpellier Parade
Cheltenham
Glos GL50 1UA
UK

Edward Elgar Publishing, Inc.
William Pratt House
9 Dewey Court
Northampton
Massachusetts 01060
USA

A catalogue record for this book
is available from the British Library

Library of Congress Cataloguing in Publication Data

Handbook of research on entrepreneurship policy/edited by David B. Audretsch,
    Isabel Grilo, A. Roy Thurik.
        p. cm. — (Elgar original reference)
    Includes bibliographical references and index.
    1. Entrepreneurship—Government policy. I. Audretsch, David B. II. Grilo,
Isabel. III. Thurik, A.R. (A. Roy).
HB615.H26597   2007
338'.04—dc22

                                                            2007000704

ISBN 978 1 84542 409 1 (cased)

Printed and bound in Great Britain by MPG Books Ltd, Bodmin, Cornwall

Contents

Contributors

David B. Audretsch, Max Planck Institute of Economics, Jena, Germany; Ameritech Chair of Economic Development, Indiana University, Bloomington, Indiana, USA.

Philip E. Auerswald, George Mason University, Fairfax, Virginia, USA.

Iris A.M. Beckmann, Max Planck Institute of Economics, Jena, Germany.

Francis J. Greene, University of Warwick, UK.

Isabel Grilo, Directorate-General for Enterprise and Industry, European Commission, CORE, Université catholique de Louvain, Belgium; GREMARS, Université de Lille 3, France.

Magnus Henrekson, Research Institute of Industrial Economics, Stockholm, Sweden.

Anders N. Hoffmann, Danish Ministry of Economic and Business Affairs, Denmark.

Marcel Hülsbeck, University of Augsburg, Germany.

Erik E. Lehmann, University of Augsburg, Germany.

Albert N. Link, University of North Carolina at Greensboro, USA.

Anders Lundström, Swedish Foundation for Small Business Research, Sweden.

Simon C. Parker, Durham University, Durham, UK.

Jesper Roine, Stockholm School of Economics, Stockholm, Sweden.

Donald S. Siegel, Rensselaer Polytechnic Institute, Troy, New York, USA.

Lois Stevenson, International Development Research Centre, Middle East Regional Office, Cairo, Egypt.

David J. Storey, University of Warwick, UK.

A. Roy Thurik, Centre for Advanced Small Business Economics, Erasmus University Rotterdam; EIM Business and Policy Research, Zoetermeer, The Netherlands; Max Planck Institute of Economics, Jena, Germany.

Charles W. Wessner, National Academies of Science, Washington, DC, USA.

1 Explaining entrepreneurship and the role of policy: a framework*

David B. Audretsch, Isabel Grilo and A. Roy Thurik

Introduction

This book has two cornerstones. The first is that entrepreneurship has emerged as a bona fide focus of public policy, particularly with respect to economic growth and employment creation. For example, the primary role played by entrepreneurship was identified by Romano Prodi during his tenure as President of the European Commission, 'Our lacunae in the field of entrepreneurship needs to be taken seriously because there is mounting evidence that the key to economic growth and productivity improvements lies in the entrepreneurial capacity of an economy' (Prodi, 2002, p. 1).

The European Union does not have a monopoly on the concern about entrepreneurship. From the other side of the Atlantic, Mowery (2005, p. 40) observes:

> During the 1990s, the era of the 'New Economy,' numerous observers (including some who less than 10 years earlier had written off the US economy as doomed to economic decline in the face of competition from such economic powerhouses as Japan) hailed the resurgent economy in the United States as an illustration of the power of high-technology entrepreneurship. The new firms that a decade earlier had been criticized by such authorities as the MIT Commission on Industrial Productivity (Dertouzos et al., 1989) for their failure to sustain competition against large non-U.S. firms were seen as important sources of economic dynamism and employment growth. Indeed, the transformation in U.S. economic performance between the 1980s and 1990s is only slightly less remarkable than the failure of most experts in academia, government, and industry, to predict it.

In fact, it is not just at the broad national level of the European Union or the United States that entrepreneurship has emerged as an important focus of public policy. The view that entrepreneurship is increasingly viewed to be the engine of economic growth and employment creation spans a broad spectrum of national but also regional and local contexts (Carree and Thurik, 2003). Public policy has looked to entrepreneurship to spawn economic growth and foster new jobs. Cities, regions, states and entire countries have turned to entrepreneurship to generate economic development.

The second cornerstone of this book is the observation that neither scholars nor policy makers are presently equipped to understand the public policy role for entrepreneurship (Audretsch, 2007). This is because the scholarly field of economics most concerned with economic growth and (un)employment, macroeconomics, has largely not considered the role that entrepreneurship plays in generating economic growth and employment. At the same time management – the academic discipline most squarely focused on entrepreneurship – has typically not considered implications for the broader economic context, and certainly not the link between that most micro of business phenomena – an individual starting a new business – and the broader macroeconomic performance. This seeming scholarly disconnection has stranded a generation of policy makers looking towards entrepreneurship to deliver economic prosperity and security without the intellectual foundation from which to understand, devise and implement policy.

The purpose of this volume is to provide such a foundation for entrepreneurship policy. In particular, six main questions are addressed:

1. What is entrepreneurship policy?
2. What is the economic rationale for (not) undertaking entrepreneurship policy?
3. Why has entrepreneurship policy become so important?
4. What are the main instruments of entrepreneurship policy?
5. Who implements entrepreneurship policy?
6. What is the impact of entrepreneurship policy and how should it be assessed?

The chapters that follow in this book provide some of the first serious, systematic analyses to address these questions. They do not, however, provide unequivocal, unanimous answers to these questions. This reflects the infancy of the field and early stages of a domain of inquiry where experiments predominate and where the importance of the questions asked prevails over the certainty of the proposed answers. Thus what emerges is a reflection of experienced scholars, serious researchers and dynamic policy makers grappling with a novel question of considerable policy relevance that few had posed just a few years earlier. Hence, this book is a prerequisite for students, scholars and practitioners in the incipient world of entrepreneurship policy.

An important conclusion of this book is that, in fact, entrepreneurship policy is not modernized policy promoting small and medium-sized enterprises (SMEs), or what is termed small business policy in the United States. Such SME or small business policy typically involves specific government agencies mandated with assisting specific types of enterprises (fewer than 500 employees in the case of the United States and fewer than 250 in the European Union).

By contrast this book argues that entrepreneurship policy is considerably more pervasive, embracing a broad spectrum of institutions, agencies and different constituency groups. This stems from the reflection of what Audretsch and Thurik (2001) identified as the shift away from the *managed economy* and towards the *entrepreneurial economy*. This shift has had a significant impact on a series of tradeoffs that range from those related to the competitiveness of large-scale production and economies of scale, to the role of diversity, finance and even geography. One implication arising from Audretsch and Thurik (2001) and confirmed in this book, is that the term 'entrepreneurship policy' is misleading in that it suggests a specific set of instruments are implemented by a restricted set of agencies affecting only a few enterprises or a particular industrial sector. Rather, it follows from Audretsch and Thurik (2001) that, just as the *managed economy* dictated a cohesive policy approach, the *entrepreneurial economy* also mandates a cohesive and pervasive policy approach that spans all facets of society, not just economic policy. The incremental approach would suggest that the rest of the economy – and certainly most aspects of public policy – remains unaltered, but that new instruments are introduced to spur new startups. The conclusions from this book build on the Audretsch and Thurik (2001) insight that what is at stake is not just a few entrepreneurial startup firms, but rather an entire economic approach. The entrepreneurial economy dictates a decidedly new public policy direction that not only spans many, if not most, institutions, but also leaves virtually no aspect of the economy untouched. Thus entrepreneurship policy may actually be less about specific new instruments or agencies and more about how traditional policies and agencies need to be redirected from their traditional role in the managed economy to a very different orientation in the entrepreneurial economy.[1] Thus rather than focus on the addition of entrepreneurship policies to the arsenal of public policy instruments, the debate should perhaps focus instead on the changing role of public policy in the entrepreneurial economy. As Audretsch and Thurik (2001) point out, public policy towards finance, immigration, labor markets, retirement, education, family, wages and income distribution, international trade, health, and social security becomes dramatically different as the entrepreneurial economy replaces the managed economy.

The policy framework
Entrepreneurship is not a field known for its consensus. Scholars have proposed a plethora of definitions and measures (Hébert and Link, 1989; van Praag, 1999; Davidsson, 2004), and the origins of entrepreneurship span a wide spectrum of theories and explanations (Brock and Evans, 1989; Gavron et al., 1998; OECD, 1998; Carree et al., 2002; Parker, 2004; Grilo and Thurik, 2005). Entrepreneurship is a multidimensional concept, the definition of which depends largely on the focus of the research undertaken (Wennekers et al., 2002). However, entrepreneurship scholars appear to agree that the level of entrepreneurial activity varies systematically both across countries and over time (Rees and Shah, 1986; de Wit and van Winden, 1989; Blanchflower and Meyer, 1994; Blanchflower, 2000; Wennekers et al., 2002) and seem to have reached consensus about the 1970s and the 1980s being a turning point in the reversal of a long-term downward trend in entrepreneurship rates (Blau, 1987; Acs and Audretsch, 1993; Acs et al., 1999; Carree and Thurik, 2000; Carree et al., 2002; van Stel, 2005).

Comparing the level of entrepreneurship across nations is difficult for several reasons. The lack of a universally agreed set of indicators (OECD, 1998) and of a generally accepted definition of entrepreneurship makes measurement and comparison of the level of entrepreneurship for different time periods and countries a challenging exercise. One can take a 'static' or a 'dynamic' perspective (Wennekers, 1997; Wennekers and Thurik, 1999). The self-employment or business ownership rate is an important 'static' indicator of the level of entrepreneurship[2] as is the number of small and medium-sized enterprises in a country. The 'dynamic' perspective focuses on nascent and startup activity,[3] as well as on the net entry rate and the turbulence rate (measuring firm entry and exit).

The multidimensional aspects of entrepreneurship include both stock and flow variables (the 'static' and the 'dynamic' aspect) and should distinguish between more qualitative aspects ('mom and pop' entry, high growth ventures, cutting-edge technological firms, etc.). The goals justifying policy intervention (from poverty eradication in developing countries to comparative advantage creation and technological frontier advances in developed countries) are crucial in defining the most relevant dimensions of the variable here summarily called 'entrepreneurship'.

One of the reasons policy makers and scholars have had such little guidance in understanding why entrepreneurship varies both temporally and geographically is that it is inherently an interdisciplinary subject spanning a broad range of fields, including management, finance, psychology, sociology, economics, political science and geography. The interdisciplinary nature of entrepreneurship research reflects a phenomenon that crosses the boundaries of multiple units of observation and analysis, such as the individual, groups, enterprises, cultures, geographic locations, industries, countries, and particular episodes of time. While each particular discipline may be well suited to analyze any particular analytical unit of observation, no discipline is equipped to analyze them all.

In this introductory chapter we present a framework of the determinants of entrepreneurship that attempts to integrate in an orderly way the different strands from the relevant fields of inquiry.

The Framework, inspired by the earlier works of Verheul et al. (2002) and Wennekers et al. (2002), explains the level of entrepreneurship by making a distinction between the supply side of entrepreneurship (labor market perspective, where the capabilities are the outcome) and the demand side of entrepreneurship (product market perspective, where the carrying capacity of the market in terms of business opportunities is the outcome).[4] The Framework integrates those factors shaping the demand for entrepreneurship on the one hand, with those influencing the supply of entrepreneurs on the other. While both the demand and supply sides are influenced by many factors, what results is a level of entrepreneurship that is determined by these two sides. The Framework also creates insight into the role of government policy by identifying the channels of intervention and policy instruments that will shift either the demand or the supply side (curves) (see Figure 1.1).

The determinants of entrepreneurship can be examined from three distinctive levels of analysis – the micro, industry and macro levels of entrepreneurship. The objects of study tied to these levels of analysis are the individual entrepreneur or business, sectors of industry and the national economy, respectively. Studies at the micro level focus on the individuals' decision-making processes and their motives for becoming self-employed. Research into the decisions of individuals to become either wage-earners or self-employed focuses primarily on personal factors, such as psychological traits, formal education and other skills, financial assets, family background and previous work experience. Studies at the industry level of entrepreneurship often focus on market-specific determinants of entrepreneurship, such as profit opportunities and opportunities for entry and exit. The macro perspective focuses on a range of environmental factors, such as technological, economic and cultural variables as well as government regulation. In short, the Framework demonstrates that there are many ways in which the level of entrepreneurship can be influenced.

The business opportunities created by technology developments and demand shifts given resource availability, can *a priori* be exploited either through existing firms[5] or through the creation of new ventures by new entrepreneurs entering the market. The extent to which incumbents rather than new firms fill the market gap created by technological or preference evolution depends on a variety of elements, some of which can be influenced by governmental intervention. Competition policy, protection of intellectual property rights, and the product and labor market regulatory environment are examples of interventions influencing this partitioning of the exploitation of opportunities between incumbent firms and potential new entrants. In Figure 1.1, the 'Business Opportunities' box and its dotted line schematically represent this.

For opportunities to materialize into market entry, potential entrepreneurs have to recognize they exist, possess the ability and resources to pursue them and be willing to do so rather than taking up other potentially rewarding outside options (such as present or alternative employment positions or unemployment).[6] The 'Capabilities' box in Figure 1.1

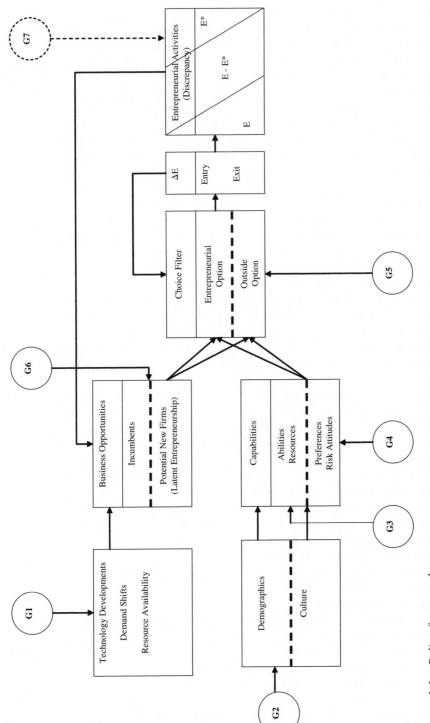

Figure 1.1 Policy framework

represents the individual characteristics of potential entrepreneurs, their abilities, their access to resources necessary to start a business and their intrinsic preferences between leisure and income, as well as their attitudes towards risk.

The 'Choice Filter' box stands for the individual decision process that potential entrepreneurs go through when confronted with the choice between the entrepreneurial venture suggested by the opportunities (that best matches their capabilities) and the best 'outside' option open to them. The risk reward profile of each available option will depend on the entrepreneur's abilities and resource access, while the final arbitrage between the entrepreneurial option and the outside option will be driven by individual preferences and in particular by risk attitudes.[7] This is represented by the arrows linking 'Capabilities' to 'Choice Filter'. Figure 1.1 shows two arrows from 'Business Opportunities' to 'Choice Filter' because the spectrum of available opportunities influences not only the risk–reward profile of the 'best to the individual' entrepreneurial venture, but also the profile of the outside option. This second link takes into consideration the effect that opportunities taken up either by incumbent firms or by other potential entrepreneurs may have on alternative employment possibilities (outside options).

Broadly speaking, the 'Business Opportunities' box can be thought of as the demand for entrepreneurship perspective (which is in the end a derived demand resulting from developments in the services and product markets); while the 'Capabilities' box relates to the supply side of entrepreneurship.[8] Feeding into the 'Capabilities' box we show factors that are not individual-specific but rather aggregate characteristics of the country or society to which the individual belongs. These factors, while having a quantitative demographic dimension as well as a qualitative cultural one, are nevertheless also important in shaping the supply side of entrepreneurship.

The occupational choices made at the individual level materialize as entry and exit rates of entrepreneurship at the aggregate level. Hence, there is an arrow from the 'Choice Filter' box to the 'ΔE' box (Entry and Exit). People have various employment alternatives to evaluate. Employed people can trade in their wage jobs (or unemployment) for self-employment; they can remain in the type of employment they are currently in, or they can exit from self-employment – either voluntarily or involuntarily. These occupational decisions determine the actual level of entrepreneurship, E, in the 'Entrepreneurial Activities (Discrepancy)' box. We assume that there is a feedback effect where entry and exit impact on the occupational choice made in the 'Choice Filter'. According to this 'demonstration effect' the dynamics of entry and exit influence the (perceived) attractiveness of self-employment for individuals. If many people enter self-employment other people may be persuaded to also make that choice, independent of the regular evaluation of the entrepreneurial option versus the outside option on the basis of capabilities and business opportunities for new firms.

The actual rate of entrepreneurship may deviate from the 'equilibrium' rate of entrepreneurship, E* in the 'Entrepreneurial Activities (Discrepancy)' box. There are different views on the factors determining this 'equilibrium' rate (Lucas, 1978; de Wit and van Winden, 1991). Carree et al. (2002) present theoretical and empirical evidence of a long-term relationship between the stage of economic development and the 'equilibrium' level of business ownership,[9] also suggesting that countries where the business ownership rate does not equal the 'equilibrium' rate suffer from a lower rate of macroeconomic growth.[10] In this respect the 'equilibrium' level can also be interpreted as an 'optimal' level.

Many forces may cause the actual number of entrepreneurs to differ from the long-term 'equilibrium' rate (Carree et al., 2002). This discrepancy, $E - E^*$ in the 'Entrepreneurial Activities (Discrepancy)' box, may stem from cultural forces and institutional settings, such as the regulation of entry, incentive structures and the functioning of the capital market (Davis and Henrekson, 1999; Henrekson and Johansson, 1999). The 'discrepancy' can be restored either through market forces or government intervention. The restoring capacity of the market works through (the valuation of) the number and type of business opportunities. Therefore, we have introduced a feedback loop from the 'Entrepreneurial Activities (Discrepancy)' box to the 'Business Opportunities' box to reflect the fact that a surplus or lack of business opportunities may be the consequence of the entry and exit of entrepreneurs in earlier periods. For instance, in the late 1970s and the early 1980s the structurally low number of businesses is likely to have contributed to a high level of unemployment (Carree et al., 2002). A high level of unemployment can push people into self-employment due to the relatively low opportunity costs of entrepreneurship (Evans and Leighton, 1989; Storey, 1991; Audretsch and Thurik, 2000).[11] Moreover, when the number of business owners exceeds the 'equilibrium' rate this is assumed to lead to diminishing profitability, because of increased competition, resulting in higher exit or failure rates and lower entry rates.

Besides the discrepancy between actual and long-term 'equilibrium' entrepreneurship, which can conceivably be bridged through the dynamics set in motion by market forces as described above, one can also take a more normative stance and discuss the concept of E^* from the perspective of the policy-making government. In other words, E^* can also be viewed as the (government)-perceived 'optimal' or target entrepreneurship, the level of which depends on the social choice function of the government, on its perception of the existence of market failures and distortions and on its beliefs concerning the leeway to correct these market failures. These elements will determine the extent to which the government will be willing to intervene in the economy and through which channels the intervention is thought to be most successful. These elements shaping the government-perceived 'optimal' or target entrepreneurship are represented in Figure 1.1 by the dashed circle labeled 'G7'.

The government can try to link the actual and 'equilibrium' rate of entrepreneurship through intervention.[12] Depending on the nature of the (assumed) discrepancy, it can try to intervene using policies that foster or restrict entrepreneurship. Different perspectives exist on the role of the government in the economic process. Austrian and Chicago School theories consider government intervention in the national economy harmful and disturbing, whereas 'antitrust' schools of thought argue that the government has an important role in giving direction to the economic process; that is, addressing market failure. Implicit in the different strands of thought is the argument that government intervention is responsible for either corroding or restoring the discrepancy between actual and long-term 'equilibrium' entrepreneurship. The channels through which policy intervention may occur are dealt with below but first we discuss the economic rationale of intervention.

The economic rationale of public intervention

Even if entrepreneurship is conceivably linked to enhanced economic performance this is no automatic economic justification for public policy intervention. The economic rationale for public intervention relies on the existence of distortions and market failures.[13] In particular, the presence of externalities is an important element leading to market failures in the context of entrepreneurship.

The incipient entrepreneurial culture in European societies has often been identified as one of the reasons for the gap in Europe's entrepreneurial activity relative to the US (Grilo and Irigoyen, 2006; Freytag and Thurik, 2007; Thurik, 2007). The under-development of Europe's entrepreneurial culture has multiple manifestations ranging from the so-called stigma of failure to people's low awareness of entrepreneurship as a career option. Education policy can play a role in changing young people's mindsets and skills by making them more aware and prepared for an entrepreneurial career. Given the alleged externalities associated with education, this in an area where public intervention can be defended as welfare enhancing.[14]

The concept of a 'level playing field' for businesses addresses a possible source of distortions in the treatment of different types of enterprises (according to their size, their sector or their origin). The establishment of a 'level playing field' is therefore an aim of enterprise policy over and above entrepreneurship itself. Taxation rules, labor and product market regulations as well as administrative burdens fall within these parameters.

Access to finance is an aspect where economic theory has identified a strong potential for market failures; the presence of these market failures has been confirmed by empirical work. Because the market for credit is particularly vulnerable to information asymmetries, situations of credit rationing may emerge when these asymmetries are too strong.[15] Because the amount of information about a firm and the cost of obtaining it is not neutral to the firm's size it follows that small and young firms are more exposed to information asymmetries and therefore to credit rationing.

For the US, there is empirical evidence that liquidity constraints are more binding as firm size decreases (Fazzari et al., 1988). This type of evidence has also been found for the UK and other European countries. The case of Germany appears to be different and some authors believe that the bank-based financial system together with the banks' representation on firms' supervisory boards prevents liquidity constraints from being significant.[16] The incipient arrival of high-technology firms in emerging industries in Germany could be attributed to this very system of financing.

Other compelling cases for public intervention in the field of entrepreneurship stem from potential market failures resulting from the existence of three types of externalities: network externalities, knowledge externalities and learning externalities.

Network externalities result from the value of an individual's or a firm's capabilities being conditional on the geographic proximity of complementary firms and individuals. This makes the value of an entrepreneurial firm greater in the (local) presence of other entrepreneurial firms, either because of the existence of a pool of specialized workers or suppliers, or because of increased potential for informational, technological and knowledge spillovers.[17]

Knowledge and the new ideas that it brings about has, at least partially, the nature of a public good. Because of these public good characteristics, private provision will be sub-optimal, opening the case for public intervention. This issue is in part related to intellectual property rights since the non-exclusivity of property,[18] and therefore the non-appropriability of research outcomes, is exacerbated in cases where rights to exploit or commercialize new ideas are not properly assigned.[19]

For firms conducting early-stage research this externality is of exceptional importance and often compounds with market distortions in the credit market, strengthening the rationale for public policies in this area. This theory-driven reasoning is backed by empirical evidence on the higher divergence between social and private research and development (R&D) returns for early-stage research projects.[20]

Finally a subtler source of externalities is the learning effect on third parties resulting from the activity of other firms, even if they fail. Ideas and projects created by failed firms often become integral parts of successful products and projects in other firms. This externality, from which other successful firms benefit, involves no counterpart compensation for the failed firm which can only appropriate the returns to its investment if it succeeds. This effect, together with the positive demonstration effects on potential entrepreneurs, leads to a level of entrepreneurial activity below the optimum (E*).

Clearly, the increasing shift in the comparative advantages of developed, high labor cost economies towards knowledge-based activities has made these sources of market failure a pervasive phenomenon, creating a compelling argument in favor of policies in areas such as venture capital markets, knowledge commercialization, R&D and skill-upgrading efforts, and clustering.

Besides these dedicated policy areas, other horizontal policy domains have also been identified by the European Commission as targets for action in order to improve the business environment and the attractiveness of investing and working in the European Union. The relaunch of the Lisbon strategy by the European Union in 2005 under the Partnership for Growth and Jobs clearly recognizes the importance of private initiative in creating jobs and spurring growth, while at the same time acknowledging the role of governments in setting up the right framework conditions to free investors and workers from unnecessary constraints and to allow them to strive, and by doing so, to generate the jobs and growth required to improve Europe's standards of living.[21]

Channels of public intervention

In our framework of entrepreneurship determinants, policy intervention channels are defined for each of the boxes.

'Channel 1' government intervention, as represented by arrow 'G1' in Figure 1.1, involves the demand side of entrepreneurship. This type of intervention impacts on the type, number and accessibility of entrepreneurial opportunities. A distinction can be made between demand side policies creating room for entrepreneurship and policies affecting the accessibility of markets. Policies stimulating technological developments and income policy belong to the first category of policies, whereas competition policy and establishment legislation pertain to the latter category of policies. The latter type of intervention enables entrepreneurs to make use of the available room and is dealt with under 'Channel 6'. Technological advancements create opportunities for entrepreneurial ventures through new ideas or new application processes. These advancements can be stimulated by the government through (subsidizing) expenditures on R&D. Income policy can create opportunities for entrepreneurship through higher wealth or income disparity, inducing demand for tailor-made products and services and thereby stimulating demand for entrepreneurship. 'Channel 2' government intervention, as represented by arrow 'G2', is intervention affecting the number of potential and future entrepreneurs at the aggregate (population) level, or the 'supply' side. Policies that pertain to 'type 2' intervention include immigration policy and regional development policy (dealing with (sub)-urbanization processes), influencing the composition and the dispersion of the population, respectively. Moreover, the fiscal treatment of families with children, including family allowances or child benefits, may influence the age structure of the population and the number of (potential) entrepreneurs in the long run. 'Channel 3' government intervention, as represented by arrow 'G3', impacts on the abilities and resources of potential entrepreneurs. Government policy can overcome finance and knowledge gaps through increasing the availability of financial and informational resources, respectively. For example, policies aimed at the (development of the) venture capital market can help improve the access of business owners to the financial capital needed to start or expand a business. Direct financial support, such as subsidies, grants and loan guarantees, can also increase the availability of resources of (potential) entrepreneurs. The knowledge base of (potential) entrepreneurs, consisting of both skills and knowledge, can be influenced through the direct provision of relevant 'business' information (i.e. advice and counseling) or through the education system. However, immutable characteristics, such as learning capacity and personality traits, are difficult to develop through education and training.[22] 'Type 3' policies can be typified as input-related policies, since they refer to both material factors, such as financial capital, and immaterial factors, such as knowledge inputs in the entrepreneurial process.

'Channel 4' government intervention, as represented by arrow 'G4', works through the preferences of individuals toward becoming an entrepreneur. Preferences of people, as expressed through values and attitudes, are developed during upbringing. These preferences include their evaluation of risks. Because preferences are, to a large extent, determined by cultural background, they are difficult to influence or modify (OECD, 2000). The government can try to influence individual preferences by fostering an entrepreneurial culture. For example, entrepreneurial values and attitudes can be shaped by introducing entrepreneurial elements in the education system and by paying attention to entrepreneurship in the media. 'Channel 4' policies are characterized by the assumed broadness of the concept of government policy, including the education system, and overlap, to some extent, with culture.

'Channel 5' government intervention, as represented by arrow 'G5', is directed at the decision-making process of individuals who are potential entrepreneurs. Given opportunities, abilities, resources and preferences, the evaluation of the entrepreneurial option versus outside options like unemployment and employment can be influenced by this type of government intervention. Relevant policies are taxation, influencing business earnings; social security arrangements, influencing the willingness of people to give up their present state of (un)employment to become an entrepreneur; and labor market legislation regarding hiring and firing, thereby determining the flexibility of the business and the attractiveness of starting or continuing a business. Bankruptcy policy can also influence the risk–reward profile. For example, when the legal consequences of bankruptcy are severe, this may discourage people from self-employment.

'Channel 6' government intervention, as represented by arrow 'G6', involves intervention on the demand side of entrepreneurship influencing the accessibility of markets. 'Channel 1' policies influence the size of the markets. Competition policy improves the accessibility of markets, for instance through reducing the market power of large firms and lowering barriers to entry for small businesses. Through establishment and bankruptcy legislation the government can also influence the accessibility of markets. When establishment requirements and bankruptcy legislation are strict and opaque (potential) entrepreneurs can be discouraged from filling in the market gaps and opportunities. Protection of property rights and the regulatory environment of product and labor markets are further examples.

Next to the six channels of public intervention discussed above we introduce a seventh element. This concerns the economic or political economy arguments that shape the determination of the level of E*. Schematically, the dashed circle at the top right of Figure 1.1 represents some of the sources of the possible discrepancy between the actual and the 'optimal' or 'equilibrium' level of entrepreneurship that have been discussed in the section dealing with the economic rationale for public intervention. We refer to this element as channel 'G7'.

The chapters of the present book and the channels of government intervention
While all chapters in this book are separately readable and practically all contain a mix of descriptions, justifications and consequences of entrepreneurship policy, some classification can be made. Chapters 2 to 5 (Auerswald, Audretsch and Beckmann, Parker, and Henrekson and Roine) emphasize the rationale of entrepreneurship policy, Chapters 6 to 9 (Stevenson and Lundström, Link, Hoffmann, and Wessner) deal with its role, and Chapters 10 to 12 (Siegel, Hülsbeck and Lehmann, and Greene and Storey) provide specific examples.

In Chapter 2 Auerswald ('The simple economics of technology entrepreneurship: market failure reconsidered') concentrates on the specific set of innovative entrepreneurs and discusses the facts and justifications (normative and positive approach) for supporting early stage technology development. It argues that for these ventures, informational asymmetries at the heart of incomplete contracting are far more important than incomplete appropriability, although this latter category of market failure – leading to R&D spillovers – is more often invoked to justify policy intervention in technology/R&D support. The chapter challenges the claim that, presently, there is enough 'private' funding of early stage technology development for public support not to be needed. The author proposes a shift from using the market failure criterion to justify policy action to the more pragmatic 'additionality' criterion: does the proposed policy action result in private decisions that otherwise would not have been taken, and do these create social benefits that cover the costs incurred (including deadweight losses resulting from revenue gathering)?

The implementation of entrepreneurship policies as a new phenomenon since the 1990s is described in Chapter 3 by Audretsch and Beckmann ('From small business to entrepreneurship policy'). The objective of these policies is to foster economic growth and job creation by stimulating new business startups in particular, and the development of an entrepreneurial economy in general. Looking at previously implemented policy strategies like small business policy, for example, one can see a fundamental shift in economic policy with regard to policy goals, instruments and implementation strategies. The chapter analyzes how and why public policy has turned towards entrepreneurship as a mechanism for generating economic growth and employment. First, differences between previous economic growth strategies and the new entrepreneurship policies are worked out, followed by an analysis of the rationale behind the different economic policies. As there are a great variety of entrepreneurship policies implemented, the chapter provides insights into different entrepreneurship policy strategies using the US and Germany as examples. The chapter concludes that the choice of entrepreneurship policy instruments is determined by context.

In 'Policymakers beware!' (Chapter 4) Parker makes a passionate case against financial support for new and small businesses, using provocative arguments. In particular, he warns against the negative effects of policies that do not anticipate the perverse incentives they create and that are rendered ineffective by the response of private agents. He argues that there is too much entrepreneurship/entry/investment and this should be discouraged be it through taxation of entrepreneurial revenue or of resource cost (using loan/interest taxation to increase capital cost).

In Chapter 5 ('Promoting entrepreneurship in the welfare state') Henrekson and Roine examine how the supply of entrepreneurship and its distribution across activities is affected by the typical tax and welfare arrangements that characterize the mature welfare state. Using Sweden as an illustration, they argue that merely complaining about the negative effects of high taxation and large public programs is insufficient to illustrate their impact since there are positive effects as well. Moreover, welfare environments appear to create particular incentives, directing entrepreneurial activities but curtailing its supply. They conclude that there is room for a mature welfare state to reform itself away from the hostility towards entrepreneurship.

In 'Dressing the emperor: the fabric of entrepreneurship policy' (Chapter 6) Stevenson and Lundström provide insights into the construction of entrepreneurship policy based on the experiences and actual policy practices of national level government in 13 economies. They discuss the broad policy challenges it seeks to address, present a framework of entrepreneurship policy measures, describe their typology of entrepreneurship policy contrasting the different dimensions of each type, introduce a process for assessing the comprehensiveness of a government's entrepreneurship policy, and identify how the particular configuration and development of entrepreneurship policy reflects the idiosyncratic economic, social, political and cultural contexts of specific countries.

In Chapter 7 ('Public policy and entrepreneurship') Link discusses four areas where public policies of the US provide resources that extend opportunities for perception and action related to innovative behavior. The areas are tax incentives aimed at innovation and R&D, direct support of innovation and R&D, collaborative research arrangements reducing the cost of being perceptive, and infrastructure technologies reducing market transaction costs. US public policies related to these four areas can be characterized under the public–private partnership policy rubric.

In his creative and useful 'A rough guide to entrepreneurship policy' (Chapter 8) Hoffmann suggests a broad and encompassing roadmap to entrepreneurship policy. His chapter compares the various ways in which entrepreneurship policy is defined and measured, defines the business environment for entrepreneurship, and provides an empirical link between specific entrepreneurship measures and entrepreneurship policy. The roadmap provided by Hoffman should serve as a guide to policy formulation spanning a broad spectrum of policy makers.

In Chapter 9 ('Government programs to encourage innovation by start-ups and SMEs: the role of US innovation awards') Wessner reminds us that success in innovation has helped the US to become the world's leading economy. It faces new challenges as the innovative edge has shifted from the large to the small business sector. This has consequences for the market of early-stage financing where a funding gap plays the role of the 'valley of death'. Examples of two complementary US business support programs are described: the Small Business Innovation Research program (SBIR) and the Advanced Technology Program (ATP). SBIR is a public–private partnership designed to draw on the inventiveness of small high-technology firms through competitive innovation awards. ATP is also designed to help bring new technologies to the market, but has a focus on high-risk, enabling and innovative civilian technologies.

In 'Quantitative and qualitative studies of university technology transfer: synthesis and policy recommendations' (Chapter 10) Siegel synthesizes a rapidly growing literature to draw out what has been learned about entrepreneurship policy facilitating the transfer of university technology. He provides a coherent framework for analyzing and understanding university technology transfer policy. The framework starts with the licensing of university technology and then considers university spin-offs, before focusing on lessons that can be drawn from entrepreneurship policy focusing on the transfer of university technology.

The purpose of the contribution of Hülsbeck and Lehmann ('Entrepreneurship policy in Bavaria: between laptop and lederhosen') in Chapter 11 is to show that Bavarian policy makers used the (dis)advantages of the past when formulating a new entrepreneurship policy. At the heart of their endeavors lay the combination of preserving traditional roots (lederhosen) and introducing tomorrow's products (laptop). They zoom in on the spillover effects of the Munich universities and conclude that the use of existing, and hence local, resources should be promoted even in the face of the uncertainties of non-existent and sometimes global products.

The contribution of Greene and Storey called 'Issues in evaluation: the case of Shell Livewire' (Chapter 12) discusses some issues in evaluating enterprise programs. It deals with questions of whether programs are well managed, and of understanding the objectives of evaluation and the problems arising from the fact that an evaluation typically takes place at a particular point in the program's development. The chapter discusses methods to aid development of enterprise programs using as illustration an evaluation conducted on Shell Livewire, a large youth enterprise development program in the UK. This example illustrates the process of converting stated targets into identifiable measures despite the presence of unclear objectives. This example also illustrates the circular nature of an evaluation process, with the assessment findings feeding into the objectives of the organization and eventually helping to refocus the organization.

Finally, using the policy framework shown in Figure 1.1 we are able to provide an overview of the dimensions of entrepreneurship policy discussed in the respective chapters of our *Handbook of Research on Entrepreneurship Policy*. In Table 1.1 the chapters are characterized in terms of the seven policy channels. See Figure 1.1 for their specific roles as determinants of entrepreneurship.

Table 1.1   The 12 chapters and the seven channels of policy intervention, G1 to G7

Chapter	G1	G2	G3	G4	G5	G6	G7
2. Auerswald	X		X				X
3. Audretsch and Beckmann			X	X	X	X	
4. Parker		X		X	X	X	X
5. Henrekson and Roine	X				X	X	
6. Stevenson and Lundström	X	X	X	X		X	X
7. Link	X					X	
8. Hoffmann	X	X	X			X	X
9. Wessner	X		X			X	
10. Siegel	X		X			X	X
11. Hülsbeck and Lehmann	X		X			X	
12. Greene and Storey		X	X	X			

Notes

*   The present chapter benefited from several visits of Isabel Grilo to the Max Planck Institute in Jena, to the Institute of Development Studies at Indiana University and to Erasmus University Rotterdam. The Framework presented is inspired by earlier ones proposed in Verheul et al. (2002) and Wennekers et al. (2002). The views expressed here are those of the authors and should not be attributed to the European Commission. The assistance of Iris Beckmann, Hugo Erken, Adam Lederer, Kerstin Schueck, Don Siegel, Lois Stevenson and Sander Wennekers is much appreciated. The *Handbook of Research on Entrepreneurship Policy* is the result of a joint effort of the Max Planck Institute of Economics in Jena and EIM Business and Policy Research in Zoetermeer. The EIM activities are part of the research program SCALES, which is financed by the Dutch Ministry of Economic Affairs.

1.   This is not denying that new innovative entrepreneurship policy avenues have been created by governments. See the contribution by Audretsch and Beckmann in Chapter 3 of this book.

2.   The term 'self-employment' sometimes only refers to people who provide employment for themselves and not for others. Not only in the present introduction but often also in the remaining chapters of this book the terms business ownership and self-employment are used as equivalent to entrepreneurship.

3.   The data of the Global Entrepreneurship Monitor (GEM) show that there are substantial differences in the *dynamics* of entrepreneurship across countries, with the developed Asian and Central European countries ranking lowest, followed by Europe. Substantially higher levels are found in the former British Empire Anglo countries (including the US), and Latin America and developing Asian countries rank still higher (Reynolds et al., 2002; Acs et al., 2005).

4.   This distinction is sometimes referred to as that between push and pull factors (Vivarelli, 1991).

5.   When this exploitation of opportunities takes place in large incumbent firms it is commonly referred to as 'corporate entrepreneurship' or 'intrapreneurship'. Although intrinsically part of the entrepreneurial economy this form of entrepreneurial behaviour is not the theme of the present book.

6.   See Sarasvathy et al. (2003).

7.   In the words of occupational choice literature, a potential entrepreneur chooses by comparing the expected utility from the two alternatives.

8.   See Verheul et al. (2002) and Wennekers et al. (2002) for a more elaborate treatment of the demand and supply interpretation.

9.   There is some evidence that this relationship is U-shaped. Carree et al. (2002) mention a 'Schumpetarian regime switch' as the cause of the recent reversal of the prolonged downward trend in the 'equilibrium' rate of entrepreneurship. Piore and Sabel (1984) use the term 'Industrial Divide' and Jensen (1993) refers to the 'Third Industrial Revolution'. Audretsch and Thurik (2001 and 2004) make a distinction between the 'managed economy' and the 'entrepreneurial economy'.

10.   See also Audretsch et al. (2002) who introduce the term 'growth penalty'.

11.   At the aggregate level (high) unemployment may also correlate with recession and declining entrepreneurial opportunities (Audretsch et al., 2005).

12.   In order to adequately intervene in the national economy, it is important that the government is able and willing to perceive a deviation from the 'optimal' rate of entrepreneurship. Moreover, the government will have its own (economic or political economy) ideas about the target level of entrepreneurship and its importance in the economy.

13. Note however that even if such failures exist, it still needs to be discussed whether public intervention does not create further distortions when addressing the original ones.
14. The European Commission has recently outlined a set of recommendations aimed at enhancing the role of education in creating a more entrepreneurial culture in European societies. See 'Implementing the Community Lisbon Programme: Fostering entrepreneurial mindsets through education and learning', COM(2006)0033. In the context of the Lisbon strategy and following the recommendations in the framework of the Charter for Small Enterprises, several EU member states have announced the introduction of elements of entrepreneurship training into school curricula.
15. See for example Stiglitz and Weiss (1981) for a model of credit rationing.
16. Contrary to other studies for Germany, Winker (1999) finds evidence that German firms are liquidity constrained and that the degree of these constraints is inversely related to size.
17. It is argued that local proximity is essential for these knowledge spillovers to fully take place (Jaffe et al., 1993; Ogawa, 1997; Feldman and Audretsch, 1999) though other authors contend that knowledge externalities are so important and forceful that there is no compelling reason for a geographic boundary to limit the spatial extent of the spillover (Krugman, 1991).
18. A public good displays both non-rivalry in consumption and non-exclusivity (meaning that, either due to technological or legal reasons, once the good is available it is so for all those who wish to use it). Public goods can be seen as an extreme case of externalities.
19. In some cases the non-codifiable nature of knowledge makes it impossible to properly define property rights and therefore excludes a market solution for the production and allocation of new ideas.
20. See Mansfield et al. (1977), Link and Scott (1997) and Martin and Scott (2000) for follow-up research.
21. See 'Working together for growth and jobs: a new start for the Lisbon Strategy', COM(2005)24 and the 2005 Communication to the Spring European Council, 'Working together for growth and jobs – integrated guidelines for growth and jobs (2005–08)' at http://europa.eu.int/growthandjobs/.
22. See van der Kuip and Verheul (2003).

References

Acs, Z.J. and D.B. Audretsch (1993), 'Conclusion', in Z.J. Acs and D.B. Audretsch (eds), *Small Firms and Entrepreneurship: An East–West Perspective*, Cambridge: Cambridge University Press, pp. 227–31.
Acs, Z.J., B. Carlsson and C. Karlsson (1999), *Entrepreneurship, Small and Medium-Sized Enterprises and the Macroeconomy*, Cambridge: Cambridge University Press.
Acs, Z.J., P. Arenius, M. Hay and M. Minniti (2005), *Global Entrepreneurship Monitor: 2004 Executive Report*, Babson Park, MA: Babson College and London: London Business School.
Audretsch, D.B. (2007), *The Entrepreneurial Society*, New York: Oxford University Press.
Audretsch, D.B. and A.R. Thurik (2000), 'Capitalism and democracy in the 21st century: from the managed to the entrepreneurial economy', *Journal of Evolutionary Economics*, **10** (1), 17–34.
Audretsch, D.B. and A.R. Thurik (2001), 'What is new about the new economy: sources of growth in the managed and entrepreneurial economies', *Industrial and Corporate Change*, **10** (1), 267–315.
Audretsch, D.B. and A.R. Thurik (2004), 'A model of the entrepreneurial economy', *International Journal of Entrepreneurship Education*, **2** (2), 143–66.
Audretsch, D.B., M.A. Carree, A.R. Thurik and A.J. van Stel (2005), 'Does self-employment reduce unemployment?', Discussion Paper DP5057, London: Centre for Economic Policy Research.
Audretsch, D.B., M.A. Carree, A.J. van Stel and A.R. Thurik (2002), 'Impeded industrial restructuring: the growth penalty', *Kyklos*, **55** (1), 81–97.
Blanchflower, D.G. (2000), 'Self-employment in OECD countries', *Labour Economics*, **7** (5), 471–505.
Blanchflower, D.G. and B.D. Meyer (1994), 'A longitudinal analysis of the young self-employed in Australia and the United States', *Small Business Economics*, **6** (1), 1–19.
Blau, D. (1987), 'A time-series analysis of self-employment in the United States', *Journal of Political Economy*, **95** (3), 445–67.
Brock, W.A. and D.S. Evans (1989), 'Small business economics', *Small Business Economics*, **1** (1), 7–20.
Carree, M.A. and A.R. Thurik (2000), 'Market structure dynamics and economic growth', in G. Galli and J. Pelkmans (eds), *Regulatory Reform and Competitiveness in Europe No. 1: Horizontal Issues*, Cheltenham, UK and Northampton, MA, USA: Edward Elgar Publishing, pp. 430–60.
Carree, M.A., A.J. van Stel, A.R. Thurik and A.R.M. Wennekers (2002), 'Economic development and business ownership: an analysis using data of 23 OECD countries in the period 1976–1996', *Small Business Economics*, **19** (3), 271–90.
Davidsson, P. (2004), *Researching Entrepreneurship*, International Studies in Entrepreneurship, New York: Springer Science+Business Media Inc.
Davis, S.J. and M. Henrekson (1999), 'Explaining national differences in the size and industry distribution of employment', *Small Business Economics*, **12** (1), 59–83.

de Wit, G. and F.A.A.M. van Winden (1989), 'An empirical analysis of self-employment in the Netherlands', *Small Business Economics*, **1** (4), 263–84.
de Wit, G. and F.A.A.M. van Winden (1991), 'An m-sector, n-group behavioral model of self-employment', *Small Business Economics*, **3** (1), 49–66.
Dertouzos, M., R. Lester and R. Solow (1989), *Made in America*, Cambridge, MA: MIT Press.
European Commission (2005a), 'Working together for growth and jobs: a new start for the Lisbon Strategy', COM(2005)24, Brussels.
European Commission (2005b), Communication to the Spring European Council, 'Working together for growth and jobs – integrated guidelines for growth and jobs (2005–08)', available at http://europa.eu.int/growthandjobs/
European Commission (2006), 'Implementing the Community Lisbon Programme: fostering entrepreneurial mindsets through education and learning', COM(2006)0033, Brussels.
Evans, D.S. and L.S. Leighton (1989), 'The determinants of changes in U.S. self-employment, 1968–1987', *Small Business Economics*, **1** (2), 111–19.
Fazzari, S., R.G. Hubbard and B.C. Petersen (1988), 'Financing constraints and corporate investment', *Brookings Papers on Economic Activity*, 141–95.
Feldman, M.P. and D.B. Audretsch (1999), 'Innovation in cities: implications for innovation', *European Economic Review*, **43** (2), 409–29.
Freytag, A. and A.R. Thurik (2007), 'Entrepreneurship and its determinants in a cross-country setting', *Journal of Evolutionary Economics*, forthcoming.
Gavron, R., M. Cowling, G. Holtham and A. Westall (1998), *The Entrepreneurial Society*, London: Institute for Public Policy Research.
Grilo, I. and J.M. Irigoyen (2006), 'Entrepreneurship in the EU: to wish and not to be', *Small Business Economics*, **26** (4), 305–18.
Grilo, I. and A.R. Thurik (2005), 'Latent and actual entrepreneurship in Europe and the US: some recent developments', *International Entrepreneurship and Management Journal*, **1** (4), 441–59.
Hébert, R.F. and A.N. Link (1989), 'In search of the meaning of entrepreneurship', *Small Business Economics*, **1** (1), 39–49.
Henrekson, M. and D. Johansson (1999), 'Institutional effects on the evolution of the size distribution of firms', *Small Business Economics*, **12** (1), 11–23.
Jaffe, A.B., M. Trajtenberg and R. Henderson (1993), 'Geographic localization of knowledge spillovers as evidenced by patent citations', *The Quarterly Journal of Economics*, **108** (3), 577–98.
Jensen, M.C. (1993), 'The modern industrial revolution, exit, and the failure of internal control systems', *Journal of Finance*, **48** (3), 831–80.
Krugman, P. (1991), 'Increasing returns and economic geography', *Journal of Political Economy*, **99** (3), 483–99.
Link, A.N. and S.J. Scott (1997), 'Evaluating technology-based public institutions: lessons from the National Institute of Standards and Technology', in G. Papaconstantinou and W. Polt (eds), *Policy Evaluation in Innovation and Technology*, Paris: OECD, pp. 255–77.
Lucas, R.E. (1978), 'On the size distribution of business firms', *Bell Journal of Economics*, **9** (2), 508–23.
Mansfield, E., J. Rapoport, A. Romeo, S. Wagner and G. Beardsley (1977), 'Social and private rates of return from industrial innovations', *Quarterly Journal of Economics*, **91** (2), 196–240.
Martin, S. and J.T. Scott (2000), 'The nature of innovation market failure and the design of public support for private innovation', *Research Policy*, **29** (4–5), 437–47.
Mowery, D. (2005), 'The Bayh–Dole Act and high-technology entrepreneurship in U.S. universities: chicken, egg, or something else?', in G.D. Libecap (ed.), *University Entrepreneurship and Technology Transfer*, Amsterdam: Elsevier, pp. 39–68.
OECD (1998), *Fostering Entrepreneurship, the OECD Jobs Strategy*, Paris: OECD.
OECD (2000), *OECD Employment Outlook*, Paris: OECD.
Ogawa, S. (1997), 'Does sticky information affect the locus of innovation? Evidence from the Japanese convenience-store industry', *Research Policy*, **26** (7–8), 777–90.
Parker, S.C. (2004), *The Economics of Self-employment and Entrepreneurship*, Cambridge: Cambridge University Press.
Piore, M.J. and C.F. Sabel (1984), *The Second Industrial Divide Possibilities for Prosperity*, New York: Basic Books.
Prodi, R. (2002), 'For a New European Entrepreneurship' (public speech 7 February), Madrid, Instituto de Empresa.
Rees, H. and A. Shah (1986), 'An empirical analysis of self-employment in the UK', *Journal of Applied Econometrics*, **1** (1), 95–108.
Reynolds, P.D., W.D. Bygrave, E. Autio, L.W. Cox and M. Hay (2002), *Global Entrepreneurship Monitor, 2002 Executive Report*, Babson Park, MA: Babson College, London: London Business School, and Kansas City, MO: Kauffman Foundation.
Sarasvathy, S.D., N. Dew, S.R. Velamuri and S. Venkataraman (2003), 'Three views of entrepreneurial oppor-

tunity', in D.B. Audretsch and Z.J. Acs (eds), *Handbook of Entrepreneurship Research*, Boston/Dordrecht: Kluwer Academic Publishers, pp. 141–60.

Stiglitz, J. and A. Weiss (1981), 'Credit rationing in markets with imperfect information', *American Economic Review*, **71** (3), 393–410.

Storey, D.J. (1991), 'The birth of new firms – does unemployment matter? A review of the evidence', *Small Business Economics*, **3** (3), 167–78.

Thurik, A.R. (2007), *On Entrepreneurship, Economic Growth and Policy*, Jena: Max Planck Institute of Economics, forthcoming.

van der Kuip, I. and I. Verheul (2003), 'Early development of entrepreneurial qualities: the role of initial education', *International Journal of Entrepreneurship Education*, **2** (2), 203–26.

van Praag, M.C. (1999), 'Some classic views on entrepreneurship', *De Economist*, **147** (3), 311–35.

van Stel, A. (2005), 'COMPENDIA: Harmonizing business ownership data across countries and over time', *International Entrepreneurship and Management Journal*, **1** (1), 105–23.

Verheul, I., S. Wennekers, D. Audretsch and R. Thurik (2002), 'An eclectic theory of entrepreneurship: policies, institutions and culture', in D.B. Audretsch, A.R. Thurik, I. Verheul and A.R.M. Wennekers (eds), *Entrepreneurship: Determinants and Policy in a European–US Comparison*, Boston/Dordrecht: Kluwer Academic Publishers, pp. 11–81.

Vivarelli, M. (1991), 'The birth of new enterprises', *Small Business Economics*, **3** (3), 215–23.

Wennekers, A.R.M. (1997), 'The revival of entrepreneurship in the Netherlands', in P.J.J. Welfens and C. Graack (eds), *Technologieorientierte Unternehmensgründungen und Mittelstandspolitik in Europa*, Heidelberg: Physica-Verlag, pp. 185–94.

Wennekers, A.R.M. and A.R. Thurik (1999), 'Linking entrepreneurship and economic growth', *Small Business Economics*, **13** (1), 27–55.

Wennekers, A.R.M., L. Uhlaner and A.R. Thurik (2002), 'Entrepreneurship and its conditions: a macro perspective', *International Journal of Entrepreneurship Education*, **1** (1), 25–64.

Winker, P. (1999), 'Causes and effects of financing constraints at the firm level', *Small Business Economics*, **12** (2), 169–81.

2 The simple economics of technology entrepreneurship: market failure reconsidered*
Philip E. Auerswald

> Technological progress fuels economic growth. The Administration's technology initiatives aim to promote the domestic development and diffusion of growth- and productivity-enhancing technologies. They seek to correct market failures that would otherwise generate too little investment in R&D. The goal of technology policy is not to substitute the government's judgment for that of private industry in deciding which potential 'winners' to back. Rather the point is to correct [for] market failure. (*1994 Economic Report of the President*, p. 191)[1]

Introduction

Among policy practitioners, few concepts are used at once as widely, or as imprecisely, as that of 'market failure'. In contexts ranging from terrorism insurance to technological innovation, both advocates and opponents of government programs point to market failure as the basic test of a government role. The logic is presumably simple: a role for government exists if, but only if, a market failure exists. Policy discussions premised on the market failure test invariably are reduced to debates over the strength of evidence that markets are not competitive – and, therefore, a government role is warranted.

A fundamental problem with this approach is that 'market failure' as properly defined is neither a necessary nor a sufficient condition for government action. The first reason is an obvious one: a perfectly competitive market achieves an efficient outcome but not necessarily an equitable one. Consequently, even in the absence of market failure, concerns over equity rather than efficiency may suggest an important and legitimate role for government action. Thus market failure is not a necessary condition for a government role. More to the point, conditions for rigorously defined market failure are present nearly everywhere. Yet the same fundamental factors that cause market failure can also bedevil the implementation of policy. Thus, in practice, a market failure is also not a sufficient condition for a government role.

In this chapter I survey the evidence regarding two broad categories of market failure: imperfect appropriability and challenges to contracting. My main point is that where economists and policy-makers alike have for over a decade emphasized the former, the latter is far more important. Better understanding the multiple aspects of market failure that combine to create fundamental challenges to contracting for technical information will lead to better policy making, implementation, and assessment.

I reconsider the 'market failure' test as applied specifically to entrepreneurship policy. While I use the generic term 'entrepreneurs' throughout this chapter, I am primarily concerned with Schumpeter's notion of the entrepreneur as an innovator, as contrasted with the Kirznerian (alternately, neo-Austrian) notion of the entrepreneur as the seeker of arbitrage opportunities, or the Knightian (alternately, neoclassical) notion of the entrepreneur as the bearer of risk.[2]

By 'technology entrepreneurship' I intend the subset of entrepreneurial activity that involves the conversion of basic knowledge in science and/or engineering to products and/or services ready for market – a process elsewhere termed the transition from invention to innovation.[3] I use 'invention' as shorthand for a commercially promising product or service, based on new science or technology, which is protectable (though not necessarily by patents or copyrights). By 'innovation' I mean the successful entry into a market of a new science or technology-based product; that is, the commercialization of an 'invention'. Technology entrepreneurs thus specialize in the technical and business activities that transform a commercially promising 'invention' into a business plan that can attract enough investment to enter a market successfully, and through that investment become a successful innovation. This requires reducing the needed technology to practice, defining a production process with predictable product costs, and relating the resultant product specifications to a defined market.

In the next section I explore two categories of market failures inherent in technology entrepreneurship: (1) imperfect appropriability and (2) various informational problems that together complicate contracting. I then consider the role of policy in addressing these market failures. In the fourth section I propose an alternative to the market failure criterion in the design and evaluation of entrepreneurship policy, and I conclude in the final section.

Market failures inherent in technology entrepreneurship
The emerging area of entrepreneurship policy is a particularly interesting one within which to analyze the limits of the market failure test. To the layman, entrepreneurship and competition are almost synonymous. A widely held view is that the tenacity and creativity of entrepreneurs enforce discipline on markets. Public policy to support entrepreneurship means simply the removal of obstacles created by government that impede the ability to pursue opportunities. In stark contrast, within the formal model of perfect competition that is the point of reference for a rigorous definition of 'market failure', entrepreneurs quite simply do not exist.[4]

In actuality, entrepreneurship is neither synonymous with, nor antithetical to, competition. Entrepreneurship and entrepreneurship policy necessarily exist in a world of 'second-best' options addressing the various linked challenges that face entrepreneurs – including uncertainty, asymmetric information, indivisibilities, and high transactions costs. Informed practitioners may believe in the independent and creative spirit of entrepreneurs, but they are also sensitive to the manner in which government unavoidably creates the context for entrepreneurial activity – not only through the enforcement of property rights, but also through tax and fiscal policy, the creation and maintenance of infrastructure, support of educational and research institutions, and the centuries-old practice of creating special rights to induce invention and innovation (i.e. the patent system and other forms of intellectual property protection). At the same time, in a partial equilibrium context, economists may plausibly claim that active public policies to support entrepreneurs 'interfere' with the functioning of private markets. For example, while disequilibria and/or market failure in product markets clearly may provide opportunities for entrepreneurs, if financial markets serving entrepreneurs are close to being competitive, a role for certain categories of policy may be obviated.

Arrow (1962, p. 609) describes the three fundamental classes of market failures that characterize inventive activity: indivisibility (marginal cost pricing rules apply imperfectly), incomplete appropriability (social and private benefits diverge), and uncertainty (future states of nature are unknown). Clearly, all three of these attributes characterize basic research, as well as 'early stage' technology development projects that convert basic science 'inventions' into market ready 'innovations'. In particular, Arrow points out that invention is an activity with particular characteristics that make it difficult for inventors to relieve themselves of risks. Arrow (1962, p. 613) notes that success in 'highly risky business activities, including invention' depends on:

> an inextricable tangle of objective uncertainties and decisions of the entrepreneurs and is certainly uninsurable. On the other hand, such activities should be undertaken if the expected return exceeds the market rate of return, no matter what the variance. The existence of common stocks would seem to solve the allocation problem . . . But then again the actual managers no longer receive the full reward of their decisions; the shifting of risks is again accompanied by a weakening of incentives to efficiency.

Of the three fundamental classes of market failures that characterize inventive activity, incomplete appropriability tends to receive the most attention in the literature – in particular as a motivation for the existence of 'knowledge spillovers' as the key driver of long-term growth. For this reason I discuss appropriability first.

Imperfect appropriability and 'knowledge spillovers'

> [R]apid imitation of new drugs is difficult in pharmaceuticals for a number of reasons. One of these is that pharmaceuticals has historically been one of the few industries where patents provide solid protection against imitation. Because small variants in a molecule's structure can drastically alter its pharmacological properties, potential imitators often find it hard to work around the patent. Although other firms might undertake research in the same therapeutic class as an innovator, the probability of their finding another compound with the same therapeutic properties that did not infringe on the original patent could be quite small. (Henderson et al., 1999, p. 279)

A good is rivalrous if its consumption by one person precludes its consumption by another; it is excludable if access to it can be limited. An automobile is rivalrous and excludable; sunshine is neither. Perfect competition concerns trade of goods that are rivalrous and excludable. In competitive markets, all information is shared, all factors of production are paid their marginal products, and all goods are priced at marginal cost. Any inventions or innovations that occur are instantly adopted by all.

Imperfect appropriability is one well recognized form of market failure. It results directly from lack of excludability (and not rivalrousness). It is a general concept, as applicable to the dredging of a river to minimize the risk of flooding as it is to the creation of a nursery rhyme. In the case of dredging, the lack of excludability results from the diffuse impact of the investment. In the case of the nursery rhyme, the lack of excludability results from ease of copying. Activities subject to imperfect appropriability are, generically, ones for which private and social returns to investment diverge.

The creation of new ideas is widely thought to be subject to imperfect appropriability for reasons both of diffuse impact and of ease of copying. Each use of a new vaccine, for instance, will create lower susceptibility to contagion for an entire population. Thus, while a particular dose of a vaccine is both rival and excludable, its benefits are neither. Price will not reflect marginal social benefits (or costs, as the case may be).

The notion that knowledge is a public good rests in part on the premise that ideas are non-excludable in the sense of being easily copied. This premise holds in many settings, but not all. Particularly questionable is the invocation of imperfect appropriability as the motivation for the concept of 'knowledge spillovers', inspired in part by the oft-quoted passage from Marshall (1890, pp. 267–77) that begins: 'The mysteries of the trade become no mysteries, but are as it were in the air.' Keeping others from copying one's ideas or methods (preventing 'knowledge spillovers') is conceptually distinct from making sure that one fully captures the benefit that can be derived from whatever novelty those ideas or methods contain (fully appropriating returns). Even a product-market monopolist whose intellectual property is 100 percent secure will only be able to capture the full benefits of an innovation if perfect price discrimination among consumers is possible; otherwise, the monopolist will derive a persistent profit, but will not capture all the social value the innovation creates. Where external effects are present (as in the dredging example above), lack of appropriability will exist even where knowledge spillovers are not present. At the other end of the spectrum, a company can, in theory, freely share its ideas and technology, yet secure most if not all of the returns from its innovations as a consequence of non-technological barriers to entry in the relevant product market – for example, the sunk costs of establishing branding or legal protection in the product market. Indeed, the entire patent system arguably is constructed on the principle that appropriability can be separated from knowledge spillovers. Yet even accepting the validity of the conceptual link between imperfect appropriability and knowledge spillovers, as is done in much of the literature, significant questions remain concerning the extent to which either concept is important to decision making by entrepreneurs and to entrepreneurship policy.

The influential work by Romer (1986, 1990) provides a point of reference. Following broadly in the tradition of Marshall, Romer (1986, 1990) famously proposed that innovation will not only continue indefinitely, but may advance at a rate exceeding the growth of conventional inputs, because ideas are fundamentally non-rival and non-excludable. While acknowledging that the concept of non-rivalry is an idealization, he asserted that product design is inherently subject to increasing returns due to ease of copying: 'What is unambiguously true about a design is that the cost of replicating it with a drafter, a photocopier, or a disk drive is trivial compared to the cost of creating the design in the first place' (Romer, 1990, p. S75).

Romer (1990, p. S72) defines technological change as 'improvements in the instructions for mixing together raw materials'. The 'instructions' (in later work, 'recipes') on which Romer bases his theory are verbally described, but nowhere explicitly modeled.[5] Yet the transfer from one firm to another of knowledge regarding production – the essence of the concept of 'instructions' that is the core of Romer (1986, 1990) – is likely to be subject to errors and imperfections.[6] This, in itself, is not a serious challenge to the argument in Romer (1986, 1990). But what of codified knowledge – the sort of 'designs' that Romer (1990) asserts can be easily copied? The argument here is weak as well. While codified knowledge may be non-rivalrous, in most cases it is either excludable (patents, documents protected by trade secret) or not directly applicable to production (basic research papers). The exceptional cases of published unprotected 'designs' are, for obvious reasons, not likely to offer significant opportunities for Schumpeterian entrepreneurs – unless combined with other information in novel and not easily imitable ways.[7] Furthermore, patent protection is available to innovators in all industries, yet significant inter-industry differences exist in the extent to which patents allow persistence of profits. As suggested by the earlier quote from Henderson et al. (1999), the differentiation is due to ease of imitability. With regard to codified knowledge that is partially excludable, a critical issue is the extent to which partial imitation, or copying, preserves the quality of the original. In many, perhaps the majority, of economically important contexts, it will not.

In recent years economists, sociologists, geographers and historians have addressed the transmission of knowledge, particularly increasing returns resulting from knowledge spillovers, in a large and varied literature. Economic theorists have explored implications for growth and trade of many different assumptions regarding the mechanisms by which knowledge spillovers occur. In most such models, 'knowledge' of some type is aggregated into a single scalar. As a rule knowledge networks are implicit, but are not explicitly represented. This theoretical, mostly macroeconomic, literature on knowledge spillovers has been complemented by an empirical, mostly microeconomic, literature. The empirical literature has assessed evidence for the existence of knowledge spillovers (see review by Griliches, 1992) and measured the extent of their geographical localization.[8] A number of pathways for localized knowledge spillovers have been studied empirically, including learning directly from neighbors (Foster and Rosenzweig, 1995), transfer of knowledge via 'star' researchers (Zucker et al., 1998a, 1998b), and transfer of knowledge through buyer–supplier co-development efforts (Appleyard, 2003).

The empirical literature on knowledge spillovers and parallel historical work have documented what the theoretical studies largely missed: the decline, during the twentieth century, of small-scale craft-based production, and the corresponding rise of science-based innovation and complex system development projects.[9] Consider the Marshallian formulation of knowledge that is 'in the air'. For the sort of craft-based production that necessarily provided the inspiration for this observation – glass making in Bohemia (Czech Republic), Champagne in Rheims (France), windmill production in Herning (Denmark) – there are solid reasons to believe that knowledge is 'in the air'. Masters share tacit knowledge with apprentices, whose core capability lies in replicating centuries-old techniques.[10] New approaches are viewed with suspicion, and are accepted into common practice only after considerable scrutiny.

Science-based innovation and system development are another matter. That Marshall's observations predated Romer's by nearly a century is of significance. The introduction of new products today (as opposed to a century ago) typically involves overcoming both technical and market risks.[11] When products are based on truly novel technology, or create new markets, their introduction often requires new organizational forms.[12] The knowledge that drives long-term growth in a modern economy is thus detailed, highly technical, and context specific.[13] It is an asset of the firm, whose development may be a consequence of explicit investments, 'passive learning', or both. Ideas that are easy to copy will not represent opportunities for entrepreneurs.[14] Yet, to the extent that the knowledge developed by an incumbent firm is the solution to a complex problem, even slightly imperfect copying is likely to lead to substantial degradation of performance. Active investment may be required to develop the 'absorptive capacity' needed to make use of the information.[15] Whether knowledge pertinent to modern science-based innovations is 'in the air' or not is – literally and figuratively – immaterial. Only specialists will understand what it means.

There is no disputing that ideas created by one person, or within one firm, can reach other people or firms through multiple pathways, many of which do not involve direct compensation of the innovator by the beneficiary. If one chooses to refer to such pathways as 'knowledge spillovers', then such spillovers will everywhere be in evidence. However, the critical point is that when such pathways involve economic benefit derived from technology entrepreneurship, they also in most cases involve significant costs: recruiting a key employee from a competitor firm or industry leader; undertaking research to invent around a patent; reverse engineering a product; paying for employee attendance at conferences; hiring consultants; building a trusted relationship with a buyer or supplier. Furthermore, to the extent that the public benefits not captured by the entrepreneur (resulting from 'knowledge spillovers' or other mechanisms) are temporally far off or uncertain, it is unlikely that they will be of greater importance to entrepreneurial decision-making than will be the immediate, first order challenges of organizing and financing the firm's operations. We next discuss the set of market failures associated with such organizational and financial challenges, referred to here and in Zeckhauser (1996) as those of contracting for technical information.

The challenge of contracting for technical information

> [The Band of Angels] got its start in January '95 with a dozen people. I invited 25 people to come, and about half of them showed up. I made sure the food was good, the wine was good, and there was a certain spirit of camaraderie, and this all happened. We now have grown to 150 people, and one of the tricks is to keep that spirit of camaraderie when the group gets larger. We have put a limit on it. We feel we have enough people. About half of them show up for dinners, as this whole thing has evolved into a protocol of dinner meeting where companies make elevator pitch presentations, generally three per evening. They are guests at dinner. We pay for it all. And we follow it up with lunch meetings for each company, where those who are truly interested can meet the management and can sit down and spend hours together. And that works. (Hans Severiens, founder, Band of Angels)[16]

A world in which technical and market knowledge relating to innovation is 'in the air' is a world in which private investments in knowledge creation yield broadly shared social benefits without the actions of intermediaries – entrepreneurs, venture capitalists, 'angel' investors, patent lawyers, corporate technology managers, and so forth. It is not the world in which we live.

In the world of the twenty-first century, knowledge pertinent to modern science-based innovation is subject to systematic uncertainties and information asymmetries that render communication difficult and contracting costly. Trust is a prerequisite to the creation of value. In this world – the world in which we do live – technology entrepreneurs perform a valuable economic function of seeking and evaluating opportunities; financial intermediaries capable of ascertaining the prospects of new ventures earn high returns, in large part because their skills and networks of contacts are not easily imitated.

Coase (1937) established the foundation for the modern theory of the firm with the observation that firms exist to minimize transactions costs. Coase (1960) elaborates, emphasizing that when entrepreneurs act to expand a firm in such a manner they will 'internalize externalities' – incorporating into the firm precisely those activities for which contracts are difficult to negotiate. This is critical. Entrepreneurs and firm managers are thus typically charged with solving complex coordination problems.[17]

Multiple barriers of information, valuation, trust and culture render particularly severe the contracting challenges for entrepreneurs seeking to realize the economic value of a science-based invention. Building on Arrow (1962), Zeckhauser (1996) identifies distinguishing characteristics of technical information that complicate contracting. To begin with, technical information is difficult to count and value. To value technical information, it may be necessary to 'give away the secret' – an aspect of the appropriability problem discussed above. Furthermore, to prove its value, technical information is often bundled into complete products (e.g. a computer chip or a pharmaceutical product). Sellers' superior knowledge about technical information makes buyers wary of overpaying. Inefficient contracts are often designed to secure rents from technical information.

Technologists and investors have long referred to the invention to innovation transition as the 'Valley of Death' in the process of creating a new technology-based firm. Looking beyond contracts to incentives and institutional cultures, Branscomb and Auerswald (2001) identify five core challenges facing technology entrepreneurs in seeking to turn science-based inventions into market-ready innovations:

1. *Differing motivations for research.* Initially an innovator demonstrates to his or her own satisfaction that a given scientific or technical breakthrough could form the basis for a commercial product (proof of principle). However, a substantial amount of difficult and potentially costly research (sometimes many years' worth) will be needed before the envisioned product is transformed into a commercial reality with sufficient function, low enough cost, high enough quality, and sufficient market appeal to survive competition in the marketplace. Few scientists engaged in academic research (or the agencies funding their work) have the necessary incentives or motivation to undertake this phase of the reduction-to-practice research.

2. *Disjuncture between technologist and business manager.* On each side of the 'Valley of Death' stands a quite different archetypal character: the technologist on one side, and the investor/manager on the other. Each has different training, expectations, information sources, and modes of expression. The technologist knows what is scientifically interesting, technically feasible, and fundamentally novel in the proposed approach. In the event of failure, the technologist risks a loss of reputation, as well as forgone pecuniary returns. The technologist is deeply invested in a vision of what could be. The investor/manager knows about the process of bringing new products to market, but may have to trust the technologist when it comes to the technical particulars of the project in question. What the investor/manager is generally putting at risk is other people's money. The investor is deeply committed to producing a profitable return on his or her investment, independent of the technology or market through which it is realized. To the extent that the technologist and the investor/manager do not fully trust one another or cannot communicate effectively, the Valley of Death between invention and innovation becomes deeper still.[18]

3. *Sources of financing.* Research funds are available (typically from corporate research, government agencies, or more rarely, personal assets) to support the creation of the idea and the initial demonstration that it works. Investment funds generally can be found to bring to market a product based on a viable prototype, supported by a validated business case. In between, however, aspiring innovators compete for scarce funds available from a diversity of sources: 'angel' investors (wealthy individuals, often entrepreneurs who have 'cashed-out' of prior successful ventures); established firms making equity investments in high-tech startups to get a look at emergent

technologies; venture capital firms specialized in early stage or 'seed' investments; military or other public procurement; state or federal government programs specifically designed for the purpose; and university funding from public or private sources.

4. *Infrastructure.* Another critical obstacle typically facing champions of early stage technology development projects is the absence of the necessary infrastructure. By infrastructure we mean not only the large scale infrastructure required for final products in the marketplace (e.g. gas stations for internal combustion automobiles, or software to run on a new operating system), but also all of the 'complementary assets' that may be required for market acceptance – suppliers of new kinds of components or materials, new forms of distribution and service, training in the use of the new technology, auxiliary products and software to broaden market scope.

5. *Creating value.* Even where a technology has demonstrated promise to create value for consumers, the question remains: how much of that value will the innovative firm be able to capture? Understanding the mechanism by which value will not only be created, but also captured, is a necessary component of the business system that allows an invention to become a successful commercial innovation. In order to execute the given strategy for value capture, the firm in question must have the internal capabilities and other resources necessary to leverage its first mover advantage into longer term market success. At every stage, firms weigh opportunities for value creation and value capture against risks and anticipated costs. All things being equal, a large corporation will develop a given technology platform first in markets where mechanisms for value capture are better established and production costs are lower.

Of these generic challenges, only the last relates to imperfect appropriability. Overwhelmingly, the market failures that matter in technology entrepreneurship – and in entrepreneurship policy – are those that relate to the presence of information asymmetries and uncertainty, not 'knowledge spillovers'.

The role of policy: an 'innovation gap'?

> As the years go by in our highly industrialized society, the funds available for new enterprise tend to concentrate in fiduciary hands. This in itself is a natural process, but it does make it more and more difficult, as time goes on, to finance new undertakings. The continued maintenance of prosperity and the continued increase in the general standard of living depend in a large measure in finding financial support for that comparatively small percentage of new ideas and developments which give promise of expanded production and employment and an increased standard of living for the American people. We cannot float along indefinitely on the enterprise and vision of preceding generations. To be confident that we are in an expanding, instead of a static or frozen economy, we must have a reasonably high birth rate of new undertakings. (Ralph Flanders, co-founder, American Research & Development)[19]

The multiple challenges that confront technology entrepreneurs seeking to traverse the 'Valley of Death' have led some to argue that a persistent 'innovation gap' exists even in countries with relatively strong and productive innovation systems. Gompers and Lerner (1999; p. 2) quote former Undersecretary of Commerce Mary Good's testimony to the Senate Committee on Governmental Affairs in 1998:

> As the competitive pressures of the global marketplace have forced American firms to move more of their R&D into shorter term product and process improvements, an 'innovation gap'

has developed. . . . Sit down with a group of venture capitalists. The funding for higher risk ventures . . . is extraordinarily difficult to come by.

In its edited form, the statement appears to suggest that venture capitalists are reluctant to provide risk capital. Gompers and Lerner point out that this is not the case: the venture capital mode of finance is precisely that which is specialized in providing finance in contexts where uncertainty is high and information asymmetries are severe. Indeed, they argue that the venture capital industry was founded with the very goal of providing financial support to finance high-risk new business undertakings – a claim consistent with the above quote from venture capital pioneer Ralph Flanders in 1945.

Particularly controversial is the further claim that the presence of an 'innovation gap' implies that corrective government action is needed. Lerner (2002; p. F73) provides a clearly stated articulation of the skeptics view:

> The initial reaction of a financial economist to the argument that the government needs to invest in growth firms is likely to be skepticism. A lengthy literature has highlighted the role of financial intermediaries in alleviating moral hazard and information asymmetries. Young high-technology firms are often characterized by considerable uncertainty and informational asymmetries, which permit opportunistic behavior by entrepreneurs. Why one would want to encourage public officials instead of specialized financial intermediaries (venture capital organizations) as a source of capital in this setting is not immediately obvious.

In this view, entrepreneurship policy is not subject to a global market failure test, but rather to a much narrower test focused on financial markets.

At first glance, there appears little evidence that government support for technology entrepreneurs would do anything but 'crowd out' private investment. The financial system specialized in investing in high-risk new enterprises – the venture capital industry – grew dramatically in the last decade, even when the dramatic downturn in 2001–02 is taken into consideration. As is well known, venture capital funds disbursed to United States firms reached a peak of over $100 billion in the year 2000, before dropping off to $37 billion in 2001. Interpretations vary. In 2002 the White House justified reductions in support to the Commerce Department's Advanced Technology Program with the statement that 'the overall growth in venture capital suggests private funding is available for high-technology projects'. In contrast, technology business leader Bill Joy of Sun Microsystems observed in July of 2001 that 'a couple of years ago, even the bad ideas were getting capital. Now we have gone too far in the opposite direction, shutting down investment in good ideas.'[20]

Some pre-boom numbers regarding technology entrepreneurship place the role of venture capital in context. In 1998, for example – probably a more reliable benchmark of innovation funding activities than 2000 when markets where at their historic peaks – the Small Business Administration reports that more than 600 000 new firms (with employees) were founded. That year approximately 450 000 individuals described themselves as technology entrepreneurs of one type or another.[21] About 10 percent of those entrepreneurs, involved in approximately 20 000 start up firms, received roughly $20 billion in funding from Angel investors.[22] In contrast, only about 300 companies received 'seed stage' funding from venture capitalists; slightly more than 1000 firms received first time venture funding in all categories.[23] Current numbers are not markedly different.

Branscomb and Auerswald (2002) report that, overall, of $266 billion that was spent on national R&D by various sources in the US in 1998, substantially less than 14 percent flowed into early stage technology development activities. The exact figure is elusive, because public financial reporting is not required for these investments. Our method of arriving at a reliable estimate was to create two models based on different interpretations of our 'early stage technology development' definition – one very restrictive (i.e. biased toward a low estimate) and the other quite inclusive (i.e. biased toward a high estimate). With this approach we conclude that between $5 billion (2 percent) and $36 billion (14 percent) of overall R&D spending in 1998 was devoted to early stage technology development. The balance supported either basic research, or applied research, engineering and testing.

Although the range between our lower and upper estimates differs by several billions of dollars, the proportional distribution across the main sources of funding for early stage technology development activities is surprisingly similar regardless of whether we employ restrictive or inclusive models. Given either model, expenditures on early stage technology development by angel investors, the federal government and large corporations funding 'out-of-the-core business' technology development are comparable in magnitude. Early stage technology development funds from each of these sources greatly exceed those from state programs, university expenditures, and the small part of venture capital investment that goes to support early stage technology projects. Notably – even excluding as we do the impact of government procurement – the federal role in this process is substantial: in our estimates roughly 20 to 25 percent of total early stage technology development funding comes from federal sources.

Investments by corporations in advancing established product and process technologies to better serve existing markets comprise a dominant source of national R&D spending. But, as Auerswald et al. (2005) report, corporate technology entrepreneurs who create an innovative idea lying outside their firm's core competence and interest face risks and financial challenges similar to those faced by CEOs of newly created firms. While corporations will indeed spend lavishly on technological innovations that support their core businesses, they are systematically disinclined to support technological innovations that challenge existing lines of business, require a fundamental shift of business model, or depend on the creation of new complementary infrastructure.

Venture capital firms are critical financial intermediaries supporting new high-growth firms. Why, then, is the role of the venture capital industry in funding early stage technology development not dominant? Popular press accounts notwithstanding, venture capital firms are not in the R&D business. Rather, they are in the financial business. Their fiduciary responsibility is to earn maximal returns for their investors. They do this through a complex set of activities that can be summarized as buying firms low and selling them high. Venture capitalists do indeed back high-growth, new ventures. In many cases, though not the majority, they support firms that are bringing radical new technologies to market.

When venture capitalists do support technology-based enterprises, they prefer to support firms that have at least proceeded beyond the product development stage – that is, firms that have completed the early stage technology development that is the focus of this chapter. As Morgenthaler (2000) and other venture capitalists report, the risk–reward ratio for seed stage technology-based ventures is not as attractive to venture capital firms as that for slightly later stage ventures.[24] As the median size of venture capital deals has increased and the pressure to provide attractive returns to investors in mammoth funds has intensified, venture capital has tended increasingly to flow to projects in the later stages of development and to already proven technologies. A decade or more can be required for the transition from invention to innovation. Given technical and market uncertainties, venture capitalists, angels and bankers prefer to wait to see the business case for a new technology rather than funding speculation. The technical content of the business proposal must be sufficiently well established to provide reliable estimates of product cost, performance and reliability in the context of an identified market that can be entered in a reasonable length of time. For all of the above reasons, trends in venture capital disbursements should not be confused with trends in the funding of early stage technology development.

The skepticism to which Lerner refers regarding the advisability of the government investing in growth firms is valid precisely because the 'specialized' skills of financial intermediaries such as venture capitalists are not easily imitated. Early stage development involves not only high quantifiable risks, but also daunting uncertainties. When the uncertainties are primarily technical, investors are ill-equipped to quantify them. For new technologies that have the potential to create new product categories, market uncertainties are also high and similarly difficult to quantify. The 'due diligence' that investors in venture capital funds require of managing partners, and that angel investors require of themselves, is intrinsically difficult – and is becoming more so as both technologies and markets become increasingly complex.

As Lerner implies, simple labor economics suggests that a public official on a government salary will be less capable of evaluating the market prospects of a new technology than will a highly paid venture capitalist. To suggest otherwise is, rightly, to invite derision. However, the same set of basic principles suggests that venture capitalists are, typically, highly compensated because their skill set is not easily imitated. Barriers to entry and high compensation both imply that the venture capitalist's opportunity cost of time is much higher than that of the public official. For that reason, the efforts of public officials to evaluate the commercial dimensions of technical proposals – for example, the review of applications for competitive government awards such as those given by the US Small Business Innovation Research (SBIR) program – are better understood as complements to, rather than substitutes for, the due diligence performed by venture capitalists. The very success of the venture capital industry has driven it away from funding technology entrepreneurs in the early stages. High 'hurdle rates' for expected returns to venture capital investments translate into high hurdle rates for reading business plans. The gap between the resources required by early stage technology entrepreneurs (typically, in the $100K to $2 million range) are inconsistent with the deal size required by mature venture capital firms to support operations given their current scale of operations.

Differences between venture capital and public modes of support for technology entrepreneurs go beyond both the capabilities of specialized intermediaries as compared with those of public officials and the quantity of funding sought. As work by Hsu (2004) and others has documented, entrepreneurs who seek venture capital investments are typically seeking more than funding. They also seek mentoring, access to contacts, and strategic guidance. In return they relinquish a degree (sometimes large) of control over their organizations. In contrast, a technology entrepreneur seeking a government award cannot expect to benefit from mentoring and other such forms of support. At the same time, however he or she can be assured that his or her equity stake will not be diluted. The risk–reward profile of the two forms of financing is thus sufficiently different to call into question the appropriateness of terms such as 'public venture capital' that are frequently used to describe various modes of public financial support to technology entrepreneurs. While the funds supplied may be public, the mode of support bears very little resemblance to venture capital.

To the extent that the sort of 'innovation gaps' referred to at the start of this section not only exist but persist over time, they do so because the skill set of individuals specialized in evaluating linked technical and commercial opportunities is very difficult to imitate. For this reason, varied contractual arrangements coexist, each offered within one of a diverse set of institutional contexts. Taken together, these arrangements provide technology entrepreneurs with a menu of options each with a distinct risk–reward profile. Design and implementation of effective policies to support technology entrepreneurs begins not by looking at one or another category of support in isolation, but rather with an understanding of, and appreciation for, the entirety of this menu of options.

Market failure reconsidered

> [I]t is possible to conceive of better worlds than the one in which we live. But the problem is to devise practical arrangements which correct defects in one part of the system without causing more serious harm in other parts.
>   . . . [W]hatever we may have in mind as our ideal world, it is clear that we have not yet discovered how to get to it from where we are. A better approach would seem to be to start our analysis with a situation approximating that which actually exists, to examine the effects of a proposed policy change and to attempt to decide whether the new situation would be, in total, better or worse than the original one. (Coase, 1960; pp. 34, 43)

In keeping with foundational work by Nelson (1959) and with further impetus from Romer (1986, 1990), both academics and policy-makers have for more than a decade emphasized imperfect appropriability as the specific market failure 'justifying' a government role in supporting entrepreneurs involved in the development of new technologies.[25] Accordingly, the evaluation of policy to support technology entrepreneurs has heavily emphasized the identification and measurement of 'knowledge spillovers' of various types as evidence of potential benefits to be realized by policy.

Arguably, it is when the path taken by 'new growth' theory led to policy that its lack of micro-foundations became all too apparent. Proponents of government support could claim that any investment in the support of technology development was justifiable because of 'increasing returns' to knowledge creation; skeptics would argue that such support was wasteful corporate welfare, and that decisions regarding the rate and direction of inventive activity were best left to better informed private actors.

In the United States, the decision to base policies for technology entrepreneurship on a market failure criterion has led to a policy deadlock. The political instability of the Advanced Technology Program (ATP) within the US Department of Commerce is instructive. In its 2004 assessment of the program, the White House Office of Management and Budget (OMB) noted that:

> ATP was initially established to address concerns about U.S. competitiveness in the late 1980s and early 1990s. However, one could argue that this concern has lessened in recent years. Studies show that there are many non-governmental entities investing in early-stage technology development,

such as corporate research labs, venture capital firms, angel investors, and universities. Given the amounts available from other sources, it is not evident that there is a clear need for federal subsidies for private technology development.

As evidence, the OMB cites the figures concerning sources of funding for early stage technology development in Branscomb and Auerswald (2002).

To be sure, where a narrow range of institutional sources of equity and debt capital typically support the incremental growth of existing businesses, the invention to innovation transition is financed by a great variety of mechanisms, as discussed above.[26] Yet the foregoing arguments suggest that the observed proliferation of institutional responses should be taken as an indication of the persistence – and possibly even growing severity – of the conditions complicating contracting for technical information.

A reconsideration of the market failure criterion for a government role provides a potential way out of the policy deadlock. If the market failure test is inappropriate and misleading, what is the alternative? The appropriate test is one of marginal impact or 'additionality'. Does government involvement result in actions being taken that would not have been taken otherwise by private actors in the absence of the policy? If so, did the policy result in societal benefits net of costs, taking into account the inefficiencies associated with revenue gathering? As Coase (1960) states, it is necessary to establish that the situation resulting from the envisioned policy will be 'in total, better . . . than the original one'. Market failure is important to policy not in its generalities but in its specifics.

The main point of this chapter is that market failures related to information asymmetries affect the extent and the nature of technology entrepreneurship far more than those related to incomplete appropriability. What does this particular observation mean for the formulation and implementation of entrepreneurship policy? Three principles follow directly:

1. *Assess policies according to deal-flow, not dollar-flow.* Transactions, not spillovers, are the measure of success in entrepreneurship policy. When public programs encourage private transactions that would not have occurred otherwise, the test of additionality is satisfied. The volume and quantity of such deals are tangible outcomes that can be measured. In contrast, when public programs are constructed with the aim of maximizing spillover benefits, they essentially focus first on dollar-flow into firms in the form of grants or contracts, and second on dollar-flow out of firms to the public in the form of spillover benefits. While it is easy to measure the flow of public funds into private firms, it is extremely difficult to measure the marginal impact of public investments on firm-level outcomes, and all but impossible to trace this through to 'knowledge spillovers' and other unpriced societal benefits. All other dimensions being equal, policies whose impacts are measurable should be preferred to policies whose impacts are not.
2. *Consider the information a program creates as part of its impact.* Impartiality, and the trust it can engender, is potentially one of the greatest assets of public sector actors. When public entities are broadly perceived to make decisions based on merit, the decisions themselves convey information. Such information is particularly valuable in settings where information asymmetries are severe, as they are in markets for technological information. Competitive public programs in support of technology entrepreneurs may serve an important function not only by directing resources to

promising projects that otherwise would not receive financing, but perhaps even more importantly by signalling quality to others in the market.[27]

3. *Understand the incentives and constraints of existing actors in the system.* Policies constructed to satisfy an additionality criterion must start with an understanding of the information, incentives and institutions that drive outcomes absent the policy intervention. In the case of the financing of technology entrepreneurs, for example, it is not adequate to observe that new technologies create economic and other social benefits, therefore public investment is warranted. It is also not adequate to state that many private entities are engaged in supporting technology entrepreneurs, therefore public investment is not warranted. Rather, it is necessary to understand the motivations and constraints that guide the decisions of private actors, and then to consider the outcomes of those decisions in the aggregate in the context of the public interest. If the public interest is not served by decentralized decision-making given existing information, incentives and institutions, then public action may be justified to add information, change incentives and create new institutions.

Conclusion

The challenges faced today by those involved in crafting and implementing entrepreneurship policy, particularly at the federal level, bear some similarity to those faced by the leading technology corporations in the United States in the 1960s, 1970s and 1980s. These large companies generated many basic science breakthroughs in noted research facilities such as Bell Labs and the Xerox Palo Alto Research Center (PARC). Yet, in many well-documented and widely discussed cases, these companies missed significant opportunities to turn inventions into profitable innovations. What is worse – in many cases the companies lost not only the inventions but also the inventors, as a result of inadequate support for the invention to innovation transition.

As the founder of Intel, Gordon Moore (noted also as the originator of 'Moore's Law') observed in recollections published in 2001:

> [i]n a pattern that clearly carries over to other technological ventures, we found at Fairchild that any company active on the forefront of semiconductor technology uncovers far more opportunities than it is in a position to pursue. And when people are enthusiastic about a particular opportunity but are not allowed to pursue it, they become potential entrepreneurs. As we have seen over the past few years, when these potential entrepreneurs are backed by a plentiful source of venture capital there is a burst of new enterprise.[28]

How much technology entrepreneurship and innovation is the right amount in a large corporation? A region? A nation? In every case, some 'leakage' occurs of ideas, people, projects. Moore continues:

> One of the reasons Intel has been so successful is that we have tried to eliminate unnecessary R&D, thus maximizing our R&D yield and minimizing costly spin-offs. But successful start-ups almost always begin with an idea that has ripened in the research organization of a large company (or university). Any region without larger companies at the technology frontier or research organizations of large companies will probably have fewer companies starting or spinning off. (Moore and Davis, 2001, p. 245)

A similar tension faces regions and nations as they struggle to encourage the 'horizontal' connections between researchers to spur invention, at the same time as they encourage 'vertical' connections between technologists and business executives in achieving the invention to innovation transition. In his Industrial Research Institute Medalist's Address provocatively titled 'The customer for R&D is always wrong!', Robert Frosch (former head of research at General Motors and Administrator of NASA, among other distinctions), offered the following observation:

> There is a kind of Heisenberg uncertainty principle about the coordination connections that are necessary in R&D. One needs all of these deep connections among kinds of knowledge, and the ability to think about the future, that works best in an institution that puts all those people together. One also needs connection with the day-to-day, market thinking, and the future thinking of the operating side of the business, which suggests to many that the R&D people should be sitting on the operating side of the business.
>
> This is an insoluble problem; there is no organizational system that will capture perfectly both sets of coordination . . . There is no perfect organization that will solve this problem – the struggle is inevitable. (Frosch, 1996, p. 24)

Neither the United States, nor its venture capital firms, nor its large corporations, have arrived at the perfect organizational structure to manage technology entrepreneurship and innovation. No such perfect organization exists elsewhere. If Frosch is correct, even in theory, fundamental contradictions inherent in the 'planning' of entrepreneurship and innovation suggest that it is misguided to aspire toward elegance, symmetry, and efficiency in this context. A better approach is to begin located within the complex and rapidly changing world in which technology entrepreneurs actually operate, and to undertake those feasible and cost-effective adjustments to the business environment that will facilitate the conclusion of deals that otherwise would not have taken place.

Notes

* This chapter derives in part from joint work with Lewis Branscomb, including Branscomb and Auerswald (2001) and Auerswald and Branscomb (2002). Funding from the National Institute of Standards and Technology is gratefully acknowledged. All errors are my own.
1. Quoted in Audretsch et al. (2002, p. 173).
2. The definition offered by Carree and Thurik (2003, p. 441) provides a more comprehensive expression of what I intend by the term entrepreneur: 'Entrepreneurship is the manifest ability to willingness of individuals, on their own, in teams, within and outside existing organizations to perceive and create new economic opportunities (new products, new production methods, new organizational schemes, and new product–market combinations), and to introduce their ideas in the market, in the face of uncertainty and other obstacles, but making decisions on the location, form, and use of resources and institutions.'
3. Kuznets (1962), Branscomb and Auerswald (2002).
4. This is not a critique of the theory any more than it is a critique of entrepreneurs. It is simply a description of the relevant axioms. The market equibrating role potentially attributable to entrepreneurs is proxied by the fictional figure of the 'Walrasian auctioneer' who calls out prices until the market clearing set of prices is found. The very existence of entrepreneurial opportunities – at the limit, proverbial $20 bills lying on sidewalks – indicates either the presence of some manner or another of market failure, or (in the spirit of Viner, 1932) that a competitive market is on a transitional path toward equilibrium.
5. Knight (1925), cited by Romer (1986), characterized this more general notion of increasing returns external to the firm as 'an empty economic box'.
6. Auerswald (2007).
7. The phenomenon of 'orphan drugs' is illustrative.
8. See, for example, Jaffe et al. (1993), and Mansfield (1995).
9. See, for example, Rosenberg and Birdzell (1985). Schumpeter (1928, 1942) emphasized the emerging role of large corporations. Papers in Nelson (1962) emphasize this phenomenon. Trends in the last 20 years have belied Schumpeter's prediction of the demise of knowledge-intensive entrepreneurial firms. Auerswald and Branscomb (2005) discuss this in detail.
10. Hirshman (1958) describes this with regard to medieval guilds.

11. Branscomb and Auerswald (2001, 2002).
12. Auerswald and Branscomb (2005).
13. Zeckhauser (1996).
14. Auerswald (2007).
15. Cohen and Levinthal (1989).
16. The Band of Angels (www.bandangels.com) was the first organized network of individual private equity investors, or 'angel' investors.
17. A classic paper by Reiter and Sherman (1962) titled 'Allocating indivisible resources affording external economies or diseconomies', anticipates recent work (e.g. Weitzman, 1998; Auerswald et al., 2000) on the firm as a solver of hard combinatorial optimization problems.
18. This phenomenon is at least a century old. As Schumpeter (1912 [1934]; p. 12) observes: 'This second "side" of production makes it, from the outset, an economic problem. It must be distinguished from the purely technological problem of production. There is a contrast between them which we frequently witness in economic life in the personal opposition between the technical and the commercial manager of the enterprise. We often see changes in the productive process recommended on one side and rejected on another. For example, the engineer may recommend a new process which the commercial head rejects with the argument that it will not pay.'
19. Passage quoted in Hsu (2001). Founded in June 1946, American Research & Development was among the first venture capital firms in the United States, and the first to raise funds from institutional investors. As described in detail by Hsu (2001), the firm was set up by Ralph Flanders, President of the Boston branch of the Federal Reserve and a trustee at MIT, Georges Doriot, a professor of industrial administration at Harvard Business School, and Karl Compton, President of MIT.
20. Green (2001).
21. US National Panel Survey of Business Start-ups, preliminary results.
22. Estimate from Jeff Sohl, University of New Hampshire.
23. Venture Economics and the National Venture Capital Association. It is also interesting to note that, according to the data gathered by the Association of University Technology Managers, only approximately 260 firms were created from university license or intellectual property.
24. The Band of Angels founder Severiens noted in 2001 that most larger venture capital firms were no longer focused on new firm creation, as opposed to the development of existing firms: '[At the time we started the Band of Angels] the big venture funds were getting bigger and bigger. What used to be a normal venture capital partnership, which maybe managed $50 million, all of a sudden, they were managing ten times as much. Nowadays one hears of billion-dollar ones. And as a result of that, the average amount of money going in per deal had to go up. Of course, you're certainly not going to increase your staff by a large number. You don't need to, because you only need to make fifty, sixty, seventy investments to get adequate diversity to mitigate the risks. The bigger funds were not funding quite as much as they used to. There seemed to be an opportunity for some of us.' Comments from Severiens shared at the 'Between Invention and Innovation' workshop held on 1–2 May, 2001, at the Kennedy School of Government, Harvard University.
25. The literature on entrepreneurship in general, rather than technology entrepreneurship in particular, has tended to place relatively greater emphasis on financing constraints.
26. A report from the National Commission on Entrepreneurship (Zacharakis et al., 1999, p. 33) notes that 'the substantial amount of funding provided through informal channels, orders of magnitude greater than provided by formal venture capital investments and heretofore unknown and unappreciated, suggests some mechanisms for filling the gap may have developed without recognition.'
27. In the limit, awards programs realize signaling benefits without any direct financing in the form of grants or contracts.
28. Moore and Davis (2001, pp. 23–4).

References

Appleyard, M.M. (2003), 'The influence of knowledge accumulation on buyer–supplier co-development projects', *The Journal of Product Innovation Management*, **20** (5), 356–73.

Arrow, K.J. (1962), 'Economic welfare and the allocation of resources from invention', in R.R. Nelson (ed.), *The Rate and Direction of Inventive Activity: Economic and Social Factors*, Princeton, NJ: Princeton University Press.

Audretsch, D.B., B. Bozeman, K.L. Combs, M. Feldman, A.N. Link, D.S. Siegel, P. Stephan, G. Tassey and C. Wessner (2002), 'The economics of science and technology policy', *Journal of Technology Transfer*, **27**, 155–203.

Auerswald, P.E. (2007), 'Entrepreneurship in the theory of the firm', *Small Business Economics*, (forthcoming).

Auerswald, P.E. and L.M. Branscomb (2005), 'Reflections on Mansfield, technological complexity, and the "Golden Age" of U.S. corporate R&D', *Journal of Technology Transfer*, **30** (1/2), 139–57.

Auerswald, P.E., L.M. Branscomb, J.N. Demos and B.K. Min (2005), 'Understanding private-sector decision making for early-stage technology development: a between invention and innovation project report', report for the Advanced Technology Program, National Institute of Standards and Technology (NIST), US Department of Commerce, September.

Auerswald, P.E., S. Kauffman, J. Lobo and K. Shell (2000), 'The production recipes approach to modeling technological innovation: an application to learning by doing', *Journal of Economic Dynamics and Control*, **24**, 389–450.

Branscomb, L.M. and P.E. Auerswald (2001), *Taking Technical Risks: How Innovators, Executives and Investors Manage High-tech Risks*, Cambridge, MA: MIT Press.

Branscomb, L.M. and P.E. Auerswald (2002), 'Between invention and innovation: an analysis of funding for early stage technology development', Report GCR 02'U841, Advanced Technology Program, National Institute for Standards and Technology NIST, US Department of Commerce, November.

Carree, M.A. and A.R. Thurik (2003), 'The impact of entrepreneurship on economic growth', in Z.J. Acs and D.B. Audretsch (eds), *Handbook of Entrepreneurship Research*, Boston, MA, Dordrecht, The Netherlands: Kluwer Academic Publishers.

Coase, R. (1937), 'The nature of the firm', *Economica*, **4**, 386–405.

Coase, R. (1960), 'The problem of social cost', *Journal of Law and Economics*, **3**, 1–44.

Cohen, W.A. and D.A. Levinthal (1989), 'Innovation and learning: the two faces of R&D', *Economic Journal*, **99** (397), 569–96.

Foster, A.D. and M.R. Rosenzweig (1995), 'Learning by doing and learning from others: human capital and technical change in agriculture', *Journal of Political Economy*, **103** (6), 1176–209.

Frosch, R.A. (1996), 'The customer for R&D is always wrong!', *Research-Technology Management*, **39** (November/December), 22–7.

Gompers, P.A. and J. Lerner (1999), *The Venture Capital Cycle*, Cambridge, MA: MIT Press.

Green, H. (2001), 'Innovation drought', *Business Week e.biz*, 9 July, p. 14.

Henderson, R., G.P. Pisano and L. Orsenigo (1999), 'The pharmaceutical industry and the revolution in molecular biology: interactions among scientific, institutional, and organizational change', in D. Mowery and R. Nelson (eds), *Sources of Industrial Leadership*, Cambridge: Cambridge University Press, pp. 267–311.

Hirshman, A.O. (1958), *The Strategy of Economic Development*, New Haven, CT: Yale University Press.

Hsu, D.H. (2001), 'The evolution of organizational practices at an early venture capital firm: a study of American Research & Development, 1946–1973, unpublished manuscript.

Hsu, D.H. (2004), 'What do entrepreneurs pay for venture capital affiliation?', *Journal of Finance*, **59** (4), August, 1805–44.

Jaffe, A., M. Trajtenberg and R. Henderson (1993), 'Geographic localization of knowledge spillovers as evidenced by patent citations', *Quarterly Journal of Economics*, **63** (3), 577–98.

Griliches, Z. (1992), 'The search for R&D spillovers', *Scandinavian Journal of Economics*, **94**, Supplement, S29–47.

Kuznets, S. (1962), 'Inventive activity: problems of definition and measurement', in R.R. Nelson (ed.), *The Rate and Direction of Inventive Activity: Economic and Social Factors*, Princeton, NJ: Princeton University Press.

Lerner, J. (2002), 'When bureaucrats meet entrepreneurs: the design of effective "public venture capital" programmes', *The Economic Journal*, **112** (February), F73–F84.

Mansfield, E. (1995), 'Academic research underlying industrial innovations: sources, characteristics and financing', *Review of Economics and Statistics*, **77** (1), 55–65.

Marshall, A. (1890), *The Principles of Economics*, London: Macmillan.

Moore, G. and K. Davis (2001), 'Learning the Silicon Valley way', Working Paper 00-45, Stanford Institute for Economic Policy Research.

Morgenthaler, D. (2004), 'Assessing technical risk', in L.M. Branscomb and K.P. Morse (eds), *Managing Technical Risk: Understanding Private Sector Decision Making on Early Stage, Technology-based Projects*, National Institute of Standards and Technology (NIST) Report No. GCR 00-787, Washington, DC: NIST.

Nelson, R.R. (1959), 'The simple economics of basic scientific research', *Journal of Political Economy*, **67**, 297–306.

Nelson, R.R. (ed.) (1962), *The Rate and Direction of Inventive Activity: Economic and Social Factors*, Princeton: Princeton University Press.

Reiter, S. and G.R. Sherman (1962), 'Allocating indivisible resources affording external economies or diseconomies', *International Economic Review*, **3** (1), 108–35.

Romer, P.M. (1986), 'Increasing returns and long-run growth', *Journal of Political Economy*, **94**, 1002–37.

Romer, P.M. (1990), 'Endogenous technological change', *Journal of Political Economy*, **98** (5), S71–S102.

Rosenberg, N. and L.E. Birdzell Jr (1985), *How the West Grew Rich: The Economic Transformation of the Industrial World*, New York: Basic Books.

Schumpeter, J.A. (1912), *Theorie der wirtschaftlichen Entwicklung*, Leipzig: Duncker and Humblot. Revised English translation (1934) by Redvers Opie, *The Theory of Economic Development*, Cambridge, MA: Harvard University Press.

Schumpeter, J.A. (1928), 'The instability of capitalism', *The Economic Journal*, **38** (51), 361–86.
Schumpeter, J.A. (1942), *Capitalism, Socialism and Democracy*, New York: Harper and Row.
Viner, J. (1932), 'Cost curves and supply curves', *Zeitschrift für Nationalökonomie*, **3**, 23–46.
Weitzman, M.L. (1998), 'Recombinant growth', *Quarterly Journal of Economics*, **113** (2), 331–60.
White House Office of Management and Budget (2004), *2004 PART Assessment of the US Department of Commerce, Advanced Technology Program*, available at http://www.whitehouse.gov/omb/budget/fy2004/pma/advancedtech.xls.
Zacharakis, A., P.D. Reynolds and W.D. Bygrave (1999), 'National entrepreneurship assessment: United States of America, 1999 executive report', report for National Commission on Entrepreneurship.
Zeckhauser, R.J. (1996), 'The challenge of contracting for technological information', *Proceedings of the National Academy of Sciences*, **93** (12), 12743–8.
Zucker, L.G., M.R. Darby and J. Armstrong (1998a), 'Geographically localized knowledge: spillovers or markets?', *Economic Inquiry*, **36**, 65–86.
Zucker, L.G., M.R. Darby and M.B. Brewer (1998b), 'Intellectual human capital and the birth of U.S. biotechnology enterprises', *American Economic Review*, **88** (1), 290–306.

3 From small business to entrepreneurship policy*
David B. Audretsch and Iris A. M. Beckmann

Policy makers' emerging interest in entrepreneurship

The emergence of entrepreneurship policy as a mechanism to stimulate economic growth, employment generation, and competitiveness in global markets is a phenomenon in many countries. In fact, a shift in economic policy started during the 1990s and the promotion of start-ups turned into an important policy strategy to achieve these goals. Just a few years earlier entrepreneurship and, in particular new and small firms, were viewed as imposing a burden on the economy. For example, the Small Business Administration in the United States was created with a clear and compelling mandate to protect and pre-serve firms that were burdened with size-inherent inefficiencies rendering them uncom-petitive. Traditionally, the public policy focus on economic growth has revolved around macroeconomic instruments involving monetary and fiscal policies.

The shift in policy focus can be best illustrated looking at the new growth policy of the EU that would have been unimaginable only a few years earlier. The European Union devised a new strategy to spur economic growth, create jobs and reduce unemployment. With the 2000 Lisbon Strategy, Romano Prodi, who was at the time serving as President of the European Commission, committed Europe to becoming the economic leader by 2010 in order to ensure prosperity and a high standard of living throughout the continent. More to the point, Prodi declared in a speech given in 2002 that the promotion of entre-preneurship was a central cornerstone of European economic growth policy: 'Our lacunae in the field of entrepreneurship need to be taken seriously because there is mount-ing evidence that the key to economic growth and productivity improvements lies in the entrepreneurial capacity of an economy' (Prodi, 2002, p. 1).

The purpose of this chapter is to explain how and why public policy has turned toward entrepreneurship as a mechanism for generating economic growth and employment. The following section reviews the public policy approach consistent with first the capital-driven, or Solow economy, during the post-war era, which subsequently gave way to the knowledge-based, or Romer economy, toward the end of the last century. In the third section the determinants of the shift from SME (small and medium-sized enterprise) policy to entrepreneurship policy are explained. Why entrepreneurship policy diffused across many different national and regional contexts is explained in the fourth section. The policy instruments to create an entrepreneurial economy differ however across coun-tries and regions. The fifth section takes a closer look at the commonalities and differences in entrepreneurship policy instruments using the United States and Germany as exam-ples. The chapter concludes by suggesting that entrepreneurship policy is the deliberate attempt to create an entrepreneurial economy. Thus this chapter does not advocate any particular set of policies and certainly no specific policy instruments to promote entre-preneurship. As Gordon Moore, who is 'widely regarded as one of Silicon Valley's found-ing fathers' (Bresnahan and Gambardella, 2004, p. 7) and Kevin Davis warn, the policy rush to emulate the Silicon Valley success is somewhat misguided: 'The potential disaster lies in the fact that these static, descriptive efforts culminate in policy recommendations and analytical tomes that resemble recipes or magic potions such as combine liberal amounts of technology, entrepreneurs, capital, and sunshine; add one university; stir vigorously' (Moore and Davis, 2004, p. 9). It is argued that the correct choice of entrepreneurship policy instruments is determined by context. This chapter brings light to the rationale behind entrepreneurship policy and explains why it is regionally rooted and focused on the individual entrepreneur.

Policy in the Solow economy: SME policy
The role of entrepreneurship in the economy has changed significantly over the last 50 years (Audretsch, 2007). During the early post World War II era, the importance of entrepreneurship and small business seemed to fade away. While alarm was expressed that small businesses needed to be preserved and protected for social and political reasons (Anglund, 1998; Beyenburg-Weidenfeld, 1992), few argued on the basis of economic efficiency. This position has been drastically reversed in recent years. Entrepreneurship has come to be perceived as an engine of economic and social development around the world.

Along with these changes in the economy a considerable economic policy shift occurred. Economic policy in the post World War II era dealt with the negative impact of market concentration on the welfare and the inefficiency of small and medium-sized enterprises. In the 1990s new types of economic policy instruments were used that were very different from previous approaches. These entrepreneurship policies differ with regard to the objective and mechanism used to achieve economic growth. While SMEs and start-ups were once perceived as inefficient entities that had to be preserved for social and political reasons, now there is strong interest by policy makers to promote entrepreneurship in order to stimulate economic growth. It is important to analyze the policy approach of the Solow economy in order to be able to show the differences between previous and current economic policy regimes.

In the Solow economy, public policy toward business revolved around finding solutions to the perceived tradeoff between scale and efficiency on the one hand, and decentralization and inefficiency on the other hand. The key public policy question of the day was 'How can society reap the benefits of the large corporation in an oligopolistic setting while avoiding or at least minimizing the costs imposed by a concentration of economic power?' The policy response was to constrain the freedom of firms to contract. Such policy restraints typically took the form of instruments involving public ownership, regulation and competition policy (as it was called in Europe) or antitrust law as in the United States.

At that time macroeconomic policy played a large role in the strategies for economic growth. The principal mechanism in the post-war economy for inducing higher growth rates was usually physical capital investment. This model of the economy was capital-driven. Increasing the labor factor could increase the level of economic output, but not the overall rate of economic growth.

While monetary policy advocates focused on using interest rates to induce capital investments, fiscal policy advocates wanted to use taxes and government spending to generate short-term growth to induce investments into new physical capital, thereby ensuring long-term growth. Ultimately, however, while the specific instruments remained at the center of intellectual and political debate, near consensus left the overarching mechanism to achieve economic growth essentially unchallenged.

Different countries blended these three policy instruments in very different proportions (Audretsch and Thurik, 2001). France and Sweden were at the vanguard of governmental business ownership. The Netherlands and Germany, in contrast, emphasized regulation. The United States placed more weight on antitrust enforcement.

While the context was considerably different, the policy mechanism choices to foster economic growth were no different for developing countries. The intellectual and policy focus on how to foster growth and prosperity in developing countries revolved around instruments to encourage inward foreign direct investment. The context of developing countries may have suggested a selection of different instruments uniquely suited for the development context, but the mechanism used to attain the policy goal of economic growth remained the same – physical capital investment. Also, while the particular instruments may have varied across countries, they were, in fact, manifestations of a singular policy approach – how to restrict and restrain the power of large corporations.

The policy focus on capital as the driving input for economic growth during the post World War II era generated simultaneous concern about the organization of that capital, both at the industry and the firm level. In particular, the emerging field of industrial organization was charged with the task of identifying how capital organization, or industry structure, influenced economic performance. A generation of scholars produced theoretical and empirical evidence suggesting that physical capital in many, but not all, industries dictated a concentration of production resulting in an oligopolisitic market structure characterized by an ownership concentration with relatively few producers (Scherer, 1970).

Scholars spanning a broad spectrum of academic fields and disciplines attempted to sort out the perceived tradeoff between economic efficiency on the one hand and political and economic decentralization on the other. The large corporation was not just thought to have superior productive efficiency but was also assumed to be the engine of technological innovation. Ironically, the literature's obsession with oligopoly was combined with essentially static analysis. There was considerable concern about what to do about the existing industrial structure but little attention was paid to where it came from and where it was going. Oliver Williamson's classic 1968 article 'Economies as an antitrust defense: the welfare tradeoffs', published in the *American Economic Review*, became something of a final statement demonstrating that gains in productive efficiency could be obtained through increased concentration, and that gains in terms of competition, and implicitly democracy, could be achieved through decentralizing policies. But it did not seem possible to have both, certainly not in Williamson's completely static model.

While a heated debate emerged about which approach best promoted large-scale production while simultaneously constraining the ability of large corporations to exert excessive market power, there was less debate about public policy toward small business and entrepreneurship. The only issue was whether public policy makers should simply allow small firms to disappear as a result of their inefficiency, or intervene to preserve them for social and political reasons (Beyenburg-Weidenfeld, 1992; May and McHugh, 2002). Those who perceived small firms to contribute significantly to growth, employment generation and competitiveness were few and far between.[1] Thus, in the post-war era, small firms and entrepreneurship were viewed as a luxury, perhaps needed by the West to ensure the decentralization of decision making, but in any case obtained only at a cost to efficiency. Small businesses were perceived as a drag on economic efficiency and growth, generating lower quality jobs in terms of direct and indirect compensation, and generally on the way to becoming less important to the economy, if not threatened by long-term extinction. Certainly systematic empirical evidence, gathered from both Europe and North America, documented a sharp trend towards a decreased role of small firms during the post-war period (Acs and Audretsch, 1993).

Public policy toward small firms generally reflected the view of economists and other scholars. Some countries, such as the Soviet Union, Sweden and France, adopted the policy of allowing small firms to gradually disappear and account for a smaller share of economic activity (Geroski, 1989; Hjalmarsson, 1991).

US public policy, on the other hand, reflected the long-term political and social valuation of small firms that seemed to reach back to the Jeffersonian traditions of the country. After all, in the 1890 debate in Congress, Senator Sherman vowed, 'If we will not endure a King as a political power we should not endure a King over the production, transportation, and sale of the necessaries of life. If we would not submit to an emperor we should not submit to an autocrat of trade with power to prevent competition and to fix the price of any commodity.'[2]

Thus public policy toward small businesses in the United States was oriented towards preserving what were considered to be inefficient enterprises, which, if left unprotected, might otherwise become extinct. An example of such preservationist policies toward small businesses was provided by the enactment and enforcement of the Robinson–Patman Act. Even advocates of small businesses agreed that small firms were less efficient than big companies. These advocates were willing to sacrifice a modicum of efficiency, however, because of other contributions – moral, political and otherwise – made by small businesses to society (e.g. Scherer, 1975). Small business policy was thus 'preservationist' in character.

The same political rationale was clearly at work with the creation of the US Small Business Administration. In the Small Business Act of 10 July 1953, Congress authorized the creation of the Small Business Administration, with an explicit mandate to 'aid, counsel, assist and protect . . . the interests of small business concerns'.[3] The Small Business Act was an attempt by Congress to halt the continued disappearance of small businesses and to preserve their role in the US economy.

Thus SMEs and entrepreneurship were not important for economic growth in the Solow economy. Economic growth was solely capital-driven. Hence, large corporations had an advantage with regard to innovations, because they could invest more in R&D, and could realize scale economies. Policy makers were also preoccupied by the welfare effects of particular market structures. Unemployment was not such a big issue in societies, and it is important to note that SME policy was not implemented for job growth. It was believed that the largest number of jobs were created by large companies until David Birch published his study on job creation of small businesses in 1979 (Birch, 1979). Today, job creation is a major, if not the most important, economic policy issue in many countries, and policy makers aim at stimulating economic growth and job creation at the same time. These objectives differ considerably from the motivations for previous SME policies.

In the following section the determinants of economic change that led to the emergence of a new economic policy for the promotion of entrepreneurship are analyzed. The next section deals with the rationale behind the new entrepreneurship policies and the determinants that caused the shift in economic policy focus during the 1990s.

The emergence of the entrepreneurship policy mandate
The emergence of entrepreneurship policies in many countries is a phenomenon of the 1990s. This emergence emanates from the failure of traditional policy instruments corresponding to the Solow model, or those based on instruments promoting investment in physical capital, to adequately maintain economic growth and employment in globalized markets on the one hand. The second push for the entrepreneurship policy mandate came from the opposite direction: the failure of the so-called new economy policy instruments, corresponding to the Romer model or those promoting investment into knowledge capital, to adequately generate economic growth and employment. Although coming from opposite directions, both try to cope with unacceptable economic performance, which is to say that the mandate for entrepreneurship policy is rooted in dissatisfaction – dissatisfaction with the status quo economic performance.[4]

Fundamental changes in the economy caused by what is generally termed globalization are responsible for immense problems policy makers face, particularly in the industrialized countries. The rationale behind entrepreneurship policy stems from these changes. Regions and even countries that had prospered during the post-war economy characterized by the Solow model were now adversely affected by globalization and loss of competitiveness in traditional industries, resulting in an adverse economic performance.

Corporations across the developed countries faced increased international competition. Pressed to maintain competitiveness in traditional low- and medium-level technology industries, where economic activity can be easily transferred across geographic space to access lower production costs, large corporations throughout the OECD countries deployed two strategic responses (Audretsch et al., 2006). The first was to offset greater wage differentials between Europe and low-cost locations by increasing productivity through the substitution of technology and capital for labor. The second was to locate new plants and establishments in lower cost locations, through either outward foreign direct investment, outsourcing, or both.

What these strategic responses have in common is that the companies have downsized the number of employees in their home countries. This has happened both in Europe and in the United States. For example, between 1991 and 1995 manufacturing employment in German plants decreased by 1 307 000 while it increased in foreign subsidiaries by 189 000 (BMWi, 1999). In the chemical sector, the decrease of domestic employment was 80 000, while 14 000 jobs were added by German chemical companies in plants located outside Germany. In electrical engineering, employment in German plants decreased by 198 000. In automobile manufacturing employment in Germany decreased by 161 000, while German firms added 30 000 jobs outside their home territories (see Table 3.1).

Developments in the international economy have caused changes to market structures leading to high unemployment rates, particularly in the European countries, and this has had significant effects on government budgets. The massive changes in the economic environment have affected the effectiveness of existing national policies and institutions that were designed for a capital-driven Solow economy. Consequently, past economic policy strategies guaranteeing stability and economic growth for the long haul are today outdated. Michigan's institutions and public policies once channeled capital and labor into the

Table 3.1 Change in employment figures in Germany and at foreign subsidiaries (1991–95, in thousands)

Employment sector	Foreign	Domestic
Manufacturing	189	−1.307
Chemicals	14	−80
Electrical engineering	−17	−198
Automotive	30	−161
Mechanical engineering	16	−217
Textiles	−6	−68
Banking and insurance	21	28

automobile industry; while in Pittsburgh, Gary and Cleveland these were channeled on behalf of steel. In Europe, the same processes functioned for steel in the Ruhr Valley and automobiles in Baden-Würtenberg. Most recently, such regions have been subjected to losses of traditional competitive advantage in traditional industries, along with the corresponding downsizing, outsourcing and loss of employment resulting from globalization.

The implementation of entrepreneurship policy has to be seen in this context. The loss of jobs caused by downsizing made policy makers look for new mechanisms to create jobs. Unable to force job creation by existing companies, the focus turned to new businesses and the stimulation of an entrepreneurial climate.

As knowledge has become more important as a factor of production, knowledge spillovers have also become more important as a source of economic growth (Romer, 1986). Entrepreneurship takes on new importance in a knowledge economy because it serves as a key mechanism by means of which knowledge created in one organization becomes commercialized in a new enterprise.

Initially start-ups do not create as many jobs as foreign direct investment or the establishment of a plant. However, by focusing on research-based start-ups policy makers try to stimulate internationally competitive start-ups that will ultimately create high quality jobs.

Policy makers identified knowledge as a source of economic growth. If physical capital was at the heart of the Solow economy, knowledge capital became the heart of the Romer economy. In a global economy the competitive advantage of high cost countries stems from innovation, consequently, universities and research institutes gained attention from policy makers who developed policy instruments to invest in knowledge.

The first generation of new policy instruments corresponding to the knowledge-driven economy, or the Romer model, generally involved inducing investments not necessarily in physical capital, but rather in knowledge capital. However these instruments were not very successful. Substantial investments in universities as well as research and development (R&D) were undertaken but had a disappointing yield in terms of economic growth and employment creation. Shifting policy focus to knowledge capital using instruments to induce knowledge capital investment has been successful in generating economic growth for many regions. However as the Knowledge Spillover Theory of Entrepreneurship (Audretsch et al., 2006) suggests, investments in knowledge capital may be a necessary but not sufficient condition to ensure that such investments are actually commercialized and generate economic growth. The existence of a strong knowledge filter impedes the spillover and commercialization of investments in new knowledge, thereby choking off the economic growth potential.

Perhaps it is at the country level where the failure of knowledge investments to generate economic growth is most striking. Consider Sweden: throughout the post-war era, Sweden has consistently ranked among the highest in the world in terms of investments in new knowledge. Whether measured in terms of private R&D, levels of education, university research or public research, Sweden has exhibited strong and sustained investment in new knowledge. As recently as 2003, Sweden had the highest ratio of GDP invested in R&D. Yet, despite these investments in knowledge, the return in terms of employment creation and economic growth has been modest, at best, and disappointing to Swedish policy makers (Goldfarb and Henrekson, 2003).

Similar examples of large investments in new knowledge yielding a low performance in terms of economic growth can be found across Europe (Tjissen and van Wilke, 1999; Archibugi and Coco, 2005), spanning Germany and France, leading the European Union to invent a new term for the European failure to commercialize investments in new knowledge – *The European Paradox* (European Commission, 1995).

Examples of high investments in knowledge but low growth performance are not limited to Europe – one Asian example is Japan. Investments in private R&D and human capital have ranked among the highest in the world, yet, Japan had low and stagnant growth for over a decade.

As the traditional policy instruments targeting either physical capital or knowledge capital failed to generate sustainable economic growth, employment and competitiveness in globally linked markets, policy makers began to look elsewhere. The political mandate for entrepreneurship was to replace or at least augment physical capital, and augment knowledge capital as the missing link. Entrepreneurship is the mechanism facilitating the return on investments made in knowledge that were not previously being accrued in terms of economic growth and employment by those regions making such investments.

Thus the inadequate economic performance of specific regions and/or entire countries and the inability of the traditional policy approaches to deliver sustainable economic performance led to a refocusing of public policy toward entrepreneurship as the engine of economic growth and employment creation. Whether or not this disappointment was with the traditional economic policy strategy of investment in physical or knowledge capital, apparently something had been missing in the economic growth strategy. This missing link in economic growth has been entrepreneurship.

In many countries one can observe that new policies have included this missing link – the promotion of entrepreneurship – from policy conception through implementation. Entrepreneurship policy emerged as the cornerstone in the strategic management of economies. These new policies are not designed to support existing businesses, as was the case with previous small business policies, or just to invest in the creation of knowledge. Instead, the new entrepreneurship policies focus on knowledge commercialization; that is, they support the creation of business ideas.

Diffusion

Governments around the world typically have the same goals: to reduce unemployment and stimulate economic growth. However, there are significant national and regional differences in the nature of these problems, and some countries and regions seem better able to cope with these challenges than others. While some regions have success in the entrepreneurial economy, others do not. Observing these differences, policy makers have started to look for effective solutions and ways to positively influence economic development in the new economic environment.

The earliest sighting of an entrepreneurial economy was California's Silicon Valley during the 1980s. As Gordon Moore, the co-founder of Intel, who has been attributed to be one of the founding fathers of Silicon Valley, suggests, 'We hold that the central element in the history of Silicon Valley is the founding of a previously unknown type of regional dynamic, high-technology economy' (Moore and Davis, 2004, p. 7). Certainly at that point in time, innovation and new technology were generally associated with the large flagship corporations, such as IBM, Wang and DEC, which seemed invincible with their large armies of engineers and scientists. These scientists demonstrated undying loyalty to their employers forged from life-time contracts and a generally paternalistic stance towards their employees.

In the 1984 best seller by Peters and Waterman, *In Search of Excellence*, which documented the top 50 US corporations, these characteristics not only placed IBM at the top of the list, but also served as a shining example for corporate America to learn from and imitate. The incipient entrepreneurial economy of Silicon Valley provided a striking contrast, where people were quick to leave their companies to start new firms and, on occasion, entirely new industries.

While IBM was large and bureaucratic with rules and hierarchical decision making, the emerging Silicon Valley entrepreneurial economy thrived on spontaneity, participation, openness and a general disdain for rules and hierarchy. If obedience and conformity were trademarks of the capital-driven economy corresponding to the Solow model, the entrepreneurial economy above all values creativity, originality, independence and autonomy (Audretsch and Thurik, 2001).

The entrepreneurial economy subsequently diffused to places such as Boston's Route 128, Research Triangle in North Carolina and Austin, Texas. More recently, the diffusion of the entrepreneurial climate in the United States has been more pervasive, including not just the Washington DC region, San Diego, Los Angeles, Salt Lake City, and Seattle, but also smaller cities such as Madison, Wisconsin.

As previously described, the entrepreneurial economy's institutions focus chiefly on networks and linkages and include research universities, such as technology parks, and non-traditional sources of early stage capital, such as angel capital and venture capital. These institutions are a departure from the Solow economy stalwarts, which were unions, big government programs and corporate hierarchies.

Diffusion of the entrepreneurial economy has in some cases occurred organically in the absence of dedicated and targeted public policies. In other cases, public policy, including a broad spectrum of public–private partnerships, has been directed toward encouraging the transition to an entrepreneurial economy.

The central issue for policy makers is to find the key mechanisms for economic prosperity. Policies encouraging entrepreneurship have been chosen by policy makers in many different countries. Thus entrepreneurship policy as a bona fide approach to generating economic growth has not just emerged in a few places, but rather has diffused across a broad spectrum of national, regional and local contexts.

Entrepreneurship policy: instruments
There are significant differences in entrepreneurship policy from country to country. However, they all have the same policy goal. This section deals with two questions: What constitutes entrepreneurship policy and a bona fide entrepreneurship policy instrument? And who actually implements entrepreneurship policy?

In distinguishing entrepreneurship policy from more traditional approaches towards business, a shift has occurred away from the focus on the traditional triad of policy instruments essentially constraining the freedom of firms to contract – regulation, competition policy or antitrust in the US, and public ownership of business. The policy approach of constraint was sensible as long as the major issue was how to restrain large firms in possession of considerable market power. The fact that this policy approach toward business is less relevant in a global economy is reflected by the waves of deregulation and privatization throughout the OECD.

Instead, a new policy approach has emerged: one that focuses on enabling the creation and commercialization of knowledge. Probably the greatest and most salient change in small business policy over the last 15 years has been a shift from trying to preserve small businesses that are confronted with a cost disadvantage due to size-inherent scale disadvantages, toward promoting the start-up and viability of new and small firms involved in the commercialization of knowledge, or knowledge-based entrepreneurship.

Small business policy typically refers to policies implemented by governmental agencies charged with the mandate to promote small businesses. The actual definition of a small business varies considerably across countries, ranging from enterprises with fewer than 500 employees in the United States and Canada, to fewer than 250 employees in the European Union, to 50 employees in many developing countries.

Small business policy typically takes the existing enterprises within the appropriate size class as exogenous, or given, and then develops instruments to promote the continued viability of those enterprises. Thus small business policy is almost exclusively targeted at the existing stock of enterprises and virtually all the instruments included in the policy portfolio are designed to promote the viability of these small businesses.

In contrast, entrepreneurship policy has a much broader focus. The definition, introduced by Stevenson and Lundström (2001, p. 19) for OECD countries, is 'Entrepreneurship policy consists of measures taken to stimulate more entrepreneurial behaviour in a region or country . . . We define entrepreneurship policy as those measures intended to directly influence the level of entrepreneurial vitality in a country or a region.'

There are at least two important features that distinguish entrepreneurship policy from small business policy (Stevenson and Lundström, 2005). The first is the breadth of policy orientation and instruments. While small business policy focuses on the existing stock of small firms, entrepreneurship policy is more encompassing because it includes potential entrepreneurs. Entrepreneurship policy also has greater sensitivity to contextual conditions and frameworks that shape the decision-making process of entrepreneurs and potential entrepreneurs.

While small business policy is primarily concerned with one organizational level, the enterprise, entrepreneurship policy encompasses multiple levels of organization and analysis. These range from the individual to the enterprise level and focus on clusters or networks. The various perspectives might involve an industry or sectoral dimension, or a spatial dimension, such as a district, city, region, or even an entire country. Just as each of these levels is an important target for policy, the interactions and linkages across these disparate levels are also important. In this sense, entrepreneurship policy tends to be more holistic than small business policy.

The second way of distinguishing entrepreneurship policy from traditional small business policy is that virtually every country has a governmental agency charged with promoting the viability of the small business sector. These ministries and agencies have by now developed a large arsenal of policy instruments to promote small businesses. However, no agencies exist to promote entrepreneurship. Part of the challenge of implementing entrepreneurship policy is this lack of agency-level institution. Rather, aspects relevant to entrepreneurship policy can be found across a broad spectrum of ministries, ranging from education to trade and immigration. Thus, while small businesses have agencies and ministries to protect their issues, no analogous agency exists for entrepreneurs.

Not only is entrepreneurship policy implemented by radically different agencies from those implementing either the traditional policy instruments constraining the freedom of firms to contract or those implementing traditional small business policy, it involves a very different and distinct set of policy instruments. Stevenson and Lundström (2005) meticulously classified the broad and diverse range of instruments that are being used around the globe to promote entrepreneurship. Examples of the emerging entrepreneurship policy abound. Still, the point to be emphasized here is not so much the efficacy of the policy, but rather the clearly stated goal – to promote the spillover of knowledge from universities for commercialization that will foster innovation and ultimately economic growth.

Not only are the instruments of entrepreneurship policy decidedly distinct from those traditionally used toward business, and small business in particular, but the locus of such enabling policies is also different. The instruments constraining the freedom of firms to contract – antitrust, regulation and public ownership – were generally controlled and administered at the national level. By contrast, the instruments of entrepreneurship policy are generally applied at decentralized levels: state, city and local government.

As Stevenson and Lundstrom (2005) point out, entrepreneurship policy uses a wide variety of instruments such as changing regulations, taxes, immigration and education, as well as more direct instruments such as the provision of finance or training. If entrepreneurship policy can be viewed as the deliberate attempt to create an entrepreneurial economy, entire institutions that were the cornerstone of the Solow economy are being challenged and reconfigured in favor of the entrepreneurial economy.

However, the shape of entrepreneurship policies differs and it is worthwhile to look at specific entrepreneurship policies in different countries. The first example deals with the effects of changing regulation – in the United States, the implementation of the Bayh–Dole Act boosted entrepreneurial action by universities. The second example presents entrepreneurship policy programs – Germany is a good example to show specific entrepreneurship policies, particularly with regard to previous start-up support programs in the framework of small business policy.

Entrepreneurship policy in the United States: the Bayh–Dole Act
One example of a successful change in regulations that boosted research-based entrepreneurship is the Bayh–Dole Act of 1980.[5] This legislation gave academic institutions

property rights for the results of federally funded research. Before, universities that had received federal funds for research had to engage in complex negotiations with government agencies who owned the patents before commercialization could occur. With the Bayh–Dole Act the incentives for universities to promote and profit from the commercialization of inventions and license their technologies increased significantly. This new policy instrument reflects a policy shift concentrating on enabling the creation and viability of entrepreneurial firms. *The Economist* (2002) wrote:

> Possibly the Bayh–Dole Act is the most inspired piece of legislation to be enacted in America over the past half-century. Together with amendments in 1984 and augmentation in 1986, this unlocked all the inventions and discoveries that had been made in laboratories through the United States with the help of taxpayers' money. More than anything, this single policy measure helped to reverse America's precipitous slide into industrial irrelevance. Before Bayh-Dole, the fruits of research supported by government agencies had gone strictly to the federal government. Nobody could exploit such research without tedious negotiations with a federal agency concerned. Worse, companies found it nigh impossible to acquire exclusive rights to a government owned patent. And without that, few firms were willing to invest millions more of their own money to turn a basic research idea into a marketable product.[6]

The Bayh–Dole Act coupled with other legal, economic and political developments was perceived as a trigger to major national economic growth, because universities started to have a great interest in licensing (Mowery, 2005). The President of the Association of American Universities claimed, 'Before Bayh–Dole, the federal government had accumulated 30,000 patents, of which only 5% had been licensed and even fewer had found their way into commercial products. Today under Bayh–Dole more than 200 universities are engaged in technology transfer, adding more than $21 billion each year to the economy.'[7]

Mowery (2005, p. 2), however, argues that such an enthusiastic assessment of the impact by the Bayh–Dole Act is exaggerated:

> Although it seems clear that the criticism of high-technology startups that was widespread during the period of pessimism over U.S. competitiveness was overstated, the recent focus on patenting and licensing as the essential ingredient in university–industry collaboration and knowledge transfer may be no less exaggerated. The emphasis on the Bayh–Dole Act as a catalyst to these interactions also seems somewhat misplaced.

The Bayh–Dole Act is one major example of the new policy focus that pursued the goal of promoting the spillover of knowledge from universities for commercialization that would foster innovation and ultimately economic growth. That such a policy goal did not have a high enough priority to come to fruition in the post-war era characterized by the Solow model reflects the shift in policy priorities, and ultimately instruments, as the economy evolved from being capital-driven, to knowledge-driven and ultimately to become the entrepreneurial economy.

Additionally, numerous other instruments exist that are decidedly distinct from those traditionally used for businesses and small businesses in particular. Furthermore, the locus of the policies has also changed. The instruments constraining the freedom of firms to contract – antitrust, regulation and public ownership – were generally controlled and used at the federal or national level. In contrast, the instruments of entrepreneurship policy are generally applied at the decentralized level of a state or city or local level.

Entrepreneurship policies in Germany

Entrepreneurship policies in Germany are a good example to show the diversity of approaches and the change in focus from small business policy to entrepreneurship policy. In Germany, policies encouraging start-ups have been in place within the framework of small business policy for decades. However, the 1990s saw the implementation of a new type of entrepreneurship policy that was considerably different from the previous start-up policies. The next section provides insights into the range of Germany's entrepreneurship policies and shows that entrepreneurship promotion has become established in economic policy.

Start-ups support programs in the framework of small business policy   Germany has a strong support infrastructure for small and medium-sized enterprises. Within this framework programs for supporting business start-ups have been available for decades. The focus of these programs has been on financial assistance and the provision of start-up specific information for the entrepreneur. For example, the Kreditanstalt für Wiederaufbau (KfW), a bank that was established after World War II, issued financial assistance programs for start-ups to bridge financial difficulties that they face with market entry. One example is the Eigenkapitalhilfe-Programm. For a long time these policies were insignificant within the overall economic growth policies. However, during the 1990s the political interest in start-ups grew dramatically and institutions like the KfW increased their range of assistance programs for start-ups.

New entrepreneurship policies   With the increasing political interest in the promotion of entrepreneurship, new policy instruments have been created and implemented since the mid-1990s. These new policies differ considerably in terms of instrumentation, targets and goals from start-up support policies described so far.

   One specific feature of the new entrepreneurship policies is that they do not target existing businesses. They have instead a systemic focus on supporting the individual (potential) entrepreneur. The motivation behind these policies is to create an entrepreneurial climate that encourages business start-ups and leads to innovative ventures. Clearly, the objective is to facilitate knowledge commercialization and research. Bringing together different forms of expertise is regarded as a mechanism to support the exchange of knowledge and ideas.

   The new instruments facilitate the institutionalization of regional cooperation and network building[8] in order to stimulate start-ups out of universities or research institutes, because start-ups are perceived as vehicles to commercialize new economic knowledge. A special feature of these new policies is the regionalization of policies.[9] Policies are initiated by the federal or state governments. However, their implementation is at the regional level. Geographic proximity has been found to be an important precondition for innovations. Consequently, the region has been identified as the appropriate level of implementation. Policies build on existing regional capacities, for example a university or an industrial cluster. The following paragraphs describe the new entrepreneurship policies in detail.

Contests for cooperation: creating an entrepreneurial environment   A range of new programs are targeted towards the creation of regional networks for cooperation between regional key actors.[10] One type of instrument brings together key regional actors from industry, science and government. All have in common that they follow a similar procedure. The program initiators at one of the federal ministries conduct contests and evaluate the concepts that have been handed in by interested regions. Only a small percentage of the proposals are funded; 80 to 90 per cent are rejected.

The BioRegio program was the first of its kind and started in 1995. The motivation was to create regions of excellence and promote the emergence of biotechnology clusters in selected regions. The Exist program,[11] initiated by the Federal Ministry of Education and Research (BMBF), followed in 1998. This program is designed to increase the number of knowledge-intensive start-ups by academics and create a regional entrepreneurial climate. The focus is on supporting the process from seed to start-up phase. Exist built regional institutions and a university-based support infrastructure, establishing university education in entrepreneurship, as well as stimulating the commercialisation of research. In the first phase (through 2002) five regions[12] were chosen. For the second wave (through 2005) 10 additional regions[13] were added. Regions had to compete for funding and the BMBF chose the 15 regions on the basis of their applications. Every participating region developed its own concept. Federal funding stopped in 2005, but networks were still functional as of 2006.

Exist offices have been established at most universities participating in the program, counselling services are available within the network, and information can also be accessed via the Internet. The inclusion of regional actors has been one of the major objectives of the program. Within the Exist framework, universities work together with regional actors such as firms, politicians and other research institutes. Networks are designed to publicize the support infrastructures and consulting services to potential entrepreneurs and to make starting a business a viable career option. Hence, visibility is regarded as essential for the success of Exist. Extensive marketing mechanisms have been implemented within the regions; for example, one mechanism has been business plan competitions.

Furthermore, the establishment of entrepreneurship education has been a major goal of the Exist program. Seminars and lectures were started to teach students about the start-up process. The establishment of 'Gründerlehrstühle', or chairs that focus their teaching on various aspects of the start-up process, has been sponsored by several corporations, the Deutsche Ausgleichsbank and individual Länder. The stimulation of greater commercialization of research is the third element in the Exist program. Techniques to search for business ideas have also been taught in cooperation with local companies. Importantly, the Exist program is only one example of government policies that were implemented to create regional support networks that facilitate business start-ups.

Supporting future entrepreneurs: jobs for developing a business idea   In addition to programs with a systemic approach, another type of program targets individual entrepreneurs. One type of program that diffused across Germany is designed for nascent entrepreneurs from a university environment. Prior to these programs, financial assistance was only available after the business had been started or the process of turning the business idea into a start-up was well under way.

The program Exist Seed[14] was established by the BMBF to complement the Exist program. It provides students, graduates or researchers with a monthly income to develop their business idea into a viable business plan. The salary potential entrepreneurs earn is comparable to that of a part-time job for postdocs. Program participants have access to university infrastructure and usually get an office. The university provides assistance and counselling, while a mentor guides the process. Similar programs were created at the federal and state level. Some of the state programs complement Exist Seed.

Exist Seed was evaluated in 2005 and can serve as an example. The evaluation gives an impression of the effect and impact of these programs. Of the 420 applications that had been received by June 2005, 245 projects and 430 entrepreneurs were supported. Two thirds of the projects had been developed by teams. Business ideas were supported in the fields of biotechnology, medical engineering, and information technology. More than 80 per cent of these projects received continued support after their initial year long period of support.

Second wave of entrepreneurship policies in Germany: focus on innovation systems After federal funding for Exist regions was phased out in 2005, the focus of federal policies shifted. Although the decentralized regional approach is still followed, policies no longer focus explicitly on university-based start-ups and the creation of support infrastructures for start-ups. Instead, the creation of regional innovation systems has become the most important objective, and recent policies build on regional strengths that exist in a particular industry.

Under the auspices of the initiative 'Entrepreneurial Regions'[15] five programs have been implemented so far. As the name of the program indicates, regions are regarded as enterprises that have to organize their capacities and resources in an optimal way. The goal is to facilitate the development of regional networks of excellence that have a unique economic and research profile. Some regions might have more than one network of excellence. All of these second wave programs are only available in the New German Länder. Regional actors apply for funding by handing in a concept for regional development and cooperation that must be compatible with the program's guidelines (see Table 3.2).

Table 3.2   Entrepreneurial regions: federal support programs for regions

Program	Program start	Supported initiatives	Budget
InnoRegio	1999	23 chosen from 444 applicants	€255.6 million (2000–06)
Innovative regional growth cores	2001	17	Continual selection process (every year five more initiatives)
Interregional alliances for tomorrow's markets – innovation forums	2001	67	Max €85 000 over a time period of six months (continual selection process)
Centers for innovation competence	2002	6	€60 million (until 2010)
InnoProfiles	2005	A minimum of 10 projects each year	€150 million (until 2012)

Source: Table based on information at www.unternehmen-region.de/en/index.php.

All instruments build on the idea that sustainable jobs are created when the commercialization of innovations is at the center of any effort, and where research institutions network with firms and universities as well as with political decision makers. The establishment of publicly funded networks should facilitate knowledge exchange in order to stimulate innovation. Programs differ and are adapted in light of the pre-existing regional cooperation levels. Support to establish regional cooperation is available, as well as financing for projects that build on existing networks. Research institutes and universities play a central role in the concept of 'Entrepreneurial Regions'. One program is specifically designed to develop an attractive research environment for young scientists. Although these programs are limited to the New German Länder, similar programs exist for Western Germany as well. One example is the program 'Kompetenznetze' that creates centers of excellence and serves as a marketing instrument for regions.

Enable program: enabling European entrepreneurship   A shift in economic policy has also occurred within the European Union. Similar entrepreneurship programs were started with a European perspective. The program 'Enable: Enable European Entrepreneurship' is similar to the 'Entrepreneurial Regions' program, but supports pan-European cooperation. The program supports technology transfer and the creation of networks of small and medium-sized enterprises, and encourages start-ups. However, one important element of this program is the exchange of knowledge and best practices for economic development strategies. A network connecting Carinthia (Austria), Western Norway, Kaunas (Lithuania) and Thuringia (Germany) has been established. The program was started in 2005 with a total budget of € 5 770 500.

A new field of German economic policy: the promotion of entrepreneurship   In Germany, entrepreneurship promotion has emerged as an important component of economic policy since the 1990s. Start-up support instruments implemented in the framework of small business policy have been expanded and new innovative policy instruments have been created. Both types of policies coexist and have the common objective of increasing the entrepreneurial activity within Germany.

With the emergence of entrepreneurship policy one can observe a change in the institutional environment. Federal entrepreneurship policies are not implemented by the Federal Ministry of Economics and Labor, although entrepreneurship policies are strongly related to economic growth strategies. Instead, all the entrepreneurship policies described so far have been implemented by the Federal Ministry of Education and Research.[16] The Federal Ministry of Economics and Labor, on the other hand, continues to deal with traditional small business policies and industrial policy.[17]

Conclusions

Entrepreneurship policy emerged in the 1990s as a new economic policy strategy for growth. This is in line with the changing role of entrepreneurship in the economy. In particular, the drivers of economic growth have changed and the impact of entrepreneurship on economic growth and employment has evolved considerably since World War II. While economic activity was previously organized in efficient large-scale operations, today entrepreneurship and small businesses contribute significantly to economic growth.

The downsizing of federal agencies charged with business regulation combined with widespread privatization throughout the OECD countries has been interpreted by many scholars as the eclipse of government intervention (e.g. Brenner, 1999; Kelly, 1999; Sassen, 2003). But to interpret deregulation, privatization and the decreased emphasis of competition policies as the end of government intervention in business misses the emergence of entrepreneurship policies. Rather, the public policy approach to constraining the freedom of firms to contract through regulation, public ownership and antitrust has given way to a new, more diffused and decentralized set of policies that enable the creation and commercialization of new ideas, especially in new firms. The new entrepreneurship policies recognize that knowledge has become a key factor shaping economic growth. They aim at creating an entrepreneurial environment in order to stimulate new business start-ups.

The shift in economic policy was caused by the growing ineffectiveness of previous economic growth strategies that focused on market structure regulation in order to sustain competition in the market. Experiencing the rise of strong political challenges such as increasing unemployment rates, policy makers realized that businesses are not given. On the contrary, the emergence of new businesses is key to economic growth and policy makers are now trying to stimulate an entrepreneurial climate. A strong motivation for entrepreneurship policies is job creation, because large corporations that previously were a guarantee for many jobs, now change location and downsize in the globalized economy. Knowledge is an important factor in the new entrepreneurial economy, so that the commercialization of knowledge has become an important goal. New policy mechanisms have been developed in the fields of research, intellectual property and human capital.

There is no recipe for public policy to create an entrepreneurial economy, so while the goals remain the same – economic growth and employment creation – the mechanism and instruments are strikingly different. Examples of entrepreneurship policies from different countries, the US and Germany, have been presented.

All entrepreneurship polices have in common the fact that policy makers have recognized that their competitive advantage in the regional and national competition for higher economic growth rates lies in the development and improvement of existing regional capacities. The key to stimulating start-ups and the commercialization of knowledge lies in mobilizing and developing regional strengths.

Notes

* The authors gratefully acknowledge the financial support from the European Commission (FP6) Project: KEINS – Knowledge-Based Entrepreneurship: Innovation, Networks and Systems, contract n.: CT-2-CT-2004-506022.
1. See for example the Bolton Report (1971).
2. Quoted from Scherer (1977, p. 980).
3. http://www.sba.gov/aboutsba/sbahistory.html.
4. A third direction contributing to the mandate for entrepreneurship policy may be in the context of less developed regions and developing countries. Such regions have had endowments of neither physical capital nor knowledge capital but still look to entrepreneurship capital to serve as an engine of economic growth.
5. Public Law 98-620.
6. 'Innovation's golden goose', *The Economist*, 12 December 2002.
7. Cited in Mowery (2005, p. 2).
8. These have sometimes been referred to as new innovation policies.
9. Editorial (2005), in *Research Policy*, **34**, 1123–7.
10. Eickelpasch and Fritsch (2005) have described these new policies and analyzed benefits and limitations.
11. www.exist.de.

12. Bizeps (Wuppertal–Hagen), dresdenexists (Dresden), GET UP (Ilmenau–Jena–Schmalkalden–Weimar), KEIM (Karlsruhe–Pforzheim), PUSH (Stuttgart).
13. BEGiN (Potsdam–Brandenburg), BRIDGE (Bremen), fit-exist (Trier), G-Dur (Dortmund), GROW (Ostbayern), Gründerflair MV (Mecklenburg–Vorpommern), KOGGE (Lübeck–Kiel), Route A 66 (Frankfurt–Wiesbaden–Offenbach), START (Kassel–Fulda–Marburg–Göttingen) sowie SAXEED (Südwestsachsen).
14. www.exist.de/existseed/index.html.
15. www.unternehmen-region.de/en/index.php.
16. http://www.bmbf.de/.
17. http://www.bmwi.de/English/Navigation/economy.html.

Bibliography

Acs, Z. and D.B. Audretsch (eds) (1993), *Small Firms and Entrepreneurship. An East–West Perspective*, Cambridge: Cambridge University Press.
Almus, M. and S. Prantl (2001), *Bessere Unternehmensentwicklung durch Gründungsförderung?*, Bonn: Deutsche Ausgleichsbank.
Anglund, S.M. (1998), 'How American core values influence public policy: lessons from federal aid to small business 1953–1993', *Governance*, **11** (1), 23–50.
Archibugi, D. and A. Coco (2005), 'Is Europe becoming the most dynamic knowledge economy in the world?', *Journal of Common Market Studies*, **43** (3), 433–59.
Audretsch, D.B. (2007), *The Entrepreneurial Society*, New York: Oxford University Press.
Audretsch, D. and R. Thurik (2001), 'What's new about the new economy? Sources of growth in the managed and entrepreneurial economies', *Industrial and Corporate Change*, **10**, 267–315.
Audretsch, D.B., M.C. Keilbach and E.E. Lehmann (2006), *Entrepreneurship and Economic Growth*, New York: Oxford University Press.
Beyenburg-Weidenfeld, U. (1992), *Wettbewerbstheorie, Wirtschaftspolitik und Mittelstandsförderung: 1948–1963, die Mittelstandspolitik im Spannungsfeld zwischen wettbewerbstheoretischem Anspruch und wirtschaftspolitischem Pragmatismus*, Stuttgart: Vierteljahresschrift für Sozial- und Wirtschaftsgeschichte Beihefte.
Birch, D. (1979), *The Job Generation Process*, MIT Program on Neighborhood and Regional Change, Cambridge: MIT.
BMBF (2002), 'Erfahrungen aus EXIST – Querschau über die einzelnen Projekte', Bundesministerium für Bildung und Forschung, Referat Öffentlichkeitsarbeit.
BMWi (1999), *Wirtschaftsbericht 1999*, Berlin: Bundesministerium für Wirtschaft und Technologie.
BMWi (2000), *Annual Report 2000*, Berlin: Bundesministerium für Wirtschaft und Technologie.
Bolton Report (1971), *Committee of Inquiry on Small Firms*, Cmnd 4811, London: HSMO.
Brenner, N. (1999), 'Beyond state-centrism? Space, territoriality, and geographical scale in globalization studies', *Theory and Society*, **28**, 29–78.
Bresnahan, T. and A. Gambardella (2004), *Building High-tech Clusters: Silicon Valley and Beyond*, Cambridge: Cambridge University Press.
Editorial (2005), 'Regionalization of innovation policy – introduction to the Special Issue', *Research Policy*, **34**, 1123–7.
Eickelpasch, E. and M. Fritsch (2005), 'Contest for cooperation – a new approach in German innovation policy', *Research Policy*, **34**, 1269–82.
European Commission (1995), *Green Paper on Innovation*, Brussels: European Commission.
Geroski, P.A. (1989), 'European industrial policy and industrial policy in Europe', *Oxford Review of Economic Policy*, **5** (2), 20–36.
Goldfarb, B. and M. Henrekson (2003), 'Bottom-up versus top-down policies towards the commercialization of university intellectual property', *Research Policy*, **32** (4), 639–58.
Hjalmarsson, L. (1991), 'The Scandinavian model of industrial policy', in M. Blomström and P. Meller (eds), *Diverging Paths: Comparing a Century of Scandinavian and Latin American Economic Development*, Baltimore, MD: Johns Hopkins University Press.
IfM Institut für Mittelstandsforschung (2001), *Bilanz der Gründungsoffensive NRW 'GO!' 1996–1999*, Bonn: IfM.
Kelly, P. (1999), 'The geographies and politics of globalization', *Progress in Human Geography*, **23**, 379–400.
May, T. and J. McHugh (2002), 'Small business policy: a political consensus?', *Political Quarterly*, **73** (1), 76–85.
Moore, G. and K. Davis (2004), 'Learning the Silicon Valley way', in T. Bresnahan and A. Gambardella (eds), *Building High-tech Clusters. Silicon Valley and Beyond*, Cambridge: Cambridge University Press, (pp. 7–39).
Mowery, D. (2005), 'The Bayh–Dole Act and high-technology entrepreneurship in U.S. universities: chick, egg, or something else?', paper presented at the Eller Centre Conference on Entrepeneurship Education and Technology Transfer, University of Arizona, 21–22 January.

Peters, T. and R. Waterman (1984), *In Search of Excellence*, New York: Harper and Row Publishers.
Prodi, R. (2002), 'For a New European Entrepreneurship' (Public Speech), Instituto de Empresa in Madrid, p. 1.
Romer, P. (1986), 'Increasing returns and long-run growth', *Journal of Political Economy*, **94**, 1002–37.
Sassen, S. (2003), 'Globalization or denationalization', Annual RIPE lecture, *Review of International Political Economy*, **10**, 1–22.
Scherer, F. (1970), *Industrial Market Structure and Economic Performance*, Chicago: Rand McNally.
Scherer, F.M. (1975), 'Prepared statement, US House of Representatives, Committee on Small Business, Hearings, Recent Efforts to Amend or Repeal the Robinson–Patman Act, Part 2, Washington, December 1975', in F.M. Scherer (2000), *Competition Policy, Domestic and International*, Cheltenham, UK and Northampton, MA, USA: Edward Elgar, pp. 145–50.
Scherer, F. (1977), *The Economic Effects of Compulsory Patent Licensing*, New York: New York University Press.
Sternberg, R. (2001), 'Evaluation des Programms zu finanziellen Absicherung von Unternehmensgründern aus Hochschulen (PFAU)', Überarbeitete Fassung des Abschlussberichtes, Wirtschafts- und Sozialgeographisches Institut, Köln.
Stevenson, L. and A. Lundström (2001), *Entrepreneurship Policy for the Future*, Stockholm: Swedish Foundation for Small Business Research.
Stevenson, L. and A. Lundström (2005), *Entrepreneurship Policy. Theory and Practice*, International Studies in Entrepreneurship Series, Vol. 9, New York: Springer.
Tijssen, R.J.W. and E. van Wilke (1999), 'In search of the European paradox: an international comparison of Europe's scientific performance and knowledge flows in information and communication technologies research', *Research Policy*, **28** (5), 519–43.
Williamson, O. (1968), 'Economies as an antitrust defense: the welfare tradeoffs', *American Economic Review*, **58**, 18–36.

4 Policymakers beware!
Simon C. Parker

Introduction

This chapter casts a skeptical eye over pro-entrepreneurship public policies. I explain why intervention might backfire or be rendered ineffective by the responses of entrepreneurs and financiers. In addition, I discuss why some apparently innocuous pro-entrepreneurship policies are actually misguided. Some examples of inappropriate and ineffective entrepreneurship policies are given; and a case for discouraging rather than promoting entrepreneurship is made.

In this short chapter, I do not offer a detailed survey of pro-entrepreneurship and small business policies. This task has been performed elsewhere: see, for example, Storey (2003) and Parker (2004, Chapter 10). Nor is it my aim to discredit the viewpoint that entrepreneurship might generate positive spillovers (though it seems likely that negative externalities from entrepreneurship will exist as well). I simply want to discuss important drawbacks to public policy interventions in this area, in the interests of stimulating a more balanced debate about the merits of public policies that take a (sometimes instinctively) pro-entrepreneurship stance.

The chapter has the following layout. The next section focuses on two logical fallacies involved with policies that target particular groups of entrepreneurs. The third section discusses five examples of pro-entrepreneurship policies that are either misguided or frustrated by private sector responses. The fourth section makes a case for discouraging support for start-ups, and the fifth section concludes with a discussion of some of the practical dangers of government intervention in entrepreneurship.

Two problems with policies that target entrepreneurial groups

I make two points in this section. First, any targeting of entrepreneurial groups should be done with an eye to the marginal, rather than average, benefits that are generated; and second, incentive problems generally accompany targeting policies. More generally, it is not unusual for policy advice to be given on the basis of average benefits; and it is even more common for policy makers to ignore the reactions of private sector entrepreneurs to the imposition of their policies.

Average benefits are not the same as marginal benefits

Consider two different types of entrepreneur, A and B. Each entrepreneurial type generates output using production functions that exhibit the same diminishing marginal returns to inputs. Consider just one input, capital k that is thought to be in short supply, and which generates greater social than private returns, perhaps because of borrowing constraints. A government policy is proposed that makes extra capital available to entrepreneurs, at constant marginal cost.

An expert now appears on the scene, and makes the following proposal: 'You should focus scarce public resources on the entrepreneurial type that is proven to be the most successful', the expert tells the government, 'and give the subsidy to A-type entrepreneurs. You want to back winners, not losers, after all'. This is precisely the kind of advice discussed by Westhead and Wright (1999) in their descriptive treatment of serial, novice and habitual entrepreneurs.

However, if government allocates resources on the basis of average benefits, and if these correspond to lower marginal benefits, then the extra benefits are lower than they could be, for any given marginal cost.

The problem just described arises when the targeting is performed ex post, that is, after the different entrepreneurial groups are discerned. A more challenging problem arises when targeting must be done ex ante. Problematically, the two entrepreneurial types might not be easily distinguishable. Both types want the subsidy, so both have incentives to claim to be the type that is favored by the policy maker. Now the government must invest extra resources into trying to distinguish which type is which. Arguably, it is hard enough for seasoned lenders to accomplish this, let alone bureaucrats who lack business experience.

Private sector responses: incentive problems
Thirty years ago, Robert E. Lucas (1976) pointed out that government policies imposed on private sector agents that do not fully take into account the responses of those agents lead to unintended, and sometimes perverse, consequences. This includes the possibility that private sector agents respond to the policy in such a way that they weaken, undo, or even reverse the government's desired outcomes. Despite its prominence in macroeconomic research, this critique has not yet been widely acknowledged in entrepreneurship policy circles.

That is a pity, as the following example testifies. Li (2002) evaluated a US federal government policy that subsidizes interest payments to new business start-ups. Calibrating a computable general equilibrium model, Li demonstrated that this policy decreases the incentives for would-be entrepreneurs to save. So total investment rises by less than the government (which assumed entrepreneurs would not change their behavior in response to the policy) hoped. This is a straightforward example of *crowding out* of private sector saving by public sector capital. Worse, the taxes needed to finance the rather ineffective subsidy also blunt incentives to work. Li concluded that interest subsidies to entrepreneurs have the consequence of *decreasing* rather than increasing net output.[1]

What if the objective of this policy was merely to increase the number of entrepreneurs? Even then it cannot be regarded as an unqualified success. Li observed that the number of entrepreneurs switching into the targeted group would increase, but the number in the untargeted group would decrease. It turns out that the latter generally outnumber the former, so the policy – which seemed so obviously bound to promote entrepreneurship – backfires completely. Lest this appear just an extreme example, it is worth pointing out that Gale's (1991) evaluation of a wide range of US federal government lending programs targeted on particular groups, also showed them to have large allocation effects but only modest investment effects – for similar reasons. Nor is strategic switching by entrepreneurs in response to policy initiatives confined to the issue of start-up finance. For example, in their study of affirmative action programs in the US, Blanchflower and Wainwright (2005) discovered that some women appear to have served as 'fronts' for a business actually owned by their husbands, in order to benefit from the positive gender discrimination at the heart of the program. And in a study of German regulations designed to maintain the authenticity of Chinese restaurants by restricting the kinds of individuals allowed to work as chefs in these establishments, Leung (2003) documented that an unintended outcome is for some restaurateurs to move into fast food, with lower skill requirements – and presumably less authenticity!

Five examples of inappropriate policies
In this section I discuss five inappropriate pro-entrepreneurship policies. The first two demonstrate how private agents can completely neutralize well-meaning government policies, leading to policy irrelevance. The last three examples illustrate policies that may look superficially attractive but turn out to be counter-productive.

First, consider Zazzaro's (2005) analysis of credit allocation to entrepreneurs. It might seem that stricter enforcement of debt contracts, for example more draconian bankruptcy laws, might afford greater protection to banks' asset base and so improve banks' willingness to lend to entrepreneurs. But if anything, such a policy weakens banks' incentives to screen borrowers, and leads to higher business failure rates. In response, banks might actually *decrease*, not increase, their lending to entrepreneurs. Zazzaro points out that a better policy would be to improve accounting standards to reduce the costs of screening and hence improve the quality of credit allocation.

Second, consider the effects of income taxation on entrepreneurship. Entrepreneurs are a particularly risk-prone group, and so can benefit from redistributed income taxation as a risk-sharing device (Boadway et al., 1991; Black and de Meza, 1997; Parker, 1999). However, income taxation might be ineffective if risk bearing fulfills a socially useful purpose. For example, suppose venture capitalists fund a risky entrepreneurial project and pay entrepreneurs a combination of base salary and profit share in order to counteract moral hazard and elicit optimal entrepreneurial effort. For optimal effort to be forthcoming, entrepreneurs must bear risk; so venture capitalists will redesign entrepreneurs' compensation packages and thereby undo a non-redistributive tax with social insurance characteristics in order to restore incentives (Keuschnigg and Nielsen, 2004). So in this case a policy of using the tax system to make entrepreneurship more attractive is neutralized by the responses of the private sector.[2]

Third, consider a policy that gives small firms a tax break to encourage entry. For example, the UK Corporation Tax rate levied on small firms is about two thirds of that levied on firms above a certain threshold (in 2005/06, the threshold is taxable profit above £300 000). This policy might appear reasonable and justifiable, but it has important secondary effects. It reduces the pre-tax rate of return that entrepreneurs require to launch a new venture, and encourages investment in inefficient projects, since rational investors might forsake investments with higher (pre-tax) rates of return in favor of the less productive tax-favored investments (Holtz-Eakin, 2000). A further problem is that tax-favoring small but not large firms involves withdrawing the subsidy as small firms grow. This acts as a perverse tax on growth.

Fourth, consider a policy designed to encourage innovation by new firms. Public support for innovation might be justified on the grounds that innovators are unable to prevent free riders from imitating their innovation. Innovators bear all of the costs while imitators bear only part of them, leading in the end to under-investment in innovation (Klette et al., 2000). Also, greater entry might promote competition and reduce the appropriation of rents by incumbents. These kinds of argument certainly seem to be the rationale for policies like the Small Business Innovation Research program in the US, the budget of which in 1997 exceeded $1 billion, and the SMART scheme in the UK. But there are several reasons to believe that there is already too much innovation by entrants. As Boadway and Tremblay (2005) point out, entrants do not internalize the value of the rents that they destroy by displacing established firms, so they innovate too much. The problem of excessive entry is especially pronounced when entrepreneurs engage in a contest to be the first to make a new discovery (Futia, 1980), or when product markets are imperfectly competitive. In the latter case, innovation by entrants generates too much product diversity and too little informative advertising (Grossman and Shapiro, 1984). Thus there may be too little innovation by incumbents and too much by entrants, suggesting that while pro-innovation policies may be worthwhile on balance, they should, if anything, favor incumbents rather than new entrants.

Finally, consider the policy of health insurance deductibility. Since 2003, the self-employed in the US have been able to deduct the entire health premium from their business expenses. In fact, according to Perry and Rosen (2004), the health of self-employed Americans (and that of their children) is no worse, and if anything is slightly better, than that of their employee counterparts. The self-employed also utilize similar levels of health services to employees; and transitions to self-employment appear to be independent of workers' health. Hence in terms of the self/paid employment occupational choice this does not obviously appear to be an appropriate policy.[3] Perhaps the best case that can be made for it is that it promotes some degree of horizontal equity with wage and salary workers.

The case for discouraging new start-ups

In this section I make a case for governments to adopt policies that discourage, rather than encourage, new start-ups. There are two primary justifications for discouraging entrepreneurship. One is based on excessive participation in entrepreneurship owing to problems of asymmetric information in credit markets. The other relates to over-optimism by entrepreneurs. No doubt additional reasons could also be proposed that are based on underlying objections to the value of entrepreneurship itself. For example, small firms destroy as well as create numerous jobs (Davis et al., 1996); small business failures often disproportionately harm customers, employees and suppliers; and entrepreneurship often imposes enormous strains on personal relationships (Blanchflower, 2004). I will not delve into these objections here.

Over-investment

In a classic article, de Meza and Webb (1987) proposed a model of credit markets operating under asymmetric information. Entrepreneurs are well informed about their projects but banks are not; but able entrepreneurs cannot credibly signal their higher ability to banks. Banks therefore have to offer the same ('pooled') debt contract to all loan applicants. De Meza and Webb assumed that able entrepreneurs have a greater probability of business success than less able entrepreneurs, and so are more likely to repay their debt to the bank. Under a pooling debt contract, the ablest entrepreneurs end up cross-subsidizing the least able, which entices into entrepreneurship individuals with projects that do not cover their resource and opportunity costs. The outcome of investment in projects that do not cover their social and opportunity costs is called *under-investment*.

It arises because of asymmetric information, since if information were symmetric lenders would be able to charge the less able riskier types higher payments, which could allow them to break even. The problem is that banks cannot distinguish able from less able types and have to pool them together, leading to the cross-subsidy. De Meza and Webb showed that over-investment is *bound* to occur when projects' returns are ranked by first-order stochastic dominance. In effect, too many entrepreneurial projects are undertaken. Everyone could be made better off if the least able individuals were discouraged from becoming entrepreneurs.

This conclusion is surprisingly robust to extensions of the model that relax its assumptions. Introducing costly screening (de Meza and Webb, 1988), variable venture sizes (de Meza and Webb, 1989), risk aversion (de Meza and Webb, 1990), and moral hazard (de Meza and Webb, 1999) does not change the basic result that there are too many entrepreneurs. When ability also affects returns from non-entrepreneurial activities, and individuals make free occupational choices, the over-investment result is no longer guaranteed to hold; but it does re-emerge in many special cases (Parker, 2003).

The other principal model of credit markets and entrepreneurial finance, by Stiglitz and Weiss (1981), assumes that entrepreneurs differ in terms of the *risk* of their projects. This model generates under-investment rather than over-investment. But it turns out that the Stiglitz–Weiss model is subject to logical objections that the over-investment model is immune to, including the fact that debt finance is no longer the financial instrument of choice in that model (de Meza, 2002). Furthermore, structures that 'mix' aspects of the de Meza–Webb and Stiglitz–Weiss models (e.g. de Meza and Webb, 2000) generate outcomes in which over-investment occurs once again. It is true that other, less structured, mixture models generate more ambiguous results (e.g. Hillier and Ibrahimo, 1992). But as Boadway and Keen (2002) showed, when equity contracts as well as debt contracts are available on competitive terms, and there is no costly state verification of ex post project returns, over-investment in these less structured models once again emerges.

The policy implications of over-investment are clear-cut. Subsidizing credit reduces efficiency, a conclusion that is strengthened if agency and deadweight costs are entailed by subsidies. A better policy is to discourage inefficient entrepreneurs without deterring their efficient counterparts whose ventures add value. Fortunately, despite the presence of hidden types caused by asymmetric information, this kind of policy is relatively easy to implement in practice. Any policy that taxes loans, deposits or interest will suffice. These policies have the added advantage of avoiding distortions in labor supply – though taxing the incomes of entrepreneurs would do just as well in the absence of such distortions. These policies can even end up increasing the equilibrium number of entrepreneurs if they improve sufficiently the average quality of the borrower pool such that banks reduce interest rates and fund more entrepreneurs (de Meza, 2002). Note that government action is needed to increase the cost of capital in order to improve the average quality of the borrower pool. Banks cannot do it themselves because the pressure of competition forces each one to price capital at the lowest possible rate.

Finally, equity contracts can also be beset by excessive entrepreneurial participation. With too much entry by entrepreneurs, output prices are competed downwards: this decreases venture capitalists' returns, which reduces their incentives to add value via the provision of costly managerial advice to entrepreneurs (Keuschnigg and Nielsen, 2005). While there are potential gains from lower prices in terms of higher consumer surplus, the appropriate policy here is nevertheless to tax, rather than to subsidize, the investment costs of new start-ups.

Unrealistic optimism
Psychologists have established that most human beings are prone to unrealistic optimism. Numerous studies have shown that optimism tends to be highest when individuals have emotional commitments to outcomes they believe to be partly under their control, and about which objective information is not widely diffused (see Manove and Padilla, 1999, for references to this literature). This is relevant to entrepreneurship because entrepreneurs commonly tie up their personal wealth in their businesses and so have tangible emotional commitments; setting up new ventures is likely to entail illusions of control; and starting entirely new ventures is inevitably uncharted territory so there is scope for unchecked fantasizing (Coelho et al., 2004).

Evidence certainly suggests that entrepreneurs are more unrealistically optimistic than non-entrepreneurs. Entrepreneurs have more unrealistic upward-biased expectations about their future incomes (Arabsheibani et al., 2000) and longevity (Puri and Robinson, 2005) than employees do – and more than is warranted. Entrepreneurs also over-estimate their prospects of business survival and relative performance (Cooper et al., 1988; Pinfold, 2001). This creates two kinds of problems: one borne by the entrepreneurs themselves and the other by society as a whole.

At the individual level, optimists are more likely to self-select into risky entrepreneurship and to devote excessive amounts of their own time and money to an endeavor (new venturing) that has only a low probability of paying off (de Meza and Southey, 1996). Thus many entrepreneurs end up ruining themselves and possibly also their families, while banks act like pawnbrokers and seize the entrepreneurs' collateral when business failures occur. And it is not only those entrepreneurs who have actually launched their venture who bear the personal costs of failure. In a study of Canadian inventors between 1976 and 1993, Åstebro (2003) calculated the proportion of new innovations reaching the market to be only 7 percent. Of these 'lucky' 7 percent, some 60 percent realized negative returns, and the average realized return among those that commercialized their inventions was –7 percent, even ignoring the cost of the inventor's often enormous efforts. (The fact that half of the inventors persisted with their idea even when paid advice recommended abandonment, is suggestive of pronounced over-optimism.) In short, over-optimistic entrepreneurs who are denied loans may be better off than those who obtain them; and government policies designed to provide funds to the former group may be particularly harmful.

There are also social costs to over-optimism. Even if entrepreneurs have unbiased profit expectations on average, the most optimistic entrepreneurs will crowd out the realists by over-producing, and possibly driving output prices below the industry break-even price. The over-optimistic entrepreneurs impose a negative externality on others because the realists could have made positive profits in the absence of the over-optimists. And, when factor markets are characterized by upward-sloping supply curves, over-optimistic entrepreneurs may overuse scarce resources in equilibrium and bid up input prices that realists must pay (Manove, 1998). Manove cites Warren Buffett in this context: 'It's optimism that is the enemy of the rational buyer.' Furthermore, Manove and Padilla (1999) rebutted the common lament that banks are too conservative and withhold credit from worthy entrepreneurs. Manove and Padilla showed that, in the presence of over-optimistic entrepreneurs, the opposite is generally the case. Over-optimistic low-ability entrepreneurs pass up the chance to apply for smaller investments that would make them a profit, requesting unprofitable larger loan sizes because they over-estimate their ability. This causes a social efficiency loss, which competitive banks do not price into their loan repayments, since they do not bear any loss incurred by forgone efficient investment by over-optimists. Hence competitive interest rates are generally too low for the social good, which only encourages optimists further, leading to too much investment. Hence conservative bank policies may well be justified despite loquacious criticism from the small-business lobby.

To summarize, individuals and society could be made better off if policy makers discouraged individuals from becoming entrepreneurs. One practical way that this can be done is by relaxing bankruptcy laws (de Meza, 2002; and see also the discussion in the section on examples of inappropriate policies). With weaker asset protection in the event of bankruptcy, banks would have to raise interest rates to make their required rate of return, and reduce their lending. As noted in the preceding section, this is the correct response to over-investment in credit markets.[4] Another appropriate government response, at least in principle, might be to promote the transfer of information, education and management skill acquisition, to moderate and counteract the effects of over-optimism. However, we know of little extant research on this issue to date.

Practical dangers of intervention
So far, this chapter has made the case on theoretical and empirical grounds for policy makers to restrain their urge to intervene in support of small and new enterprises. I conclude this article by mentioning several practical dangers of intervention when government cannot resist these urges, some of which are specific to entrepreneurship and some of which are not.

First, government intervention is not always justified when a market failure is identified. Not every problem is worth fixing, especially if it is costly to do so. For example, subsidies directed to entrepreneurs must be financed. The cost of public funds is often greater than unity, since taxation crowds out private effort and capital, and distorts incentives. If crowding out is substantial, the 'cure' might be worse than the 'disease'. Also, governments rarely possess information that is any better (it is often worse) than the private sector, making effective intervention difficult. So, for instance, it is hard to justify public expenditure on government-organized forums designed to connect business angels and entrepreneurs. An incentivized private sector could presumably do this job just as well, if not better. For similar reasons, one can also question government-funded assistance and advisory support to small businesses, which suffer from low take-up rates and vigorous competition from the private sector (Robson and Bennett, 2000).

Second, governments do not always intervene wisely. Large firms often have incentives to lobby for regulations that restrict competition (Holmes and Schmitz, 2001). Bad regulations come in many forms. One is paperwork that imposes a fixed compliance cost on firms, which large firms can spread over a greater scale, putting their smaller competitors at a competitive disadvantage (Brock and Evans, 1986). Other examples are local zoning ordinances that designate home-based businesses illegal in some cities, or that restrict the scope of their operations; while other legislation restricts the number of trading licenses in certain occupations (Dennis, 1998). On a related issue, government interventions can sometimes encourage entrepreneurs to engage in unproductive activities ('rent-seeking') rather than in productive ones (Baumol, 1990; Murphy et al., 1993). This can hinder productive effort, whether entrepreneurial or not; restrict competition; and attenuate economic growth (Dennis, 1998; Djankow et al., 2002).

Third, there is now a large literature in political economy and public finance arguing that politicians and interest groups may direct subsidies in ways that benefit themselves, rather than increasing social welfare (Stigler, 1971; Becker, 1983). For instance, in the specific context of entrepreneurship, Lerner (2004) chronicled instances of 'regulatory capture' in US public venture capital programs. One simply cannot assume that government will always act in the public's best interest when it decides to intervene. And, once government departments are charged with delivery of particular programs, they can be very hard to remove after they have outlived their usefulness.

Fourth, the foregoing discussion presumes that governments have clear objectives – whether benign or otherwise. In fact many public programs have unclear or multiple objectives. As I have written elsewhere:

> Governments invariably face conflicting aspirations and objectives. They want to target resources to achieve focus but are unable to pick winners; they want to make assistance selective to control budgetary costs but wish also to both remain inclusive and avoid spreading resources too thinly; and they want policies to make a big impact for political reasons while minimizing costs and program deadweight losses. These trade-offs are deep-rooted and probably inescapable. (Parker, 2004, p. 269).

A good example of a public program caught on the horns of this dilemma is unemployment assistance programs designed to encourage unemployed workers to start new businesses. These schemes, which have been widespread in Europe, subsidize unemployed workers who start a business to compensate for loss of welfare benefits, and often provide advice and assistance in the start-up process. As evaluators of these schemes have pointed out (Bendick and Egan, 1987; Storey, 1994), these schemes face a tradeoff between economic objectives (high survival rates, profitability and employment creation) and social objectives (e.g. putting to work the hardest to employ). On this point Bendick and Egan concluded:

> The programmes in these countries [France and Britain] have succeeded in turning less than one per cent of transfer payment recipients into entrepreneurs, and an even smaller proportion into successful ones. They cannot be said to have contributed greatly to solving either social or economic problems, let alone both. (1987, p. 540).

Finally, multiple objectives can make specific government entrepreneurship programs difficult to evaluate. And when program evaluations are conducted in practice (which is usually infrequently), they are often selective, choosing to focus on particular interventions that place the government of the day in the most favorable light (Dennis, 1998; Storey, 2003). This might explain why some entrepreneurship programs, such as loan guarantee schemes, are most frequently reassessed, while other programs are effectively ignored. A plea for more consistent, regular, and wide-ranging entrepreneurship policy evaluations – ideally taking account of joint effects of different programs where this is relevant – seems an appropriate point with which to close.

Notes
1. For Swedish evidence that capital subsidies are associated with lower total factor productivity growth, see Bergström (2000).
2. See also Keuschnigg and Nielsen (2001), who showed that while government spending on entrepreneurial training, subsidies to equipment investment and output subsidies stimulate entrepreneurship, they are at best welfare neutral.
3. The authors did not consider whether this policy additionally distorts the decision to become incorporated rather than remaining a sole proprietor.
4. Also, asset protection in the default state provides optimistic but risk-averse entrepreneurs with valuable insurance, even though they do not think they will need it (Berkowitz and White, 2004). This enhances social welfare.

References

Arabsheibani, G., D. de Meza, J. Maloney and B. Pearson (2000), 'And a vision appeared unto them of a great profit: evidence of self-deception among the self-employed', *Economics Letters*, **67**, 35–41.
Åstebro, T. (2003), 'The return to independent invention: evidence of risk-seeking, extreme optimism or skewness-loving?', *Economic Journal*, **113**, 226–39.
Baumol, W.J. (1990), 'Entrepreneurship: productive, unproductive, and destructive', *Journal of Political Economy*, **98**, 893–921.
Becker, G. (1983), 'A theory of competition among pressure groups for political influence', *Quarterly Journal of Economics*, **98**, 371–400.
Bendick, M. and M.L. Egan (1987), 'Transfer payment diversion for small business development: British and French experience', *Industrial and Labor Relations Review*, **40**, 528–42.
Bergström, F. (2000), 'Capital subsidies and the performance of firms', *Small Business Economics*, **14**, 183–93.
Berkowitz, J. and M.J. White (2004), 'Bankruptcy and small firms' access to credit', *Rand Journal of Economics*, **35**, 69–84.
Black, J. and D. de Meza (1997), 'Everyone may benefit from subsidising entry to risky occupations', *Journal of Public Economics*, **66**, 409–24.
Blanchflower, D.G. (2004), 'Self-employment: more may not be better', *Swedish Economic Policy Review*, **11**, 15–74.
Blanchflower, D.G. and J. Wainwright (2005), 'An analysis of the impact of affirmative action programs on self-employment in the construction industry', Discussion Paper No. 1856, 12A, Bonn.
Boadway, R. and M. Keen (2002), 'Imperfect information and public intervention in credit markets', Mimeo, Queens University, Kingston, Canada.
Boadway, R. and J.-F. Tremblay (2005), 'Public economics and start-up entrepreneurs', in V. Kanniainen and C. Keuschnigg (eds), *Venture Capital, Entrepreneurship and Public Policy*, Cambridge, MA: MIT Press, pp. 181–219.
Boadway, R., M. Marchand and P. Pestieau (1991), 'Optimal linear income taxation in models with occupational choice', *Journal of Public Economics*, **46**, 133–62.
Brock, W.A. and D.S. Evans, (1986), *The Economics of Small Businesses: Their Role and Regulation in the US Economy*, New York: Holmes and Meier.
Coelho, M.P., D. de Meza and D.J. Reyniers (2004), 'Irrational exuberance, entrepreneurial finance and public policy', *International Tax and Public Finance*, **11**, 391–417.
Cooper, A.C., C.Y. Woo and W.C. Dunkelberg (1988), 'Entrepreneurs' perceived chances for success', *Journal of Business Venturing*, **3**, 97–108.
Davis, S.J., J.C. Haltiwanger and S. Schuh (1996), *Job Creation and Destruction*, Cambridge, MA: MIT Press.
de Meza, D. (2002), 'Overlending?', *Economic Journal*, **112**, F17–F31.
de Meza, D. and C. Southey (1996), 'The borrowers curse: optimism, finance, and entrepreneurship', *Economic Journal*, **106**, 375–86.
de Meza, D. and D.C. Webb (1987), 'Too much investment: a problem of asymmetric information', *Quarterly Journal of Economics*, **102**, 281–92.
de Meza, D. and D.C. Webb (1988), 'Credit market efficiency and tax policy in the presence of screening costs', *Journal of Public Economics*, **36**, 1–22.
de Meza, D. and D.C. Webb (1989), 'The role of interest rate taxes in credit markets with divisible projects and asymmetric information', *Journal of Public Economics*, **39**, 33–44.
de Meza, D. and D.C. Webb (1990), 'Risk, adverse selection and capital market failure', *Economic Journal*, **100**, 206–14.
de Meza, D. and D.C. Webb (1999), 'Wealth, enterprise and credit policy', *Economic Journal*, **109**, 153–63.
de Meza, D. and D.C. Webb, (2000), 'Does credit rationing imply insufficient lending?', *Journal of Public Economics*, **78**, 215–34.
Dennis, W. (1998), 'Business regulation as an impediment to the transition from welfare to self-employment', *Journal of Labor Research*, **19**, 263–76.

Djankow, S., R. La Porta, F. Lopez-de-Silanes and A. Shleifer (2002), 'The regulation of entry', *Quarterly Journal of Economics*, **117**, 1–37.

Futia, C. (1980), 'Schumpeterian competition', *Quarterly Journal of Economics*, **93**, 675–95.

Gale, W.G. (1991), 'Economic effects of federal credit programs', *American Economic Review*, **81**, 133–52.

Grossman, G. and C. Shapiro (1984), 'Informative advertising with differentiated products', *Review of Economic Studies*, **51**, 63–82.

Hillier, B. and M.V. Ibrahimo (1992), 'The performance of credit markets under asymmetric information about projects means and variances', *Journal of Economic Studies*, **19**, 3–17.

Holmes, T.J. and J.A. Schmitz (2001), 'A gain from trade: from unproductive to productive entrepreneurship', *Journal of Monetary Economics*, **47**, 417–46.

Holtz-Eakin, D. (2000), 'Public policy toward entrepreneurship', *Small Business Economics*, **15**, 283–91.

Keuschnigg, C. and S.B. Nielsen (2001), 'Public policy for venture capital', *International Tax and Public Finance*, **8**, 557–72.

Keuschnigg, C. and S.B. Nielsen (2004), 'Start-ups, venture capitalists, and the capital gains tax', *Journal of Public Economics*, **88**, 1011–42.

Keuschnigg, C. and S.B. Nielsen (2005), 'Public policy for start-up entrepreneurship with venture capital and bank finance', in V. Kanniainen and C. Keuschnigg (eds), *Venture Capital, Entrepreneurship and Public Policy*, Cambridge, MA: MIT Press, pp. 221–50.

Klette, T.J., J. Moen and A. Griliches (2000), 'Do subsidies to commercial R&D reduce market failure? Microeconometric evaluation studies', *Research Policy*, **29**, 471–95.

Lerner, J. (2004), 'When bureaucrats meet entrepreneurs: the design of effective "public venture capital" programs', in D. Holtz-Eakin and H.S. Rosen (eds), *Public Policy and the Economics of Entrepreneurship*, Cambridge, MA: MIT Press, pp. 1–22.

Leung, M.W.H. (2003), 'Beyond Chinese, beyond food: unpacking the regulated Chinese restaurant business in Germany', *Entrepreneurship and Regional Development*, **15**, 103–18.

Li, W. (2002), 'Entrepreneurship and government subsidies: a general equilibrium analysis', *Journal of Economic Dynamics and Control*, **26**, 1815–44.

Lucas, R.E. Jr (1976), 'Econometric policy evaluation: a critique', in K. Brunner and A. Meltzer (eds), *The Phillips Curve and Labor Markets, Vol. 1 of the Carnegie-Rochester Conference Series on Public Policy*, Amsterdam: North-Holland, pp. 19–46.

Manove, M. (1998), 'Entrepreneurs, optimism, and the competitive edge', Mimeo, Boston University, Boston, MA.

Manove, M. and A.J. Padilla (1999), 'Banking (conservatively) with optimists', *Rand Journal of Economics*, **30**, 324–50.

Murphy, K.M., A. Shleifer and R. Vishny (1993), 'Why is rent-seeking so costly to growth?', *American Economic Review Papers and Proceedings*, **83**, 409–14.

Parker, S.C. (1999), 'The optimal linear taxation of employment and self-employment incomes', *Journal of Public Economics*, **73**, 107–23.

Parker, S.C. (2003), 'Asymmetric information, occupational choice and government policy', *Economic Journal*, **113**, 861–82.

Parker, S.C. (2004), *The Economics of Self-employment and Entrepreneurship*, Cambridge: Cambridge University Press.

Perry, C.W. and H.S. Rosen (2004), 'The self-employed are less likely to have health insurance than wage earners. So what?', in D. Holtz-Eakin and H.S. Rosen (eds), *Public Policy and the Economics of Entrepreneurship*, Cambridge, MA: MIT Press, pp. 23–57.

Pinfold, J.F. (2001), 'The expectations of new business founders: the New Zealand case', *Journal of Small Business Management*, **39**, 279–85.

Puri, M. and D.T. Robinson (2005), 'Optimism, entrepreneurship and economic choice', Working Paper, Duke University.

Robson, P.J.A. and R.J. Bennett (2000), 'The use and impact of business advice by SMEs in Britain: an empirical assessment using logit and ordered logit models', *Applied Economics*, **32**, 1675–88.

Stigler, G. (1971), 'An economic theory of regulation', *Bell Journal of Economics*, **2**, 3–21.

Stiglitz, J. and A. Weiss (1981), 'Credit rationing in markets with imperfect information', *American Economic Review*, **71**, 393–410.

Storey, D.J. (1994), *Understanding the Small Business Sector*, London: Routledge.

Storey, D.J. (2003), 'Entrepreneurship, small and medium sized enterprises and public policies', in Z.J. Acs and D.B. Audretsch (eds), *Handbook of Entrepreneurship Research: An Interdisciplinary Survey and Introduction*, Boston, MA: Kluwer, pp. 473–511.

Westhead, P. and M. Wright (1999), 'Contributions of novice, portfolio and serial founders located in rural and urban areas', *Regional Studies*, **33**, 157–73.

Zazzaro, A. (2005), 'Should courts enforce credit contracts strictly?', *Economic Journal*, **115**, 166–84.

5 Promoting entrepreneurship in the welfare state*
Magnus Henrekson and Jesper Roine

Introduction

Over the past decades endogenous growth theory has developed models that come closer to making explicit what drives long-term economic development. More specifically, explicit incentives for innovation have been included so as to explain why individuals would engage in creating new technologies and better ways of producing goods and services (see Barro and Sala-i-Martin, 1995; Aghion and Howitt, 1998). However, the actual agents of change, the entrepreneurs, are still defined rather narrowly and theory does not capture the wide-ranging and complex functions suggested outside mainstream economics (see for example Glancey and McQuaid, 2000; Swedberg, 2000; and Bianchi and Henrekson, 2005).

Typically theories of endogenous growth emphasize the (expected) pay-offs from innovation or, more generally, the gains from the activities that improve production and organization. Consequently, taxes and benefits that reduce the incentives for engaging in such activities, or policies that decrease their return, should be expected to reduce growth. It is commonly thought that the welfare state's large marginal tax wedges reduce incentives to save and accumulate capital, ultimately discouraging innovation. If this is the case, the welfare state should have less innovation and consequently less growth. However, the disincentive effects from taxes could be countered by spending on growth-enhancing activities such as schooling, infrastructure, or well functioning institutions. It is also possible – as was pointed out by Steinmo (1993) and Lindert (2004), among others – that taxes in a welfare state can be raised in ways that are more pro-growth and less progressive than is typically imagined. In short, there is no simple theoretical relation between high taxes and a large public sector, and negative effects on economic performance of a country. This mixed view seems to be supported by the empirical literature as well.[1]

However this does not imply that the welfare state does not affect economic performance. On the contrary, the fact that a welfare state reaches into more aspects of its citizens' lives means that it, to a larger extent than a low-welfare state, shapes 'the rules of the game in society' (North, 1990, p. 3). The ultimate question about the impact of the welfare state on economic growth therefore concerns the particular incentive structures that result in the welfare state, and to what extent these form the set of 'appropriate institutions' for a given economy.[2]

This chapter addresses a specific subset of questions revolving around the interrelationship between endogenous growth theory, the welfare state and entrepreneurship. The purpose is to examine how the supply of entrepreneurship – and to a lesser extent its distribution across activities – is affected by the kind of tax and welfare arrangements that prevail in a typical mature welfare state. In particular, we emphasize that it is not simply a question of high taxation or large public programs, as their undisputed negative effects can in principle be countered by positive ones, but rather we focus on the particular incentives created by the system.

Given that Sweden is probably the most extensive welfare state (Lindbeck, 1997), the country offers a 'laboratory', or testing ground, for such an examination. We argue that the Swedish welfare state, through attempting to combine high taxation and the creation of large public programs with sustained incentives for growth, has instead created an incentive structure in which long-term economic success depends heavily on the success of established large companies. A key assumption for this view – largely inspired by Schumpeter (1942) and later advanced by Galbraith (1956) – was the idea that innovative activity was best performed by large firms, while individual entrepreneurs and new firms were considered less important.

Our analysis is greatly influenced by Baumol's (1990) study, but since 'the structure of payoffs' for entrepreneurship is examined in a modern welfare state, both the institutional analysis and the relative performance measures are more precise than in Baumol's broad historical comparisons. Similar studies are needed for nations to find out if the findings of this chapter have general validity.

The chapter is organized as follows. In the next section entrepreneurship is precisely defined and some useful distinctions are made. We also discuss why entrepreneurship is likely to be particularly important for economic development in a modern economy. In the third section the modern welfare state is characterized, and specifically its implementation in Sweden is outlined, focusing on aspects relevant to an entrepreneurial perspective. The fourth section outlines a political economy theory of the Swedish model as a compromise between the large established firms and the representatives of workers, which leads to the combination of a high average tax rate and a large public sector, but relatively low taxes on capital and relatively favorable conditions for certain types of industries and business entities. This section makes a number of broad predictions that are followed up in the remaining sections. In the fifth section we look in more detail at what kind of policies this leads to, while in the sixth section we study the extent to which the empirical evidence regarding entrepreneurial activity in Sweden is consistent with what may be predicted from the incentive structure. The final section concludes.

Defining entrepreneurship and its links to economic growth

The entrepreneur and entrepreneurship are elusive concepts. In the literature one can find at least 13 distinct themes developed around these concepts (Hébert and Link, 1989). The most influential view is probably the one proposed by Schumpeter (1934, 1942), who saw the entrepreneur as somebody who caused disequilibrium by introducing new technologies ('creative destruction'). Kirzner (1973, 1997), on the other hand, emphasized the role of pushing the economy back towards equilibrium by exploiting previously unperceived opportunities to reach the production possibility frontier. A third influential view was originally proposed by Knight (1921), who saw entrepreneurs as agents who receive a rate of return for bearing what he dubbed 'genuine uncertainty', that is, non-calculable risk.

In the context of this chapter these subtleties are of less importance, and to capture the most important mechanisms we define entrepreneurship, in line with Wennekers and Thurik (1999), as the ability and willingness of individuals, both on their own and within organizations to: (1) perceive and create new economic opportunities; (2) introduce their ideas in the market, in the face of uncertainty and other obstacles, by making decisions on location, form and the use of resources and institutions; and (3) compete with others for a share of that market.

Thus in order for an activity to be defined as entrepreneurial it needs to be novel, at least in some sense, but whether it is novel because it applies new knowledge or uses existing knowledge in new ways does not matter. There must also be an ambition to grow. As a result, one cannot define entrepreneurship as self-employment or firm formation per se. A person may be entrepreneurial both in his or her role as business owner/self-employed or as an employee (intrapreneur).

Baumol (1990) and Murphy et al. (1991) specifically deal with the effect of institutions/ the social payoff structure on the distribution of entrepreneurship between productive and unproductive/destructive activities. Baumol assumes that the supply of entrepreneurship (i.e. the application of entrepreneurial talent) is roughly a constant, while its distribution between productive and unproductive activities is affected by the social payoff structure. This assumption is unnecessarily restrictive; there are a priori reasons to assume that the incentive structure will affect both the total supply of entrepreneurial talent and its distribution across activities that are more or less socially productive.

Baumol's broad historical analysis makes it clear that the factors that 'forge the structure of payoffs' for entrepreneurship are multi-faceted, but it is also obvious that the incentive structure cannot be characterized in much detail using this historical method. This is of course easier if one chooses to study contemporary institutional contexts.

By the 1930s the idea had gained strength that economic development from then on would be possible without the entrepreneurial function. In particular, Schumpeter argued forcibly in favour of this view in his 1942 classic *Capitalism, Socialism and Democracy*, where he claimed that by means of modern techniques and modern modes of organization, the innovation process would become increasingly automated. Innovations would no longer be associated with the efforts and brilliance of specific individuals.

The notion that large-scale production and a social order with strong collectivist elements would promote economic development had many advocates at the time. In particular, Galbraith (1956, 1967) provided an important rationale for economic policy oriented towards large corporations. He argued that in a modern industrial society, innovative activity as well as improvements in current products and production processes could be carried out most efficiently within the realm of the large industrial corporation. Individual efforts, and hence individual incentives, would dwindle in importance, and small firms and entrepreneurs came to be seen as marginal elements in the process of economic development. We will come back to these ideas as they have been of particular importance in the Swedish case.

The long period during which large firms had predominated and small firms had been increasingly marginalized came to an end in the 1970s. Entrepreneurship and small firms experienced a global resurgence (Brock and Evans, 1986; Loveman and Sengenberger, 1991). Several reasons why this occurred have been suggested:

1.   Technological change in recent decades has resulted in large reductions in transaction costs in the market, fostering increased specialization across firms and sharper focus on each firm's core activity. Outsourcing and corporate downsizing are concrete manifestations of this change (Carlsson, 1999; Piore and Sabel, 1984).

2. Since the 1960s, there has been a sizeable shift away from industries characterized by large firms (manufacturing, extraction, construction) towards service industries where firms and establishments tend to be smaller (see e.g. Davis et al., 1996).
3. In tandem with increased incomes, consumers have come to demand more differentiated products rather than standardized products suitable for large-scale production and distribution (Piore and Sabel, 1984; Carree and Thurik, 1999).
4. In many cases, large, mature firms cannot introduce genuinely new products and production methods efficiently. In the long run, radically new technology is required to sustain a high growth rate, since firms in other countries at lower income levels will sooner or later imitate current technologies. Large firms often excel in increasing productivity in the manufacture of existing products, while totally new products are often produced more efficiently in newly established firms, which have been started with the purpose of producing these very products (Baldwin and Johnson, 1999; Audretsch, 1995).
5. Small entrepreneurial firms can often act as crucial *agents of change*. When such firms are motivated to grow they are likely to play a particularly important role in the growth process (Audretsch, 1995).
6. The small-business sector can function as an inexpensive mechanism for identifying and developing entrepreneurial and managerial talent (Lucas, 1978).

The first three mechanisms contribute to an increased tendency for more goods and services to be produced more efficiently in smaller firms and establishments – for structural as well as technological reasons. The last three mechanisms are more dynamic.

Lately, the importance of entry, exit and turnover of firms – especially in countries close to the technological frontier – has also been emphasized, for example in Aghion and Howitt (2005). In general, the importance of turnover could be seen as the standard Schumpeterian idea that faster growth implies a higher rate of firm turnover as new innovators enter, replacing the former, who exit. However, as noted by Aghion et al. (2005) there are several effects going in opposite directions in terms of how increased competition affects incentives to innovate. On the one hand, stricter competition may reduce growth by reducing post-innovation returns to successful innovators. On the other hand stricter competition induces more 'escape competition', that is, incentives for innovation so as to break away from one's competitors through superior technology. They also emphasize that exit may be positive for productivity growth because it replaces less efficient firms (or inputs) by better ones. The relative size of these effects depends, in their framework, on the distance to the technological frontier and, more specifically, the closer a country (or a sector) is to the frontier, the more important is entry.

Carree et al. (2002) hypothesize that there ought to be a U-shaped relationship between the degree of entrepreneurial activity and the level of development. Empirically, this is tested by using the rate of self-employment as a proxy for entrepreneurial activity. Some support for the hypothesis is found, in particular for the existence of a downward-sloping segment up to a certain level of income. Wennekers et al. (2005) instead measure entrepreneurial activity as the rate of 'nascent entrepreneurship' from the 2002 GEM study (Reynolds et al., 2005; see section 6) for 36 countries. In this case the hypothesized U-shape is more evident in the data. Furthermore, Nicoletti and Scarpetta (2003) show that high entry costs and a lower degree of turnover in Europe compared to the US are important for explaining Europe's relatively disappointing growth performance over the past decades, and Sapir et al. (2003) argue that an important reason for the fact that Europe stopped catching up with the US GDP per capita in the mid-1970s has been the failure to switch institutions to ones that promote the entry of new firms.

The mature welfare state
In line with Lindbeck (1988) the term 'welfare state' is reserved for the array of publicly financed provision or subsidization of personal services, notably for health, education, child care and care of the elderly, and for social security systems, transfers and subsidies. The welfare state may of course be defined more broadly by including a number of non-budget or regulatory measures such as price and rent controls and regulations of labor and capital markets, where these measures are intended to benefit particular groups or activities that are considered to be in need of extra support or protection.

The expansion of the welfare state was a salient feature of almost all industrialized countries, in particular during the 1960s and 1970s (Castles, 1998; Beck, 1981). This tendency was most pronounced in Sweden. In 1960 Sweden was not an exceptional case; the relative size of the public sector was only marginally above the OECD average.[3] But over the following quarter of a century this situation changed dramatically, and since the late 1960s Sweden has had the largest public sector measured as a share of GDP in the OECD. In particular, government consumption as a share of GDP became very high by the 1980s (close to 30 percent of GDP), which resulted in a very large share of public employment; public sector employment has constituted approximately one third of total employment since about 1980. Total government expenditures as a share of GDP were almost 25 percentage points above the OECD average by the early 1980s. During the latter half of the 1980s the difference diminished somewhat on the expenditure side, but measured from the income side, the public sector remained at a level that was more than 20 percentage points larger as a share of GDP than the OECD average. In the early 1990s the expenditure ratio exploded, largely reflecting the abysmal downturn of the economy. During the latter half of the 1990s the government spending share decreased substantially as a combined effect of austerity measures and the strong recovery after the crisis of the early 1990s. Still, in the first years of the twenty-first century, the public sector was almost 50 percent larger than the OECD average.

The Swedish welfare state is so large because ambitions are high regarding both social insurance and public service production. The welfare state cares for its citizens from 'cradle to grave' through a large number of schemes (parental leave, child care, medical and dental care, sickness cash benefits, disability pensions, unemployment benefits and public pensions). Income-related, as opposed to flat rate, programs are the rule, which makes the programs costly, and furthermore a number of measures have been introduced over the years that have raised the lower threshold for disposable income. See Forslund (1997) and Aronsson and Walker (1997) for an overview of the programs. The consensus view is that the Swedish welfare state has been successful in a number of ways, notably in eliminating poverty and equalizing income, wealth, hours of work and consumption in virtually every respect (over the life cycle, across individuals, across households) (Freeman et al., 1997; Forslund, 1997; Lindbeck, 1997).

Increasingly, economists recognized the disincentive effects created by a welfare state as extensive as the Swedish one, and these effects were found to be multidimensional, affecting not just the choice of work or quantity of market work but also the intensity of work and the investment in human and physical capital, as well as a host of other factors. By the 1990s there were also studies that showed that the overall effect of the welfare systems made it unprofitable to work at all for substantial groups in society (see e.g. Ds 1994:81 and Ds 1997:73).[4] It is impossible to give a short summary of the numerous studies, but it is fair to say that overall, economists have emphasized the accumulated disincentive effects of regulations in the capital, product and labor markets and how these have interacted with the disincentive effects emanating from high marginal effects caused by the tax and transfer systems (Agell, 1996; Lindbeck, 1997). However, surprisingly little attention has been given to the incentive effects of welfare state arrangements on the supply of entrepreneurial effort and its distribution across activities.

The political economics of entrepreneurial policy in the Swedish welfare state
Above we have discussed aspects of entrepreneurship, endogenous growth theory and some features of the Swedish welfare state. A reoccurring theme has been to point to the importance of the incentives created by policy and in particular that appropriate policies may be highly context specific. However, so far we have said nothing about how policy is chosen. In this section we first briefly discuss some standard theories of growth where policy is endogenous. We then discuss some early key ideas about growth policy in the Swedish context and see how the presented political economy ideas could be modified to understand these policies as well as how they can persist, even if they no longer constitute what would be appropriate for enhancing growth.

Early endogenous growth theory focused on capital accumulation as the engine of economic growth (Barro and Sala-i-Martin, 1995). With this view, economic growth is ultimately a function of individual decisions about capital accumulation, and the policy that affects these decisions has an effect on growth. A number of political economy models (i.e. models where policy is determined endogenously through a political process) have been developed to study how, for example, income inequality maps into the choice of broad policies like taxation and redistribution. In models developed by, for example, Alesina and Rodrik (1994) and Persson and Tabellini (1994), high inequality will raise the demand for redistribution, which in turn will lead to high taxes, lowering the returns on investment, thus lowering growth. If, on the other hand, the increased revenue is used to promote infrastructure, to support education or to finance some other policy that may be conducive to accumulation and investment, this could outweigh the negative effect of the tax wedge.[5] Combining these ideas we get the much debated tradeoff between the negative effects from high taxes on investment and savings on the one hand, and the possibility of using tax revenue to promote growth.

A central idea – not present in the above theories of endogenous policy choice – around the time of the expansion of the Swedish welfare state was that high taxes were possible without hurting capital accumulation. As long as taxes did not harm the incentives of those who were thought to be important for the growth-enhancing investments (which would create employment) disincentive effects on others were less of a concern. In particular, detrimental effects on the entrepreneurial function were not thought to be important, since – as already noted – the dominant view at the time was that the entrepreneur was waning in importance. The notion that large-scale production and a social order with strong collectivist elements were conducive to economic development had considerable appeal.[6]

Key elements of the Swedish model are in line with this vision: the large corporations and the public sector as engines of economic development, the perceived unimportance of individual incentives for entrepreneurship, effort and human capital investment, and the claim that not just large-scale production but also innovative activity and renewal could be subordinated to Fordist organizational principles. By the late 1960s it was clear that the ruling party, the Social Democrats, considered small firms and individual entrepreneurs as marginal elements in the process of economic development, and in due course such phenomena were expected to be totally anachronistic (Henrekson and Jakobsson, 2001). Johansson and Magnusson (1998) describe how a vision of 'capitalism without capitalists' developed. They claim that this vision is crucial, because it constitutes 'the link uniting collectivism and market dynamics. As a result, capitalism can be salvaged – without requiring powerful owners or capitalists. Redistribution of income can co-exist with high profits in the most dynamic firms' (p. 121).

Could such a policy be an endogenous outcome of a political process? Could there be an outcome where policy is characterized by high redistributive ambitions, a high general tax rate, but relatively favorable conditions for large incumbent firms? The short answer is 'yes'. As shown in Roine (2006) it is possible, even in a purely redistributional setting, to have political equilibria characterized by a coalition where those with the very highest initial resources can agree with those with the smallest initial resources to tax the middle group heavily as long as they (the top group) do not pay (full) taxes themselves.[7] Applying a similar logic to the build up of the Swedish welfare state, the (owners of the) initially large firms could agree with (the representatives of) the workers (i.e. the unions) to have generally high taxes, as long as there were some concessions for them. In fact, such an agreement can even be seen as more beneficial to the large firms than a generally lower tax rate, since high taxes act as a barrier to entry for initially small firms that have growth ambitions but are too small to be part of the initial coalition. As we shall see in the next section, there are several indications regarding both the structure of taxation and the size distribution of firms over time, which support this view.

A set of institutions that benefit incumbent firms in certain sectors is obviously favorable to them. But is it also possible that this outcome contributes to growth? Again the short answer is 'yes'. As has already been pointed out, policies favoring large incumbent firms can be appropriate if there are important economies of scale making larger firms more efficient in production as well as better suited for innovative activities. Indeed, if this is the case, individual efforts can be seen as a waste of resources as well as entrepreneurial talent and the role of new entrants is small.

What kind of institutions should we expect to evolve as a result of the unusual coalition between the (representatives) of the workers and the initially important firms (the large capital holders)? The theory, of course, says nothing about the exact policies (only that general taxes and redistributive ambitions should be high, while there are exemptions for large firms and capital owners) but in terms of incentive structure we could expect institutions favoring:

- Large established firms over smaller, new entrants;
- Industry that is intensive in physical rather than human capital;
- Intrapreneurship over entrepreneurship.

And in terms of outcomes we should expect:

- An industry structure dominated by large and relatively old firms;
- A tax system where investment in physical capital is treated favorably (especially relative to human capital);
- Most innovation taking place within existing corporations;
- A declining share of total taxable income being business income;
- A political rapport between established firms and large capital owners and representatives of the workers and unions.[8]

It is important to emphasize once again that it is not theoretically possible to conclude that this set of policies is good or bad for growth. In line with Gerschenkron's idea of 'appropriate institutions', policies favoring large corporations could be growth conducive compared to an 'incentive-neutral' policy (holding total taxation and redistribution constant). However, if it turns out to be the case that the initially favored firms are not the ones best suited for continued growth and innovation, or that exogenous changes make human-capital intensive firms become increasingly important, this kind of policy may be inimical to growth. In particular, if it is the case that the entry, turnover and exit of firms and individual entrepreneurship are important, a set of policies favoring large incumbents is not the best for growth.

Welfare state policies and incentives for entrepreneurship
In this section we explore in more detail how a number of institutions of the Swedish welfare state affect incentives for entrepreneurship.

Taxation of entrepreneurial income
Income emanating from successful entrepreneurial activity is often capitalized in the form of ownership of equity that appreciates in value. However, over time the Swedish tax code evolved in a way that was highly congruent with a vision of a market economy without individual capitalists and entrepreneurs. This is clear from Table 5.1 where effective marginal tax rates for different combinations of owners and sources of finance are presented for selected years from 1980 until 2001. Three categories of owners and sources of finance are identified, and the effective marginal tax rate is calculated assuming a pre-tax real rate of return of 10 percent. A negative number means that the real rate of return is greater after tax than before tax.[9]

Table 5.1 highlights three important aspects of the Swedish tax system (for further details and additional years, see Davis and Henrekson, 1997). First, by 1980 debt financing consistently received extremely favorable tax treatment relative to new share issues. Second, the taxation of households as owners is much higher than for other categories, and their rate of taxation started to increase sharply in the 1960s, whereas the reverse occurred for insurance companies and tax-exempt institutions.[10] From some point in the 1960s until the 1991 tax reform, more than 100 percent of the real rate of return was taxed away for a household buying a newly issued share. Third, tax-exempt institutions benefit from a large tax advantage relative to the other two categories of owners, and this advantage increased strongly during the 1960s and 1970s.

Table 5.1   *Effective marginal tax rates for different combinations of owners and sources of finance, 1980, 1991 and 2001 (10% real pre-tax rate of return at actual inflation rates)*

	Debt	New share issues	Retained earnings
1980			
Households	58.2	136.6	51.9
Tax exempt institutions	−83.4	−11.6	11.2
Insurance companies	−54.9	38.4	28.7
1991			
Households	31.3	62.0	54.6
Tax exempt institutions	−10.0	7.3	20.4
Insurance companies	14.0	33.5	32.0
2001			
Households	29.7/24.7†	61.0/51.0†	44.1/34.1†
Tax exempt institutions	−1.4	23.6	23.6
Insurance companies	19.6	47.2	44.7

Notes:
† Excluding wealth tax; the wealth tax on unlisted shares was abolished in 1992.
  All calculations are based on the actual asset composition in manufacturing. The following inflation rates were used: 1980: 9.4%, 1991: 5%, 1994: 3%, 2001: 3%. These calculations conform to the general framework developed in King and Fullerton (1984). The average holding period is assumed to be 10 years.

Source: Calculations provided by Jan Södersten; see also Södersten (1984, 1993).

Households owning a successful business typically faced an even higher tax rate because of the combined effect of wealth and income taxation. Until 1992, wealth tax was levied on 30 percent of the net worth of a family-owned company. As of the mid-1980s, the maximum wealth tax rate was 3 percent. Since the wealth tax was not deductible at the company level, funds required to pay the wealth tax were first subject to the personal income tax and the mandatory payroll tax. From around the mid-1960s until the late 1980s the taxation of individually owned firms that could not work with extreme debt–equity ratios was so high that it could be seen as confiscatory in real terms (see Södersten, 1984). This spurred the formation of a number of so-called bank-connected investment companies that acquired a large share of the medium-sized family-owned businesses (Petersson, 2001).

This makes clear the extraordinary extent to which the Swedish tax system favored, and still favors, institutional ownership and discouraged direct household ownership of firms, which is a prerequisite for entrepreneurial firms, at least in the early phase of their life cycle.

In order to analyze how the tax system impacts on entrepreneurial behavior it is not sufficient to focus on the taxation of owners of firms. To a large extent the return on entrepreneurial effort is taxed as wage income. First, a large part of income accruing from closely held companies has to be paid out as wage income, since there are severe restrictions on the room for dividends even if the firm is profitable, and the capital gains tax is normally 43 percent for small closely held firms instead of the regular 30 percent, since half the capital gain is taxed as wage income. Second, a great deal of the entrepreneurial function is carried out by employees without an ownership stake in the firm, and the total marginal tax wedge for high-income earners has been high in Sweden throughout the post-war period. Defining the total marginal tax wedge as all taxes paid as a percentage of total labor compensation paid by the employer, the marginal tax wedge for an average wage of an executive (just below the CEO level) went from 50 percent in 1952 to a peak of 91 percent in 1979, while the marginal tax wedge for the average white-collar worker peaked at 85 percent. The comprehensive tax reform in 1991 simplified and lowered the income tax schedule, but as a result of increased local and consumption taxes the total tax wedge was still 75 percent in the late 1990s for executives and the average white-collar worker alike (Du Rietz, 1994; Nordling and Damsgaard, 1998). In the early 2000s local taxes have continued to increase while some consumption taxes and property taxes have been lowered. In 2005 the overall tax wedge was still in the order of 75 per cent for these groups.

Furthermore, the use of stock options to encourage and reward intrapreneurship is highly penalized by the tax system, since gains on options are taxed as wage income when the stock options are tied to employment in the firm. Thus they are subjected both to mandatory social security (33 percent) and the marginal tax rate. Since the marginal tax rate is roughly 57 percent this entails a total tax rate of roughly 68 percent (2005).[11] In practice, stock options can therefore not be used as a means to reward entrepreneurial behavior among wealth-constrained individuals.[12]

Finally, it is now widely recognized that venture capital firms can play a crucial role in the development of a small entrepreneurial venture by converting high-risk opportunities to a more acceptable risk level through portfolio diversification, and adding key competencies that the firm may be lacking. This is achieved by means of developing arrangements that align the incentives of the three agents – investors, venture capitalists and entrepreneurial startups (Zider, 1998; Gompers and Lerner, 2001). However, the above-described tax schedules apply to this industry as well, which means that a highly competent venture capital industry where high-powered incentives can be used to reward investment managers, cannot develop in Sweden.[13]

Incentives for savings and individual wealth formation
Welfare state provisions remove a number of savings motives for the individual. As long as unemployment insurance, income-dependent pensions and sick-leave benefits, higher education and highly subsidized health and care services are provided by the government, most of the essential savings motives for the average person disappear. Means-tested schemes such as social assistance may exacerbate this effect at the lower end since it is conditional on the individual not having any assets (Hubbard et al., 1995). Moreover, pay-as-you-go pension systems tend to lower national savings and investment compared to funded systems (Feldstein, 1996). Thus, in an extensive welfare state system, total savings motives are much reduced. Individual savings rates and average holdings of readily available assets are also very low in Sweden by international comparison – see Table 5.2 and Pålsson (2002).

There are numerous research results suggesting that such disincentives to savings and individual wealth accumulation are likely to lower the propensity to supply entrepreneurial effort. The availability of equity financing is a critical factor for both startups and the expansion of existing firms. In general, the riskier the business, the greater the need to

Table 5.2   Household net saving as a share of disposable income in Sweden, OECD and OECD Europe, 1960–2004 (percent)

	1960–69	1970–79	1980–89	1990–97	1998–2004
Sweden	*6.1*	*4.0*	*1.1*	*5.4*	*2.5*
OECD	9.7	12.1	11.2	9.8†	6.2
OECD Europe	12.0	13.6	11.6	10.9‡	10.9

Notes:
† 1990–95, ‡ 1990–96.
Savings in equity pension funds are excluded. OECD Europe 1998–2004 is defined as the Euro-12 countries.

Sources: OECD, *Historical Statistics 1960–1980* and *1960–1995*; OECD, *Economic Outlook*, Vol. 65, 1999 and Vol. 77, 2005.

rely on equity relative to debt financing and the smaller and newer the firm, the more difficult for outside financiers to assess the viability and profitability of the proposed investment project. Thus, *ceteris paribus*, small and newly established firms are more dependent on equity financing than large, well-established firms. Low private savings also exacerbate the inherent problem caused by asymmetric information, since wealth-constrained would-be entrepreneurs are unable to signal forcibly to outside investors by means of making sizeable equity infusions of their own.

There is substantial scientific evidence supporting the idea that the individual wealth position has important effects on the probability of becoming an entrepreneur and the propensity to expand. For example, Lindh and Ohlsson (1996, 1998) find that the likelihood of starting a business in Sweden increases significantly among those who receive an inheritance or a lottery gain. They also find that a more unequal wealth distribution covaries positively with the share of self-employed. Similar evidence is found for the US by Holtz-Eakin et al. (1994). This is probably the most well-established finding in the small business economics literature, and there are a host of further studies pointing to the importance of personal assets for the degree to which entrepreneurial talent is exploited, see for example Blanchflower and Oswald (1998) and Taylor (2001), and the overview of this literature in Parker (2004, Chapters 5–6).

In addition to the welfare state reducing the need for savings for precautionary as well as life-cycle reasons, taxation has created additional disincentives. The *real* rate of taxation on financial savings was extremely high in Sweden for individuals before the 1990/91 tax reform. On interest income it typically exceeded 100 percent by a wide margin during the 1970s and 1980s. The rate of taxation on saving and wealth accumulation remains high. First, the high tax rates on wage income make it hard to save a substantial portion of income that can subsequently be used for equity financing. Second, total taxation on accumulated wealth is high (2005): 30 percent on the nominal current return, 30 percent nominal capital gains tax and 1.5 percent wealth tax on real estate, interest-bearing instruments and prime listed stock.

The combination of low private savings and an extremely even distribution (Lindh and Ohlsson, 1998) of these low savings implies that few people are able to raise the requisite equity, either themselves or from their associates, friends or relatives, to realize their business projects.

In recent decades private saving has been encouraged through favorable tax treatment. This concerns both fully tax-deductible pension plans paid individually and supplementary occupational schemes. Through these schemes a person may accumulate substantial wealth. However, following the welfare state logic this is primarily seen as a complement to the income security provided by the government, and hence these funds are by law channeled to traditional financial institutions and the wealth is locked in, at least until age 55, and it cannot be lifted in large chunks. This is likely to reduce the supply of equity financing for potential entrepreneurs and extant small businesses, since pension funds are less suitable for channeling funds to entrepreneurs compared to business angels or venture capital firms. Hence, if the system is designed so that ordinary people are in effect obligated to carry out most of their savings through large collective systems, small business financing will suffer relative to alternative policies and institutional arrangements that allow for greater choice by individuals regarding their savings and investments.

Government production of income-elastic services
No doubt Schumpeter and Galbraith almost exclusively dealt with the industrial, mostly goods-producing, sector of the economy. However, in Sweden the large-scale production in the manufacturing sector came to be seen as a role model also for central parts of the production of highly income-elastic services such as health care, child care, elderly care and education (Rojas, 2001). In these cases it was seen as natural that the public sector substituted for the large corporations, and as a result Fordist principles of planning, standardization and large-scale production came to characterize society as a whole – Rojas (2001) speaks of 'social Fordism'. This strategy had a profound effect on employment growth across sectors; from 1960 until the mid-1990s all net employment growth in Sweden took place in the local government sector (Rosen, 1997).

These publicly produced private services are in many cases highly suitable for production in private and often also small firms. The political decision to produce these services primarily through a public sector monopoly has largely barred this area from both startup activity and the emergence of high-growth firms. Table 5.3 summarizes the share of private production for the major services that are fully or primarily tax-financed. The private production share is very low in activities like child care, care of the elderly and after-school care, despite the fact that these activities are highly amenable to private, small-firm production. The potential market is huge. The operating costs incurred by local governments for schooling, child care and care of the elderly exceeded 10 percent of GDP per year in the mid-1990s, and the health care sector was almost as large.

Hence, due to the *de facto* monopolization by the public sector of the production of many income-elastic services, vast areas of the economy have remained unexploited as sources of commercial growth. In particular in the health sector, it is easy to imagine how a different organizational mode could have provided a basis for the emergence of new high-growth firms.[14]

Household-related services out of reach for entrepreneurial exploitation
A large percentage of all work, most notably household work, is performed outside the market. Cross-country comparisons of industry-level employment also point to considerable scope for substitution of certain economic activities between the market and non-market sectors (Davis and Henrekson, 2005). For Sweden, studies indicate that more time

*Table 5.3   Private sector production share for major services that are primarily publicly
funded, 1996 and 2000 (percent)*

Service	1996	2000
Institutional child care (pre-school)	12.5	11.8
Child care in the home (of the professional)	2.2	8.6
After-school care	4.5	
Compulsory schooling	2.4	3.9
High school	1.9	4.4
Care of the elderly in nursing homes	8.3	10.0
Care of the elderly in special apartments	5.1	
Care of the elderly in their own home	2.6	
Hospital care	4.3	
Medical consultations	28	
Share of doctors privately employed	10	
Psychiatric wards	24	
Children's dental care	5	

Source: Werenfels Röttorp (1998) for 1996 and Jordahl (2002) for 2000.

is spent on production in the household than in the market. According to the 1997 Service Sector Taxation Report (SOU 1997:17), 7 billion hours were devoted to household work in 1993, while production of goods and public and private services accounted for 5.9 billion hours. Furthermore, paid work not reported to the tax authorities was estimated to represent approximately 10 percent of the hours worked in the marketplace. The same report also presents evidence that the private service sector is exceptionally small in Sweden compared to other OECD countries. This is particularly the case for the whole-sale and retail trade, hotels and restaurants and miscellaneous services. In a detailed industry level comparison of Sweden and the US, Davis and Henrekson (2005) demonstrate that relative employment in the US is considerably greater in household-related services, such as repair of durable goods, hotel and restaurant, retail sales, laundry and household work.[15]

In a well-functioning, decentralized market economy, entrepreneurs can be expected to detect and act on the potential for starting new operations or expand existing ones, thereby creating job opportunities. US trends in recent decades indicate that new jobs primarily arise through the rapid growth of an increasingly differentiated service sector. So why does Sweden not display a similar trend? A fundamental reason emanates from high rates of personal taxation. Personal taxes raise the full price of goods and services. For many goods (e.g. high-tech products like computers), a high price may cause the consumer to forgo a purchase, or to buy a lower quality version of the good. This need not be the case with services – high labor taxes often induce the consumer to produce the service himself. This basic insight constitutes an important point of departure in recent work in the theory of optimal taxation. The theoretical results of Jacobsen et al. (2000) and Piggott and Whalley (2001) strongly suggest that the optimal tax structure involves a relatively low tax rate on those market-produced services that could alternatively be produced in the household sector.[16] High rates of taxation of labor tend to make it more profitable to shift a large share of the service production to the informal economy, in particular into the 'do-it-yourself' sector. In the case where the cost of the service consists of labor cost only, one can show that it is profitable to produce the service in the market when (Pålsson, 1997; Davis and Henrekson, 2005):

$$\frac{\text{Buyer's hourly wage before tax}}{\text{Seller's hourly wage before tax}} \cdot \frac{\text{Seller's productivity}}{\text{'Do-it-yourself' productivity}}$$

$$> \frac{(1 + \text{the VAT rate})(1 + \text{social security rate})}{1 - \text{buyer's marginal tax rate}}$$

Let us call the right-hand side of this expression the tax factor.[17] The expression describes a fundamental economic relation, which, given wage and productivity differentials, is a crucial determinant of the demarcation line between taxed and untaxed work. Low rates of taxation on labor require smaller wage differentials before tax and/or productivity differences in order to avoid unpaid work crowding out professional work in cases where unpaid (or black market) work is feasible.

The tax factor in Sweden is in the range 2.7–4.1 (1997 tax code). In the US the tax factor is generally in the 1.4–1.9 range. Comparisons between Sweden and the US (California) show that in order for a professional service producer to be competitive vis-à-vis unpaid household production, the professional must have a productivity edge of 170–310 percent in Sweden, whereas 40–90 percent is sufficient in the US (in the case of equal market wage). Alternatively, in the case of equal productivity (e.g. child care) the hourly wage of the buyer must exceed that of the seller by a factor of 2.7–4.1 in Sweden, whereas a factor of 1.4–1.9 is sufficient in the US.

As a result, the emergence of a large, efficient service sector competing successfully with unpaid work is less likely in a large welfare state than in countries with lower rates of labor taxation (and higher wage dispersion). As a corollary, an important arena for commercial exploitation and entrepreneurial business development becomes less accessible. Given that more than half of the total volume of work remains commercially unexploited in Sweden, this is likely to be of great economic significance, particularly in the long run. When services are provided by professionals, incentives emerge to invest in new knowledge, to develop more effective tools, to develop superior contractual arrangements, to create more flexible organizational structures and so forth. Put simply, higher rates of personal taxation discourage the market provision of goods and services that substitute closely for home-produced services. As a consequence, higher rates of personal taxation reduce the scope for entrepreneurial expansion into new market activities that economize on time use or that supply close substitutes for home-produced services.

Incentives for necessity entrepreneurship
In the empirical literature on the determinants of the supply of entrepreneurship, a distinction is often made between pull and push factors (Storey, 1994). An individual can either be pulled into entrepreneurship in order to pursue a business opportunity (rather than having a regular job) or he or she can be pushed into it because there is no better choice for work or for making a living. Reynolds et al. (2001, 2005) explicitly distinguish

Table 5.4   Number of tax-financed and market-financed individuals in Sweden, 1960, 1990 and 2002 (millions)

	1960	1990	2002
1. Tax-financed individuals†	1143	3887	4021
2. Employed in market-sector‡	2989	2569	2490
Ratio (1/2)	0.38	1.51	1.63

Notes:
† The sum of public sector employees, old age pensioners, people on early retirement, paid sick leave, paid parental leave, refugee applicants and people receiving unemployment benefits or participating in labor market programs.
‡ Including the self-employed and those working in public utilities and government owned corporations but excluding those on paid sick leave and parental leave.

Source: Lindbeck (1997) for 1960 and 1990, and authors' own corresponding calculation for 2002.

between 'opportunity-based' and 'necessity' entrepreneurship in their multi-country effort to measure the rate of entrepreneurial activity.[18]

The effects of the welfare state discussed so far – taxation of entrepreneurial income and institutional impediments to commercial exploitation in large parts of the service sector – has primarily, at least implicitly, been concerned with the problem that a comprehensive welfare state curbs opportunities for entrepreneurs. But the welfare state also provides ample opportunities for receiving income from the public budget, either as a government employee or as a transfer recipient. Aggregate figures clearly show that these opportunities have increased sharply in Sweden during the post-war period. According to Table 5.4 there were more than 1.6 persons getting most of their income from the public budget for each person employed in the market sector in 2002. The corresponding figure in 1960 was 0.38.

For the most part, the ambition of the welfare state to equalize outcomes is formally focused on individuals and households. However, there are enormous differences across regions in labor market opportunities, and as a result large interregional differences in employment levels may persist indefinitely, as large sums are transferred from high-employment to low-employment regions in the form of unemployment benefits, disability pensions, compensation through labor market programs and so forth. Table 5.5 reports the share of household income consisting of labor income paid by private employers in Swedish municipalities. This share varies from roughly 23 percent up to two thirds. The country average is slightly below 50 percent. Thus these data clearly indicate that the push towards necessity entrepreneurship in low-employment regions or in a region suffering from a negative shock is very weak.

The high tax on labor creates difficulties from another standpoint – a decent net wage presupposes high pre-tax earnings. This problem is particularly acute in Sweden, which places a heavy tax burden on the low-income earners. For someone who earns 75 percent of the average wage of an industrial worker, 61 percent of the total labor cost consists of taxes and mandatory social security contributions. This is the highest rate among industrialized countries (Norrman, 1997).

It seems reasonable to assume that there is a connection between the net wage the individual demands and the minimum income he or she is guaranteed by the social security

Table 5.5   Market income as a share of total household income in Swedish municipalities, 1995 and 1998 (percent)

Top 5 municipalities	1995	1998	Bottom 5 municipalities	1995	1998
Gnosjö	64.8	68.1	Pajala	22.8	23.5
Håbo	61.1	63.9	Boden	24.7	25.4
Täby	60.2	63.9	Haparanda	25.7	26.7
Gislaved	60.1	62.8	Övertorneå	27.5	27.4
Sollentuna	58.4	62.5	Sollefteå	29.3	29.3
Country average	45.7	48.9			

Note: Market income as a share of total income is defined as the share of total household income emanating from labor income paid by private employers. Income from capital is excluded.

Source: SAF (2000).

system. The net wage demanded corresponds to a certain gross pre-tax wage, the reservation wage. The ingredients that determine the reservation wage are complex and dependent on a number of circumstances. The social safety nets play an important role in the determination of the reservation wage. Ultimately an individual is entitled to social welfare, which guarantees the household a politically defined minimum standard of living.[19]

Thus the social safety nets provide a yardstick for measuring an appropriate reservation wage. Although other types of compensation, such as unemployment benefits for the uninsured and housing allowances, may provide less coverage, supplementary assistance can often be obtained up to the level guaranteed by the Social Security Act. A 1994 Swedish Government study (Ds 1994:81) demonstrated that a significant percentage of those who are active or potentially active in the work force, and who live in typical family constellations, fell below this basic level. The study concluded that 'jobs offering wages below or near what the ultimate social safety net provides are likely to disappear over the long run' (p. 201).

The social safety nets affect what is considered a reasonable wage, the unions' wage claims, and the kinds of businesses that entrepreneurs are willing to start. To the extent that social safety nets in welfare states push up reservation wages, they affect both types of entrepreneurship. They discourage necessity-based entrepreneurship by providing an alternative source of income at a reasonable level and they curb opportunity-based entrepreneurship by pushing up reservation wages so that many activities that are (initially) low-productivity activities are largely barred from entrepreneurial exploitation, since entrepreneurs have low incentives to start businesses that presuppose wages below the level guaranteed by the ultimate safety net.

Miscellaneous aspects

In this subsection a few additional aspects that are likely to impede productive entrepreneurship are dealt with. Although important, they are deemed to be of lesser importance than the factors elaborated on in the preceding subsections.

1.   Firms may be eligible for subsidies if they locate in low-income regions or if existing firms expand in those regions. A host of measures including both direct subsidies

and tax breaks have been used to this effect. But as shown by Bergström (2000) it appears that in the long-run firms that have received support perform worse than other comparable firms. This kind of support increases the risk that entrepreneurial talent (a scarce resource) is attracted to inherently less productive activities (Murphy et al., 1991).[20]

2. In order to equalize income across municipalities and regions a municipal tax-equalization scheme was introduced in 1966 and the redistributive stance of this scheme has been strengthened on several occasions, to the extent that there is virtually no correlation between local/regional government net tax receipts and per capita income in the municipality or county (Fölster, 1998; Kommunförbundet, 2000). In fact, it is easy to point to cases where a boom in the local economy will worsen the financial situation of the municipality in question. This equalization of outcomes in yet another dimension has made it at best economically indifferent for local government officials to promote entrepreneurial activity.

3. The Swedish Employment Security Act (LAS) from 1974 gives employees extensive protection against unfair dismissal, and it is hence intended as an additional means to enhance economic security for individuals. The only legal grounds for dismissal are gross misconduct and redundancies. In the latter case, LAS stipulates a 'last in – first out principle'. Strict employment security provisions are likely to be more harmful for smaller and potentially fast-growing employers. For many firms – and in particular for firms with a good growth potential in terms of productivity and employment – there is a great need for flexibility both to increase the number of employees in response to rising demand and likewise to be able to contract rapidly when demand falls short of expectations. The road from small to large for a fast-growing firm is far from straight, since the activities of new firms in particular are subject to genuine uncertainty. If, in such circumstances, rules are imposed that reduce the firms' leeway for rapid adjustment, one should expect both a lower willingness to expand in general and that fewer firms, despite a good product or a viable idea, grow from small to large in a short period of time.[21] In addition, a strictly applied 'last in – first out' principle in the case of redundancies implies that tenure at the present employer becomes relatively more important for labor security than individual skill and productivity. This fact increases the individual's opportunity cost of changing employers or of leaving a secure salaried job to become an entrepreneur.

The emerging picture of policy and its effects on entrepreneurial incentives
In the section on the political economics of entrepreneurial policy we sketched some broad predictions regarding this policy in the Swedish welfare state, with the starting point that an overriding theme has been the attempt to combine high taxation and ambitious welfare programs with favorable conditions for economic growth. We argued that the particular way of combining these has relied on preferential treatment of large established firms at the expense of individuals and smaller firms, and preferential treatment of physical-capital intensive activities compared to human-capital intensive ones. In this section we have looked at an array of different policies, which suggests an emerging picture in line with what was predicted in the earlier section. In the respective subsections we have shown that the tax system has in various ways favored established large firms over small new ones, institutional ownership over household ownership, as well as physical

capital over human capital. The emphasis on public provision in certain sectors has also hindered entrepreneurial efforts in these sectors. Overall the incentive structure has been one that both directs entrepreneurial activity and curtails its supply. We now turn to an examination of the outcomes of this particular incentive structure.

Empirical evidence

A first, although crude, measure consistent with the described weak incentives for entrepreneurship is the slow aggregate growth of the Swedish economy. Beginning in the mid-1960s the rate of growth began to lag relative to the OECD average, and from 1965 until the mid-1990s, Swedish PPP-adjusted GDP per capita fell by close to 30 percentage points relative to the weighted average of the 23 richest OECD countries (Lindbeck, 1997; Henrekson, 2001). Although the relative decline has stopped, catching up in terms of relative GDP per capita has been only some 2 percentage points since the mid-1990s (OECD, *National Accounts*, February 2005).[22] Aggregate private sector employment performance is also very weak. The entire growth in employment after 1950 until the early 2000s took place in the public sector; that is, no new jobs were created in the business sector during that 50-year period despite population growth of more than 20 percent and a rapid growth in female participation rates (Davidsson and Henrekson, 2002). Hence, both the aggregate growth and private sector employment performance are consistent with what one would expect if incentives for entrepreneurship are important.

In our context it is, however, more relevant to examine data that directly speak to the issue of the supply of entrepreneurship. Although one should not equate entrepreneurship with self-employment, it is still worth noting that from the early 1970s until 1990, Sweden exhibited the lowest ratio of non-agricultural self-employment to civilian employment among all OECD countries (OECD, *Employment Outlook*, July 1992). The European Observatory for SMEs (1995) reports that Sweden had a lower self-employment rate in 1992 than any of the then 12 member countries of the European Community (EC). The number of self-employed has also decreased in recent decades; comparing 2004 with 1980 and 1994, the number of self-employed is down by 7 and 5 percent, respectively (Statistics Sweden, 2005).

In recent work Roine and Waldenström (2006) have studied top incomes in Sweden over the twentieth century. Of particular interest for the arguments here is the decomposition of income by source. As shown in Figure 5.1 the share of business income has gone down from close to 20 percent of an income earner in the top half of the distribution in 1945 to almost nothing in the year 1997. The pattern is virtually identical for the top decile as well as for the top percentile. This is in itself not proof that self-employment has gone down, and even less so that entrepreneurship has decreased over this period. It could be argued that particular tax laws make it profitable to choose different forms of compensation. What is undeniable, however, is that this reflects either a decrease in the activity in itself or, at least, the fact that the tax system discourages earning business income to such an extent that it does not show up in the tax statistics (instead it shows up as wage or capital income). Either way it seems clear that policy over this period has discouraged the earning of business income.

More directly comparable estimates of the extent of entrepreneurial activity across countries can be derived from a major collaborative research effort, namely the Global Entrepreneurship Monitor (GEM; see Reynolds et al., 2001, 2005). Its main goal is to

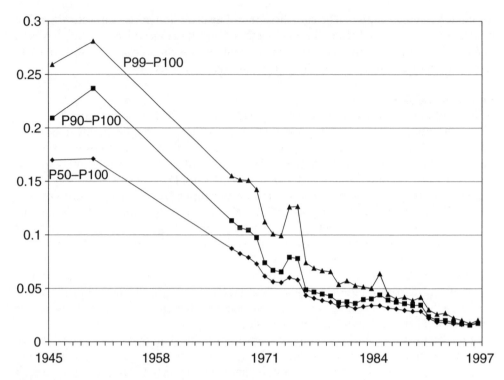

Note: Total income is the sum of wage income, capital income and business income and the figure shows the share of total income that derives from business income for the upper half of the income distribution (P50–P100), the top decile (P90–P100) and the top percentile (P99–P100) in the period 1945–97. See Roine and Waldenström (2006) for series including capital gains and for more on the composition of income over time.

Source: Roine and Waldenström (2006).

Figure 5.1   The share of total income (excluding capital gains) stemming from business income 1945–97, for different groups in the income distribution

arrive at internationally comparable estimates of the prevalence of 'nascent entrepreneurs'; that is, people who are in the process of starting a new business at a given point in time, or who have recently started a business that is still running. In Figure 5.2 the result of the GEM study for 2004 is displayed. It is clear that the level of nascent entrepreneurs is low in Sweden: roughly 3.7 percent of the population is engaged in starting a business or running a business founded within the last 42 months. This is the third lowest level among the 19 rich OECD countries participating in the GEM study in 2004. The expected pattern is also found for the prevalence of necessity-based entrepreneurial activity. The lowest activity in this category is experienced in the most extensive welfare states: Sweden, Denmark, Belgium, and the Netherlands.

There are also a number of indicators of the disproportionate importance of large firms in the Swedish economy. The European Observatory for SMEs (1995) reports that among 16 European countries, Sweden showed the largest value for mean enterprise size in 1990. Average enterprise size was 13 employees in Sweden, more than twice the corresponding average value for the 16 countries. Jagrén (1993) found that relative to GDP, Sweden

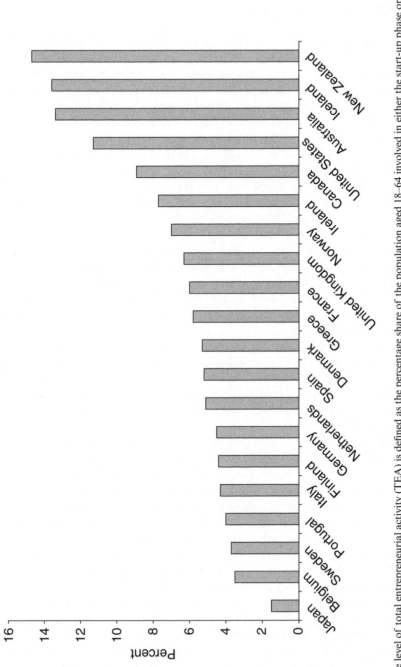

Note: The level of total entrepreneurial activity (TEA) is defined as the percentage share of the population aged 18–64 involved in either the start-up phase or managing a new business less than 42 months old.

Source: Reynolds et al. (2005).

Figure 5.2 Level of total entrepreneurial activity in rich OECD countries, 2004

proved to have twice as many Fortune-500 firms as Japan and the UK, and four times as many as the US and Germany. Even compared to other countries dominated by large firms, such as Finland and South Korea, the number of large firms relative to GDP was substantially greater. Henrekson and Johansson (1999) document that Sweden had the greatest number of large industrial firms (500+ employees) per capita in Europe in 1990.

Hence, by the late 1980s there were no clear signs of a resurgence of entrepreneurship and small firms, a pattern that began to emerge almost two decades earlier in the US (Loveman and Sengenberger, 1991). This picture is also consistent with studies where the growth of firms is examined. Birch and Medoff (1994) maintain that all new jobs in the US are created in a fairly small number of rapidly growing firms (gazelles). Storey (1994, p. 113) reports that out of 100 small firms in the UK at a certain point in time, the four fastest-growing firms will generate half of the total number of jobs created by these 100 firms. According to the OECD (1998) there is now 'general agreement' that the share of jobs created by small firms has increased since the early 1970s in most high-income countries. In contrast, little support for the gazelle hypothesis is found in Sweden (Davidsson et al., 1994, 1996). Instead they find that the contribution of small and medium-sized enterprises to net job creation is largely the result of many small startups. More specifically, Davidsson and Henrekson (2002) and Davidsson and Delmar (2003) study the employment contribution of the 10 percent fastest-growing firms. Regardless of how they conduct the analysis (unit, period, type of growth) they are unable to find a small group of 'elite' firms that collectively account for a substantial share of total job creation.

A final indication that the policy environment is unfavorable for entrepreneurial ventures is given by the experience of new technology-based firms. Sweden has the highest R&D expenditure both in total and in the university sector as a share of GDP in the OECD, and Sweden is second only to Israel in terms of publications of scientific and technical articles relative to the size of the economy (OECD, 2001). Utterback and Reitberger (1982) carried out a comprehensive interview study of 60 firms, based on new technology, which had been founded between 1965 and 1974. The 60 firms constituted roughly half of the total population of such firms founded during that period. By 1980 the studied firms together contributed no more than roughly 0.5 percent of total manufacturing employment. Rickne and Jacobsson (1996) updated the Utterback and Reitberger study by following the 53 firms still fulfilling the original selection criteria through 1992. Of the 53 firms only nine had grown to have more than 200 employees in 1992. Taken jointly, the 53 firms employed no more than 3400 persons in Sweden in 1992.

Rickne and Jacobsson (1999) studied all new technology-based firms founded between 1975 and 1993 (and still in existence in 1993) in Sweden. The main results from their study are summarized in Table 5.6. The employees of the new technology-based firms accounted for 2.2 percent of employment in the industries they belonged to (either manufacturing or manufacturing-related services). Thus their share of total employment was very small and not a single one of the firms had more than 300 employees.

Given the overall picture conveyed by these studies, it is hardly surprising that not a single one of the 50 largest firms in Sweden in 2000 was founded after 1969 (Figure 5.3). This may be compared to the very different situation in the US in recent decades, where new and fast-growing firms have generated not just most of the jobs but also the new industries (Audretsch and Thurik, 2000).

Table 5.6   The distribution of the stock of new technology-based firms by size in 1993 (all firms covered by the definition were founded in 1975–93)

Size	Number of firms in the category	Number of employees in the category	Percentage of employees
3–19	1022	7702	39.5
20–49	196	5886	30.2
50–99	48	3187	16.4
100–199	15	2009	10.3
200+	3	704	3.6
Total	1284	19488	100.0

Source: Rickne and Jacobsson (1999).

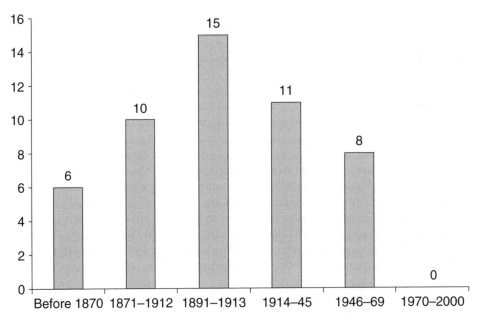

Source: NUTEK and ALMI (2001).

Figure 5.3   Sweden's 50 largest private corporations (turnover) – period of establishment

Conclusions

Are mature welfare states at a disadvantage when it comes to economic growth, innovativeness and employment creation? There is no doubt that high tax and benefit wedges have disincentive effects, but advocates can also point to likely advantageous effects. In the end, this remains an empirical question, which is not yet conclusively resolved. In this chapter we systematically explored a number of aspects of one factor that had been largely overlooked in the discussion so far, namely, how a wide array of typical welfare state arrangements may influence the incentives for individuals to supply entrepreneurial effort, and, to a lesser extent, how this effort is distributed across productive and unproductive activities. We also emphasized how some of the ideas underlying the early Swedish welfare state were likely to have encouraged large established firms and capital intensive production, at the expense of new firms, especially in the service sectors. Such an incentive structure could in theory form the 'appropriate institutions' for growth if large corporations are superior in terms of both productivity and innovation. However, if it turns out that entry, turnover and exit of firms as well as individual entrepreneurship are important, the set of policies that favor large incumbents are more problematic.

In recent years evidence suggesting that entrepreneurship is increasingly important for growth and employment creation has accumulated at a rapid rate. Leading scholars of the field speak of 'the emergence of the entrepreneurial society' (Acs and Audretsch, 2001). But the entrepreneur has been an alien figure in the welfare state. This is not so surprising given that the main ideas underlying the (Scandinavian) welfare state model were principally developed when it was widely believed that individual entrepreneurs were waning in importance.

Our examination of how the welfare state arrangements in Sweden, allegedly the most mature of all welfare states, have structured payoffs suggests negative effects on the return to entrepreneurial behavior in both relative and absolute terms. A number of channels contributing to this effect have been examined: taxation of entrepreneurial income, muted savings incentives and savings encouraged to take forms that withdraw funds from entrepreneurial ventures, comprehensive government service provision and very high tax rates on labor that bar large parts of the economy from entrepreneurial exploitation. Furthermore, policies for redistribution across individuals and regions along with a high-level minimum standard of living guaranteed by the government render necessity entrepreneurship irrelevant, and strict labor laws discourage individual job mobility.

In recent years Swedish economic performance has not contradicted the hypothesis that favorable incentives for entrepreneurship are important for economic performance. In particular, the lack of new high-growth firms in Sweden is striking, despite record levels of R&D spending, and with an industry structure well-suited for taking advantage of the boom in the IT and biotech sectors in the 1990s (Elg, 2005). As emphasized by Audretsch (2002) it is imperative that the really promising startups act in an environment where they can grow rapidly, because if scale economies are anything other than negligible, then the new firms have to grow in order to survive. Ultimately, they will have to attain the minimum efficient scale level of output, or they will go out of business. According to our analysis the government has a key role in creating an environment fostering the success and viability of firms, so that good ideas have the maximum chance to be translated into successful commercial ventures attaining their full potential.

So is there scope for changing the incentive structure? In light of our analysis of the endogenous determination of policy, some problems clearly stand out. The reliance on large incumbent firms and the public sector as the creators of employment opportunities and economic progress has made them seem indispensable. Their dominance has also turned these groups into powerful lobbyists for the continuation of traditional policies to foster future growth. As pointed out by Lindbeck (e.g. 1995) it may be a difficult collective problem to unwind a welfare system in which most individuals have stakes. Similarly, it may be difficult to change industrial policy in a situation where many people have become dependent on the success of the incumbent large firms, and where vested interests have substantial political clout.

Nevertheless, quite a few things can be done that cost fairly little and give strong incentives to individual entrepreneurs:

1. Ownership taxation can be lowered considerably by removing double taxation and giving more room for closely held firms to pay dividends. Furthermore, capital gains taxation on long-term holdings of firms where the individual takes an active part could be abolished (long-term capital gains taxation is in fact zero in the majority of the EU-15 countries). Such measures would send strong signals to existing and potential entrepreneurs, while costing very little in terms of taxes forgone.
2. Savings can be 'deinstitutionalized' so that a large part of the pension wealth becomes available for equity investments in entrepreneurial firms.
3. The public sector can implement a strategy for encouraging entrepreneurs to substitute for tax-financed public sector service production. A further step would be to allow service producers to offer additional services on top of what is granted through a tax-financed voucher system, while monitoring that tax-financed services are distributed solidaristically.
4. Retention rates can be marginally lowered across the board and qualification criteria can be made more stringent for transfer programs. This would not jeopardize the welfare state, but it would contribute to making entrepreneurship more attractive on the margin.
5. A more radical measure would be to announce that since the welfare state protects the individual through a number of cushions, the obligations for firms could be eased substantially: more liberal job security mandates, fewer demands on firms to take responsibility for sick leave, rehabilitation programs, and so on.[23]
6. Rights 'earned' through tenure with the present employer could be made portable, for instance through a system of severance pay.[24] After all, labor market inflexibility is an element inherently inconsistent with the flexibility, non-hierarchical structures, networking and labor mobility across firms distinguishing an entrepreneurial business culture (Saxenian, 1996).

Still, a mature welfare state will almost by definition have a high aggregate tax burden, and this necessarily implies high tax rates on labor and on locally produced services. As a result, it will be difficult to develop the household-related service sector as much as in low-tax countries. Likewise, individual savings incentives will be lower and reservation wages will be pushed up to higher levels by more generous social assistance schemes (relative to average income).

Finally, a continued almost exclusive reliance on taxation for the financing of key services like education, health care, child care and care of the elderly can be expected to become increasingly problematic. These services are highly income-elastic, they suffer from Baumol's disease (Baumol, 1993), and technological breakthroughs are likely to increase the supply of services in the health sector in the future. As long as private purchasing power is not allowed into these sectors, they risk turning into a tax-financed 'cost problem' rather than becoming potential growth industries attracting talented entrepreneurs.

All in all, there seems to be some room for a mature welfare state to reform itself in ways that promote entrepreneurship, while the core of the welfare model remains intact. However, a vibrant entrepreneurial culture and the set of institutions that underpin such a culture seem very remotely related to the welfare state culture and its institutions, perhaps they are even negatively related.

Notes

*   Both authors gratefully acknowledge financial support from the Jan Wallander and Tom Hedelius Research Foundation.

1.   Studies that find negative coefficients on 'government consumption' in cross-country growth regressions are for example Easterly and Rebelo (1993), Barro (1997). Fölster and Henrekson (2001) also find negative growth effects from a large public sector. However, Slemrod (1995), Mendoza et al. (1997), and Agell et al. (1997) find no clear costs from social spending. In an overview Temple (1999) concludes that there seems to be no convincing evidence that growth is harmed by having a large public sector.

2.   The term 'appropriate institutions' was coined by Gerschenkron (1962) and has recently received renewed attention in Acemoglu et al. (2003), and others. They focus on differences in what constitutes good policy depending on a country's 'distance to the technological frontier'. We will use it in a broader sense where institutions may be 'appropriate' with respect to a number of other aspects of the economy such as distribution of firms in different industries, the size of these firms, and so on. But more importantly we will stress that policies that were initially 'appropriate' may persist due to vested interests even after exogenous changes (or catch-up to the frontier) have made these policies 'inappropriate'.

3.   Going back to 1950 the ratio of total public expenditure to GDP was among the lowest to all industrial countries at roughly 26 percent, the same level as Switzerland and the United States.

4.   According to one influential welfare state scholar, Gøsta Esping-Andersen (1990), this is in line with the ultimate aim of the Nordic welfare state model, namely, to achieve 'the decommodification of labor'.

5.   Some examples of political economy formalizations of such ideas are Saint-Paul and Verdier (1993), Perotti (1996) and Bénabou (1996).

6.   We will not go into details of how this vision changed over time. In particular, we will not deal with the (failed) attempt to introduce wage-earner funds. See for example Pontusson (1992) and Henrekson and Jacobsson (2001) for more on this.

7.   In Roine (2006) the setting is one where taxes can be avoided by paying a (large) fixed cost. This results in a situation where only those with high income optimally choose to invest in tax avoidance. If their taxable income (i.e. income after avoidance) is low enough they face a tradeoff between taxation and redistribution similar to those with lower incomes, leading to the unusual coalition. A similar logic could be used on the politics of the Swedish welfare state. If there is, for example, a high entry cost for gaining political influence, such influence would only be possible for initially large firms. They could then support high general taxes, as long as they get special treatment (avoidance possibilities). This would lead to a situation with generally high taxes, which hurts investment (and growth) in small firms but has no adverse effects on the large incumbent firms. Indeed, one can even see an additional motive for them to favor the generally high taxes, namely that they act as a barrier to entry for small firms with growth ambitions.

8.   See for example Pontusson (1992) and Steinmo (1993) and their extensive references on this topic. As pointed out above we do not go into details of, for example, the differences within the Social Democratic Party regarding this policy.

9.   The effective real tax rates presented in Table 5.1 result from a complex interaction of a vast array of different tax rates, accounting and valuation rates, asymmetric effects of inflation, and so on. This is described in depth in Södersten (1984, 1993).

10. Tax-exempt institutions by definition pay no tax on interest receipts, dividends or capital gains. This category includes charities, scientific and cultural foundations, foundations for employee recreation set up by companies, pension funds for supplementary occupational pension schemes, and the National Pension Fund (now seven funds). In terms of industry ownership and control, tax-exempt institutions have a dominant position in Sweden.

11. This stands in stark contrast to the US where an employee who accepts stock options can defer the tax liability to the time when the stocks were sold rather than when the options were exercised. In general, there are (1) no tax consequences to the employee on the grant or the exercise of the option; (2) the employee is taxed at capital gains rates when the stock acquired on the exercise of the option is sold after

a specified holding period; and (3) there is no deduction available to the employer. This change in the law shifted the tax risk in the options back to the government, and thus accomplished two things: it increased the potential profit from the stock options and it allowed budget-constrained individuals to sell stocks whenever they chose to do so (Misher, 1984).

12. Stock options are also mostly offered to the top level management in large listed firms. In this case, there is more room for arrangements where stock-option gains are taxed largely as capital income, that is, at 30 percent rather than 68 percent.

13. See Henrekson and Rosenberg (2001) for a fuller exposition of this issue.

14. Compare the development in the US health sector during the 1990s, where strong competition between health care organizations has led to large cost reductions and efficiency gains, not least because modern information technology is systematically applied (Cutler et al., 2000; Litan and Rivlin, 2002).

15. This finding is also consistent with time-use studies reported in Juster and Stafford (1991). There were marked differences between Swedish and US men. US men worked more in the market, while Swedish men performed substantially more household work. In particular, Swedish men were the clear international leaders in home improvement time, averaging 4 hours per week, compared to 2.8 hours for US men and less than 1 hour for Japanese men. Total work time for Swedish and US men was virtually identical (57.9 vs. 57.8 hours). The amount of leisure time was approximately 3 hours longer per week in the US compared to Sweden for both men and women. Thus, 'Swedish men, compared to US men, have less market work time, more home production time, and less leisure time' (Juster and Stafford, 1991, p. 498).

16. This result can apply even if these services are complementary to leisure.

17. The marginal tax rate includes the employee's mandatory contributions to social security.

18. Strictly speaking, necessity entrepreneurship is not consistent with the definition of entrepreneurship given earlier. However, what was initially necessity entrepreneurship may in many cases at a later stage become opportunity-based entrepreneurship, when the entrepreneur discovers a growth opportunity in his or her business idea.

19. See Siebert (1997) for an interesting discussion of the interplay between the reservation wage and the social safety nets from a broader European perspective.

20. Leonard and Audenrode (1993) find that transfers to ailing industries have negative growth effects.

21. Davis and Henrekson (1997) discuss these issues more fully.

22. Given that the real growth rate has been high compared to the EU and OECD averages since 1994 this may seem puzzling. However, in the same period Swedish terms-of-trade have declined rapidly.

23. In this respect Denmark differs greatly from Sweden. State provision of income security is at least as generous, while labor security legislation is among the least protective of insiders relative to outsiders in Europe.

24. Severance pay is common in Italy, where large firms set aside a thirteenth salary payment every year, which is paid out on termination of the job; these arrangements are called TFR (*trattamento di fine rapporto*). The tax rate is only 10 percent, and allegedly this institution has made it possible for many redundant workers to start their own businesses.

Bibliography

Acemoglu, D., P. Aghion and F. Zilibotti (2003), 'Vertical integration and distance to frontiers', *Journal of the European Economic Association*, **1** (2), 630–38.

Acs, Z.J. and D.B. Audretsch (2001), 'The emergence of the entrepreneurial society', Prize lecture, *The International Award for Entrepreneurship and Small Business Research*, Stockholm, May.

Agell, J. (1996), 'Why Sweden's welfare state needed reform', *Economic Journal*, **106** (459), 1760–71.

Agell, J., T. Lindh and H. Ohlsson (1997), 'Growth and the public sector: a critical review essay', *European Journal of Political Economy*, **13** (1), 33–52.

Aghion, P. and P. Howitt (1998), *Endogenous Growth Theory*, Cambridge, MA: MIT Press.

Aghion, P. and P. Howitt (2005), 'Appropriate growth policy: a unifying framework', 2005 Joseph Schumpeter Lecture delivered at the conference of the European Economic Association, 25 August.

Aghion, P., R. Burgess, S. Redding and F. Zilibotti (2005), 'Entry liberalization and inequality in industrial performance', *Journal of the European Economic Association, Papers and Proceedings*, **3** (2–3), 291–302.

Alesina, A. and D. Rodrik (1994), 'Distributive politics and economic growth', *Quarterly Journal of Economics*, **109** (2), 465–90.

Aronsson, T. and J.R. Walker (1997), 'The effects of Sweden's welfare state on labor supply incentives', in R.B. Freeman, R. Topel and B. Swedenborg (eds), *The Welfare State in Transition*, Chicago: University of Chicago Press.

Audretsch, D.B. (1995), *Innovation and Industry Evolution*, Cambridge, MA: MIT Press.

Audretsch, D.B. (2002), 'The dynamic role of small firms: evidence from the US', *Small Business Economics*, **18** (1), 13–40.

Audretsch, D.B. and A.R. Thurik (2000), 'Capitalism and democracy in the 21st century: from the managed to the entrepreneurial economy', *Journal of Evolutionary Economics*, **10** (1), 17–34.
Baldwin, J.R. and J. Johnson (1999), 'Entry, innovation and firm growth', in Z.J. Acs (ed.), *Are Small Firms Important? Their Role and Impact*, Dordrecht: Kluwer.
Barro, R.J. (1997), *Determinants of Economic Growth: A Cross Country Empirical Study*, Cambridge, MA: MIT Press.
Barro, R.J. and X. Sala-i-Martin (1995), *Economic Growth*, New York: McGraw-Hill.
Baumol, W.J. (1990), 'Entrepreneurship: productive, unproductive, and destructive', *Journal of Political Economy*, **98** (5), 893–921.
Baumol, W.J. (1993), 'Health care, education and the cost disease: a looming crisis for public choice', *Public Choice*, **77** (1), 17–28.
Beck, M. (1981), *Government Spending, Trends and Issues*, New York: Praeger.
Bénabou, R. (1996), 'Inequality and growth', in B. Bernanke and J. Rotemberg (eds), *NBER Macroeconomics Annual 1996*, Cambridge, MA: MIT Press.
Bergström, F. (2000), 'Capital subsidies and the performance of firms', *Small Business Economics*, **14** (3), 83–93.
Bianchi, M. and M. Henrekson (2005), 'Is neoclassical economics still entrepreneurless?', *Kyklos*, **58** (3), 353–77.
Birch, D.L. and J. Medoff (1994), 'Gazelles', in L.C. Solmon and A.R. Levenson (eds), *Labor Markets, Employment Policy and Job Creation*, Boulder and London: Westview Press.
Blanchflower, D.G. and A.J. Oswald (1998), 'What makes an entrepreneur?', *Journal of Labor Economics*, **16** (1), 26–60.
Brock, W.A. and D.S. Evans (1986), *The Economics of Small Firms*, New York: Holmes & Meier.
Carlsson, B. (1999), 'Small business, entrepreneurship, and industrial dynamics', in Z.J. Acs (ed.), *Are Small Firms Important? Their Role and Impact*, Dordrecht: Kluwer.
Carree, M. and A.R. Thurik (1999), 'Industrial structure and economic growth', in D.B. Audretsch and A.R. Thurik (eds), *Innovation, Industry Evolution and Employment*, Cambridge, MA: Cambridge University Press.
Carree, M., A. van Stel, A.R. Thurik and S. Wennekers (2002), 'Economic development and business ownership: an analysis using data of 23 OECD countries in the period 1976–1996', *Small Business Economics*, **19** (3), 271–90.
Castles, F.G. (1998), *Comparative Public Policy*, Cheltenham, UK and Lyme, USA: Edward Elgar.
Cutler, D.M., M. McClellan and J.P. Newhouse (2000), 'How does managed care do it?', *Rand Journal of Economics*, **31** (3), 526–48.
Davidsson, P. and F. Delmar (2003), 'Hunting for new employment: the role of high growth firms', in D.A. Kirby and A. Watson (eds), *Small Firms and Economic Development in Developed and Transition Economies: A Reader*, Aldershot: Ashgate.
Davidsson, P. and M. Henrekson (2002), 'Institutional determinants of the prevalence of start-ups and high-growth firms: evidence from Sweden', *Small Business Economics*, **19** (2), 81–104.
Davidsson, P., L. Lindmark and C. Olofsson (1994), *Dynamiken i svenskt näringsliv*, Stockholm: Almqvist & Wiksell.
Davidsson, P., L. Lindmark and C. Olofsson (1996), *Näringslivsdynamik under 90-talet*, Stockholm: NUTEK.
Davis, S.J. and M. Henrekson (1997), 'Industrial policy, employer size and economic performance in Sweden', in R.B. Freeman, R. Topel and B. Swedenborg (eds), *The Welfare State in Transition*, Chicago: University of Chicago Press.
Davis, S.J. and M. Henrekson (2005), 'Tax effects on work activity, industry mix and shadow economy size: evidence from rich-country comparisons', in R. Goméz-Salvador, A. Lamo, B. Petrongolo, M. Ward and E. Wasmer (eds), *Labour Supply and Incentives to Work in Europe*, Cheltenham, UK and Northampton, MA, USA: Edward Elgar.
Davis, S.J., J. Haltiwanger and S. Schuh (1996), *Job Creation and Destruction*, Cambridge, MA: MIT Press.
Ds 1994:81, *En social försäkring*, Report to ESO, Stockholm: Ministry of Finance.
Ds 1997:73, *Lönar sig arbete?*, Report to ESO, Stockholm: Ministry of Finance.
Du Rietz, G. (1994), *Välfärdsstatens finansiering*, Stockholm: City University Press.
Easterly, W. and S. Rebelo (1993), 'Fiscal policy and economic growth', *Journal of Monetary Economics*, **32** (10), 417–58.
Elg, L. (2005), 'Innovation policy and performance in Sweden', in OECD, *Innovation Policy and Performance: A Cross-country Comparison*, OECD: Paris.
Esping-Andersen, G. (1990), *The Three Worlds of Welfare Capitalism*, Cambridge: Polity.
European Observatory for SMEs (1995), *Third Annual Report 1995*, Zoetermeer, The Netherlands: EIM Small Business Research and Consultancy.
Feldstein, M.S. (1996), 'The missing piece in policy analysis: social security reform', *American Economic Review*, **86** (2), 1–14.
Fölster, S. (1998), *Kommuner kan! Kanske!*, Stockholm: Expertgruppen för studier i offentlig ekonomi.

Fölster, S. and M. Henrekson (2001), 'Growth effects of government expenditure and taxation in rich countries', *European Economic Review*, **45** (8), 1501–20.
Forslund, A. (1997), 'The Swedish model: past, present, and future', in H. Giersch (ed.), *Reforming the Welfare State*, Berlin: Springer Verlag.
Freeman, R.B., R. Topel and B. Swedenborg (eds) (1997), *The Welfare State in Transition*, Chicago, MA: University of Chicago Press.
Galbraith, J.K. (1956), *American Capitalism: The Concept of Countervailing Power*, Boston, MA: Houghton Mifflin.
Galbraith, J.K. (1967), *The New Industrial State*, London: Hamish Hamilton.
Gerschenkron, A. (1962), *Economic Backwardness in Historical Perspective*, Cambridge, MA: Harvard University Press.
Glancey, K.S. and R.W. McQuaid (2000), *Entrepreneurial Economics*, New York: Palgrave.
Gompers, P.A. and J. Lerner (2001), *The Money of Invention: How Venture Capital Creates New Wealth*, Cambridge, MA: Harvard University Press.
Hébert, R.F. and A.N. Link (1989), 'In search of the meaning of entrepreneurship', *Small Business Economics*, **1** (1), 39–49.
Henrekson, M. (2001), 'Swedish economic growth: a favorable view of reform', *Challenge*, **44** (4), 38–58.
Henrekson, M. and U. Jakobsson (2001), 'Where Schumpeter was nearly right – the Swedish model and *Capitalism, Socialism and Democracy*', *Journal of Evolutionary Economics*, **11** (3), 331–58.
Henrekson, M. and D. Johansson (1999), 'Institutional effects on the size distribution of firms', *Small Business Economics*, **12** (1), 11–23.
Henrekson, M. and N. Rosenberg (2001), 'Designing efficient institutions for science-based entrepreneurship: lessons from the US and Sweden', *Journal of Technology Transfer*, **26** (3), 207–31.
Holtz-Eakin, D., D. Joulfaian and H.S. Rosen (1994), 'Sticking it out: entrepreneurial survival and liquidity constraints', *Journal of Political Economy*, **102** (1), 53–75.
Hubbard, R.G., J. Skinner and S.P. Zeldes (1995), 'Precautionary savings and social insurance', *Journal of Political Economy*, **103** (2), 360–99.
Jacobsen, H., W.F. Richter and P.B. Sørensen (2000), 'Optimal taxation with household production', *Oxford Economic Papers*, **52** (3), 584–94.
Jagrén, L. (1993), 'De dominerande storföretagen', in *Den långa vägen*, Stockholm: Research Institute of Industrial Economics.
Johansson, A.L. and L. Magnusson (1998), *LO – andra halvseklet. Fackföreningsrörelsen och samhället*, Stockholm: Atlas.
Jordahl, H. (2002), *Vad har hänt med de enskilda alternativen?*, Stockholm: Reforminstitutet.
Juster, F.T. and F.P. Stafford (1991), 'The allocation of time: empirical findings, behavioral models, and problems of measurement', *Journal of Economic Literature*, **29** (2), 471–522.
King, M.A. and D. Fullerton (eds) (1984), *The Taxation of Income from Capital. A Comparative Study of the United States, the United Kingdom, Sweden and West Germany*, Chicago: University of Chicago Press.
Kirzner, I.M. (1973), *Competition and Entrepreneurship*, Chicago: University of Chicago Press.
Kirzner, I.M. (1997), 'Entrepreneurial discovery and the competitive market process: an Austrian approach,' *Journal of Economic Literature*, **35** (1), 60–85.
Knight, F.H. (1921), *Risk, Uncertainty and Profit*, New York: Houghton Mifflin.
Kommunförbundet (2000), *Utjämning mellan kommunerna – en kort beskrivning av dagens system*, Stockholm.
Leonard, J.S. and M.A. Audenrode (1993), 'Corporatism run amok: job stability and industrial policy in Belgium and the United States', *Economic Policy*, **17**, 356–400.
Lindbeck, A. (1988), 'Consequences of the advanced welfare state', *The World Economy*, **11** (March), 19–37.
Lindbeck, A. (1995), 'Hazardous welfare-state dynamics', *American Economic Review, Papers and Proceedings*, **85** (2), 9–15.
Lindbeck, A. (1997), 'The Swedish experiment', *Journal of Economic Literature*, **35** (3), 1273–319.
Lindert, P. (2004), *Growing Public: Social Spending and Economic Growth since the Eighteenth Century*, Cambridge: Cambridge University Press.
Lindh, T. and H. Ohlsson (1996), 'Self-employment and windfall gains: evidence from the Swedish lottery', *Economic Journal*, **106** (439), 1515–26.
Lindh, T. and H. Ohlsson (1998), 'Self-employment and wealth inequality', *Review of Income and Wealth*, **44** (1), 25–42.
Litan, R.E. and A.M. Rivlin (2002), *Beyond the dot.coms*, Washington, DC: Brookings.
Loveman, G. and W. Sengenberger (1991), 'The reemergence of small-scale production: an international comparison', *Small Business Economics*, **31** (1), 1–37.
Lucas, R.E. Jr (1978), 'On the size distribution of business firms', *Bell Journal of Economics*, **9** (3), 508–23.
Mendoza, E., G.M. Milesi-Ferretti, and P. Asea (1997), 'On the ineffectiveness of tax policy in altering long-run growth', *Journal of Public Economics*, **66** (1), 99–126.

Misher, N. (1984), 'Tax consequences of exercising an incentive stock option with stock of the granting corporation', *The Tax Executive*, **36**, 357–63.
Murphy, K.M., A. Shleifer and R.W. Vishny (1991), 'The allocation of talent: implications for growth', *Quarterly Journal of Economics*, **106** (2), 503–30.
Nicoletti, G. and S. Scarpetta (2003), 'Regulation, productivity and growth', *Economic Policy*, **36**, 11–72.
Nordling, D. and N. Damsgaard (1998), 'Så höga är skatterna 1998', Report 1998:1, Stockholm: Swedish Taxpayers' Association.
Norrman, E. (1997), *Skatterna på arbete i Sverige och omvärlden 1996*, Stockholm: Swedish Taxpayers' Association.
North, D.C. (1990), *Institutions, Institutional Change and Economic Performance*, Cambridge: Cambridge University Press.
NUTEK & ALMI (2001), *Tre näringspolitiska utmaningar – Allianser för hållbar tillväxt*, Stockholm: NUTEK Förlag.
OECD (1992), *OECD Employment Outlook*, Paris: OECD.
OECD (1998), *Fostering Entrepreneurship*, OECD: Paris.
OECD (2001), *OECD Science, Technology and Industry Scoreboard 2001*, OECD: Paris.
OECD (2005), *National Accounts*, Paris: OECD, online: Source OECD.
Pålsson, A.-M. (1997), 'Taxation and the market for domestic services', in I. Persson and C. Jonung (eds), *Economics of the Family and Family Policies*, London: Routledge.
Pålsson, A.-M. (2002), 'Myt och verklighet om de svenska hushållens förmögenheter', *Ekonomisk Debatt*, **30** (8), 679–91.
Parker, S.C. (2004), *The Economics of Self-employment and Entrepreneurship*, Cambridge: Cambridge University Press.
Perotti, R. (1996), 'Growth, income distribution, and democracy: what the data say', *Journal of Economic Growth*, **1** (2), 149–88.
Persson, T. and G. Tabellini (1994), 'Is inequality harmful for growth?', *American Economic Review*, **84** (3), 600–21.
Petersson, T. (2001), 'Promoting entrepreneurship: bank-connected investment development companies in Sweden 1962–1990', in M. Henrekson, M. Larssson and H. Sjögren (eds), *Entrepreneurship in Business and Research. Essays in Honour of Håkan Lindgren*, Stockholm: Probus.
Piggott, J. and J. Whalley (2001), 'VAT base broadening, self supply, and the informal sector', *American Economic Review*, **91** (4), 1084–94.
Piore, M. and C. Sabel (1984), *The Second Industrial Divide*, New York: Basic Books.
Pontusson, J. (1992), *The Limits of Social Democracy – Investment Politics in Sweden*, Ithaca and London: Cornell University Press.
Reynolds, P.D. and Project Team (2001), *Global Entrepreneurship Monitor. 2000 Executive Report*, Wellesley, MA/London/Kansas City: Babson College, London Business School and Kauffman Center for Entrepreneurial Leadership.
Reynolds, P.D. and Project Team (2005), *Global Entrepreneurship Monitor. 2004 Executive Report*, Wellesley, MA/London/Kansas City: Babson College, London Business School and Kauffman Center for Entrepreneurial Leadership.
Rickne, A. and S. Jacobsson (1996), 'New technology-based firms – an exploratory study of technology exploitation and industrial renewal', *International Journal of Technology Management*, **11** (3/4), 238–57.
Rickne, A. and S. Jacobsson (1999), 'New technology-based firms in Sweden – a study of their direct impact on industrial renewal', *Economics of Innovation and New Technology*, **8** (2), 197–223.
Roine, J. (2006), 'The political economics of not paying taxes', *Public Choice*, **126** (1–2), 107–34.
Roine, J. and D. Waldenström (2006), 'The evolution of top incomes in an egalitarian society: Sweden, 1903–2004', SSE/EFI Working Paper Series in Economics and Finance No. 625, Stockholm School of Economics, forthcoming in *Journal of Public Economics*.
Rojas, M. (2001), *Beyond the Welfare State: Sweden and the Quest for a Post-industrial Welfare Model*, Stockholm: Timbro.
Rosen, S. (1997), 'Public employment and the welfare state in Sweden', in R.B. Freeman, R. Topel and B. Swedenborg (eds), *The Welfare State in Transition*, Chicago: University of Chicago Press.
SAF (2000), *Strukturrapport 2000. Ett gyllene tillfälle!*, Stockholm: SAF.
Saint-Paul, G. and T. Verdier (1993), 'Education, democracy and growth', *Journal of Development Economics*, **42** (2), 399–407.
Sapir, A. and Panel (2003), *An Agenda for a Growing Europe*, Oxford: Oxford University Press.
Saxenian, A. (1996), *Regional Advantage. Culture and Competition in Silicon Valley and Route 128*, Cambridge, MA: Harvard University Press.
Schumpeter, J.A. (1934), *The Theory of Economic Development*, Cambridge, MA: Harvard University Press.
Schumpeter, J.A. (1942), *Capitalism, Socialism and Democracy*, New York: George Allen & Unwin.

Siebert, H. (1997), 'Labor market rigidities: at the root of unemployment in Europe', *Journal of Economic Perspectives*, **11** (4), 37–56.
Slemrod, J. (1995), 'What do cross-country studies teach about government involvement, prosperity, and economic growth?', *Brookings Papers on Economic Activity*, **2**, 373–431.
Södersten, J. (1984), 'Sweden', in M.A. King and D. Fullerton (eds), *The Taxation of Income from Capital. A Comparative Study of the United States, the United Kingdom, Sweden and West Germany*, Chicago: University of Chicago Press.
Södersten, J. (1993), 'Sweden', in D.W. Jorgenson and R. Landau (eds), *Tax Reform and the Cost of Capital. An International Comparison*, Washington, DC: Brookings.
SOU 1997:17, *Skatter, Tjänster och Sysselsättning*, Stockholm: Ministry of Finance.
Statistics Sweden (2005), *Swedish National Accounts*, Stockholm, available at www.scb.se.
Steinmo, S. (1993), *Democracy and Taxation*, New Haven and London: Yale University Press.
Storey, D.J. (1994), *Understanding the Small Business Sector*, London: Routledge.
Swedberg, R. (2000), *Entrepreneurship: The Social Science View*, Oxford: Oxford University Press.
Taylor, M.P. (2001), 'Self-employment and windfall gains in Britain: evidence from panel data', *Economica*, **68** (272), 539–65.
Temple, J. (1999), 'The new growth evidence', *Journal of Economic Literature*, **37** (1), 112–56.
Utterback, J.M. and G. Reitberger (1982), 'Technology and industrial innovation in Sweden: a study of new technology based firms', Center for Policy Alternatives, MIT and STU, Stockholm.
Wennekers, S. and A.R. Thurik (1999), 'Linking entrepreneurship and economic growth', *Small Business Economics*, **13** (1), 27–55.
Wennekers, S., A. van Stel, A.R. Thurik and P.D. Reynolds (2005), 'Nascent entrepreneurship and the level of economic development', *Small Business Economics*, **24** (3), 293–309.
Werenfels Röttorp, M. (1998), 'Den offentliga sektorns förnyelse – vad har hänt under de senaste 15 åren?', in H. Lundgren et al., *På svag is*, Stockholm: Timbro.
Zider, B. (1998), 'How venture capital works', *Harvard Business Review*, November–December, 131–9.

6 Dressing the emperor: the fabric of entrepreneurship policy
Lois Stevenson and Anders Lundström

Introduction

Since the 1990s we have observed a noticeable shift in the policy orientation of governments in many countries towards encouraging and facilitating entrepreneurship. This has been largely a response to the rapidly changing economic and social environment: the acceleration of technological advancements, growing global competition, rise of the knowledge-based economy, economic and industrial restructuring, a higher level of acceptance of the importance of democratic values and private sector development and so on. Governments are increasingly focusing on entrepreneurship as a vehicle to address a range of problems including the need for employment generation, labour force integration, social cohesion, improvement in sector productivity and competitiveness, economic renewal, innovation, and wealth creation. Governments are at different stages of adopting entrepreneurship policies and emphasize different approaches and measures depending on the economic and social circumstances of the country and their perception of the role and importance of entrepreneurial activity in the economy.

Because entrepreneurship policy is a recent phenomenon there is a limited research base on which governments can rely to make more informed policy decisions in the area. There is a lack of clarity concerning what actually constitutes entrepreneurship policy and much confusion about the scope and differentiating characteristics of entrepreneurship policy compared to the more developed area of small and medium-sized enterprise (SME) policy. Although there is widespread agreement that provisions bearing on business entry and exit dynamics are central to any effective and focused strategy to create a favourable environment for the emergence of new firms, there is still limited knowledge about the construction of entrepreneurship as a policy domain.

Our study of entrepreneurship policy started in 2000 with the aim of responding to the growing interest of governments around the world for policy prescriptions leading to the creation of a more entrepreneurial society. Since then we have examined the entrepreneurship policy approach of national governments in 13 economies: Australia, Canada, Denmark, Finland, Iceland, Ireland, the Netherlands, Norway, Spain, Sweden, Taiwan, the United Kingdom and the United States (Lundström and Stevenson, 2005; Lundström, 2003; Stevenson and Lundström, 2001, 2002). Our purpose for this research was to address gaps in the knowledge base about the construction of entrepreneurship policy: what it is, what policies and measures characterize its make up and how governments make decisions about the mix of these policies, based on the actual practices of governments in a set of economies with diverse economic, social, political, cultural and structural contexts. Through this examination of approaches to entrepreneurship policy our objective was to gain insights that would be helpful to policy makers in other countries as well as to the research community.

Our approach in each economy was to provide an overview of the economic situation, review the national level economic policy agenda, examine the major programme measures and institutions and outline the evolution from SME policy to entrepreneurship policy. We used a variety of data collection and qualitative analytical techniques to arrive at our findings and conclusions,[1] including the publication of case studies on each economy (Stevenson and Lundström, 2001; Lundström, 2003).

Based on our findings this chapter sets out a definition of entrepreneurship policy as distinct from SME policy; outlines the policy challenges it seeks to address; presents a framework of entrepreneurship policies and measures; presents four broad, context-related configurations (or typologies) of these framework policies; summarizes findings from a comparison of the patterns in comprehensiveness of entrepreneurship policies across governments; and makes observations about the extent to which governments consider context when designing policy. This chapter advances understanding of the application of entrepreneurship policy in different contextual environments, draws some conclusions about how governments differ in their entrepreneurship policy orientations and comprehensiveness, and raises issues for further research and analysis.

We begin by briefly summarizing the evolution of entrepreneurship policy, defining entrepreneurship and the study of entrepreneurship, describing the scope of entrepreneurship and reviewing the major economic arguments and policy rationale in support of entrepreneurship. We then present our descriptions of the construction of entrepreneurship policy and its many dimensions and draw conclusions about the future of entrepreneurship policy and the research needed to support it. More knowledge about this will be very important for governments as entrepreneurship becomes more of a recognized force in the attainment of positive economic outcomes.

The evolution of entrepreneurship policy
The dominant approach to industrial and economic development in the latter part of the twentieth century was based on the assumption that a small number of large, established firms were the major source of economic growth and that this would produce a 'trickle-down' effect to the economy. Governments focused on efforts to ensure that 'national firm champions' were as efficient and productive as possible by employing special legislation, tax incentives and protective regulations to reduce costs or competition (Reynolds et al., 1999). This model overlooked the role of new firms as a major source of innovation and job creation, while ignoring the role of entrepreneurs in the economic development process. In fact Reynolds et al. (1999) suggest that these proposals to improve the global competitiveness of large, established firms actually discourage the emergence of new firms and, therefore, innovation, economic renewal and overall country competitiveness. Audretsch and Thurik (2001a) concur. During the industrial era the stimulation of entrepreneurial activity was at best a by-product of industrial policies.

Policy makers' recognition of the importance of small firms in the industrial economic process did not occur until the early 1980s following the Birch (1979) discovery that the majority of new jobs in the United States were being created by small (and often young) firms. This was contrary to the prevailing wisdom that large manufacturing firms were the job generators, and stimulated new thought about the role of small firms in the economy. The widespread evolution of SME policy in the late 1980s and early 1990s emphasized a level playing field for small firms. For the most part these policies focused on measures to improve the operating environment for existing small firms and generally ignored the issue of new firm creation.

In the mid-1990s growing levels of unemployment in many OECD and European countries prompted interest in policies to foster entrepreneurship as a way of creating jobs (OECD, 1995, 1997, 1998; European Commission, 1998). Growing research evidence of the link between new firms, innovation and economic growth during the latter part of the 1990s called increasing attention to entrepreneurial activity levels and ultimately to the importance of stimulating the supply of entrepreneurs.

It is now widely accepted that new business entry is a major factor in economic growth leading to job creation, innovation and productivity improvements at both the firm and industry level (Audretsch, 1995; Baldwin, 1999; Reynolds et al., 2004). Governments in developed countries may still focus some policy attention on national firm champions, but they are also moving more of their policy emphasis towards strengthening the environment for new and growing firms. Audretsch and Thurik (2001b) suggest that interest in entrepreneurship policy is a response to the shift from a 'managed' to an 'entrepreneurial' economy, the entrepreneurial economy being one characterized by the transition from an industrial economy to a knowledge-based economy, from a manufacturing base to the services sector, from large firms to small firms (reduction in plant and firm size), and from small firms to new firms.

Defining entrepreneurship
Entrepreneurship is an ill-defined, multi-dimensional concept (Carree and Thurik, 2003) in a multi-disciplinary field of scholarly inquiry (Parker, 2005) that suffers from a diversity of meanings (Koppl and Minniti, 2003). The definition of entrepreneurship depends on its source. In the management literature entrepreneurship has come to be defined as something that entrepreneurs 'do' or in relationship to aspects of an individual's behaviour (Wennekers and Thurik, 1999; Carree and Thurik, 2003). The European Commission (2004a) defines entrepreneurship as the mindset and process needed to create and develop economic activity within a new or an existing organization. According to Reynolds et al. (1999) entrepreneurship is any attempt at new business or new venture creation such as self-employment, a new business organization or the expansion of an existing business by an individual, a team of individuals or an established business. There is a lack of consensus as to whether this entrepreneurial behaviour is specific to the starting of a new firm or behaviour that leads to innovation and growth in an existing firm, and as to whether the person performing the behaviour is necessarily an owner of the firm.

Others take a more process or organizational view of the definition. Gartner and Carter (2003) state that entrepreneurship is a role that individuals undertake to create organizations and define it as an organizational phenomenon and, more specifically, as an organizing process. Koppl and Minniti (2003) define entrepreneurship as a dynamic process of change in which individuals, having in unusual degree certain personal or psychological characteristics, undertake innovative activities. To Shane and Eckhardt (2003) it is the sequential process of discovery, evaluation and exploitation of future goods and services.

Another stream of research defines entrepreneurship more broadly as an economic dynamic or societal phenomenon. According to Morris (1996) entrepreneurship is the relationship between entrepreneurs and their surroundings and the role government plays in creating the economic, political, legal, financial and social structures that characterize a society (and the environment for entrepreneurs). To Lowrey (2003) it is an economic system that consists of entrepreneurs, legal and institutional arrangements, and governments. He states that governments are important because they have the ability to foster economic growth and development by adjusting the economic institutions that work to protect individual entrepreneurs and stimulate their motives to achieve.

We adopt a definition of entrepreneurship that includes behaviours leading to the start-up and growth of a business and where business ownership is a necessary feature. In our view it is not just something that entrepreneurs 'do'; it is also a social phenomenon that emerges within the context of a broader society and involves a system comprising the many institutions, organizations and individuals that, together, support the emergence of entrepreneurs and entrepreneurial activity. In Figure 6.1 we map the extensive range of individuals, institutions and organizations that comprise this system. This systems perspective is an important dimension in the development of entrepreneurship policy but we find a notable absence of research analysing the total entrepreneurship system and the complexity of relationships between entrepreneurs and other system members.

The study of entrepreneurship
The study of entrepreneurship also means different things to different people. To Shane and Venkataraman (2000, p. 218) it is the study of why, when and how opportunities for the creation of goods and services come into existence; why, when and how some people and not others discover and exploit these opportunities; and why, when and how different

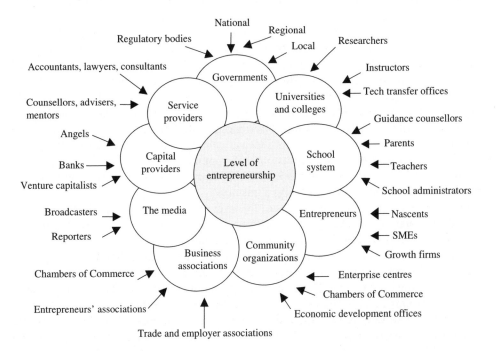

Source: Lundström and Stevenson (2005, p. 270).

Figure 6.1   The entrepreneurship system

modes of action are used to exploit opportunities. McGrath (2003) asserts that the study of entrepreneurship has fundamentally to do with the study of economic change. In Lundström and Stevenson (2005, p. 273) we define the study of entrepreneurship as the study of dimensions of the entrepreneurial process and the behaviours and practices of the total system that lead to the emergence of entrepreneurial activity in a society. By entrepreneurial process we mean 'the process whereby individuals become aware of business ownership as an option or viable alternative, develop ideas for businesses, learn the processes of becoming an entrepreneur, and undertake the initiation and development of a business' (Stevenson, 1996, p. 11). In other words the entrepreneurial process begins before the actual start-up of a business and includes behaviours leading to its growth. If the policy objective is to increase the supply of entrepreneurs within an economy, attention must be paid to all behaviours and activities leading to the conceptualization, creation, survival and growth of an enterprise, including stimulating an entrepreneurial spirit in society.

The scope of entrepreneurship
One of the primary outcome measures of the scope of entrepreneurship is the annual rate of business start-ups as a function of the level of incumbent firms, although this can also be expressed as a function of some other base.[2] The annual rate of business start-ups (or firm entry rate) is often related to the annual firm exit rate. Added together, these rates are used to measure the level of 'turbulence' within the stock of firms, which is an indicator or measure of innovation and renewal in an economy. The net value of these rates measures growth in the net stock of firms over any given time frame. Other indicators used to measure the scope of entrepreneurship include the rate of business ownership in the labour force (van Stel, 2003); the self-employment rate; the nascent entrepreneur prevalence rate[3] and the Total Entrepreneurial Activity (TEA)[4] rate (Reynolds et al., 2004; Wennekers et al., 2005); the proportion of people considering going into business (Small Business Service, 2004b); the percentage of firms that grow (OECD, 2001b); and the relative share of SMEs and SME employment of all private sector firms (Fritsch and Mueller, 2005). Grilo and Irigoyen (2005) and Thurik and Grilo (2005) introduce the concept of 'entrepreneurial engagement levels' as a measurement of the scope of entrepreneurship. This includes measures for the proportion of the population that has never thought about starting a business, is thinking about it, is taking steps to start one, has a young business, has an older business, or no longer has a business.

Our capacity to measure and compare the level of entrepreneurship for different time periods and across countries is constrained by the lack of agreed to and consistent data and indicators (OECD, 1998). Although country comparisons are still in the infancy stage considerable variance is found among countries on all current measures. For example substantial differences are found in nascent entrepreneur prevalence and TEA rates among countries in the GEM study. These rates are lowest in the developed Asian and Central European countries, followed by Europe, then by the United States, Canada, Australia and other British Empire nations, and are highest in developing Asian, Latin American and African countries (Acs et al., 2005). This variance across countries can be related to the level of economic development as well as to diverse demographic, cultural and institutional characteristics (Wennekers et al., 2005). Grilo and Irigoyen (2005) conclude that country-specific effects are important both for latent and actual entrepreneurs, and could be affected by cultural values, differences in labour market legislation, social security regimes, the tax environment, availability of bank loans, and so on. Also significant is the fact that variations in regional start-up rates within countries are greater than those between countries. More understanding of these variances is crucial for governments seeking to benefit from the positive effects of entrepreneurship on the economy.

The economic and social impacts of entrepreneurship

Entrepreneurs exist in every society and entrepreneurship is part of the fabric of every economy. Entrepreneurship exists in environments that support it or not and independent of whether government policies specifically aim to foster it. However, it tends to thrive in environments where it is supported (Baumol, 1990).

Entrepreneurs play many economic and social roles. Through the process of starting new firms, some that survive and grow and others that fail, entrepreneurs generate employment, contribute to Gross Domestic Product (GDP), increase competition, provide stability in rural areas of the country and drive innovation. Entrepreneurial activity is critical to innovation activity (Audretsch, 1995), contributes to industry and firm level productivity improvements (Baldwin, 1999), and has a positive effect on the employment growth rate (van Stel and Diephuis, 2004). Entrepreneurship also offers an option for people who do not fit within mainstream economic society (Wilken, 1979) or who prefer to pursue independent work. Hart (2003a, p. 4) asserts that the level and quality of entrepreneurship make a difference in the economic vitality of communities, regions, industries and nations as a whole and argues that policy makers may be able to enhance the economy by enhancing entrepreneurship. But does entrepreneurial activity lead to economic growth?

The role of entrepreneurship in economic growth

Investigations of the relationship between entrepreneurial activity rates and economic growth are relatively recent (Acs and Armington, 2004; Carree and Thurik, 2003; Audretsch and Thurik, 2001a; Reynolds et al., 1999). The task of relating a country's business birth rate to its economic growth rate is a complex one and findings on the relationship between turbulence rates and economic growth have been mixed (see Carree and Thurik, 2003). Although they could not find a statistically significant relationship between TEA levels and economic growth among the countries in the 2003 GEM study, Reynolds et al. (2004) observe that countries with high levels of entrepreneurial activity have above average levels of economic growth, and that no country with high entrepreneurial activity levels has low economic growth. Therefore it might be assumed that economic growth will be impeded if an economy does not develop its entrepreneurial capacity. Or to put it another way countries that do not develop their entrepreneurial capacity will miss opportunities for growth. This is notwithstanding the observation made by Lowrey (2003) that countries with low levels of individual entrepreneurship have often achieved long periods of economic growth, noting Russia, Korea and others as illustrative examples. However Eliasson (1995) concludes that in the long term the lack of entry of new firms will adversely affect economic performance.

One of the reasons it is difficult to find a causal relationship between economic growth and entrepreneurial activity levels is because there are a number of intervening variables and linkages between economic conditions and entrepreneurial propensity, and then between entrepreneurship and economic growth (Wennekers and Thurik, 1999; Friis et al., 2002). There is also evidence that entrepreneurial activity levels may be contingent on a country's level of economic development. In their study of the long-term relationship between business ownership rates and the level of economic development in OECD countries, Carree et al. (2002) found a U-shaped curve relationship between the business ownership rate and per capita GDP. Countries with lower GDP per capita in any given time period had higher business ownership rates than those in more economically developed countries. Also, a country's business ownership rate was found to decline as GDP per capita increased, until GDP per capita reached about US$18 000 at which point business ownership rates started to increase with increases in GDP per capita. The authors suggest that there may be an equilibrium rate of business ownership and that countries falling above or below the U-shaped curve may have either too few or too many business owners. Countries with too many business owners (and possibly too many marginal enterprises), usually developing economies, may not be benefiting sufficiently from economies of scale and scope. Countries falling below the curve may not have enough entrepreneurial activity, meaning that opportunities for innovation and competitive undertakings may be underdeveloped. In both cases, there is a penalty – either too few or too many business owners will lead to lower economic growth rates. Government intervention may be called for to 'adjust' the level of entrepreneurship but the implications for appropriate policy actions will differ depending on the country's level of economic development (Wennekers et al., 2005).

Carree and Thurik (2003) propose that the level of entrepreneurship will also differ depending on the economic system of a country, suggesting that it will be higher in market economies than in semi-planned and planned economies because there is more freedom of entry and exit and firms are allowed to adjust their inputs to maximize profits. Large firms are seen as the engines of progress in semi-planned economies and new firm entry is likely to be hampered by regulations and low levels of business ownership. Entrepreneurial activity really does not exist in planned economies because production and markets are controlled by government.

Building on the work of Schmitz (1989), the first to introduce entrepreneurship as a variable in endogenous growth models, Audretsch and Keilbach (2004) propose that entrepreneurship capital may be a missing link in explaining variations in the economic performance of regions and countries. Because knowledge is embedded in individuals, knowledge-based societies need entrepreneurial capacity to transfer knowledge into economic activity. This paradigm shift in thought about the role of entrepreneurship in economic growth is stimulating further interest in this area of policy development at both macro and micro levels.

The determinants of entrepreneurship
To assist in the challenge of defining the scope of entrepreneurship policy a number of researchers have developed frameworks of the determinants of entrepreneurship (Verheul et al., 2001; Reynolds et al., 1999; Wennekers and Thurik, 1999). The model of Entrepreneurial Framework Conditions introduced in Reynolds et al. (1999) includes: the availability of resources, such as financial capital and commercial and legal services; physical infrastructure; education and training; the density and intensity of competition; R&D transfer; cultural and social norms that can act to legitimize entrepreneurship in the

society; and government policies and programmes. These framework conditions act to promote entrepreneurial opportunities and build entrepreneurial capacity (skills and motivation) that will lead to the emergence of new firms and, through technical innovation and employment, contribute to national economic growth.

The framework developed by Wennekers and Thurik (1999) sets out that the conditions for entrepreneurship are shaped by culture, institutions,[5] incentives and the psychological endowments of individuals. These authors state that demographic, cultural and institutional factors will influence the rate of entrepreneurial dynamics but are difficult to change in the short term since they are structural in nature. Wennekers et al. (2005) conclude that government policy may have an impact on the level of entrepreneurship but that this will occur only through the gradual evolution of culture and institutions over time.

The eclectic framework put forward by Verheul et al. (2001) takes into consideration both the supply side and the demand side of entrepreneurship and weaves together an integrated framework consisting of aspects of culture, occupational choice, the resources available to entrepreneurs and the extent of entrepreneurial opportunities in the economy. These researchers distinguish between the supply side and the demand side of entrepreneurship and highlight the different sets of policy interventions available to governments depending on which perspective is taken. The demand side creates opportunities through market demand for products and services and is influenced by such factors as technological development, the differentiation of consumer demand, the industrial structure of the economy and the stage of economic development. The supply side is influenced by such factors as the demographic composition and density of the population, the resources and abilities of individuals and their attitudes towards entrepreneurship. These researchers outline five types of policy interventions that could have an impact on entrepreneurial activity depending on whether there is a need to adjust demand or supply side considerations. Such interventions could affect the type, number and accessibility of entrepreneurial opportunities; the supply of potential entrepreneurs (such as immigration policy); the availability of resources and knowledge for potential entrepreneurs (such as advice and counselling, direct financial support, venture capital and entrepreneurship education); the shape of entrepreneurial values in society (through the education system and the media); and the risk–reward profile of entrepreneurship directed at the decision-making process of individuals and their occupational choices (such as taxation, social security arrangements, labour market legislation and bankruptcy policy).

Casson (2003) suggests that the supply of entrepreneurship depends on natural abilities, the nature of the education system and the relative status of entrepreneurial careers, and that the demand for entrepreneurship is partly created by entrepreneurs themselves through the perceiving of opportunities. Entrepreneurial rewards in the form of profits will tend to adjust the balance of overall demand and supply but can be intermediated by financial institutions and government actions. Hart (2003a) asserts that public policy and governance can shape virtually all the contextual determinants of the demand for entrepreneurship and, over time, the supply of entrepreneurs.[6] Public policy can affect the demand for goods and services, the environment for competition and opportunities to pursue entrepreneurship. Governments can ease the burden of entry by reducing the time and costs associated with starting a new business. Entrepreneurial activity levels may be influenced by decreasing social security nets and improving labour market flexibility.

Opportunities for new businesses can be provided through deregulation, privatization of government services, competitive regimes and tax policies (such as a shift in the capital gains tax rates, which can affect investment decisions).

The rationale for public policies
The OECD has examined the various economic arguments in support of entrepreneurship policies per se (OECD, 2003, Chapter 5). Apart from the conclusion that good macroeconomic framework conditions are insufficient by themselves to produce higher levels of entrepreneurship (Reynolds et al., 1999), the primary argument for policy intervention is failures in the market for entrepreneurial activity. These failures can be caused by imperfections in the market for information (asymmetries); uncompetitive market structures; economies of scale in the supply of goods and services (for example shortcomings in the supply of debt and equity to new and small firms); shortages in physical premises, business development services and training; and the systematic failure of markets to properly allocate resources to new firms and entrepreneurs. Such market imperfections will affect the ability of small firms and new entrepreneurs (at an acceptable level of investment of both time and money) to access the information, skills, financing, advice and technical assistance that would improve their start-up, survival and growth probabilities.

Another policy argument is based on positive externalities being produced from the creation of new firms. For example valuable information is provided to other actual and potential entrepreneurs when an entrepreneur creates a business. Additionally entrepreneurship spreads in part through the influence of imitation (OECD, 2003, p. 89) and exposure to entrepreneur role-models (Reynolds et al., 2004). If potential entrepreneurs are prone to imitate actual entrepreneurs, then other things unchanged, places with low levels of entrepreneurship will be more likely to experience low rates of entrepreneurship in the future. To alter this path dependency, public policy might be justified. The extent to which path dependency is a valid argument is challenged by the OECD (2003) but certainly finds at least some support in the study by Fritsch and Mueller (2005), who conclude that regions with high or low levels of entrepreneurial activity are likely to maintain high or low levels of start-up activity and that policies to stimulate entrepreneurship in low entrepreneurship regions will need patience and persistence over the long term. Other positive externalities of entrepreneurship are associated with area regeneration,[7] although the OECD points out that this argument is undermined by the lack of empirical studies of enterprise demographics. Parker (2005) agrees that we lack sufficient firm evidence of positive spillovers from entrepreneurship.

The OECD concludes that the strongest grounds for policy intervention appear to be the correction of failures in a number of markets on which entrepreneurs depend (for example financial, training and business services), and corrective and preventive interventions to address discrimination against minorities, women, and the disabled or other groups. They further conclude that policy justifications premised on employment effects are weak (if the objective is to encourage unemployed people to become entrepreneurs) and that there is insufficient empirical evidence to base policy on regeneration and other externalities from enterprise births. The OECD review of policy rationale falls short of addressing the matter of government failures caused by overly burdensome administrative, regulatory and legislative demands on new firms.

The scope of entrepreneurship policy

When we started our policy research in 2000 there were no comprehensive descriptions or delineations of entrepreneurship as a policy domain. Policy makers were left to sort through the wide ranging literature on promoters and inhibitors of entrepreneurship for possible and relevant policy implications. Some research has had more influence on policy thinking than others, mostly that focused on SME policy (for example, Storey, 1994; Birch 1987). Prescriptions about what entrepreneurship policy *should be* have been largely derived either from the development of theoretical, conceptual frameworks (discussed earlier) or from the vast array of empirical studies of the needs and challenges of entrepreneurs attempting to create new firms.

More research specifically related to entrepreneurship policy has started to emerge (see Hart, 2003b; Holtz-Eakin and Rosen, 2004); however, much of it is limited to examining the influence of isolated policy effects on entrepreneurial activity levels (for example taxation or availability of venture capital) or the impact of entrepreneurial activity in specific industry sectors. Hart (2003b) actually refrains from defining entrepreneurship policy. He describes it as covering a large policy domain encompassing the actions of several levels of government, having a bearing on low technology and high technology activity and ranging from regional policy to economic development policy to poverty reduction policy. He states his view that entrepreneurship policy aims to foster a socially optimal level of venturing activity (that is, the starting and continual expansion of a business) including policies to raise the level of entrepreneurial activity, but admits there is limited conformity in the policy community about how to do this and that the various areas of policy making are typically uncoordinated, with some policies even pulling in opposite directions.

Hart specifically excludes education policy, macroeconomic policy and other policies that influence 'background conditions' from his discussion of the scope of entrepreneurship policy and explains this limitation on the basis that these policies do not have the direct objective of influencing entrepreneurial activity levels.[8] However when comparing entrepreneurship policies across countries, background and macroeconomic conditions and contextual factors become very important in explaining different levels of entrepreneurial activity, even if the interplay between these conditions or factors is not precisely clear (Lundström and Stevenson, 2005). Also entrepreneurship is increasingly being incorporated as an outcome of education and business environment policies and we argue that in any discussion of entrepreneurship policy it is necessary to have a more holistic view of its policy scope.

The OECD and the European Commission have produced a number of entrepreneurship policy-related publications that serve as helpful guides to governments interested in developing policies, strategies and programmes to foster higher levels of entrepreneurship (European Commission, 1998, 2004a; OECD, 1998, 2001a, 2001b, 2003), including a number of 'best practice' profiles of policy initiatives that work well in particular countries (European Commission, 2002, 2001, 2004c, 2004d; OECD, 2004b). They have also initiated efforts to benchmark enterprise, entrepreneurship and growth outcomes so countries are able to compare their relative performance on a range of statistical and quantifiable indicators (European Commission, 2004b; OECD, 2002). Those indicators used to benchmark entrepreneurship, which include many of the scope of entrepreneurship indicators, are employed by several OECD countries and EU member states to set measurable targets for their policy outcomes.[9] Indicators have also been developed to benchmark policy areas relevant to improving entrepreneurship framework conditions, specifically those related to regulation (administrative conditions, entry barriers, labour market, bankruptcy legislation, income tax, risk–reward); financing (debt and equity capital, tax policy); guidance (government policies and programmes, entrepreneurship infrastructure, advisers, incubators); entrepreneurship education; and culture (entrepreneurship culture and risk-taking) (Hoffman et al., 2005; Danish National Agency for Enterprise and Housing et al., 2004).

While existing research studies have contributed greatly to knowledge regarding the essential framework conditions for entrepreneurship and benchmark indicators, which governments will find helpful in their policy analysis and decision-making, there has been a paucity of research on the actual policy practices of governments (Lundström and Stevenson, 2001, 2005; Stevenson and Lundström, 2001, 2002; Audretsch et al., 2002; and Lundström, 2003 being exceptions).

The foundations of entrepreneurship policy
The underpinning foundations for the development of entrepreneurship policy reside in the extent to which entrepreneurial motivation, opportunity and skills exist in a society or economy (Lundström and Stevenson, 2001; Stevenson and Lundström, 2002). A large number of related variables have the potential to affect entrepreneurial activity levels as illustrated in Figure 6.2. Each of these is influenced by the prevailing culture, set of institutional arrangements and socioeconomic environment within an entrepreneurship system that is either more or less favourable to the emergence of new entrepreneurs.

The research on what motivates someone to become an entrepreneur or start a business is extensive. Shapero (1984) and Shapero and Sokol (1982) conclude that the decision to become an entrepreneur is highly situational and influenced by a range of familial, social, economic and cultural circumstances. People start businesses because they either perceive an opportunity and want to pursue it, are forced to out of economic necessity or have an intrinsic need to work for themselves. The ease with which they are able to do this is strongly influenced by the degree of access they have to support and resources. Their capacity to start and grow a viable and successful business is further dependent on the skills and know-how of a technical, entrepreneurial and managerial nature that they possess. The existence of a favourable and supportive entrepreneurial culture; opportunities to gain entrepreneurial skills, knowledge and experience; the availability of resources of a financial (such as loans, equity) and non-financial (such as advice and technical assistance) nature; and low barriers to entry will produce many of the right conditions for the emergence of entrepreneurship.

One of the first key challenges faced by governments whose aim is to produce higher levels of entrepreneurial activity will be to determine what systemic gaps or market failures exist for individuals moving through the entrepreneurial process and which policy levers will address deficiencies in the level of motivation, opportunity and skills. An analysis of areas affecting the level of motivation, opportunity and skills is a starting point for assessing the level of entrepreneurial capacity in a country or region and forms the base for the formulation of entrepreneurship policy. The optimal situation would be to have high levels of each one. (See Lundström and Stevenson, 2005 for a more extensive discussion of motivation, opportunity and skills.)

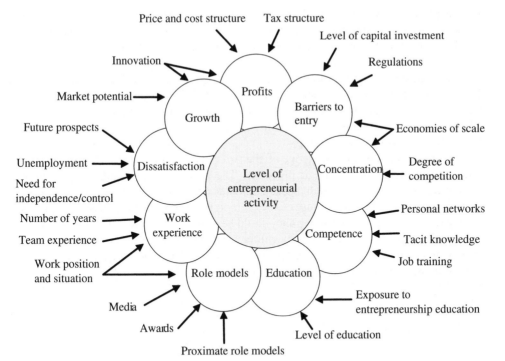

Source: Lundström and Stevenson (2005, p. 208).

Figure 6.2   *Variables influencing level of entrepreneurial activity*

Entrepreneurship policy and its construction

Based on the above we define entrepreneurship policy as policy aimed at the pre-start, the start-up and early post-start-up phases of the entrepreneurial process, designed and delivered to address the areas of motivation, opportunity and skills, with the primary objective of encouraging more people in the population to consider entrepreneurship as an option, move into the nascent stage of taking actions to start a business and proceed into the entry and early stages of the business (Lundström and Stevenson, 2001). This entails policies and measures to create favorable conditions for the emergence of entrepreneurs and new firms and to address their unmet needs through various phases of the entrepreneurial process.

Entrepreneurship policy as distinct from SME policy

Our definition of entrepreneurship policy draws some parallels with that of small business policy, a policy domain that in our view is related but distinctive. These two policy areas differ in their overall goal, specific objectives, client groups and targeting, business cycle application, policy priorities and levers, and time frames for expected results (for more discussion see Lundström and Stevenson, 2005, pp. 50–60). The primary aim of small business policy is to level the playing field for small firms through measures to overcome their disadvantages in the marketplace resulting from their 'smallness' and 'resource poverty', and to improve their competitiveness. The primary target is established firms.

The specific aim of entrepreneurship policy is to increase entrepreneurial activity levels and to foster a favourable environment for the emergence of new firms. Because 'people' start firms, this logically means that the unit of policy analysis and focus must shift away from the firm to the individual entrepreneur or potential entrepreneur. This is one of the most distinguishing features of entrepreneurship policy vis-à-vis small business policy. Entrepreneurial activity starts before a firm is created, so entrepreneurship policy also includes provision for awareness creation and specific pre-start and start-up support. SME policy assumes that assisted firms already exist and have built sufficient capacity to absorb the benefits of any assistance.

In Figure 6.3 we illustrate the scope of the two policy domains by stages of the entrepreneurial and SME development processes. The role and appropriate type of policy intervention will depend on which market, systemic or cultural failures the government is aiming to address and at what phase of the entrepreneurial or SME development process. In some respects entrepreneurship policy could be viewed as the base of SME policy. The foundation for an efficient SME policy will be limited without efforts to foster the development of positive attitudes and a supply of motivated individuals, nascent entrepreneurs, start-ups and young emerging firms.

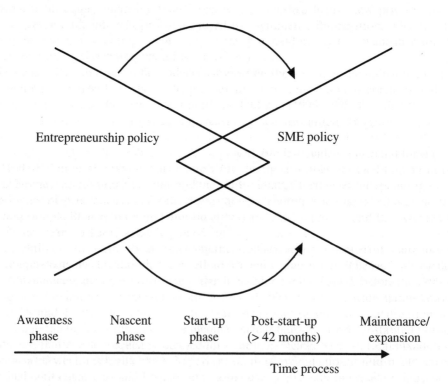

| Awareness phase | Nascent phase | Start-up phase | Post-start-up (> 42 months) | Maintenance/ expansion |

Time process

Note: The upper limit for time in business in the definition of entrepreneurship policy is 42 months, the same limit employed in the Global Entrepreneurship Monitor.

Source: Lundström and Stevenson (2002).

Figure 6.3   The interface between entrepreneurship policy and SME policy

The framework of entrepreneurship policy measures
Governments active in entrepreneurship policy formulation state their overall objective in one of three ways: to foster a stronger entrepreneurial culture and climate leading to a more entrepreneurial society; to increase the level of entrepreneurial activity in the country (or region); or to produce an increase in the number of new businesses, the stock of firms or the number of entrepreneurs (Stevenson and Lundström, 2002). Through their entrepreneurship policy governments seek to address four broad policy challenges: (1) influencing an entrepreneurial culture, (2) encouraging nascent entrepreneurs (by introducing people to the concept of entrepreneurship, instilling know-how and removing career disincentives); (3) converting nascents to actual entrepreneurs (by assisting them with access to the opportunities and necessary resources to start their businesses); and (4) supporting the first three to four years of start-up vulnerability to influence a positive survival and growth path.

The collective framework of policy measures for doing this consists of six components (see Figure 6.4):

1. entrepreneurship promotion;
2. entrepreneurship education;
3. reducing administrative, legislative and regulatory barriers to entry and exit;
4. business support for start-ups;

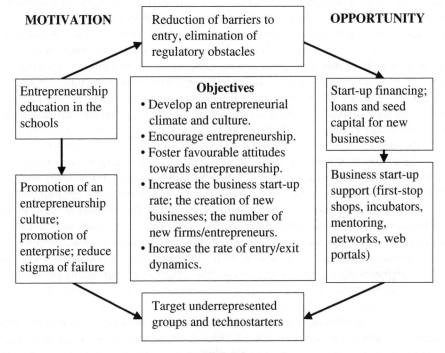

Figure 6.4   Framework of entrepreneurship policy measures

5. start-up and seed financing; and
6. target group measures.

The mapping of individual government's policies and actions within each of these framework components allowed us to identify the range of policy instruments and measures in the collective policy palette of 13 economies (illustrated in Table 6.1).

The typology of entrepreneurship policies
Individual governments emphasize some areas more than others in their policy mix, combine policies and measures in different ways and use a variety of indicators to monitor the performance of policies and measures. To some extent their choices reflect the nature of economic or social problems they are seeking to address. If a country has a high unemployment rate and there are barriers to business entry, the government may place higher priority on measures to reduce entry barriers in order to stimulate the creation of employment through new firms. If a government has an already entrenched SME policy it may choose to focus its primary attention on addressing obstacles experienced by groups of the population underrepresented as business owners (that is, adopt target group measures). If there is an already strong base of SMEs and self-employment and a high entry rate of new firms, the government may decide to prioritize policies to encourage the start-up of innovative, technology firms (although the appropriateness of this approach will depend on the level of economic development of the country and other factors). If the government has determined that the culture for entrepreneurship is weak and there are structural weaknesses in the framework conditions for entrepreneurship that will have a longer-term negative impact on the economic growth of the nation, it may adopt a more comprehensive approach with policy measures in each of the framework areas.

There appear to be four typologies that describe these different approaches adopted by governments: (1) an 'add-on' or extension to SME policy; (2) a 'niche' target group approach; (3) a 'new firm creation' approach; and (4) a 'holistic' entrepreneurship policy approach. This typology is modelled in Figure 6.5 and the distinguishing features of the four types are summarized in Table 6.2.

E-extension policy   A government with an E-extension approach is one that does not have a specified entrepreneurship policy. Any entrepreneurship-oriented policy measures are generally embedded within an existing SME policy framework and added on to offerings already provided through existing national SME programmes and services, probably in a somewhat piecemeal fashion. To a great extent this 'add-on' approach can be described as a reactive response to emerging demand for start-up services and resources or for employment alternatives in high unemployment regions. Policy measures are likely to focus on improving access to resources such as the provision of start-up information, business planning assistance, self-employment training or micro-loans.

This is most likely to be the dominant entrepreneurship policy approach in economies where the government has long-standing SME policies and well-established SME support networks in place – economies such as Australia, Canada, Sweden, Taiwan and the United States. However the primary policy focus of these governments is geared towards addressing market failures and 'levelling the playing field' for existing SMEs and the entrepreneurship-oriented measures tend to be a marginalized priority and weakly resourced

Table 6.1   Objectives and measures for each area of the entrepreneurship policy framework

Policy area	Policy objectives	Policy measures
Entrepreneurship promotion	Increase social value of entrepreneurship; create more awareness of entrepreneurship in society; promote credible role-models	Awards programmes Profiling role-models Mass media activities Entrepreneurship events
Entrepreneurship education	Increase opportunities for people to gain entrepreneurial 'know-how'; integrate entrepreneurship into various levels of the formal education system	Entrepreneurship adopted in National Curriculum Guidelines Development of entrepreneurship-related curriculum for integration into levels of the formal education system Train teachers how to teach entrepreneurship Support youth entrepreneurship and student venture activities Sponsor business plan competitions and awards Fund incubators and seed capital programmes
Barriers to entry and exit	Reduce the time and cost of starting a new business; reduce barriers to and improve opportunities for start-up and growth; remove 'disincentives' to the entrepreneurial career choice decision	Streamline business registration processes Single-window access for dealings with government Remove 'quiet disincentives' in labour market, social security, and taxation regimes Review competition policy, company law, bankruptcy laws, patent and intellectual property regimes, and regulation affecting the transfer of business ownership Relax tax and administrative burden on new firms Offer tax breaks/concessions for new firms; tax breaks to encourage investors to release capital to new firms Implement 'better regulation' units within government
Start-up business support	Provide easy access to start-up information, advice, counselling, and other institutional supports; facilitate the transfer of 'know-how'	Networks of enterprise and start-up service centres and one-stop shops for new entrepreneurs Start-up web-portals Mentoring and training programmes for new entrepreneurs National incubator strategies Support for entrepreneur networks

Table 6.1   (continued)

Policy area	Policy objectives	Policy measures
		Programmes to improve quality of business advisory services
Start-up and seed financing	Address market failures and gaps in provision of appropriate financing for new and early stage firms; reduce information asymmetries	Micro-loan, pre-venture and starter funds for new entrepreneurs Loan guarantee programmes Seed capital funds for techno-starters Incentives for angel and venture capital investments in new and early-stage firms; foster angel networks Access to information about sources and types of available financing Partnerships with banks and other financing intermediaries
Target groups	Reduce systemic barriers to raise start-up rates of groups underrepresented as business owners; reduce risks for high growth technology start-ups to foster wealth creation	Target group-specific enterprise centres, awards, promotion (role-models), advisory, training and mentoring services, peer networks, web-portals and loan programmes Procurement set-asides Incubators for techno-starts Venture capital, pre-seed funds, campus capital programmes

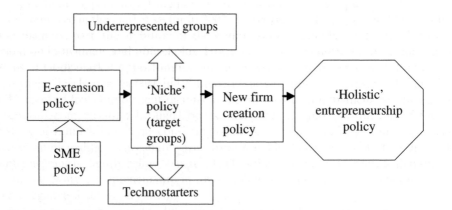

Figure 6.5   *Entrepreneurship policy typology*

compared to SME policy measures. These are economies with few regulatory or administrative barriers to the business start-up process and where it is not generally difficult, time consuming or costly to start a business. They also tend to be economies with a well-developed culture of entrepreneurship, which is certainly the case in Canada, Taiwan and the US although less so in Sweden and Australia (self-reportedly due to a lack of role

Table 6.2 A comparison of entrepreneurship policy typologies

Features	E-extension policies	New firm creation policies	'Niche' target group policies	'Holistic' E-policy
Objectives	Improve access to start-up supports through existing SME support structures; better service to starters.	Reduce barriers to business entry and exit; simplify start-up procedures and requirements; increase the start-up rate.	Increase the start-up rate among groups underrepresented as business owners or potential starters of innovative firms.	Strengthen entrepreneurial culture, enhance entrepreneurship as a career option, create dynamic start-up markets/better growth conditions.
Policy rationale	Market failures; information asymmetries.	Government failures; market failures.	Systemic failures; social equity; market failures.	Government failures; market failures; information asymmetries.
Policy areas	Business information; advisory, planning and training services; regional and community economic development programmes.	Competition; bankruptcy; company law; business registration procedures; social security regulations; employment rules and taxation.	Immigration policies; business support policies; financing; incubation; innovation policies; gender policies.	Entrepreneurship awareness; entrepreneurship in national education curricula; start-up support, information, financing; infrastructure; regional policy.
Measures	Micro-loans; business advisory services; web portals; self-employment training programmes; local services.	Flexible labour markets; open competition; less stringent bankruptcy laws; fewer business registration steps, lower cost, faster approvals; simplified incorporation processes; one-stop shops; reduced tax burden.	Tailored supports for each identified target group – enterprise centres; promotion and awards programmes; start-up loan funds; web portals; networks and mentoring programmes; incubation units; role-models.	Promotion and awards programmes; role-models; entrepreneurship in the schools; one-stop shops; enterprise centres; incubators; mentoring and peer networking programmes; start-up advice and web portals; seed capital and micro-loans.
Most likely policy structure	Vertical; limited interaction with ministries of education or regulatory departments.	More horizontal; many government departments implicated.	Vertical; limited interaction with ministries of education or regulatory departments; could be links with S&T ministry.	Horizontal, interministerial structure. Recognize that many areas of government impact on business start-up and growth.
Limitations	Start-up initiatives are 'added-on' to existing local SME support structures on a piecemeal basis; limited focus on entrepreneurship in the education system; and removing barriers to entry.	Primary focus on changes to the 'business environment'; simplifying the business start-up phase; less emphasis on longer term strategy of promoting enterprise culture and integrating entrepreneurship in schools.	Focus on target groups may lead to overlooking the growth potential of non-targeted groups or low-tech sectors; may have limited focus on regulatory changes or fail to address overall weaknesses in the culture for entrepreneurship.	Difficulty in managing policy interdependencies across departments and levels of government.

Source: Stevenson and Lundström (2002, p. 60).

models). Economies with E-extension approaches, with the exception of Sweden, are ones with high levels of self-employment, high start-up rates and/or high nascent entrepreneur prevalence rates. Because of relatively high levels of entrepreneurial dynamism in these economies their governments may not see any immediate compelling reason to make major adjustments in their policy positions to further influence an 'entrepreneurial climate'. This might explain why we found few national policy directives in these economies to foster an entrepreneurial culture, to examine specific barriers to entry or to integrate entrepreneurship in the education system. With the exception of Australia none of these economies has a national programme to integrate 'enterprise' in the K-12 education system. That being said we have seen evidence of policy shifts in some of these economies since 2001 (Lundström and Stevenson, 2005).

New firm creation policy   The new firm creation policy approach (sometimes referred to as business start-up policy) is concerned with eliminating government-induced administrative and regulatory barriers to business entry and exit and simplifying the start-up process (or simply put, adjusting for government failure). One of the big administrative/regulatory issues affecting entrepreneurial activity levels has to do with the time and cost of starting a business – the number of days it takes to obtain approvals, the number of required procedures, the number of regulations that have to be satisfied and the cost of business registration and regulatory compliance. The objective of new firm creation policy is to reduce this time and cost to a minimum so more people will be able to start (and formalize) their businesses. This entails the review of a number of government policies and structures, including regulations and policies related to competition, social security, employment, taxation, company law, and bankruptcy law or insolvency rules. A large number of government ministries, departments and regulatory agencies are implicated in this review process.

   This tends to be the dominant entrepreneurship policy approach in economies that have many structural and regulatory barriers to the business creation process. This is more likely to be the case in economies where the government has only recently focused on policy to stimulate endogenous growth through small business and entrepreneurial activity. High unemployment rates may be a feature in these economies and, although micro-firms exist, they may have limited access to the capital and resources needed to grow. This may be exacerbated by a lack of formalization among enterprises caused by regulatory and administrative barriers. Governments in such economies increasingly view entrepreneurship and new firm creation as a necessary vehicle for generating employment and growth. In response governments may establish one-stop shops to simplify the process of setting up companies (fewer forms, fewer permits and fewer steps) and reform Company Law so informal economy businesses and micro-firms can more readily become part of the formal economy. A number of initiatives may be implemented to help women, young people and the unemployed to become self-employed or to promote entrepreneurship education, particularly at the vocational level.

'Niche' target group policies   'Niche' entrepreneurship policy focuses on stimulating higher start-up rates among particular segments of the population. In this approach governments are either aiming to: (1) improve the entrepreneurial activity levels of groups of the population underrepresented in business ownership, or (2) accelerate the take-up of

high-tech, innovative entrepreneurship from among post-secondary graduates and scientifically, technologically oriented researchers and experts, often referred to as 'techno-starters'. The rationale for target group policies could be job creation, social inclusion, gender equity, labour market integration or wealth creation, and in both cases governments justify their interventions on the basis of social, systemic or market failures. Members of groups underrepresented as business owners may face social or economic barriers to the entrepreneurial process and technostarters may face market failures as a result of the uncertainty and high risk associated with their high-technology businesses.

Although it is rarely a government's dominant entrepreneurship policy approach, all of the governments in our 13-economy analysis target one or more groups for tailored entrepreneurship support (Lundström and Stevenson, 2005). Underrepresented groups include women, young people, ethnic minorities, Aboriginals, immigrants, people with disabilities and the unemployed. There has been growing interest in target group measures over the past few years, especially those directed towards young people, women and ethnic minorities, but governments differ in their selection of specific target groups and vary in the comprehensiveness of their policy supports based on differences in their demographic makeup and views about targeted initiatives. The package of policy measures for these groups, most comprehensive in the United States, Canada, and Sweden, includes support for networks of dedicated enterprise centres, micro-loan funds, awards programmes, training, counselling and mentoring services and web-based information portals specific to each of the selected groups.

The key target groups for technology-oriented innovative entrepreneurship are people with post-secondary educations, especially researchers with commercially promising technologies and potential entrepreneurs found among new graduates and within university and technology institute environments. The package of tailored policy measures includes such things as funding for community or campus incubators, pre-seed funding for commercializable R&D, campus venture capital programmes, enterprise platforms (entrepreneurial skills development, mentoring and management assistance) and post-secondary level national business plan competitions. Technostarter niche policies are found in Ireland, the Netherlands, Australia, Taiwan, Norway, Denmark and the UK – economies where governments have linked entrepreneurship to the innovation agenda.

'Niche' entrepreneurship policy is often complementary to a government's dominant entrepreneurship policy approach and may be more effective in economies where the overall entrepreneurship culture is strong but where special efforts are needed to help certain groups of the population overcome adverse effects. As a stand-alone policy it may have some limitations. If the overall culture of entrepreneurship is weak in the country, if there are general barriers to business entry, or if opportunities to gain entrepreneurial knowledge and skills are generally deficient, target groups might well still face difficulties in their entrepreneurial endeavours. Thus a 'niche' policy approach probably makes more sense within the context of a broader set of entrepreneurship-oriented policies.

'Holistic' entrepreneurship policy   'Holistic' entrepreneurship policy is the most comprehensive in the typology and incorporates the policy measures of the other three types. National government policy objectives will include reducing barriers to entry and exit, improving access to start-up resources (financing, information and assistance), and addressing the start-up needs of target groups but also promoting an entrepreneurship

culture, creating a positive climate for entrepreneurship and embedding entrepreneurship in the education system.

The main impetus for the 'holistic' approach is to achieve higher levels of dynamism, innovation, productivity and growth through robust entrepreneurial activity, in other words to produce a more entrepreneurial society. Through this more comprehensive and integrated approach governments attempt to address a range of 'failures' – systemic failures, social failures, education failures, information asymmetries, and market failures – and capitalize on the positive externalities of entrepreneurship to foster both short-term and long-term development of an entrepreneurial population.

Only four of the 13 governments in 2004 had adopted a 'holistic' policy approach, the UK, the Netherlands, Finland and Denmark, all economies with lower than average business ownership and TEA rates for the economies in the study (Lundström and Stevenson, 2005) and those demonstrating the strongest commitment to entrepreneurship policy. Setting them apart from the others are the following:

- There is a clear statement in high-level policy documents about the importance of business dynamics (rate of entry and exit activity) to economic renewal and growth and the contribution of new firm entries to productivity improvements and the overall competitiveness of the economy.
- The government's plan for accelerating entrepreneurial activity levels is presented in one policy framework document together with rationale, objectives, explicit targets, set policy lines for action and a set of stated policy and programme priorities and measures (see Small Business Service, 2004a; Ministry of Trade and Industry, 2004; Ministry of Economic Affairs, 2004; and Ministry of Economic and Business Affairs, 2003). This policy framework is likely to be reinforced in the policy documents of other ministries or government departments.[10]
- The policy includes quantified targets to increase either the number of people considering entrepreneurship as an option, the start-up rate, the number of entrepreneurs, or the level of entrepreneurial dynamism.
- A budget is included to fund implementation of the entrepreneurship initiatives (and not just for a few measures that might fit within the framework).
- There is clear responsibility in one of the main ministries for implementation of the entrepreneurship policy framework across ministries (and perhaps levels of government) and in a broad number of areas affecting the environment for entrepreneurial activity.
- Performance indicators outlining measures for improved entrepreneurial climate and culture conditions or improved conditions for actual start-ups are included in the policy framework document.

Measuring the outcome of entrepreneurship policy
Not much is actually known about how public policy measures impact on entrepreneurial activity levels at the macro level. Since entrepreneurship policy has only recently emerged as a policy domain it is not surprising that efforts to measure its impacts and identify appropriate performance indicators are not well developed. Governments are currently experimenting with the development of these policy indicators and measures of performance, the United Kingdom being one of the most advanced (Small Business

Service, 2004b). Many of the scope of entrepreneurship indicators are being used to baseline country performance and their use is accelerating. We observed some level of sophistication in the development of performance indicators for specific policy and programme areas such as in entrepreneurship education, advice and counselling services, start-up financing and administrative obstacles to business entry, but overall much work remains to be done. Work on these areas is being advanced by the OECD or the European Commission and then shared with member countries and states.

So how should a government proceed in this area? One of the first things is to determine what outcome is expected from entrepreneurship policy in terms of contributing to growth in the economy. Is it employment creation, productivity improvement, innovation or something else? Second, it is important to identify some baseline measures that can be used to monitor progress and developments over time (for example annual business entry rate; the contribution of new and growth firms to employment, net sales and value-added; or the share of female entrepreneurs among all business owners). Third, it is necessary to identify what impacts are desired from each of the specific framework policy areas (for example entrepreneurship promotion, education, seed financing). Fourth, it is necessary to set performance indicators for each of the micro-policies articulated through individual programmes or initiatives (for example micro-finance programme, women's entrepreneurial development programme). Finally some governments prepare an annual review of their entrepreneurship policy programmes and benchmark their performance outcomes against those in other countries. An annual White Paper on entrepreneurship policy or an annual report on the state of small business and entrepreneurship, including a description of entrepreneurial dynamics, should become part of the process of reporting on progress and tracking developments and changes over time. Only a few economies are actually producing such reports – with the United States, Taiwan and the Netherlands being good cases in point.

Structures for entrepreneurship policy
Policy making and programme delivery structures matter in the formulation and implementation of entrepreneurship policy. Government SME/entrepreneurship policy structures can be categorized as 'umbrella', 'silo' (vertical) or 'horizontal' (Stevenson and Lundström, 2002). The interdependency of policy jurisdictions across a large number of ministries and levels of government becomes more apparent as government policy shifts more in favour of entrepreneurship. In the case of governments with a more 'holistic' entrepreneurship policy approach we noted a tendency to adopt more horizontal administrative and policy management structures, even though horizontal structures are not easy to manage or coordinate. This suggests that a realignment of structure with the entrepreneurship policy focus may be necessary. Better mechanisms may be needed for cross-ministry coordination of policies affecting business entry as well as for coordination of the regional delivery of objectives, programmes and services. Entrepreneurship policy requires government-wide commitment, and integrated approaches to policy development and planning are optimal.

Some governments have set up entrepreneurship divisions or directorates with the mandate to carry out an advocacy function with officials from other ministries and to interface with private sector partners and the media in support of entrepreneurship. These responsibility centres may have to solicit collaboration from other departments of government, for example departments of education, immigration or labour, or ministries of science and technology, and develop linkages and alliances with regional and local governments. This networking role within government is an important one for these champion units. In some cases coordination committees are established for the purposes of exchanging views and perspectives on reducing barriers to business entry and growth among representatives of the relevant government departments and agencies. The minister responsible may put in place a Ministerial Advisory Council on Entrepreneurship and Small Business consisting of entrepreneurs and key business leaders or establish a Ministerial Council of state and/or provincial/regional ministers that aim to agree on a common vision for entrepreneurship and work cooperatively towards its realization. Annual policy forums are another vehicle used for coordination and sharing.

The move to entrepreneurship policy may also lead to the streamlining and adjustment of existing delivery structures. It was evident in our case studies that new delivery structures go hand-in-hand with the shift in policy focus, notably one-stop shops, campus-based incubators, regional enterprise centres or entrepreneurship nodes, and the establishment of entrepreneurship units in other departments and levels of government. Much work may be required in aligning new and existing organizations to the entrepreneurship agenda, as well as the skills and knowledge of the people working in them. Special efforts may be needed to better orient business advisers and other officials who interact with the entrepreneurial community regarding the provision of appropriate services to clients at each stage of the entrepreneurial process. Part of that orientation includes attention to the 'know-how' of delivering an entrepreneurship policy agenda. More learning networks may also be necessary.

Entrepreneurship policy comprehensiveness
To conduct our assessment of entrepreneurship policy it was necessary to design tools that would enable a comparison across economies. In Stevenson and Lundström (2002) we mapped the entrepreneurship-related policies and measures of each national level government for the six areas of our entrepreneurship policy framework. From this mapping we developed a checklist of the collective actions taken in each policy area. In Lundström and Stevenson (2005) we further developed this checklist into an instrument designed to crudely measure the comprehensiveness of a government's entrepreneurship policy and to facilitate a comparison across economies. The resulting entrepreneurship policy comprehensiveness (EPC) instrument consists of 90 items distributed among the six policy framework areas and an additional 17 items to measure policy commitment, structure and performance tracking. Scores from 0 to 1 were assigned to each item based on the degree of evidence that a government was implementing relevant policy actions. The final score provided an indication of the scope of actions governments were taking in each area. This policy scoring method was adapted from that employed by Hall (2002, 2003) to measure the comprehensiveness of SME policy in ASEAN and APEC countries.[11]

We found many differences in EPC between governments (Figure 6.6). Overall policy comprehensive scores ranged from a high of 92 per cent of the action items for the United Kingdom to a low of 35 per cent for Iceland. The overall average EPC score was 67.5 per cent (see Table 6.3 for individual economy scores).

The greatest variances in comprehensiveness of policy actions are in the areas of promotion, education and target group policies. For example it is interesting to note the

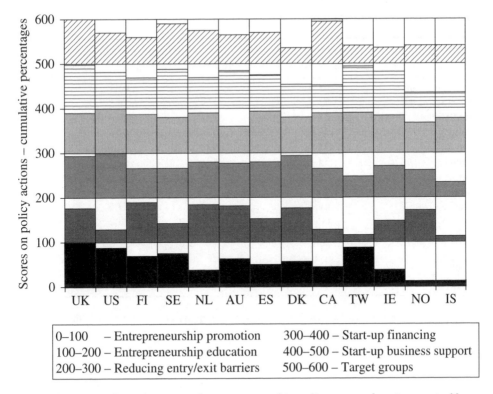

0–100 – Entrepreneurship promotion	300–400 – Start-up financing	
100–200 – Entrepreneurship education	400–500 – Start-up business support	
200–300 – Reducing entry/exit barriers	500–600 – Target groups	

Figure 6.6   Comparing the scope of entrepreneurship policy comprehensiveness in 13 economies

differences in policy emphasis on entrepreneurship education between the UK, Finland and the Netherlands compared to the US, Canada, Taiwan and Iceland. There is relatively more consistency in governments' policy attention in the areas of start-up financing, reducing barriers to entry and exit, and start-up business support.

One of the interesting observations from our comparative analysis is preliminary evidence that in economies with both higher TEA and business ownership rates governments tend to have lower EPC scores (Figure 6.7). Governments in economies with lower business ownership and TEA rates tend to demonstrate higher commitment to entrepreneurship policy and score higher on overall EPC, specifically when the business ownership rate is less than 12 per cent (of the labour force) and the TEA rate is less than seven (per 100 adults). This includes the UK, the Netherlands, Finland, Sweden and Denmark.

We also observed that governments with lower overall EPC scores scored higher on a subset of 17 policy actions[12] selected from the long list of 107 items to capture the comprehensiveness of policies to stimulate innovative (technology-based) start-up activity. In fact as overall EPC scores went down innovative EPC scores went up (see Table 6.3). This was particularly evident in Denmark, Australia, Taiwan, Ireland and Norway and to a lesser extent in the US and Iceland. With the exception of Denmark these are all economies, among those in the study, with above average business ownership rates or above average TEA rates or both. They also include all of the above average GDP per

Table 6.3   Scores and rankings for overall EPC and innovative EPC

Country	Overall EPC score (per cent of 107 items)	Rank	Innovative EPC score (per cent of 17 items)	Rank
United Kingdom	92.0	1	97.1	1
The Netherlands	77.1	2	76.5	6
United States	77.1	2	85.3	4
Finland	76.6	4	67.6	10
Denmark	73.8	5	94.1	2
Sweden	73.4	6	67.6	10
Spain	72.0	7	64.7	12
Australia	70.6	8	85.3	4
Taiwan	61.2	9	73.5	8
Ireland	60.7	10	88.2	3
Canada	56.5	11	73.5	8
Norway	51.9	12	76.5	6
Iceland	35.0	13	47.1	13
Average	67.5		76.7	

Note: Overall EPC is based on 107 items; innovative EPC is derived from a subset of 17 of the EPC items.

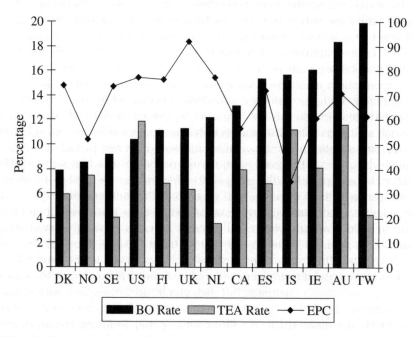

Note: BO and TEA rates are on the left axis and EPC scores are on the right axis.

Figure 6.7   Comparing EPC scores with business ownership and TEA rates

capita economies although we did not have enough variance in GDP per capita or enough economies in the study to draw any definitive conclusions about how this might have factored into the EPC outcomes.

Governments with holistic entrepreneurship policy and high policy commitment tend to score well on both overall EPC and innovative EPC. They incorporate parallel measures to stimulate development of innovative entrepreneurship activity within their comprehensive entrepreneurship policy frameworks. Governments in the other economies appear to make more of a policy choice.

Although the EPC score is a crude measure and there were only a few economies in our analysis, the observation about higher business ownership and TEA rates and EPC makes intuitive sense. Governments in these economies are less concerned about raising their entrepreneurial activity levels and will place a lower priority within their overall macro- or microeconomic policy frameworks on policies to stimulate entrepreneurship. However the observation regarding innovative EPC deserves further comment. For a number of reasons articulated in Lundström and Stevenson (2005, pp. 146–8) we would argue that an innovative entrepreneurship policy approach may be appropriate in an environment that already has a strong culture of entrepreneurship and a high density of SMEs and business owners, but that in an environment where there are cultural, regulatory, structural and other barriers to general entrepreneurship there may be an economic cost to focusing primarily on technology-based innovative entrepreneurship. We therefore propose that policies in favour of innovative entrepreneurship should be considered within the context of a holistic entrepreneurship policy framework that addresses all the other issues such as societal support for entrepreneurship; promotion of entrepreneurship; entrepreneurship education in the schools; general administrative, regulatory and legislative barriers to business entry; flexible labour markets; and business support for the development of nascent entrepreneurs regardless of the type of business idea. This is certainly the approach of the UK government, which scores highest on both sets of policy comprehensiveness actions.

The importance of context in entrepreneurship policy formulation

There will be many influences on the shape of a government's entrepreneurship policy including its views on the importance of entrepreneurship in overall economic policy, the role government could or should play in developing the policy area, the possible effects of policy actions and so on. However one of the conclusions from our study is that a country's context also matters greatly in the formulation of entrepreneurship policy. It could be logically assumed that policy makers would take their specific context conditions into consideration when assessing policy gaps and opportunities and developing their policy analysis. Given that contextual conditions will vary from one country or region to another it would also be logical to assume that governments will differ in their policy approaches. We next describe the outcome of our preliminary and exploratory attempt to examine the relationship between an economy's context conditions and its government's entrepreneurship policy orientation.

Context as an explanatory set of variables

Although 'context' could embrace a broad range of economic, social, cultural, attitudinal and structural aspects that will vary from one country to another, we quantified the notion

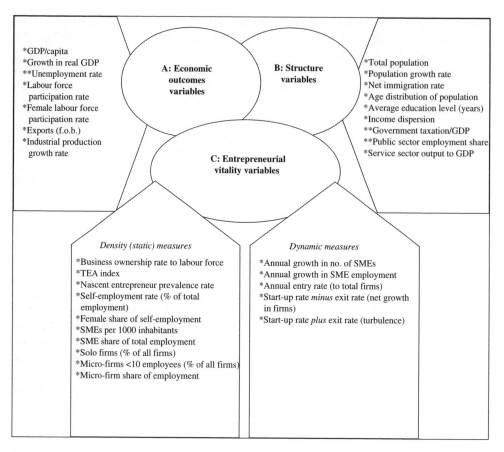

Density (static) measures

*Business ownership rate to labour force
*TEA index
*Nascent entrepreneur prevalence rate
*Self-employment rate (% of total
 employment)
*Female share of self-employment
*SMEs per 1000 inhabitants
*SME share of total employment
*Solo firms (% of all firms)
*Micro-firms <10 employees (% of all firms)
*Micro-firm share of employment

Dynamic measures

*Annual growth in no. of SMEs
*Annual growth in SME employment
*Annual entry rate (to total firms)
*Start-up rate *minus* exit rate (net growth
 in firms)
*Start-up rate *plus* exit rate (turbulence)

Notes:
* A high level of the variable is considered positive for entrepreneurial activity.
** A high level of the variable is considered negative for entrepreneurial activity.

*Figure 6.8   Context variables measuring economic outcomes, structure and
entrepreneurial vitality*

of 'context' by selecting a number of variables that could act either to constrain or promote opportunities leading to increased entrepreneurial activity (see Figure 6.8). Data for most of these variables, many of which have been referred to in earlier parts of this chapter and are known to be relevant considerations, are available from secondary sources. We categorized these variables into three clusters: (A) economic outcomes variables (EOV); (B) structure variables (SV); and (C) entrepreneurial vitality variables (EVV).

The subset of economic outcomes variables includes economic performance indicators routinely used as targets in policy making such as growth in GDP; GDP per capita; labour force participation and unemployment rate; and industrial production growth rate. The subset of structure variables consists of demographic, labour force and industrial structure variables that have an effect on opportunities for entrepreneurship (growth in consumer demand measured by size and growth of the population and level of income dispersion; the supply of potential entrepreneurs measured by the age composition and education level of the population and immigration rates; relative size of the service sector where it is easier to start businesses; and constraints on entrepreneurial opportunities measured by taxation and public sector employment levels as proxies for the size and role of government in the economy). The subset of entrepreneurial vitality variables includes measures for the level of entrepreneurial vitality in the economy both in terms of density (proportion of SMEs, business owners, self-employed persons and nascent entrepreneurs; SME employment share of total employment; and TEA rate) and dynamics (annual growth in SMEs and SME employment; and rate of business entry and exit). Economic outcomes variables, except the unemployment rate, are assumed to be positively related to the level of entrepreneurship. Except for the level of government taxation and the public sector share of employment the same is true of structure variables. All variables in EVV are positively related to the level of entrepreneurship.

Cross-country international data comparisons are very difficult because of lack of consistency, standardization and harmonization. Consequently after securing quantitative indicators for each of the context variables for each economy we used a three-step ranking procedure to determine each economy's relative context performance on subset variables.[13] On the final Borda rankings (Moulin, 1988), using a scale of +7 to −6, we found a great deal of variation in the performance rankings for each subset of variables and each economy (Figure 6.9); variation that is not easy to explain.

None of the economies had high-performing rankings for all variables in a subset and there were often contradictory results within individual economies. The US, Australia and Canada had the highest rankings on structure (supportive for entrepreneurship) and Sweden, Finland and Spain had the lowest rankings. Iceland, Norway and Denmark were the highest ranking economies for economic outcomes (although they all had negative rankings for structure, meaning their structures were less favourable for entrepreneurship) and Spain, Finland and Australia were the lowest ranking. Spain, Australia and Iceland were the highest ranking economies on entrepreneurial vitality, and Denmark, Norway and the Netherlands the lowest ranking.

We noted a number of peculiarities. For example the highest ranking economies on EOV were not necessarily the highest ranking on EVV. In fact it was often the reverse. A case in point is Norway, which had the second best ranking value for EOV and the second lowest ranking for EVV. This suggests that Norway's economic performance is relatively strong but not necessarily because of its level of entrepreneurial activity. Not even the US consistently ranked highest on all three variables subsets, ranking highest on structure but falling to seventh place on EOV and eighth on EVV.

Based on our choice of particular subset variables and our ranking procedure structure variables appear to have a significant influence on the 'context' for entrepreneurship. Economies with large public sectors (high levels of taxation to GDP and high levels of public sector employment) also tend to have lower entrepreneurial densities (that is, Denmark, Norway, Finland and Sweden). The reverse tends to be the case for Australia, Canada, Taiwan and the US (low dominance of government in the economy and higher entrepreneurial density). Raising the density of SMEs and entrepreneurs in the economy may be an important policy objective if the overall aim is to become a more entrepreneurial society. But in order to do this a policy decision may have to be made about the dominance of government's role in the economy and about other aspects of an economy's structure that influence the attractiveness of entrepreneurship as a viable employment option.

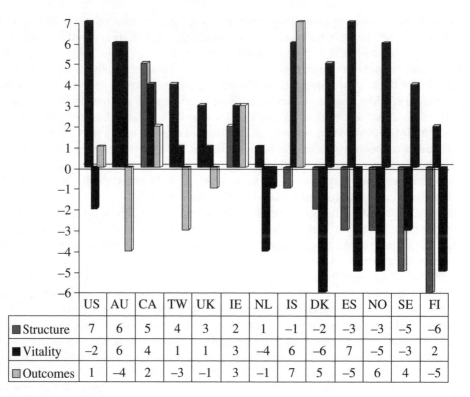

	US	AU	CA	TW	UK	IE	NL	IS	DK	ES	NO	SE	FI
■ Structure	7	6	5	4	3	2	1	–1	–2	–3	–3	–5	–6
■ Vitality	–2	6	4	1	1	3	–4	6	–6	7	–5	–3	2
☐ Outcomes	1	–4	2	–3	–1	3	–1	7	5	–5	6	4	–5

Note: Economies with the highest ranking positive values have the best overall context for entrepreneurship and economies with the highest ranking negative values have the least favourable contexts for entrepreneurship.

Figure 6.9   Borda scale rankings on economic outcomes, structure and entrepreneurial vitality

Our overall conclusion is that the importance of 'context' for entrepreneurship development is not sufficiently recognized and poorly understood. Although the level of economic development of a country is an important variable in explaining some of the context differences between economies, different contexts will produce different levels of entrepreneurial activity. 'One-size does not fit all' and a best practice approach or measure in one context will not obviously produce a best practice result in another context, given these differences. In order to design an effective entrepreneurship policy approach a 'context' description of an economy should be undertaken and analysed with a view to customizing the policy portfolio to the 'context' and tailoring the policy mix to the particular economic circumstances and the problems or opportunities to be addressed. One context configuration may not be better than another but it is quite clear that different context descriptions will lead to different assessments of the problems entrepreneurship policies and measures can solve and what needs to be adjusted to produce more entrepreneurship. The context model and description may provide a useful way for governments to systematically look at opportunities and gaps where entrepreneurship may provide a solution. Even if certain of the identified context deficiencies or gaps were seen as acceptable to a government given its overall policy priorities (and therefore not acted on) at least there would be a more conscious realization of the policy tradeoffs.

Context and entrepreneurship policy comprehensiveness
We were interested in examining the possible relationships between an economy's context description and the comprehensiveness of its government's entrepreneurship policy. Although there are really too few cases to draw definitive conclusions regarding relationship patterns, we observed that economies with both high and low rankings on EOV could have either high or low rankings on EPC but that economies with the highest EOV rankings tended to have the lowest EPC rankings. The same relationship tended to exist for entrepreneurial vitality; the higher the EVV rankings, the lower the EPC score.

It did not obviously appear that individual governments were taking the results demonstrated by the context model into consideration when organizing their different entrepreneurship policy measures. For example the Irish government was not very active with policies to support women entrepreneurs in spite of having one of the lowest female labour force participation rates and the lowest female self-employment rate among the 13 economies. We argue that a relationship between the context description and EPC should exist, and propose that the context model and EPC instrument would be useful tools for governments in identifying weaknesses and opportunities in the environment for entrepreneurship, identifying gaps, and assessing existing policy priorities to determine what new policy measures should be taken to favourably impact on entrepreneurial activity levels. More research exploring the relationships between context variables, entrepreneurship policy and changes in entrepreneurial activity levels over time would be helpful.

Conclusions
Governments in virtually every country are seeking to generate economic renewal and growth – one of the key ways to achieving this in the future will be through innovation and entrepreneurship. Technological advancements and globalization trends are accelerating. Developed and developing countries alike are becoming more knowledge driven. The average size of firms continues to shrink, the average age of firms to shorten and the rate of turbulence in the stock of firms to hasten. The increasingly rapid pace at which this is occurring will produce more demand pressures on the supply of new entrepreneurs. Developing the entrepreneurial capacity of the population will become a policy imperative even in countries that do not see much of a problem at the moment because they are experiencing good performance on entrepreneurial vitality and/or economic outcomes. There has been a significant increase in the amount of research being generated on entrepreneurial activity, rapid developments in the use of benchmarking data and policy indicators, and growing interest in entrepreneurship policy research and sharing, more of which will be needed to address the knowledge needs of government policy makers in the future.

Although there are still many things we do not know about precisely how entrepreneurship emerges within a society and how to foster it, from what we do know, certain facts are clear:

- Low barriers to the entry and exit of businesses are necessary conditions for the creation of economic dynamism and renewal. The dynamic caused by firm birth, expansion, contraction and exit fuels growth. Firm entry may be the most critical variable.

- A number of economic, social, cultural and political factors influence entrepreneurial activity levels and a country's level of economic development, its structure and its cultural context are important considerations.
- There is a great deal of regional variation in the entrepreneurial attitudes and skills of the population in most countries.
- Barriers discouraging entrepreneurship are found within the education and training system, the regulatory environment and institutional arrangements.
- To foster higher rates of firm entry public policies should be more oriented towards removing barriers to business entry (and exit) and stimulating the supply of future entrepreneurs.

We also know that policy making in the entrepreneurship field is complex and messy. A government's emphasis on entrepreneurship policy and its mix of policy options depend on a number of factors including but not limited to: the prevailing attitudes of the population towards entrepreneurship; demographic, labour force, and industrial structures; the size and role of government; the level of economic development; its history with SME development as a policy imperative; and existing levels of business ownership and entrepreneurial activity. Many areas of government policy, both at the macro and micro level, have the potential to influence entrepreneurial activity levels and several points of intervention are implicated in the systems definition of entrepreneurship.

Policies focusing primarily on producing good general economic framework conditions are unlikely to be sufficient to produce a more entrepreneurial society. Governments with the highest commitment to improving the level of entrepreneurial dynamism adopt integrated policy approaches, with efforts to promote fair and open competition, well-functioning capital markets and flexible labour markets as well as specific measures in key entrepreneurship policy areas to reduce administrative and regulatory procedures for start-ups, promote entrepreneurial values in society, increase opportunities to learn about entrepreneurship, and ensure all members of the population have access to the economic resources and supports necessary to become entrepreneurs and build viable businesses. Efforts to promote entrepreneurship and increase business entry rates will be impeded if there are many barriers to start-up and people do not have the necessary skills and knowledge. If target group policies are not in place young people may face systemic barriers because they are not taken seriously by the financial community; women may not be encouraged to pursue entrepreneurship; and innovative entrepreneurs may not be able to source the expertise and risk capital they need to develop their potentially commercializable ideas. The construction of appropriate policies and measures will be assisted by an assessment of the national or regional context with due consideration of the policy needs at different stages of the entrepreneurial process.

This chapter has provided new insights into the nature and characteristics of entrepreneurship policy, including ways to categorize, measure and assess it. The entrepreneurship typology offers a useful way to classify the approaches of governments that demonstrate varying levels of commitment to entrepreneurship policy and configure their policy measures in different ways. There is preliminary evidence that governments in economies with lower business ownership and TEA rates have a higher commitment to entrepreneurship policy and more policy comprehensiveness. Governments in economies with higher business ownership rates and TEA rates appear to have a greater tendency towards adoption of entrepreneurship policies emphasizing the start-up of innovative, technology-oriented firms and the fostering of technology entrepreneurs. The EPC instrument and context model have been useful for exploring overall as well as innovative entrepreneurship policy and for better understanding how and why governments may diverge in their policy choices and some of the opportunities and risks of taking different policy paths.

The EPC could also be a useful tool for monitoring changes in the scope of entrepreneurship policy actions over time periods and providing benchmark guidance to governments wishing to adopt a more comprehensive approach to stimulating entrepreneurship. In future research it would be useful to refine the EPC assessment process to enable a measurement of policy intensity – the depth to which governments are implementing actions in each of the policy framework areas – as well as policy scope. In addition, to reflect the many spatial dimensions and variations in entrepreneurial activity, regional-level context descriptions and entrepreneurship policy analysis would provide a more complete picture of a country's entrepreneurship policy scope. It may be equally important to explore in greater detail under what conditions different entrepreneurship policy approaches are appropriate given a country's economic, structural and political context. Here further development and use of the context model may be helpful. Applying our research approach and tools to the study of entrepreneurship policy in a larger number of countries with more divergence in GDP per capita may also provide helpful insights about how it plays out in developed versus developing economic contexts.

Essentially there is a lot more we need to know about the emergence of entrepreneurship. Unfortunately most researchers are still only looking at parts of the problem. The policy making community would benefit from more research that moves beyond the static measurement of one-to-one relationships between entrepreneurship system elements to an examination of the complexity of the system affecting entrepreneurial activity levels. Also, it would benefit from more empirical research evidence of the positive spillovers from entrepreneurship.

Notes

1. Our research was carried out in three phases. The first phase was an exploratory study of the practices of national level governments in ten developed economies that differed in population size; GDP per capita; immigration rates; political orientation; socioeconomic and cultural context; size and role of government; history with SME policy; density of SMEs; and so on. The final selection included Australia, Canada, Finland, the Republic of Ireland, the Netherlands, Spain, Sweden, Taiwan, the United Kingdom and the United States. In phase two the entrepreneurship policy frameworks developed in phase one were applied to the practices of governments in the five Nordic countries. Case studies for each of the phase one and phase two economies were published in Stevenson and Lundström (2001) and Lundström (2003) respectively. To collect our data we made site visits to each economy and conducted semi-structured interviews with government officials, academics and representatives from policy research think-tanks, key small business or entrepreneurs' associations, small business support organizations and the education community. Key areas of questioning focused on the national policy agenda, major programme measures and institutions, policies to stimulate higher levels of entrepreneurial activity, structures for policy development and implementation, and performance indicators and measures. We also reviewed a variety of economic and SME data for each economy and supplemented interview and statistical data with a review of SME and entrepreneurship-related policy documents, reports, programme materials, and evaluation studies that we obtained either from economy officials or from the national/central governments' websites. We used qualitative methodologies to 'make sense of' the case material and to map individual entrepreneurship policy approaches and initiatives. This formed the basis of a collective framework that included six major policy components. We further constructed collective maps for each of the six framework areas and analysed

these maps for key insights about the critical elements of each one from a policy analysis perspective. For the final stage of this research process, 13 economies were included. In 2004 we updated information for each economy by reviewing government websites for new policy documents and information on recent programmes and initiatives as well as policy-relevant documents and research reports prepared by the European Commission, the OECD and economy-specific think-tanks. We also updated the statistical data for each economy. We reclassified the inventory of 2004 policy measures according to the original entrepreneurship policy typology and collective framework and compared economies in terms of the scope of policy measures in each area using a instrument we developed to analyse and compare the comprehensiveness of a government's entrepreneurship policy. We used quantitative (frequency counts) and qualitative (document analysis) techniques to develop and score policy comprehensiveness. This scoring of policy comprehensiveness offered a way to examine patterns across economies and to note similarities and differences in policy approaches and emphasis.

2. For example Acs and Armington (2004) use the number of new firms per 1000 members of the labour force.
3. The nascent entrepreneur prevalence rate is defined as the number of people actively involved in starting a new venture as a percentage of the adult population (18–64 years of age).
4. The Total Entrepreneurial Activity rate is a composite of the nascent entrepreneur prevalence rate and the number of people in the adult population who have a young business that has paid salaries and wages for at least three months but less than 42 months.
5. In their definition of institutions Wennekers and Thurik (1999) include: fiscal legislation, social security systems, the education system and government policies affecting the starting of a business.
6. Hart (2003a, p. 8) defines public policy as the intentional use of the powers of government to effect a societal outcome, like a change in the number of entrepreneurial ventures, and governance as the conscious collective action that extends beyond government, deploying the capacities of businesses, community groups and academic institutions to bring about such an outcome.
7. Start-ups in a region can attract other firms by increasing the availability of services, enlarging the pool of trained workers, lowering the unit costs of providing public utilities or adding to the attractiveness of a locale as a place to live (OECD, 2003; reprinted in 2004a, p. 90).
8. Hart (2003a, p. 8) does recognize that education policies may influence the legitimacy of entrepreneurial ventures and extent of knowledge, skills and networks possessed by individuals and social groups, and that macroeconomic policies may affect things like the short-term availability of capital and thus contribute to the context for entrepreneurship.
9. Examples of indicators to benchmark entrepreneurship and set targets for policy outcomes in the European Commission (2004b) include: the number of new enterprises per year; real birth rates of high potential start-ups; the number of self-employed; the number of new enterprises supported by public incubators; the time it takes to set up a company and venture capital investment as a percentage of GDP. The OECD (2001a) indicators include: providing skills (entrepreneurship education); providing opportunities (administrative simplification, deregulation, incubators); and influencing the risk–reward trade-off (taxes, bankruptcy).
10. For example entrepreneurship and job creation would be included as one of the main policy lines of action in the government's national action plan for employment, reinforcing the top priority of the government.
11. Hall's scale consisted of 35 policy questions in seven policy areas and was used as a tool to identify patterns in the SME policy approaches adopted by ASEAN and APEC governments and to provide a basis for comparing SME policy and programmes among these economies over two time periods: 1990–94 and 2000–01.
12. These included actions such as: offering tax incentives to stimulate venture capital investments; reducing the capital gains tax; taking actions to simplify patent processes; providing pre-commercialization funding; funding national incubator strategies; and offering entrepreneurship education to science and engineering students.
13. Data for each of the context variables were obtained for the 13 economies. Each economy was ranked on each of the variables. The best performing economy was assigned the ranking number of (1) and the lowest performing economy the ranking number of (13). For the subset of structure variables, low values represented better performance, except for public sector employment and government taxation. For the economic outcomes and entrepreneurial vitality subsets low values indicated better performance for all variables. Then an average ranking score was calculated for each economy for each subset. To deal with the rank-aggregation problem and to obtain a better rank-ordering, we next used the Borda ranking procedure (see Moulin, 1988). We used this ranking procedure to help overcome a number of well-known problems in doing international statistical comparisons (economies are at different stages of economic development; international statistical data are not completely comparable, and ordinal ranking systems do not take into consideration that two rankings can be more or less similar). Based on the average ordinal rankings for each of the three subsets of variables (and including the average rankings for the two categories of density and dynamic variables within the entrepreneurial vitality subset) we assigned Borda ranking values from +7 to −6 to the ordinal rankings.

Bibliography

Acs, Z.J., P. Arenius, M. Hay and M. Minniti (2005), *Global Entrepreneurship Monitor: 2004 Executive Report*, Wellesley, MA and London: Babson College and London Business School.

Acs, Z.J. and C. Armington (2004), 'Employment growth and entrepreneurial activity in cities', *Regional Studies*, **38**, 911–27.

Acs, Z.J. and D.B. Audretsch (eds) (2003), *The Handbook of Entrepreneurship Research*, Boston, Dordrecht and London: Kluwer Academic Publishers.

Audretsch, D.B. (1995), *Innovation and Industry Evolution*, Cambridge, MA: MIT Press.

Audretsch, D.B. and M. Keilbach (2004), 'Entrepreneurship, capital and economic growth', *Regional Studies*, **38**, 949–59.

Audretsch, D.B. and R. Thurik (2001a), 'Linking entrepreneurship to growth', STI Working Paper 2001/2, Paris: OECD.

Audretsch, D.B. and R. Thurik (2001b), 'What is new about the new economy? Sources of growth in the managed and entrepreneurial economies', *Industrial and Corporate Change*, **10**, 267–315.

Audretsch, D.B., R. Thurik, I. Verheul and S. Wennekers (eds) (2002), *Entrepreneurship: Determinants and Policy in a European–US Comparison*, Boston, Dordrecht and London: Kluwer Academic Publishers.

Baldwin, J. (1999), 'A portrait of entrants and exits', Research Paper No. 121, Micro-Economic Analysis Division, Ottawa: Statistics Canada, June.

Baumol, W. (1990), 'Entrepreneurship, productive, unproductive and destructive', *Journal of Political Economy*, **98** (5), 893–921.

Birch, D. (1979), 'The job generation process', unpublished report, Massachusetts Institute of Technology (MIT) Program on Neighbourhood and Regional Change, prepared for the Economic Development Administration, Washington, DC: US Department of Commerce.

Birch, D. (1987), *Job Creation in America*, New York: Free Press.

Carree, M.A. and A.R. Thurik (2003), 'The impact of entrepreneurship on economic growth', in Z.J. Acs and D.B. Audretsch (eds), *The Handbook of Entrepreneurship Research*, Boston, Dordrecht and London: Kluwer Academic Publishers, pp. 437–71.

Carree, M.A., A. van Stel, R. Thurik and S. Wennekers (2002), 'Economic development and business ownership: an analysis using data of 23 OECD countries in the period 1976–1996', *Small Business Economics*, **19**, 271–90.

Casson, M. (2003), 'Entrepreneurship, business culture and the theory of the firm', in Z.J. Acs and D.B. Audretsch (eds), *The Handbook of Entrepreneurship Research*, Boston, Dordrecht and London: Kluwer Academic Publishers, pp. 223–46.

Danish National Agency for Enterprise and Housing, Danish Ministry of Economic and Business Affairs, FORA, ART, and Monitor Company Group (2004), 'Dynamic benchmarking of entrepreneurship performance and policy in select countries: entrepreneurship index initiative, Discussion Paper', Copenhagen, May.

Eliasson, G.E. (1995), 'Economic growth through competitive selection', paper presented at 22nd EARIE Conference, 3–6 September, mimeo.

European Commission (1998), *Fostering Entrepreneurship in Europe: Priorities for the Future*, Communication from the Commission to the Council, Brussels: Commission of the European Communities, 07.04.

European Commission (2001), 'Creating top-class business support services', Commission Staff Working Paper, Brussels: Directorate-General Enterprises, European Commission.

European Commission (2002), *Benchmarking the Administration of Start-ups*, Centre for Evaluation Studies, Brussels: Enterprise Directorate-General, European Commission, January.

European Commission (2004a), *Action Plan: The European Agenda for Entrepreneurship*, COM(2004) 70 final, Communication from the Commission to the Council, the European Parliament, the European Economic and Social Committee and the Committee of the Regions, Brussels: Commission of the European Communities, 11.02.

European Commission (2004b), *Benchmarking Enterprise Policy: Results from the 2004 Scoreboard*, Commission Staff Working Document SEC(2004)1427, Brussels: Enterprise Publications, Commission of the European Communities, 10.11.

European Commission (2004c), *Education for Entrepreneurship: Making Progress in Promoting Entrepreneurial Attitudes and Skills through Primary and Secondary Education*, Final Report of the Expert Group, Brussels: Enterprise Directorate-General, European Commission, February.

European Commission (2004d), *Good Practices in the Promotion of Women Entrepreneurship*, Brussels: Enterprise Directorate-General, European Commission.

Friis, C., T. Paulsson and C. Karlsson (2002), *Entrepreneurship and Economic Growth: A Critical Review of Empirical and Theoretical Research*, Stockholm: Swedish Institute for Growth Policy Studies.

Fritsch, M. and P. Mueller (2005), 'The persistence of regional new business formation activity over time – assessing the potential of policy promotion programs', No. 0205, Discussion Papers on Entrepreneurship, Growth and Public Policy, Jena, Germany: Max Planck Institute for Economics.

Gartner, W.B. and N.M. Carter (2003), 'Entrepreneurial behaviour and firm organizing processes', in Z.J. Acs and D.B. Audretsch (eds), *The Handbook of Entrepreneurship Research*, Boston, Dordrecht and London: Kluwer Academic Publishers, pp. 195–221.
Grilo, I. and J.M. Irigoyen (2005), 'Entrepreneurship in the EU: to wish and not to be', No. 0105, Discussion Papers on Entrepreneurship, Growth and Public Policy, Jena, Germany: Max Planck Institute for Economics.
Hall, C. (2002), *Profile of SMEs and SME Issues in APEC 1990–2000*, APEC Small and Medium Enterprises Working Group, Singapore: APEC Secretariat.
Hall, C. (2003), 'The SME policy framework in ASEAN and APEC: benchmark comparisons and analysis', paper for the Small Enterprise Association of Australia and New Zealand 16th Annual Conference, Ballarat, Australia, 29 September–1 October.
Hart, D.M. (2003a), 'Entrepreneurship policy: what is it and where it came from', in D.M. Hart (ed.), *The Emergence of Entrepreneurship Policy*, Cambridge, MA: Cambridge University Press.
Hart, D.M. (ed.) (2003b), *The Emergence of Entrepreneurship Policy*, Cambridge, MA: Cambridge University Press.
Hoffman, A., M. Larsen and N. Neilsen (2005), *Entrepreneurship Index 2005*, Copenhagen: National Agency for Enterprise and Construction, October.
Holtz-Eakin, D. and H.S. Rosen (eds) (2004), *Public Policy and the Economics of Entrepreneurship*, Cambridge, MA: MIT Press.
Keilbach, M. and D. Audretsch (2004), 'Entrepreneurship capital: determinants and impacts', No. 37, Discussion Papers on Entrepreneurship, Growth and Public Policy, Jena, Germany: Max Planck Institute for Economics.
Koppl, R. and M. Minniti (2003), 'Market processes and entrepreneurial studies', in Z.J. Acs and D.B. Audretsch (eds), *The Handbook of Entrepreneurship Research*, Boston, Dordrecht and London: Kluwer Academic Publishers, pp. 81–102.
Lowrey, Y. (2003), 'The entrepreneur and entrepreneurship: a neoclassical approach', presented at the ASSA Annual Meeting, 5 January, Washington, DC: Office of Advocacy, Small Business Administration.
Lundström, A. (ed.) (2003), *Towards an Entrepreneurship Policy – A Nordic Perspective*, Stockholm: Swedish Foundation for Small Business Research.
Lundström, A. and L. Stevenson (2001), *Entrepreneurship Policy for the Future*, Stockholm: Swedish Foundation for Small Business Research, March.
Lundström, A. and L. Stevenson (2002), *On the Road to Entrepreneurship Policy*, Stockholm: Swedish Foundation for Small Business Research.
Lundström, A. and L. Stevenson (2005), *Entrepreneurship Policy: Theory and Practice*, New York: Springer Science+Business Media Inc.
McGrath, R.G. (2003), 'Connecting the study of entrepreneurship and theories of capitalist progress', in Z.J. Acs and D.B. Audretsch (eds), *The Handbook of Entrepreneurship Research*, Boston, Dordrecht and London: Kluwer Academic Publishers, pp. 515–31.
Ministry of Economic Affairs (2004), *Action for Entrepreneurs!*, Enterprise Directorate, The Hague: Ministry of Economic Affairs, December.
Ministry of Economy and Business Affairs (2003), *Promoting Entrepreneurship – A Plan of Action*, Copenhagen: Ministry of Economy and Business Affairs, August.
Ministry of Trade and Industry (2004), *Entrepreneurship Policy Programme: An Enterprising Society in View*, Helsinki: Ministry of Trade and Industry, June.
Morris, M. (1996), 'Sustaining the entrepreneurial society', Working Paper 96-01, The Research Institute for Small and Emerging Business, Washington, DC: The Small Business Foundation of America.
Moulin, H. (1988), *Axioms of Cooperative Decision Making*, Boston, MA: Cambridge University Press.
National Agency for Enterprise and Construction (2004), *Entrepreneurship Index 2004*, Copenhagen: Danish National Agency for Enterprise and Construction.
OECD (1995), *Thematic Overview of Entrepreneurship and Job Creation Policies*, Paris: OECD.
OECD (1997), *Small Businesses, Job Creation and Growth: Facts, Obstacles and Best Practices*, Paris: OECD.
OECD (1998), *Fostering Entrepreneurship*, Paris: OECD.
OECD (2001a), 'Benchmarking of growth drivers', OECD Growth Studies, Paris: OECD.
OECD (2001b), *Entrepreneurship, Growth and Policy*, Paris: OECD.
OECD (2002), 'Policy benchmarks for fostering firm creation and entrepreneurship', DSTI/IND(2002), 13, Paris: OECD.
OECD (2003), *Entrepreneurship and Local Economic Development: Programme and Policy Recommendations*, Paris: OECD. Reprinted in 2004.
OECD (2004a), 'Fostering entrepreneurship as a driver of growth in a global economy', prepared for the Second OECD Conference of Ministers Responsible for Small and Medium-sized Enterprises (SMEs), Istanbul, June, Paris: OECD.
OECD (2004b), 'Venture capital: trends and policy recommendations', Science Technology and Industry, Paris: OECD.

Parker, S. (2005), 'The economics of entrepreneurship: what we know and what we don't', No. 1805, Discussion Papers on Entrepreneurship, Growth and Public Policy, Jena, Germany: Max Planck Institute for Economics.

Reynolds, P.D., W.D. Bygrave and E. Autio (2004), *GEM 2003 Global Report*, Wellesley, MA, London and Kansas City: Babson College, the London Business School and the Ewing Marion Kauffman Foundation.

Reynolds, P.D., M. Hay and S.M. Camp (1999), *Global Entrepreneurship Monitor, 1999 Executive Report*, Wellesley, MA, Kansas City and London: Babson College, Kauffman Center for Entrepreneurial Leadership and the London Business School.

Schmitz, J.A Jr (1989), 'Imitation, entrepreneurship and long-run growth', *Journal of Political Economy*, **97**, 721–39.

Shane, S. and J. Eckhardt (2003), 'The individual–opportunity nexus', in Z.J. Acs and D.B. Audretsch (eds), *The Handbook of Entrepreneurship Research*, Boston, Dordrecht and London: Kluwer Academic Publishers, pp. 161–91.

Shane, S. and S. Venkataraman (2000), 'The promise of entrepreneurship as a field of research', *The Academy of Management Review*, **25** (1), 217–26.

Shapero, A. (1984), 'The entrepreneurial event', in C. Kent (ed.), *The Environment for Entrepreneurship*, Lexington, MA: Lexington Books, pp. 21–40.

Shapero, A. and L. Sokol (1982), 'The social dimensions of entrepreneurship', in C. Kent, D. Sexton and K. Vesper (eds), *Encyclopaedia of Entrepreneurship*, Englewood Cliffs, NJ: Prentice Hall.

Small Business Service (2004a), *A Government Action Plan for Small Business: Making the UK the Best Place in the World to Grow a Business*, London: Department of Trade and Industry.

Small Business Service (2004b), *A Government Action Plan for Small Business: The Evidence Base*, London: Department of Trade and Industry.

Stevenson, L. (1996), *Implementation of an Entrepreneurship Development Strategy in Canada: The Case of the Atlantic Region*, Paris: OECD Territorial Services Division and the Atlantic Canada Opportunities Agency.

Stevenson, L. and A. Lundström (2001), *Patterns and Trends in Entrepreneurship/SME Policy and Practice in Ten Countries*, Stockholm: Swedish Foundation for Small Business Research.

Stevenson, L. and A. Lundström (2002), *Beyond the Rhetoric: Defining Entrepreneurship Policy and its Best Practice Components*, Stockholm: Swedish Foundation for Small Business Research.

Storey, D. (1994), *Understanding the Small Business Sector*, London and New York: Routledge.

Thurik, R. and I. Grilo (2005), 'Determinants of entrepreneurial engagement levels in Europe and the US', No. 2505, Discussion Papers on Entrepreneurship, Growth and Public Policy, Jena, Germany: Max Planck Institute for Economics.

van Stel, A. (2003), 'COMPENDIA 2000.2: a harmonized data set of business ownership rates in 23 OECD countries', Research Report H200302 (SCALES), Zoetermeer: EIM Business & Policy Research, May.

van Stel, A. and B. Diephuis (2004), 'Business dynamics and employment growth: a cross-country analysis', No. 32, Discussion Papers on Entrepreneurship, Growth and Public Policy, Jena, Germany: Max Planck Institute for Economics.

van Stel, A., M. Carree and R. Thurik (2005), 'The effect of entrepreneurial activity on national economic growth', No. 04, Discussion Papers on Entrepreneurship, Growth and Public Policy, Jena, Germany: Max Planck Institute for Economics.

Verheul, I., S. Wennekers, D. Audretsch and R. Thurik (2001), *An Eclectic Theory of Entrepreneurship: Policies, Institutions and Culture*, EIM Research Report 0012/E, Zoetermeer: EIM Business & Policy Research, March.

Wennekers, S. and R. Thurik (1999), 'Linking entrepreneurship and economic growth', *Small Business Economics*, **13**, 27–55.

Wennekers, S., A. van Stel, R. Thurik and P. Reynolds (2005), 'Nascent entrepreneurship and the level of economic development', No. 1405, Discussion Papers on Entrepreneurship, Growth and Public Policy, Jena, Germany: Max Planck Institute for Economics.

Wilken, P.H. (1979), 'The emergence of entrepreneurship and its significance for economic growth and development', in *Entrepreneurship: A Comparative and Historical Study*, Norwood, NJ: Ablex.

7 Public policy and entrepreneurship*
Albert N. Link

Introduction

Hébert and Link's (1988, 1989) studies of the history of economic thought on the evolution of the concept of the entrepreneur concluded with the following synthesis (1988, p. 155):

> [The entrepreneur is] someone who specializes in taking responsibility for and making judgemental decisions that affect the location, the form, and the use of goods, resources, or institutions.

This perception and subsequent action, in a dynamic or multi-period context, is entrepreneurship.

The Hébert and Link synthesis incorporates the ideas of risk, uncertainty, innovation, perception and change. Stated alternatively, the entrepreneur has differentiated abilities that allow him or her, within an environment of risk and uncertainty, to perceive opportunities and have the ability to act on them. In a sense, then, the entrepreneur may be said to 'perceive what normal people of lesser alertness and perceptiveness, would fail to notice' (Machlup, 1980, p. 179), and, in a dynamic context, 'creative and imaginative action [will] shape the kind of transactions that will be entered into in future market periods' (Kirzner, 1985, pp. 63–4).

Can public policy enrich environments in which individuals grasp knowledge that might otherwise go unexploited? In this chapter I argue that the answer to this question is definitely, 'yes', especially as related to innovation.

There are a number of public policies in the United States that, to varying degrees, provide resources that extend opportunities for perception and action, especially as related to innovative behavior. These include, but certainly are not limited to, tax incentives aimed at innovation and research and development (R&D), direct support of innovation and R&D, collaborative research arrangements that reduce the cost of being perceptive; and infrastructure technologies that reduce market transaction costs and hence enrich the opportunity to affect the use of goods, resources or institutions. US public policies related to each of these four categories are described in the following sections, and each is characterized under the policy rubric of a public/private partnership.

Public/private partnerships: a framework

'Public' refers to any aspect of perception or innovativeness that involves the use of governmental resources. 'Private' refers to any aspect of perception or innovativeness that involves the use of private resources. And resources are broadly defined to include financial resources, infrastructural resources, and research resources that affect the general environment in which perception and innovation take place. Finally, 'partnership' refers to any and all relationships that spur creativity.

In the United States, the concept of commingling public and private resources to enhance innovation has only recently gained acceptance (and to speculate, perhaps this recent acceptance or action was a perceptive response on the part of the public sector to the loss of world market share by many companies in advanced technology industries and the subsequent slowdown in total factor productivity growth in the early 1980s).

The US Office of Technology Policy (1996) classifies public/private partnerships, in general, along a time spectrum so as to illustrate and emphasize that public/private partnerships have evolved from a relationship wherein the government was merely a customer of private innovation to a relationship wherein the government is a partner in the underlying research (Office of Technology Policy, 1996, pp. 33–4):

> By the late 1980s, a new paradigm of technology policy had developed [in the United States]. In contrast to the enhanced spin-off programs . . . the government developed new public–private partnerships to develop and deploy advanced technologies. . . . [T]hese new programs . . . incorporate features that reflect increased influence from the private sector over project selection, management, and intellectual property ownership.

In response to the productivity slowdown in the United States and in other industrial nations, it became apparent to the nation's leadership that the private sector was more than a recipient of the outputs of public technology-based programs. The private sector was a major, yet frequently overlooked, contributor to the selection of technology strategy and also to the execution of the strategy. To academics, this realization was long overdue in light of the extant literature that had for nearly two decades quantified the strong relationship between the private-sector R&D and productivity growth.[1]

Although nearly two decades have passed, it is still too soon from an evaluation perspective to judge whether this paradigm shift has affected the entrepreneurial actions of individuals within public sector organizations or private sector firms, but certainly change is expected (Office of Technology Policy, 1996, p. 34):[2]

> The new paradigm has several advantages for both government and the private sector. By treating the private sector as a partner in federal programs, government agencies can better incorporate feedback and focus programs. Moreover, the private sector as partner approach allows the government to measure whether the programs are ultimately meeting their goals: increasing research efficiencies and effectiveness [i.e. *perception*] and developing and deploying new technologies [i.e. *action*].

To elaborate on the Office of Technology Policy's (1996) realization of the private sector as a partner in public sector technology development and deployment raises another policy issue, namely the relationship between public sector and private sector R&D in the innovation process. It has long been debated – theoretically and empirically – whether these two sources of innovation inputs complement each other or crowd each other out in the private sector's performance of R&D.[3,4]

Regardless of this, the fact is that the public sector and the private sector are direct partners in technology-based economic growth; there are obviously also indirect partners because the knowledge that results from either sector has public good characteristics and spillovers. Economic growth is spurred, at least in part, by the entrepreneurial insights and efforts of participants in the process from both the public sector and the private sector, and the level and focus of participation follow from public policies.

In the following section aspects of such partnerships are discussed within a public/private partnership framework, and this framework is illustrated with specific

Table 7.1   Public/private partnerships framework

Governmental involvement	Economic objective	
	Leverage public innovation and R&D	Leverage private innovation and R&D
Indirect	——	——
Direct		
Financial resources	——	——
Infrastructural resources	——	——
Research resources	——	——

examples of US public policies, although similar public policy programs exist in most industrialized nations. Table 7.1 illustrates this framework. The first column of the table describes the nature and scope of government's involvement in a public/private partnership. Government involvement could be indirect or it could be direct; if involvement is direct there will be an explicit allocation of resources including financial resources, infrastructural resources and research resources. The second and third columns of the table relate to the economic objectives of the partnership. With any innovation-related activity there are spillovers of knowledge and thus the a priori and ex post economic objectives of the partnership are multi-dimensional. For the purpose of illustrating the examples in the next section, a single overriding objective is posited. The objective is either to leverage public R&D activity or to leverage private R&D activity.

Examples of public/private partnerships in the United States
Four examples of general public/private partnerships with US specifics are described in this section. These innovation-based partnerships are tax incentive programs, grants-based programs such as the Small Business Innovation Research program, collaborative research arrangements, and the provision of technology infrastructures. Each example is discussed from an institutional perspective and then placed within the public/private partnership framework in Table 7.1.

Tax incentives
Tax incentives represent a public/private partnership. Tax incentives – compared to grants assistance programs – and the legislation that promulgated them, represent indirect governmental involvement in the innovation process with the objective of leveraging the efficiency of innovative activity in the private sector.[5]

Tax incentives, as a leveraging mechanism, have advantages and disadvantages. Some advantages of tax incentives are:

- *Tax incentives entail less interference in the marketplace than do other mechanisms, thus affording private sector recipients the ability to retain autonomy regarding the use of the incentives.* It has been argued that tax incentives alleviate the need for government officials to make difficult and subjective judgments, and tax incentives protect against the creation of artificial markets. The first point is probably valid, however the second point is more a function of the design of the program than of tax incentives per se.

- *Tax incentives require less paperwork than other programs and fewer layers of bureaucracy than grants assistance.* Tax incentives do require paperwork but the administrative burden is less, and government bureaucracy is already trained in auditing and tax administration. In addition, there is an administrative advantage to tax incentives because the rules of the game change less rapidly. One of the greatest administrative boons from tax incentives is predictability, and tax policies are not likely to change frequently whereas grants assistance may require yearly appropriations.
- *Tax incentives obviate the necessity to directly target individual firms in need of assistance.* There is an administrative benefit to avoiding particularistic requirements with regard to efficiency and equity. With regard to R&D, tax incentives are ideally designed to reward past behavior.
- *Tax incentives have the psychological advantage of achieving a favorable industry reaction.* While it is difficult to document the psychological advantages of tax incentives versus grants assistance, tax incentives seem to draw nourishment from the free enterprise system.
- *Tax incentives may be permanent and thus do not require annual budget review.* Firms are more likely to make fundamental changes in their investment strategies and forecasts if they perceive that a policy has stability.
- *Tax incentives have a high degree of political feasibility.* In many industrialized nations, and especially in the United States, tax incentives face less political opposition than do direct grants assistance programs.

Some disadvantages of tax incentives compared to grants assistance programs are:

- *Tax incentives may bring about unintended windfalls by rewarding firms for what they would have done in the absence of the incentive.* For strict verification, this proposition requires knowledge that is in principle unobtainable. Once a tax incentive is introduced, counterfactual analyses are difficult and at best subjective.
- *Tax incentives often result in undesirable inequities.* Tax incentives are likely not only to introduce inequities but also to mask those inequities. Tax incentives are a blunt instrument, and highly specific provisions would have to be written into the tax code to deal effectively with inequities. It is not simply that differential rewards are provided under tax incentives, but there is a tendency for lopsided benefits as well.
- *Tax incentives raid the federal treasury.* Tax expenditures represent forgone revenue and, *ceteris paribus*, the tax rate would have to be elevated just to maintain revenue. However, all else is not equal because revenue is not simply a function of tax rates. Tax expenditures can ultimately lead to an increase in revenues provided that incentives ultimately lead to productivity growth, but tax incentives are often open-ended, with few dollar upper limits.
- *Tax incentives frequently undermine public accountability.* The stabilizing influence provided by tax incentives compared to grants assistance is not without cost. With tax incentives, Congress has forfeited its oversight function. This has a number of possible ramifications. First, tax incentives are awarded a status not enjoyed by other government initiatives because they are, at least in the United States, off

budget and thus not a controllable expenditure. And second, tax expenditures are an especially pernicious form of back door spending because revenue committees rather than authorizing committees often open the back door.

● *The effectiveness of tax incentives often varies over the product life cycle.* Internal R&D investments are most effective during the growth and maturity stages of the product lifecycle. Many firms purchase technology during the introduction and decline stages; thus, during those stages, grants assistance is more valuable than a tax incentive.

In the United States, the Economic Recovery and Tax Act of 1981 included a 25 percent tax credit for qualified research and experimentation (R&E) expenditures in excess of an average amount spent during the previous three years or 50 percent of the current year's expenditures. R&E tax credits are not unique to the United States (Leyden and Link, 1993). Canada and Japan initiated such incentives in the 1960s. Over the years, the US R&E tax credit has been modified, but it has not been made permanent.

Clearly, for those involved in innovation and who benefit from a tax credit, the marginal cost of creative inquiry is reduced and thus the level of creative inquiry is increased. That said, the empirical evidence is that the tax elasticity of R&D is about unity, meaning that a 1 percent increase in the credit will increase private sector R&D by about 1 percent (Hall and van Reenen, 2000).

Direct support of innovation activity
The Small Business Innovation Research Program (SBIR), as one example of direct support of innovation activity by the US government, is a public/private partnership that leverages public R&D through direct governmental support.

The SBIR program began at the National Science Foundation (NSF) in 1977 (Tibbetts, 1999). At that time the goal of the program was to encourage small businesses and their entrepreneurial founders, long believed to be engines of innovation in the US economy, to participate in NSF-sponsored research, especially research that had commercial potential. Because of the early success of the program at NSF, Congress passed the Small Business Innovation Development Act of 1982. The Act required all government departments and agencies with external research programs of greater than $100 billion to establish their own SBIR programs and to set aside funds equal to 0.2 percent of the external research budget. As a set aside program, the SBIR program redirects existing R&D rather than appropriating new monies for R&D. Currently, agencies must allocate 2.5 percent of the external research budget to SBIR. Ten agencies participate in the program. The Department of Defense and the National Institutes of Health are the largest two in terms of dollar grants awarded.

The 1982 Act states that the objectives of the program are:

1. to stimulate technological innovation;
2. to use small business to meet federal research and development needs;
3. to foster and encourage participation by minority and disadvantaged persons in technological innovation;
4. to increase private sector commercialization of innovations derived from federal research and development.

The Act was reauthorized in 1992 with the same objectives, and in 2000 the Act was again reauthorized. This latter reauthorization extended the program to 2008.[6]

Collaborative research arrangements

Research joint ventures (RJVs) represent a public/private partnership. An RJV is a collaborative research arrangement through which those within the collaborating firms or organizations (i.e. a university can be a research partner) jointly acquire new knowledge.[7] RJVs, and the legislation that promulgates them, represent indirect government involvement in the innovation process with the objective of leveraging the efficiency of innovative activity in the private sector.

The National Cooperative Research Act of 1984 was enacted in the United States:

> . . . to promote research and development, encourage innovation, stimulate trade, and make necessary and appropriate modifications in the operation of the antitrust laws.

The Act created a registration process, later expanded by the National Cooperative Research and Production Act of 1993, under which RJVs can voluntarily disclose their research intentions to the US Department of Justice, thereby gaining two significant benefits. One, if the venture were subjected to criminal or civil antitrust action, the courts would evaluate the alleged anticompetitive behavior under a rule of reason rather than presumptively ruling that the behavior constituted a per se violation of the antitrust law. And two, if the venture were found to fail a rule-of-reason analysis it would be subjected to actual rather than treble damages.

As with any legislative initiative, there are benefits and costs associations with the collaboration of ideas through an RJV.[8] The benefits include the opportunity for participants to capture knowledge spillovers from other members; reduced research costs due to a reduction in duplicative research; faster commercialization because the fundamental research stage is shortened; and the opportunity to develop industry-wide competitive vision. And the costs include a lack of appropriability because research results are shared among the participants; and the growth of managerial tension as participants, in some cases, learn to trust each other and to work together.

Research partnerships are correctly viewed as a complementary source of technical knowledge and technical efficiency for the firm. Thus firms that participate in a research partnership leverage their own R&D process through interactions and knowledge sharing.[9]

The extant literature has addressed a number of specific issues that have stemmed from the above discussion of benefits and costs.[10] Two public policy questions for which there is sufficient literature to reach a conclusion are:

- *Have research partnerships improved research efficiency?* Yes. The evidence is overwhelming that research partnerships lower transaction costs, participation reduces duplicative R&D expenditures, R&D expenditures increase over time because of spillovers from partnership participants, partnerships yield economies of scale and scope, and knowledge from partnerships reduces research risks in general.
- *Have research partnerships increased competition in the marketplace?* Yes. The evidence is that partnerships decrease market competition, and they increase market

output and lower price through product cost reductions when spillover effects are present.

Technology infrastructures

Technology infrastructure has many dimensions. It can be classified first, legitimately, by the set of physical and virtual tools, methods and data that enable all three stages of technology-based economic activity: the conduct of R&D, the control of production processes to achieve target quality and yield, and the consummation of market place transactions at minimum time and cost. The underlying infratechnologies – including measurement and test methods, process and quality control techniques, evaluated scientific and engineering data, and the technical dimensions of product interfaces – are ubiquitous in the typical technology-based industry. The collective economic benefits of such infrastructure are therefore considerable, as are the consequences of not having it in place at critical points in a technology's life cycle.

Technology infrastructure can also, although this is done less frequently, be interpreted broadly as an organizational or institutional form, often tied to national measurement systems, that leverages knowledge creation and knowledge flows in and among technology developers and users, including research/science parks, incubators, university research centers, and focused public/private partnerships. The efficiency of these institutions in providing technology and related infrastructure services is essential to an efficiently functioning national innovation ecology and to the capacity of that ecology to form and reform innovation systems around innovation problems.

With respect to the public provision of technology infrastructure for the benefit of the private sector, it is useful to think of technology infrastructure as a prescribed set of rules, conditions or requirements concerning: definitions of terms; classification of components; specification of materials, their performance, and their operations; delineation of procedures; and/or measurement of quantity and quality in describing materials, products, systems, services or practices.

In the United States, the provision of standards represents a public/private partnership through which the government directly provides infrastructural resources to leverage the efficiency of innovation in both public and private sectors. Here, unlike with tax incentives and collaborative research arrangements, there is a long legislative history dating back to the Articles of Confederation signed in 1778, through the writing of the Constitution of the United States, and eventually to the Organic Act of 1901 which established the National Bureau of Standards (now the National Institute of Standards and Technology, NIST).

An industry standard is a set of specifications to which all elements of products, processes, formats or procedures under its jurisdiction must conform. The process of standardization is the pursuit of this conformity, with the objective of increasing the efficiency of economic activity. The complexity of modern technology, especially its system character, has led to an increase in the number and variety of standards that affect a single industry or market. Standards affect the R&D, production and market penetration stages of economic activity and therefore have a significant collective effect on innovation, productivity and market structure. Thus one concern of government policy is the evolutionary path by which a new technology or, more accurately, certain elements of a new technology become standardized. This concern is well founded. Narrowly, government provision of standards is like government provision of public or quasi-public goods so there is an issue of accountability of resources. Broadly, standards reduce transaction costs in market activity thus leveraging the efficacy with which entrepreneurial action occurs.

Standards can be grouped into two basic categories: product-element standards, and nonproduct-element standards. This distinction is important because the economic role of each type is different. Product-element standards typically involve one of the key attributes or elements of a product, as opposed to the entire product. In most cases, market dynamics determine product-element standards. Alternative technologies compete intensely until a dominant version gains sufficient market share to become the single *de facto* standard. Market control by one firm can truncate this competitive process. Conversely, nonproduct-element standards tend to be competitively neutral within the context of an industry. This type of standard can impact an entire industry's efficiency and its overall market penetration rate.[11]

There has been limited empirical research to quantify the impact of standards and other forms of technology infrastructure on firms; that is, on the creative actions of private sector economic agents. The little evidence that exists suggests that firms that invest in infrastructure technologies are more efficient in their in-house R&D than firms that do not.[12]

Conclusions

The four examples given earlier in the chapter fit within the public/private partnerships framework proffered above (see Table 7.2). More important than fitting within the framework is that these examples represent public policies designed to spur entrepreneurial activity within both public and private sector organizations. In a sense, the existence of these examples reflects the fact that in some ways government acts as an entrepreneur.

Government, as illustrated by these examples, is, in a sense, Schumpeterian in its perception of technology-based needs and the demonstration of policy revealed action. In Schumpeter's theory of entrepreneurship, successful innovation requires an act of will, not of intellect, and entrepreneurship should thus not be confused with invention. Schumpeter (1934, pp. 88–9) was explicit:

Table 7.2   Public/private partnerships framework with US examples

Governmental involvement	Economic objective	
	Leverage public innovation and R&D	Leverage private innovation and R&D
Indirect		Tax incentives Research joint ventures
Direct		
Financial resources	Small Business Innovation Research Program	
Infrastructural resources	Standards activities (through NIST)	Standards activities (through NIST)
Research resources	Standards activities (through NIST)	Standards activities (through NIST)

To carry any improvement into effect is a task entirely different from the inventing of it, and a task, moreover, requiring entirely different kinds of aptitudes. Although entrepreneurs of course may be inventors just as they may be capitalists, they are inventors not by nature of their function but by coincidence and vice versa.

The leadership that constitutes innovation in the Schumpeterian system is disparate, not homogeneous, and not unique to the private sector (although Schumpeter himself does not make that case). An aptitude for leadership stems in part from the use of knowledge. People of action – such as those who promulgated the technology-based public policies discussed in Table 7.2 – who perceive and react to knowledge do so in various ways. The public or private leader distances himself or herself from a manager by virtue of his or her aptitude.

According to Schumpeter (1928, p. 380), different aptitudes for the routine work of 'static' management result merely in differential success at what all managers do, whereas different leadership aptitude means 'some are able to undertake uncertainties incident to what has not been done before; [indeed] . . . to overcome these difficulties incident to change of practice is the function of the entrepreneur'. And technology-based public policies are a demonstration of a response to uncertainties as to what has not been done before.

Notes

*   This chapter has benefited from comments and suggestions of the editors of the *Handbook of Research on Entrepreneurship Policy* as well as those of several anonymous referees.
1. See, in particular, Mansfield (1980), Link (1981), and Griliches (1986). The history of this literature is reviewed in Link and Siegel (2003).
2. As an aside, and as a reflection on the quotation from Machlup (1980) above, the National Research Council categorizes public/private partnerships in terms of their contribution 'to the development of industrial processes, products, and services that might not otherwise emerge spontaneously' (Wessner, 2003, p. 8).
3. This debate can be traced back to the 'pump-priming' versus 'substitution' hypothesis of Blank and Stigler (1957).
4. David et al. (2000) recently reconciled this debate and concluded that some of both occur.
5. These arguments draw from Bozeman and Link (1984) and Leyden and Link (1992).
6. Audretsch et al. (2002) offer the most recent empirical evidence that SBIR innovations and related R&D do lead to commercialization, and that the benefits to the market and to society are substantial.
7. Hall et al. (2003) show that universities are invited to join a research venture to help member firms create a greater awareness of difficulties that arise during basic research.
8. See Hagedoorn et al. (2000) for a review of this literature.
9. This point has been demonstrated by Link and Rees (1990).
10. See Link and Siegel (2003) for a review of this literature.
11. See Link (1983) for evidence of this proposition.
12. See Tassey (1992, 2005) and Link and Tassey (1993) for a review of this literature.

References

Audretsch, D.B., A.N. Link and J.T. Scott (2002), 'Public/private partnerships: evaluating SBIR-supported research', *Research Policy*, **31**, 145–58.
Blank, D.M. and G.J. Stigler (1957), *The Demand and Supply of Scientific Personnel*, New York: National Bureau of Economic Research.
Bozeman, B. and A.N. Link (1984), 'Tax incentives for R&D: a critical evaluation', *Research Policy*, **13**, 21–31.
David, P.A., B.H. Hall and A. Toole (2000), 'Is public R&D a complement or a substitute for private R&D: a review of the literature', *Research Policy*, **29**, 497–529.
Griliches, Z. (1986), 'Productivity growth, R&D, and basic research at the firm level in the 1970s', *American Economic Review*, **76**, 141–54.
Hagedoorn, J., A.N. Link and N.S. Vonortas (2000), 'Research Partnerships', *Research Policy*, **29**, 567–86.
Hall, B.H. and J. van Reenen (2000), 'How effective are fiscal incentives for R&D? A review of the evidence', *Research Policy*, **29**, 449–69.

Hall, B.H., A.N. Link and J.T. Scott (2003), 'Universities as research partners', *Review of Economics and Statistics*, **85**, 485–91.

Hébert, R.F. and A.N. Link (1988), *The Entrepreneur: Mainstream Views and Radical Critiques*, 2nd edn, New York: Praeger.

Hébert, R.F. and A.N. Link (1989), 'In search of the meaning of entrepreneurship', *Small Business Economics*, **1**, 39–49.

Kirzner, I.M. (1985), *Discovery and the Capitalist Process*, Chicago: University of Chicago Press.

Leyden, D.P. and A.N. Link (1992), *Government's Role in Innovation*, Boston; MA: Kluwer Academic Publishers.

Leyden, D.P. and A.N. Link (1993), 'Tax policies affecting R&D: an international comparison', *Technovation*, **13**, 17–25.

Link, A.N. (1981), 'Basic research and productivity increase in manufacturing: some additional evidence', *American Economic Review*, **71**, 1111–12.

Link, A.N. (1983), 'Market structure and voluntary product standards', *Applied Economics*, **15**, 393–401.

Link, A.N. (2006), *Public/Private Partnerships: Innovation Strategies and Policy Alternatives*, Boston, MA: Springer.

Link, A.N. and J. Rees (1990), 'Firm size, university based research and the returns to R&D', *Small Business Economics*, **2**, 25–32.

Link, A.N. and D.S. Siegel (2003), *Technological Change and Economic Performance*, London: Routledge.

Link, A.N. and G. Tassey (1993), 'The technology infrastructure of firms: investments in infratechnology', *IEEE Transactions on Engineering Management*, **40**, 312–15.

Machlup, F. (1980), *Knowledge and Knowledge Production*, Princeton, NJ: Princeton University Press.

Mansfield, E. (1980), 'Basic research and productivity increase in manufacturing', *American Economic Review*, **70**, 863–73.

Office of Technology Policy (1996), 'Effective partnering: a report to Congress on federal technology partnerships', Washington, DC: US Department of Commerce.

Schumpeter, J.A. (1928), 'The instability of capitalism', *Economic Journal*, **38**, 361–86.

Schumpeter, J.A. (1934), *The Theory of Economic Development*, Cambridge, MA: Harvard University Press.

Tassey, G. (1992), *Technology Infrastructure and Competitive Position*, Norwell, MA: Kluwer Academic Publishers.

Tassey, G. (2005), 'Underinvestment in public good technology', *Journal of Technology Transfer*, **30**, 89–113.

Tibbetts, R. (1999), 'The Small Business Innovation Research Program and NSF SBIR commercialization results', mimeograph.

Wessner, C.W. (2003), *Government–Industry Partnerships for the Development of New Technologies*, Washington, DC: National Academy Press.

8 A rough guide to entrepreneurship policy
Anders N. Hoffmann[1]

Introduction

During the 1990s, 'entrepreneurship' was a buzzword both in the media and in the political debate. Newspapers were full of success stories about self-made billionaires. Politicians supported their endeavours and attempted to associate themselves with successful entrepreneurs. Old fashion subsidies to ineffective small firms were consequently relabelled as entrepreneurship policy and the majority of the old rhetoric related to the policies for small and medium-sized enterprises (SMEs) was adopted by the 'new' entrepreneurship policy makers. New firms are mostly small; therefore SME policies should benefit entrepreneurs. The logic behind this argument is as clear as the following statement: 'People cannot fly. Rocks cannot fly, so people are rocks.'

Although some have defined entrepreneurship policy as 'ensuring small firms can compete in the marketplace and that they are not prejudiced because of their small size, relative to large firms' (Lundström and Stevenson, 2005, p. 37), it is actually about creating a dynamic economy, which ensures that people can start new ventures and subsequently develop these ventures to become high-growth firms (Hart et al., 2003). As formulated by the Danish government, entrepreneurship policy should support and increase a country's ability to compete on knowledge, new ideas, and the ability to adapt and find new solutions to problems (Danish Government Platform, 2005).

The objective of this chapter is to provide both policy makers and scholars with a quick overview of which policy areas are essential parts of a country's overall strategy to promote entrepreneurship. The chapter also provides insights into the relative importance of each of these policy areas. The conclusions are based on a cross-country comparison of indicators measuring both performance and the underlying business environment for entrepreneurship. The chapter can be compared with a travel guide to a specific region. The guide gives you a good overview of the important things to visit, but if you want more details you have to talk to the local people and examine the region yourself.

The chapter consists of five parts. First, the methodology is presented and discussed. Second, entrepreneurship performance is measured and top performers are identified. Next, a model for the business environment affecting entrepreneurship is constructed and quantified. Fourth, the relative importance of the policy areas affecting entrepreneurship performance is determined by linking the indicators of performance with the indicators of the business environment. Finally, a brief analysis of Germany's entrepreneurship policy illustrates how the presented guide can be applied in a specific country in order to assist policy makers in policy formulation.

Methodology

The field of entrepreneurship research has two principal strands. The first focuses on linking entrepreneurship to growth (Wennekers and Thurik, 1999), while the second strand focuses on the various background factors and policy effects on entrepreneurship.

This chapter fits in the second strand of the literature as it focuses on linking policy to entrepreneurship, but it reviews evidence from the first strand to support the definitions and relevance of the policies.

The field of linking policies to entrepreneurship is new and no agreed methodology exists. Some have attempted to construct theoretical frameworks for addressing this issue (Audretsch et al., 2002; Stevenson and Lundström, 2001). Another important strand of literature has attempted to link entrepreneurial activity to characteristics specific to a spatial unit of observation like a city or region (Reynolds et al., 1994). Several authors have focused on the evaluation of specific programmes aimed at promoting entrepreneurship (Storey, 2002 and 2003), while others have focused on specific issues like entrepreneurship education (Charney and Libecap, 2001).

This chapter is based on a comparative approach that builds on cross-country comparisons of quantifiable indicators within a theoretical framework. The theoretical framework is inspired by the aforementioned work, but it is adapted to better allow for quantification and policy analysis. The quantification of the framework is new, as is the distinction between performance and the underlying business environment.

The underlying foundation of this approach is that linking indicators related to the business environment with the indicators of performance will allow for new policy insights. The methodology has five main steps. First, entrepreneurship performance is defined and, subsequently, quantified. Second, the performance of countries is compared and top-performing countries are selected. Third, the business environment for entrepreneurship is defined and quantified. Fourth, the empirical links between the indicators measuring the business environment and the indicators measuring performance are tested. Fifth, if the correlation between business environment and performance is significantly positive, then key policy areas for enhancing entrepreneurship performance will be identified based on regression and comparative techniques.

A lack of internationally comparable indicators of entrepreneurship activities has made this type of comparative policy analysis difficult, but recently several initiatives have produced comparable indicators. Attempts to overcome data shortcomings have been made by the Global Entrepreneurship Monitor (GEM) and the World Bank. GEM has compiled entrepreneurial activity data since 2000, while the World Bank has collected indicators related to the administrative barriers affecting both start-ups and existing firms. Recently, the OECD engaged in producing entrepreneurship-relevant indicators and published comparative analysis of entrepreneurship based on these indicators (OECD, 2005a).

Many of the examined policy areas are multi-dimensional and cannot be captured by a single indicator. The analysis consequently builds composite indicators to better capture the dimensions of the various policy areas. Several problems are associated with the use of composite indicators. This chapter uses an approach developed by the OECD and the Joint Research Centre of the EU Commission (Giovannini et al., 2005). The approach ensures the high quality of the composite indicator by following a specific procedure while constructing it, but it does not resolve the issue of assigning weights to the individual indicators.

No direct solution exists regarding the selection of weights. A new sensitivity technique has been developed by the OECD where weights are assigned randomly to each of the normalized indicators (OECD, 2005a). In this chapter, the calculation was repeated 10 000 times and weights were drawn randomly from a uniform distribution for each of the indicators. This exercise gives a distribution of possible rankings for each country, which is then used in the analysis. The probability of being among, for example, the top three, the top five or the top ten performing countries can be calculated based on the distribution. The figures shown in this chapter are based on these probability calculations. The randomly assigned weights vary between 0 and 1 for each indicator; therefore, the technique indirectly tests for the robustness of excluding an indicator.

A final point to be noted concerning the methodology is whether or not a country can learn from other countries and use the priorities of the top performing countries as a guide for their own policy formulation. No clear-cut answer exists to this question. Each country is unique and, therefore, there will always be limits to cross-country comparisons and the transferability of policy experiences.

This chapter makes a slightly blurry distinction between policy areas and specific policy initiatives. An example of a policy area is venture capital. The indicators for venture capital are correlated with the performance indicators and the best performing countries give high weight to their venture capital markets. The importance of venture capital for entrepreneurship is also supported by other studies. The chapter consequently concludes that venture capital is important and that countries should prioritize the development of these markets in their entrepreneurship policy. However, each country has to figure out what policy initiatives it needs to put in place in order to develop its national venture capital market. In this respect, countries can learn from each other's experience, but the initiative must to be tailored to each national context.

Defining and quantifying entrepreneurship performance

Entrepreneurship is not a single event, but a process that transforms an innovative idea into a growing firm. Most new firms exit as a result of failure, while others survive at, or near, the break-even point (Figure 8.1). Only a small minority of new firms turn into high-growth firms, also known as gazelles.

Previous analyses show that about 30 per cent of the population (16–60 years) in OECD countries responded that they would like to participate in some kind of start-up activity; around 10 per cent are already engaged in some kind of start-up activity, but only 1–2 per cent realize their wish every year and actually start a new firm (GEM, 2004;

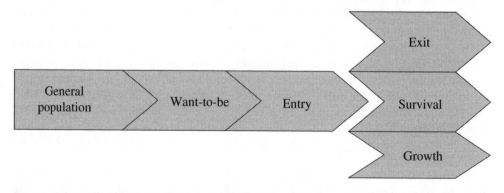

Source: Adopted from the final report from the *Panel Study of Entrepreneurial Dynamics* (Kaufmann, 2003).

Figure 8.1   The process of entrepreneurship

Eurobarometer, 2004). Other studies show that 70 per cent of the new start-ups will survive but not grow – often referred to as 'lifestyle entrepreneurs' (EU, 2003). Only about 5 per cent of the new firms will turn into high-growth firms (NCOE, 2001).

Defining entrepreneurship

Entrepreneurship policies should be designed to meet a set of macroeconomic policy objectives (Storey, 2002). Consequently the definition of entrepreneurship used in this chapter must reflect policy objectives. Three main objectives for entrepreneurship policy are identified – job creation, economic growth and poverty alleviation (OECD, 2004).

This chapter focuses on entrepreneurship as a driver of economic growth through increased productivity. Entrepreneurship is consequently defined by two parts in the process: (1) the *entry of new firms*, and (2) the *creation of high-growth firms*. Conclusive analyses show a direct link between these two parts of the entrepreneurial process and productivity growth (Audretsch and Thurik, 2000; Scarpetta et al., 2002; OECD, 2003a; Brandt, 2004a).

This definition of entrepreneurship is narrower than the holistic definitions used in most other papers and various policy reports on entrepreneurship. Most papers tempt to define entrepreneurship as an attitude, 'a willingness and ability to change' or 'as the pursuit of opportunities beyond the resources one currently controls' (Stevenson and Lundström, 2001). On the one hand, the holistic definition might better capture the many aspects of entrepreneurship, but it cannot be measured and compared across countries. On the other hand, the definition offered in this chapter is directly measurable and linked to growth, whereas the link between willingness to change and productivity growth is more difficult to measure.

The effect of new firm entry and exit on productivity can be shown in a so-called growth accounting framework (OECD, 2003a). A detailed OECD decomposition of productivity growth in eight OECD countries over a ten-year period showed that between 20 and 40 per cent of total labour productivity growth can be explained by new firm entry and exit. Normally, firms that exit the market have less labour productivity than their competitor in the industry and, thereby, their exit directly increases the average productivity within the industry. Firms that enter the market have a labour productivity near the industry average and only have, consequently, a small effect on labour productivity growth.

Effects on multifactor productivity (MFP) are different. Exiting firms have a limited role in MFP growth, while new firm entry contributes significantly to MFP growth. New firms can enter with new innovative management that utilizes the factors of production better and thus increases MFP growth (OECD, 2005a).

Other studies confirm this connection between entry and productivity using different techniques. One study, for example, relates sectoral firm entry rates to sectoral productivity growth. This approach captures both the impact that firms have via their own productivity and any indirect effect on aggregate productivity that might occur, for instance as a result of the competitive pressure created through firm entry (Brandt, 2004a and 2004b).

New high-growth firms, almost by definition, affect productivity. A new study, based on an extensive database including all Danish firms, also shows a positive correlation between the MFP level and the growth rate of new firms (Figure 8.2). OECD work also confirms this connection between high-growth firms and productivity growth (OECD, 2003a).

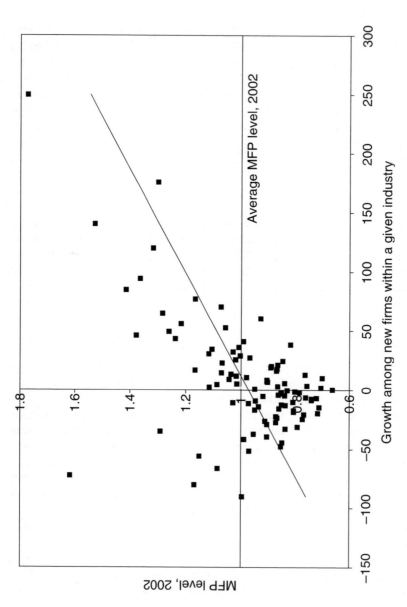

Note: All Danish firms – that have been operational for fewer than five years and have more than three employees in the initial year – are divided into 100 different industries. Each dot represents the average of the new firms within one of the 100 different industries.

Source: Calculation based on Danish Ministry of Economic and Business Affairs database on Danish firms.

Figure 8.2   Correlation between firm growth and MFP

Table 8.1   Performance indicators of entrepreneurship

Entry of firms	New high-growth firms
Firm entry rates, average 2000–02 (new firms as % existing firms)	Share of young firms with more than 60% growth rates in turnover in a three-year period, 1999–2003
Entrepreneurial activity (TEA), average 2000–02	Share of young firms with more than 60% growth rates in employment a three-year period, 1999–2003

Selecting top-performing countries
Only a few internationally comparable data exist, which can be used to measure entrepreneurship performance as it is defined in this chapter (*entry* and *creation of high-growth firms*). Four indicators are used in this analysis (Table 8.1). These data will be defined as performance indicators, as they measure the outcome of the entrepreneurial process.

Some alternative measures of entrepreneurship exist but these will not be included in this analysis as their link to productivity is less clear. For example, survival rates have often been used as a performance measure in government reports even though they are not conclusive. Northern Ireland has, for example, the highest survival rate among the regions in the United Kingdom, but it also has one of the lowest start-up rates (SBS, 2001).

EU harmonized firm level data on *entry of firms* covers ten European Union countries and Norway over the period 1998–2002. The 11 countries fall into three groups. Luxembourg and Norway are top performers with an average entry rate of new firms above 10 per cent in the period from 2000 to 2002. These two countries are followed by four other countries (Denmark, Spain, Netherlands and United Kingdom) with entry rates between 9 and 10 per cent. Finally, Portugal, Finland, Belgium and Sweden have the lowest entry rates at between 5 and 7 per cent (Eurostat, 2003).

Canada also records its yearly start-up rates using a methodology quite similar to the one used by the EU. The US does not have a central registration of new firms, so start-up rates from the US come from various sources. The available start-up rates for the US show that it falls in the top performance group with start-up rates around 10 per cent. Canadian data show much higher entry rates (around 14 per cent). Despite these differences, studies comparing the US and Canada conclude that the start-up activities are quite similar in the two countries if employment in new firms and first year survival are taken into account (Baldwin et al., 2002).

The Global Entrepreneurship Monitor (GEM) publishes the Total Entrepreneurship Activity index (TEA), which is a frequently used measure of start-up activity (GEM, 2004). TEA estimates the number of people who are entrepreneurially active in a given country. They define entrepreneurially active as: *adults in the process of setting up a business they will (partly) own and or currently owning and managing an operating young business* (Reynolds et al., 2005, p. 209). This estimation is based on the GEM adult population survey, which has a minimum sample of 2000 people in each of the participating countries, except for five developing countries. The respondents were asked a series of questions about their participation in entrepreneurial activities. These included three screening questions that determined whether or not they could possibly be considered as entrepreneurially active. Following the screening questions people have to meet a number of criteria in order to be labelled as either *Nascent entrepreneurs: involved in setting up a business* or *Owner-manager of a young firm (less than 3.5 years old)* (Reynolds et al., 2005). The advantage of using this indicator is that it is based on a standardized questionnaire for a large number of countries, rendering a priori cross-country comparisons less problematic.

However, the TEA index has some drawbacks. To some extent, it seems to measure an individual's 'intentions' and 'trials' while setting up a firm, as well as measuring those of 'real' start-ups. Corrections are needed if the TEA index is to be compared to offical data on firm registration.

The GEM data show for example that 7.6 per cent of individuals aged between 18 and 64 in the UK are either in the process of starting a new business or are the owner-managers of a newly operating business that is less than 42 months old (GEM, 2001). This equals about 2.7 million people engaged in entrepreneurial activity in the UK. In 2000, about 183 500 firms registered for value added tax (VAT), which is significantly lower than the number of people engaged in entrepreneurship. The VAT threshold is high in the UK, so a new firm does not have to register for VAT in order to start trading, although most firms do open a bank account. In 2000, approximately 400 000 new business bank accounts were opened in the UK (Barclays, 2001). This is less than 15 per cent of the number of people engaged in entrepreneurial activity according to the GEM survey.

These limitations are recognized by the GEM research team. Reynolds et al. (2005) list for example several ways to construct GEM data that are comparable with official registrations. Start-up rates are constructed for eight EU countries and the US. In these constructed data the large differences between Europe and the US found in the TEA index seem to disappear. The US has an 11.5 per cent start-up rate based on GEM data compared to a 9.7 per cent average among the eight EU countries (Reynolds et al., 2005, Table X). The TEA index shows a much greater difference (11 in the US compared to an average of 6.7 in the eight EU countries). This could suggest that the TEA index overestimates the differences between Europe and the US. Despite the limitations of the TEA indicator, it will be included in the analysis as no better alternative exists.

No internationally accepted definition exists of what constitutes a high-growth firm. The literature offers several definitions inspired by the seminal work of David Birch (1987). In some countries, a high-growth firm doubles its employment in a five-year period. In other countries, high-growth firms are, by definition, the 10 per cent fastest growing firms in the economy (OECD, 2002).

The data for calculating indicators on the share of high-growth firms in the economy is taken from Bureau van Dijk (BvD), an electronic publishing firm. BvD specializes in cleaning and organizing data supplied by national information providers in various countries to create a broader data set (e.g. Companies House in the UK, Kamers van Koophandel in the Netherlands, INPI in France, National Bank of Belgium). The database has been used by other researchers (see for example, Desai et al., 2003). The data and calculations used in this chapter are documented in Junge and Kaiser (2004) and their usefulness and quality are discussed in Hoffmann and Junge (2006b).

High-growth firms are defined as the share of young firms with a growth rate (in either employment or turnover) higher than 60 per cent in a three-year period. A young firm is less than five years old in the first year of the three-year growth period. The 60 per cent threshold is commonly used, but is not based on any hard evidence. Both turnover and employment are used as measures of high growth because of the differences in growth patterns across sectors. Knowledge intensive manufacturing firms grow in both employment and turnover, whereas service sector firms mainly have high employment growth (Delmar et al., 2003).

An extensive sensitivity analysis shows that the ranking of countries stands up to changes in the 60 per cent threshold. The ranking is also robust to corrections for differences in the industry structure across countries. Alternative definitions of high growth and different assumptions about the age of a young firm were also tested, but again with little impact on the ranking of countries.

From this analysis, the United States and Korea are performing better than the other countries studied (Figure 8.3). The superior performance of the United States is also found in OECD work on firm demography based on firm level data from the early 1990s. OECD work showed that US firms grow much faster and generate more jobs than European firms (Scarpetta et al., 2002). Korea's top performance cannot be independently confirmed as no alternatives exist.

As variables are expressed in various units, the indicators have to be normalized to render them comparable. Several techniques can be used to standardize individual indicators, including the standard deviation from the mean, the distance from the mean (where OECD = 100), the distance from the best performer (leader = 100), and the distance from the best and the worst performing country (the 'minimum–maximum method'). For this study, the 'minimum–maximum method' (leader = 100 and laggard = 0) has been selected because personal experience shows that this is the easiest method for policy makers to understand. Sensitivity analyses show that the ranking of countries is robust and stands up to other methods of normalization.[2]

No empirical data or knowledge exists comparing the relative importance of the four selected indicators. The selection of top performing countries is consequently based on a sensitivity analysis where the weights for the individual indicators are allowed to vary between zero and one drawn from a uniform distribution. The calculation is repeated 10 000 times. This results in a distribution of composite indicators for each country. This distribution is approximately normal and the average of the distribution approximately equals the average of the four indicators. Only countries with data for at least three indicators are included in the analysis, which limits the number to 18.

The distribution of composite indicators allows for an analysis to rank countries. The number of times a country is among the top three, top six and top ten can be calculated based on the distributions.

Korea, Ireland, Canada and the United States clearly outperform the rest of the countries studied; these are the only ones that are among the top three OECD countries regardless of weights used. The growth data for Ireland are biased because of a lack of data on employment, hence Ireland is not included among the top three countries (Figure 8.4).

Defining and quantifying the business environment for entrepreneurship
The number of new firms and the subsequent share of high-growth firms created each year depend on a myriad of underlying environmental and sociological factors coupled with the personal attributes of entrepreneurs. No single paradigm exists, but many important contributions to the literature have been made (Aldrich, 2000). This chapter builds on the eclectic theory developed by Audretsch, Thurik and Verheul (Audretsch et al., 2002) and the policy framework developed in the works of Lundström and Stevenson

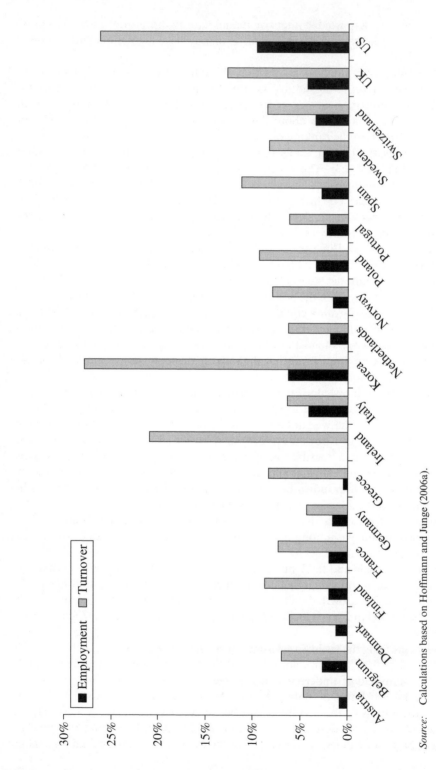

Source: Calculations based on Hoffmann and Junge (2006a).

Figure 8.3   Share of young firms with more than 60 per cent growth rates in a three-year period, average (1999–2003)

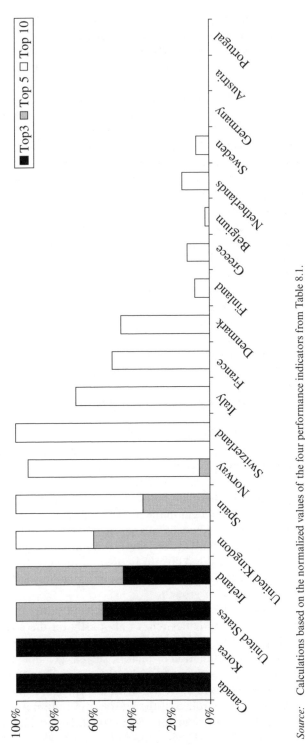

Source: Calculations based on the normalized values of the four performance indicators from Table 8.1.

Figure 8.4   Robustness analysis – performance

(2002, 2005; Stevenson and Lundström, 2001), which draws in part from sociology literature. The model is described in detail in Gabr and Hoffmann (2006).

Many words and definitions are used in the literature to describe the factors affecting entrepreneurship. The differences between various studies are often semantic; the essence of the various papers is that a new firm is created by a combination of three factors: *opportunities, skilled people* and *capital*. These three factors are then combined with the necessary condition of a *market clearing* (possible benefits of creating a new firm outweigh the cost relating to the risks) based on the occupational choice theory (Acs, 2005). The occupational choice theory emphasizes that in equilibrium the marginal entrepreneur is indifferent between entrepreneurship and paid employment. Two main streams of occupational choice theory exist (Parker, 2005). This chapter builds on the stream attributed to Lucas (1978), where differences in skills (entrepreneurial abilities) among people will determine whether or not they chose to become entrepreneurs instead of paid employees.

Opportunities are ideas that create genuine value in the minds of other people (Smilor, 2001), and they are essential for starting and growing businesses (EU, 2003; Davidsson, 1989). Opportunities are represented in the *demand* side of the model because they arise through market demand for goods and services.

Skills not only entail basic industry knowledge required to succeed in a competitive environment, but also an ability to seize entrepreneurial opportunities (Reynolds et al., 1999; Gavron et al., 1998). Skills include the competencies of the entrepreneur but also access to competencies within the entrepreneurial infrastructure (Lee et al., 2000).

Capital is a necessity for the start-up, expansion and growth of firms. Nearly all studies of entrepreneurship highlight access to capital as one of the most critical factors for success (EU, 2003). Capital covers all phases of 'business life' from access to early seed to access to the stock markets. Capital represents, together with skills, the supply side of the model.

A combination of opportunity, ability and capital does not necessarily lend itself to entrepreneurship. If costs, such as opportunity cost (e.g. forgone salary and loss of health insurance) and start-up cost, outweigh potential benefits, then the opportunity should not be pursued following the rationale of basic economic theory. These *incentives* reflect the classic market clearing condition that marginal cost equals marginal benefit in equilibrium. The incentive structure component in the model represents the various incentives and disincentives that impact the cost/benefit balance of the opportunity.

The same three factors and the market clearing condition affect high-growth firms. Opportunities are needed for growth, skills are needed to manage the growth phase, capital is needed for investment and the tradeoff between risk and reward has to be right in order to pursue the opportunity for growth.

A final component in the model is *motivation*. Previous work shows that people's willingness to pursue entrepreneurial activities relies only partly on the economic factors described above (Davidsson, 1989). Personal motivation plays a decisive role as it is unique and involves a complex combination of factors, such as personal traits, risk aversion and sociological circumstances determined by the national culture. While some people are driven by a cause, trying to solve a particular problem, others may become motivated by a new technology. Regardless of the reason, motivation is a key ingredient for both entry and success in entrepreneurship, even though empirically identifying the key motivating factors is very difficult (Davidsson, 2006). This model's understanding of

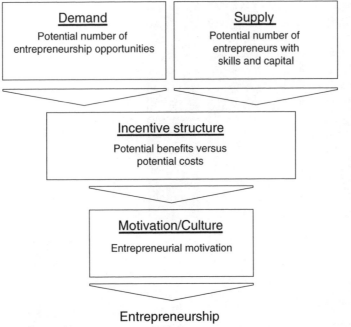

Figure 8.5   Model of factors affecting entrepreneurship

motivation is based on cognitive theory, which has its roots in psychology (Wood and Bandura, 1989).

All in all, the combination of individuals with the right *skills*, *opportunities* and *capital* along with an appropriate *incentive structure* and *motivation* is the foundation for entrepreneurship and the basis for which this policy framework has been developed (Figure 8.5).

It must be highlighted that entrepreneurship is also affected by basic macroeconomic conditions. High unemployment, for instance, will increase the number of individuals motivated to become entrepreneurs as a result of job loss. Despite the obvious importance for entrepreneurship, these conditions are excluded in the policy framework in order to focus on microeconomic structures. The framework is therefore constructed for 'opportunity-based entrepreneurs' as defined by the Global Entrepreneurship Monitor project, as opposed to 'necessity driven' entrepreneurs (GEM, 2001).

Moving from theory to policy areas
The most complete list of policy areas affecting entrepreneurship is offered in the works of Lundström and Stevenson (2002, 2005; Stevenson and Lundström, 2001) and the OECD, which has worked intensively on entrepreneurship for several years (OECD, 1998, 2001, 2003b, 2005a and 2005b). Based on these publications, a list of 24 different policy areas can be identified (Figure 8.6). Appendix 8.2 briefly defines each of the policy areas. This list spans the policy framework affecting entrepreneurship, which implies that any policy aimed at affecting growth by stimulating entrepreneurship should belong to one or more of the policy areas. Testing the comprehensiveness of the list is difficult, but it forms

Total measure of the business environment for entrepreneurship

	Opportunities	Capital	Ability	Incentives	Motivation/culture
Factors affecting entrepreneurial performance / Policy areas affecting entrepreneurial performance	Entry barriers/ deregulation	Loans	Trad. business education	Personal income tax	Entrepreneurial motivation
	Access to foreign markets	Wealth & bequest tax	Entrepreneurship education	Business tax & fiscal incentive	Initiatives towards specific groups
	Technology transfer	Business angels	Restart possibilities	Social security discrimination	Communication about heroes
	Private demand conditions	Venture capital	Entrepreneurship infrastructure (public)	Administrative burdens	
	Procurement regulation	Capital taxes	Entrepreneurship infrastructure (private)	Labour market regulation	
		Stock markets		Bankruptcy legislation	

Figure 8.6   Overview of the main policy areas at the micro-level

the basis of the Danish Entrepreneurship Policy (EBST, 2005). Various levels of aggregation and disaggregation of the 24 policy areas can decrease or increase the number of policy areas.

Each area is organized in relation to the factor it affects most, based on a qualitative judgement by the author. The level of capital taxation, for instance, affects the potential benefits of the entrepreneur, but, more significantly, it affects the amount of capital available for entrepreneurial investments, therefore it is placed under the factor *capital*. The organization of factors does not play any role in the analytical results as each policy area is analysed independently of the other areas. The organization of policy areas serves only as a framework for communicating the results in an easily comprehensible manner.

Determining the relative importance of each area of entrepreneurship policy
Out of the 24 policy areas, a total of 18 can be quantified with 61 indicators used to benchmark these areas in this chapter. Each policy area is consequently measured by one or more indicator. Appendix 8.1 shows which indicators have been included in each policy area.

Each indicator is normalized using the minimum–maximum method previously discussed. Missing values are dealt with by the simplest method possible: they are ignored. This implicit method assigns all missing values for a country with a value equal to the average of all other available indicators for that particular country.

The indicators are a mix of market outcomes, such as the venture capital market size, and the quantification of policies, such as the time for which creditors can lay claims on assets after a bankruptcy. All indicators measured by at least ten OECD countries are included in the analysis. The quality of each indicator has been evaluated on the basis of three quality dimensions – *relevance*, *accuracy* and *availability*. These dimensions are taken from the OECD's *Quality Framework* (OECD, 2003c).

The analysis shows a solid correlation between a simple average of all performance indicators and a simple average of all business environment indicators (Figure 8.7). This suggests efficient policies may have a positive effect on entrepreneurship performance. Sensitivity tests show that the correlation between the business environment and performance varies between 0.25 and 0.79 if weights assigned to the indicators are allowed to vary freely between 0 and 1. All correlation coefficients within the 95 per cent confidence interval of the median (0.43 and 0.7) are significantly different from zero.

However, the interpretation of a significant correlation is not without difficulty. The transmission mechanism between policy areas and performance varies substantially, which makes the correlation difficult to interpret. A change in bankruptcy law might take many years before it affects performance, while higher venture capital investment will affect entrepreneurship the same year the investment occurs. A system of indicators needs to exist for a large time series in order to support solid conclusions on causality. Changes in the business environment tend to be rather slow, so it is plausible that the correlation will stay significant as the data is updated.

As shown in Figure 8.7, the United States, Canada, the United Kingdom, Ireland and Korea claim top position in the overall performance index and in the index for the business environment. Canada and Ireland's positions should be treated with some caution as they are based on a limited number of indicators.

Not all of the evaluated policy areas for business environment are equally important. Based on various analytical and empirical methods, a hierarchy of priorities can be

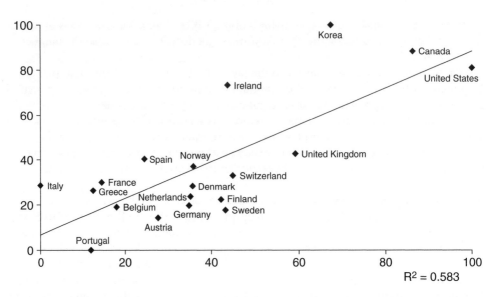

Note: The value for the business environment is based on a nested average. The normalized indicators within a given policy area are given equal weights, which results in a value for each policy area. The value for the business environment is then equal to the average of all policy areas. The performance is simply the average of the four normalized performance indicators.

Figure 8.7   Link between performance and the business environment

established. Two approaches are used in this chapter to determine the most important policy areas. First, correlation analysis is used to determine which policy areas have the highest correlation with performance. Second, analysis of the business environment in the top performing countries (Canada, Korea and the United States) provides additional insights.

Using correlation analysis to determine relative importance
Ideally, the importance of the various areas should be determined in a multi-variant regression analysis that includes all policy areas. However, data are only available for a limited number of countries and years, which makes this type of analysis impossible because of the lack of degrees of freedom. An alternative approach is to examine the correlation coefficients between the different policy areas and performance. This type of analysis identifies a number of important areas. Some of the correlations might be spurious and, therefore, produce a list of potentially important areas that would be too long to enumerate and inconclusive.

The use of bilateral correlation coefficients also makes the size of the coefficient difficult to interpret. A higher coefficient for one policy area in relation to another does not necessarily imply a higher importance of that particular policy, as the interaction of the policy areas is not taken into account. Consequently, the analysis only focuses on whether or not a policy area is significantly correlated with performance and not on the size of the correlation coefficient.

The correlation between performance and a policy indicator depends on the weights assigned to each indicator in each policy area. Instead of assuming a given weighting

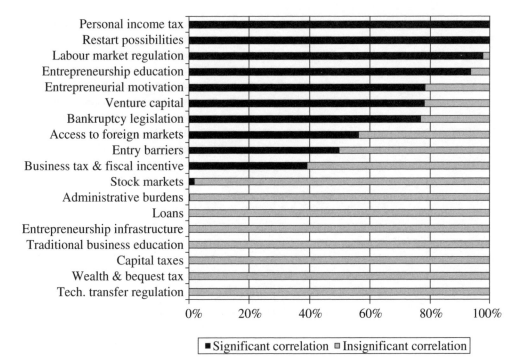

■ Significant correlation ▫ Insignificant correlation

Note: The figure shows the share of times that the correlation between a given policy area and performance was significantly different from zero at the 5 per cent level. The weights for the underlying indicators were allowed to vary between zero and one.

Figure 8.8   The share of outcome with significant and insignificant correlation with performance

scheme, this analysis is based on a Monte Carlo Simulation, where weights are allowed to vary between 0 and 1 for each indicator. The simulation was then repeated 10 000 times. This calculation shows a very stable result for 12 areas (Figure 8.8).

Four areas (*restart possibilities, personal income tax, labour market regulation* and *entrepreneurship education*) are significantly correlated with the performance indicators in more than 95 per cent of the simulations. This implies that weights do not play a role in the correlation. Regardless of weights these areas are positively correlated with performance.

Eight areas (*technology transfer, wealth and bequest tax, capital taxes, traditional business education, entrepreneurship infrastructure (public), loans, administrative burdens* and *stock markets*) are always insignificantly correlated with performance regardless of weight used. The six remaining areas remain more or less undetermined.

Using benchmarking techniques to determine relative importance
The performance indicators highlighted the United States, Canada and Korea as top performing countries. Highly prioritized policy areas in these three top performing countries could potentially be more important for performance than others.

A simple analysis shows that top performing countries tend to prioritize *entrepreneurship education, labour market regulation, personal income tax, venture capital, wealth and*

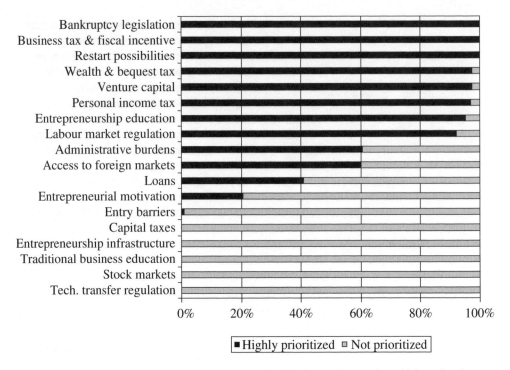

Note: The figure shows the share of random outcomes where a given policy area has a higher value than the average of all policy areas in the top three countries. The argument is that a higher value than average value indicates that the top three countries prioritize that specific policy area.

Figure 8.9   The share of outcome where the top three countries give high priority to a policy area

bequest tax, *restart possibilities*, *business tax and fiscal incentive* and *bankruptcy legisla-tion*, which have a value significantly above average in the concerned policy areas. These policy areas have a higher value in the top three countries than the average of all policy areas in these countries. This conclusion depends again on the weight assigned to each indictor, so a Monte Carlo Simulation has been applied (Figure 8.9).

How do the identified policies affect entrepreneurship?
The four areas that were significantly correlated with performance were also highly pri-oritized in the top performing countries. This suggests that these four areas (*restart pos-sibilities*, *personal income tax*, *labour market regulation* and *entrepreneurship education*) are crucial for entrepreneurship performance. Two additional areas (*venture capital* and *bankruptcy legislation*) were significantly correlated in more than 75 per cent of the out-comes and were highly prioritized in the top performing countries. Consequently, these two areas are also included as being important for entrepreneurship performance.

This section looks at how bankruptcy and restart possibilities affect entrepreneurship performance by briefly reviewing what other studies have concluded in these policy areas. Similar reviews are done for the other areas, but are not reported here to limit the length of the chapter (the reviews are available in EBST, 2005). Bankruptcy and restart possibilities are chosen because these areas are relatively new in the context of entrepreneurship policy and, significantly, several countries are currently reviewing their bankruptcy legislation.

Changes in *bankruptcy legislation* and *restart possibilities* affect entrepreneurship in two ways. First, changes can increase or decrease the risk attached to failure, which directly affects incentives to start and grow new firms. Second, changes can affect the possibility of people restarting after a failure. Often, the second effect is given a lot of emphasis as perceptions of bankruptcy are affected by the anecdotal evidence from the United States where previous failures supposedly are seen as a measure of success. Lee et al. (2000, p. 5) observed that in Silicon Valley 'there are many examples of entrepreneurs who have failed and successfully started over. These entrepreneurs (and their financiers) usually view failure as a learning experience, and they are rarely punished for it in their subsequent adventures.' Others have a similar argument (Landier, 2004; Lewis et al., 1984). However, only a limited number of studies support the claim that people perform better the second time (BCG, 2002).

However, bankruptcy legislation is also about tradeoffs. On the one hand, creditors' interests need to be protected, leading to, for example, a certain length of time for which creditors can lay claims on a bankrupt's assets. On the other hand, an entrepreneur's willingness to take chances and start a new business may be negatively affected by this time period. This tradeoff can be shown empirically. For example, in the United States the entrepreneur must surrender assets above a fixed bankruptcy exemption level for repayment to creditors, but future earnings are entirely exempt. Each US state sets its own exemption levels and the levels vary significantly from state to state. An econometric study shows the probability of a typical non-corporate firm being turned down for credit in the United States. This rate was 40 per cent higher in states with high exemptions as compared to states with low exemptions. For corporate firms, the rejection rate was 30 per cent higher (Berkowitz and White, 2000). Another study shows that the predicted probability of owning a business is 35 per cent higher for homeowners in states with high exemptions as compared to states with low exemptions. Renter households in states with high exemptions were 29 per cent more likely to own a business as compared to renters in low exemption states (Fan and White, 2000).

The time period for which a creditor can lay claims on assets varies across countries, from one year in the United States to a lifetime in Switzerland. Reducing the time too much may create problems. Bankruptcy filings in the United States have risen from fewer than 300 000 in 1984 to 1.5 million in 2001, partly because the bankruptcy system makes defaulting on consumer debt an attractive option for many borrowers (US Bankruptcy Institute, 2002). About 5 per cent of consumer loans are never repaid. This can lead to higher interest rates for other borrowers, which in some respects can be seen as a tax on borrowers who repay their debts. The average borrower in the United States pays about $500 a year in extra charges to cover lenders' losses (White, 1999). The United States is consequently changing the law relating to personal bankruptcy.

The actual time it takes to officially close a firm also plays an important role in determining the possibility for restarting another business. This period varies substantially among countries from less than half a year in Ireland to well over three years in Denmark (World Bank, 2005). Several policy options exist in order to reduce this time, including fast track procedures for estates without assets, specialized courts and strict deadlines for solicitors dealing with bankruptcy cases.

How countries can apply the analysis

The policy framework and the selected indicators provide a structure for country specific analyses. Countries can, based on these indicators, compare their business environments to those of the top performing countries and then use the previous section on relative importance to prioritize their policy actions. The current section focuses on Germany; however, this example should only be seen as an illustration of the potential of this proposed framework and not a full analysis. An analysis of the Danish business environment for entrepreneurship based on this approach took over 100 pages to fully complete (EBST, 2005).

Germany is lacking in both dimensions of entrepreneurship performance: both the start-up rates and the share of new firms with high growth are low. An analysis of their business environment also shows deep-seated problems. Germany is only among the top performing countries with respect to five out of the 18 policy areas that can be quantified. Furthermore, out of these five areas, four are low priorities for the top performing countries.

Germany lags behind the top three countries (Canada, the US, Korea) on all six policy areas that were found to be significant for performance (Table 8.2).

Germany needs to improve almost all aspects of its business environment for entrepreneurs, but most importantly, it must improve in the following policy areas: *venture capital, restart possibilities, bankruptcy legislation, entrepreneurship education, personal income tax* and *labour market regulation.*

Again, a note of caution should be added. Germany will have to figure out how to improve in these areas based on the functioning of its economy. Germany can get inspiration from top-performing countries, but the initiatives have to be tailored for the German context.

Table 8.2   Benchmarking Germany's business environment with the top performing countries

	Not significantly correlated with performance indicators	Significantly correlated with performance indicators
High priority in top three countries	*Business tax and fiscal incentive* *Administrative burdens* Wealth and bequest tax *Access to foreign markets*	*Venture capital* *Restart possibilities* *Bankruptcy legislation* *Entrepreneurship education* *Personal income tax* *Labour market regulation*
Low priority in top three countries	*Exit markets* *Capital taxes* *Traditional business education* Entrepreneurship infrastructure Loans Tech. transfer	*Entrepreneurial motivation* Entry barriers/deregulation

Note: Policy areas are shown *italics* if the value for Germany is more than 10 per cent lower than the value for that particular policy area when compared to the top three countries.

Conclusion

This chapter's objective was to provide policy makers and other interested readers a quick overview of what policy areas should be part of a country's entrepreneurship policy and some ideas on each policy area's relative importance. Three main points were put forward in the chapter.

First, it was emphasized that policies must always be designed to match the set of macroeconomic policy objectives. The focus of this analysis was productivity growth. Entrepreneurship was consequently defined as the entry and creation of high-growth firms, as past analyses show direct links between these two parts of the entrepreneurial process and productivity growth.

Second, the analysis suggested that *restart possibilities, personal income tax, labour market regulation, entrepreneurship education, venture capital* and *bankruptcy legislation* could potentially be the most important policy areas for stimulating entrepreneurship performance. The analysis was based on a cross-country analysis of performance and business environment indicators. Other studies support the importance of these six policy areas.

Finally, countries can use the analysis by benchmarking their business environment to that of the top-performing countries. This will give them an overview of those parts of their business environment that need to be improved. More importantly, they can combine the benchmarking analysis with the analysis of relative importance of the policy areas. This will provide countries with a prioritized list of policy areas in which they lag behind compared to top-performing countries.

The prioritized list of policy areas that are essential to increasing productivity through entrepreneurship is based on a comparative analysis. This analysis has some weaknesses. The main problem is a lack of time series for the applied indicators, which makes causal tests difficult. The only solution to this problem is a yearly update of the analysis. Over the years a stable pattern is likely to emerge. Missing values for many countries are also a problem. Only 18 OECD countries are included in the analysis because there were too many missing values for the other countries. Much work is needed to improve the availability of data in order to improve the quality of the analysis. A continual update of the indicators will also allow for more concrete tests of the relative importance of these selected policy areas, which in turn will allow for multiple regression analysis.

Despite the obvious limitations of the approach presented in this chapter, no real alternative exists for policy makers advising politicians on what to do about entrepreneurship in their country. Therefore, this chapter gives a first hand illustration on the effectiveness of this policy analysis tool, which can be introduced to support fact-based reforms of entrepreneurship policy. The analysis of Germany clearly showed that some countries are lagging far behind when it comes to fostering a business environment that supports entrepreneurship. Using the framework presented will give these countries a guide on where to start on their journey into the land of entrepreneurship policy.

Notes

1. This chapter builds on work I have carried out during my time at the OECD and on work I am currently undertaking for the Danish Government. I am grateful to the many people who have helped me to get a better understanding of their country's approach to entrepreneurship policy and also for the help and useful comments I have received from my colleagues in FORA. I have also benefited from comments from the brilliant editors of this book.
2. The sensitivity analysis is available on request from the author (ah@ebst.dk).

References

Acs, Z. (2005), 'A formulation of entrepreneurship policy', *The FSF-Nutek Award Winning Series*, 2005.

Aldrich, H. (2000), 'Learning together: national differences in entrepreneurship research', in D. Sexton and H. Landström (eds), *The Blackwell Handbook of Entrepreneurship*, Oxford: Blackwell Business.

Audretsch, D. and R. Thurik (2000), 'Linking entrepreneurship to growth', paper prepared for the OECD Directorate for Science, Technology and Industry.

Audretsch, D.B., R. Thurik, I. Verheulm and S. Wennekers (eds), *2002 Entrepreneurship: Determinants and Policy in a European–U.S. Comparison*, Boston/Dordrecht/London: Kluwer Academic Publishers, pp. 11–83.

Baldwin, J., D. Beckstead and A. Girard (2002), 'The importance of entry to Canadian manufacturing with an appendix on measurement issues', OECD Working Paper.

Barclays (2001), *Barclays Small Business Survey*, London: Barclays Bank.

BCG (2002), *A Report on Entrepreneurial Restarters, Setting the Phoenix Free*, Germany: Boston Consulting Group.

Berkowitz, J. and M. White (2000), 'Bankruptcy and small firms' access to credit', Working Paper, University of California, San Diego.

Birch, D.L. (1987), *Job Creation in America: How Our Smallest Companies Put the Most People to Work*, New York: Free Press.

Brandt, N. (2004a), 'Business dynamics, regulation and performance', STI Working Paper, OECD, Paris.

Brandt, N. (2004b), 'Business dynamics in Europe', STI Working Paper, OECD, Paris.

Charney, A. and G.D. Libecap (2001), *Impact of Entrepreneurship Education*, Insights Kauffman Research Series, Kansas City, MO: Kauffman Foundation.

Danish Government Platform (2005), *New Goals, Government Platform 2005*, Danish Prime Minister's Office, available at http://www.stm.dk/publikationer/UK_reggrund05/index.htm.

Davidsson, P. (1989), 'Entrepreneurship – and after? A study of growth in small firms', *Journal of Business Venturing*, **4**, 211–26.

Davidsson, P. (2006), 'Nascent entrepreneurship', *Foundations and Trends in Entrepreneurship*, **2** (1), 1–79.

Delmar, F., P. Davidson and W. Gartner (2003), 'Arriving at the high-growth firm', *Journal of Business Venturing*, **18**, 189–216.

Desai, M., P. Gompers and J. Lerner (2003), 'Institutions, capital constraints and entrepreneurial firms' dynamic: evidence from Europe', NBER Working Paper 10165.

EBST (2005), *Entrepreneurship Index 2005*, Copenhagen: National Agency for Enterprise and Construction.

EU (2003), *Entrepreneurship: A Survey of the Literature*, prepared for the European Commission, Enterprise Directorate General by D.B. Audretsch, available at http://europa.eu.int/comm/enterprise/entrepreneurship/green_paper/literature_survey_2002.pdf

Eurobarometer (2004), *Entrepreneurship*, Brussels, European Commission, available at http://europa.eu.int/comm/public_opinion/flash/fl160_en.pdf

Eurostat (2003), *Business Demography in Europe, Results for 10 Member States and Norway*, Luxembourg: European Commission.

Fan, W. and M. White (2001), 'Personal bankruptcy and the level of entrepreneurial activity', Working Paper, Department of Economics, University of Michigan.

Gabr, H. and A. Hoffmann (2006), 'A general policy framework for entrepreneurship', FORA Working Paper, available at www.foranet.dk.

Gavron, R., M.H. Cowling and A. Westhall (1998), *The Entrepreneurial Society*, IPPR, London: Central Books.

GEM (2001), *Global Entrepreneurship Monitor*. (P.D. Reynolds, S.M. Camp, W.D. Bygrave, E. Autio and M. Hay (eds)), Babson Park, MA: Babson College, London: London Business School, Kansas City, MO: Kauffman Foundation.

GEM (2004), *GEM 2004 Global Report* (Z.J. Acs, P. Arenius, M. Hay and M. Minniti (eds)), Babson Park, MA: Babson College, London: London Business School, Kansas City, MO: Kauffman Foundation.

Giovannini, E., A. Hoffmann, M. Nardo, M. Saisana, A. Saltelli and S. Tarantola (2005), 'Handbook on Constructing Composite Indicators: Methodology and User Guide', OECD Working Paper, Paris.

Hart, D.M. (ed.) (2003), *The Emergence of Entrepreneurship Policy – Governance, Start-ups, and Growth in the U.S. Knowledge Economy*, Cambridge: Cambridge University Press.

Hoffmann, A. and M. Junge (2006a), 'Comparing the number of high-growth entrepreneurs across 17 countries', FORA Working Paper forthcoming at www.foranet.dk, Copenhagen.

Hoffmann, A. and M. Junge (2006b), 'Documenting data on high-growth firms and entrepreneurs across 17 countries', FORA Working Paper, available at www.foranet.dk.

Junge, M. and U. Kaiser (2004), 'Benchmarking of small and medium size firms for twenty selected countries – construction of growth indicators', EBST and FORA Working Paper available at www.foranet.dk

Kauffman (2003), *Panel Study of Entrepreneurial Dynamics*, Kansas City, MO: Kauffman Foundation.

Landier, A. (2004), *Entrepreneurship and the Stigma of Failure*, New York: New York University Press.

Lee, C.-M., W.F. Miller, M.C. Hancock and H.S. Rowen (2000), *The Silicon Valley Edge. A Habitat for Innovation and Entrepreneurship*, Stanford, CA: Stanford University Press.

Lewis, J., A. Gibb and J. Stanworth (1984), *Success and Failure in Small Business*, Aldershot: Gower.

Lucas, R.E. (1978), 'On the size distribution of business firms', *Bell Journal of Economics*, **9**, 508–23.

Lundström, A. and L. Stevenson (2002), *On the Road to Entrepreneurship Policy*, Stockholm: Swedish Foundation for Small Business Research.

Lundström, A. and L. Stevenson (2005), *Entrepreneurship Policy – Theory and Practices*, ISEN International Studies in Entrepreneurship, New York: Springer.

National Commission on Entrepreneurship (NCOE) (2001), *High-growth Companies: Mapping America's Entre-preneurial Landscape*, Washington, DC: The Public Forum Institute, available at www.publicforuminstitute.org/nde/sources/reports/2001-high-growth.pdf.

OECD (1998), *The OECD Jobs Strategy Fostering Entrepreneurship*, Paris: OECD.

OECD (2001), *Science, Technology and Industry Outlook – Drivers of Growth: Information Technology, Innovation and Entrepreneurship*, Paris: OECD.

OECD (2002), *High-growth SMEs and Employment*, Paris: OECD.

OECD (2003a), *The Sources of Economic Growth in OECD Countries*, Paris: OECD.

OECD (2003b), *Entrepreneurship and Local Economic Development Programme and Policy Recommendations*, Paris: OECD.

OECD (2003c), *Quality Framework and Guidelines for OECD Statistical Activities, Version 2003/1*, Organization for Economic Co-operation and Development, Statistics Directorate, STD/QFS(2003)1, Paris: OECD.

OECD (2004), 'Promoting entrepreneurship and innovative SMEs in a global economy', background report to the 2nd OECD Conference of Ministers Responsible for Small and Medium-sized Enterprises (SMEs) Istanbul, Turkey, 3–5 June 2004.

OECD (2005a), *Micro-policies for Growth and Productivity*, available at www.oecd.org/sti/micro-policies.

OECD (2005b), *SME Outlook*, Paris: OECD.

Parker, S. (2005), 'The economics of entrepreneurship', *Foundations and Trends in Entrepreneurship*, **1**, 1–55.

Reynolds, P.D., M. Hay and M. Camp (1999), *Global Entreprenurship Monitor, Executive Report*, Kansas City, MO: Kauffman Center for Entrepreneurship Leadership.

Reynolds, P., D.J. Storey and P. Westhead (1994), 'Cross-national comparisons of the variation in new firm formation rates', *Regional Studies*, **28** (4), 443–56.

Reynolds, P., N. Bosma, E. Autio, S. Hunt, N. de Bono, I. Servais, P. Lopez-Garcia and N. Chin (2005), 'Global Entrepreneurship Monitor: data collection design and implementation', 1998–2003', *Small Business Economics*, **24** (3), 205–31.

SBS (2001), *Household Survey of Entrepreneurship*, London: Small Business Service.

Scarpetta, S., P. Hemmings, T. Tressel and J. Woo (2002), 'The role of policy and institutions for productivity and firm dynamics: Evidence from micro and industry data', OECD Economics Working Papers, Paris.

Smilor, R. (2001), *Daring Visionaries*, Holbrook, MA: Adams Media Corporation.

Stevenson, L. and A. Lundström (2001), 'Patterns and trends in entrepreneurship/SME policy and practice in ten economies', *The Entrepreneurship Policy for the Future Series*, Vol. 3, Stockholm: Swedish Foundation for Small Business Research.

Storey, D.J. (2002), 'Methods of evaluating the impact of public policies to support small businesses: the six steps to heaven', *International Journal of Entrepreneurship Education*, **1**, 181–202.

Storey, D.J. (2003), 'Entrepreneurship, small and medium sized enterprises and public policy', in Z.J. Acs and D.B. Audretsch (eds), *International Handbook of Entrepreneurship Research*, Dordrecht: Kluwer Academic.

US Bankruptcy Institute (2002), *US Bankruptcy Fillings Statistics*, available at http://www.abiworld.org/stats/newstatsfront.html

Wennekers, S. and R. Thurik (1999), 'Linking entrepreneurship and economic growth', *Small Business Economics*, **13**, 27–55.

White, M. (1998), 'Why it pays to file for bankruptcy: a critical look at incentives under US bankruptcy laws and a proposal for change', *University of Chicago Law Review*, **65** (3), Summer, 685–732.

White, M. (1999), 'What's Wrong with Personal Bankruptcy Law and How to Fix It', *Regulation*, **22** (3), Fall, available at http://www.cato.org/pubs/regulation/regv22n3/reg 22n3.html.

Wood, P.M. and A. Bandura (1989), 'Goal setting and monetary incentives: Motivational tools that can work too well', *Compensation and Benefits Review*, May–June, 41–9.

World Bank (2005), *Doing Business, The International Bank for Reconstruction and Development*, Washington, DC: The World Bank.

Appendix 8.1: Data description

Table 8A.1   Overview of the data

Policy area	Indicator	Source	Internet link
Tech-transfer regulation			
	University/industry research collaboration	WEF, The Global Competitiveness Report, 2004	n.a.
	Technological cooperation	IMD, World Competitiveness Yearbook, 2004	n.a.
Entry barriers			
	Barriers to competition – OECD index	OECD, Summary indicators of product market regulation, pp. 25 and 75	http://www.olis.oecd.org/olis/ 1999doc.nsf/c16431e1b3f24c 0ac12569fa005d1d99/5ef586bbe 13dd52ac125684a003a8da0/ $FILE/00075836.PDF
	Public ownership – OECD index	Same	Same
	Public involvement in business operation	Same	Same
Access to foreign markets			
	Share of new enterprises with exports	FORA	n.a.
	Access to capital markets	IMD, World Competitiveness Yearbook, 2004	n.a.
	Export credits and insurance	Same	n.a.
Loans			
	Extent of guarantees	EU Commission, p. 38	http://europa.eu.int/comm/ enterprise/enterprise_policy/ analysis/doc/smes_observatory_ 2003_report2_en.pdf
	Private credit	The World Bank, Doing Business	http://rru.worldbank.org/ DoingBusiness/ExploreTopics/
	Interest rate spread	Same	Same
	Cost to create collateral	Same	Same
	Legal rights index	Same	Same
	Country credit rating	IMD, World Competitiveness Yearbook, 2004	Same
Venture capital			
	Venture capital (early stage)	OECD, Science, technology and industry. Venture capital: trends and policy recommendations, p. 7	http://www.oecd.org/dataoecd/ 4/11/28881195.pdf
	Venture capital (expansion stage)	Same	Same

Table 8A.1   (continued)

Policy area	Indicator	Source	Internet link
Exit			
	Capitalization of secondary stock markets	OECD, Science, technology and industry. Venture capital: trends and policy recommendations, p. 25	http://www.oecd.org/dataoecd/ 4/11/28881195.pdf
	Market capitalization of newly listed companies relative to GDP	World Federation of Exchanges, Annual report and statistics, 2004	http://www.world-exchanges.org/publications/ WFE%202004%20Annual%20 Report%20and%20Statistics.pdf
	Capitalization of primary stock market	The World Bank	http://www.worldbank.org/ research/projects/finstructure/ structure_database.xls
	Turnover in primary stock market	The World Bank	Same
	Buyouts	OECD, Science, technology and industry. Venture capital: trends and policy recommendations, p. 7	http://www.oecd.org/dataoecd /4/11/28881195.pdf
Wealth and bequest tax			
	Revenue from bequest tax	OECD, 2003, Revenue Statistics	n.a.
	Revenue from net wealth tax	OECD, 2003, Revenue Statistics	n.a.
	Top marginal bequest tax rate	OECD, Directorate for science, technology and industry, Industry issues taxation, SMEs and entrepreneurship	http://www.olis.oecd.org/olis/ 2002doc.nsf/43bb6 130e5e86e5fc12569fa005d004c /2137ebc4eaa738a5c1256c10004e 37ec/$FILE/JT00130282.PDF
Capital taxes			
	Taxation of dividends – top marginal tax rate	OECD, Taxation of SMEs and entrepreneurship	http://www.olis.oecd.org/ olis/2002doc.nsf/43bb6 130e5e86e5fc12569fa005d00 4c/2137ebc4eaa738a5c1256c 10004e37ec/$FILE/JT00130282. PDF
	Taxation of dividends – top marginal tax rate for the self-employed	Same	Same
	Taxation of stock options	Eurostat, Competitiveness and benchmarking enterprise policy results from the 2002 scoreboard	http://europa.eu.int/comm/ enterprise/enterprise_policy/ better_environment /doc/ enterprise_policy_scoreboard _2002_en.pdf

Table 8A.1   (continued)

Policy area	Indicator	Source	Internet link
	Taxation of capital gains on shares – short term	OECD, Taxation of SMEs and entrepreneurship	http://www.olis.oecd.org/ olis/2002doc.nsf/43bb6 130e5e86e5fc12569fa005d004c /2137ebc4eaa73 8a5c1256c10004e37ec/$FILE /JT00130282.PDF
	Taxation of capital gains on shares – long term	Same	Same
Restart possibilities			
	Length of time that creditors still have claims on a bankrupt's assets	OECD, Science, technology and industry outlook. Drivers of growth: Information technology, innovation and entrepreneurship	http://www1.oecd.org/ publications/e-book/ 9201131e.pdf
Entrepreneurship education			
	Entrepreneurship education at primary education	Global Entrepreneurship Monitor	Schøtt, Thomas (2005), 'Undervisning i iværksætteri i Danmark og andre lande', http://www.sam.sdu.dk/~tsc/ CESFOundervisning1.doc
	Entrepreneurship education at higher education	Same	Same
Traditional business education			
	Quality of management schools	WEF: The global competitiveness report	–
Entrepreneurship infrastructure			
	Government programmes	Global Entrepreneurship Monitor	http://www.gemconsortium.org/
Personal income tax			
	Highest marginal income tax plus social contributions	OECD, Taxing Wages 2001–2002	http://emlab.berkeley.edu/users/ webfac/saez/e230b_s04/ OECD01_02taxing wages.pdf
	Average income tax plus social contributions	Same	Same
Business tax and fiscal incentive			
	SME tax rates	OECD, Directorate for science, technology and industry, Industry issues taxation, SMEs and entrepreneurship	http://www.olis.oecd.org/olis /2002doc.nsf/43bb6 130e5e86e5fc12569fa005d004c /2137ebc4eaa738a5c1256c10004e 37ec/$FILE/JT00130282.PDF
	Taxation of corporate income revenue	OECD 2003, Revenue Statistics 1965–2002	–

Table 8A.1 (continued)

Policy area	Indicator	Source	Internet link
Bankruptcy legislation			
	Actual cost to close a business	The World Bank, Doing Business	http://rru.worldbank.org/Doing Business/ExploreTopics/Closing Business/CompareAll.aspx
	Actual time to close a business	Same	Same
Administrative burdens			
	Starting a business – number of procedures	The World Bank, Doing Business	http://rru.worldbank.org/Doing Business/ExploreTopics/Starting Business/CompareAll.aspx
	Starting a business – number of days	Same	Same
	Starting a business – cost	Same	Same
	Regulatory and administrative opacity	OECD, Summary indicators of product market regulation, pp. 25 and 75	http://www.olis.oecd.org/olis/ 1999doc.nsf/c1643 1e1b3f24c0ac12569fa005 d1d99/5ef586bbe13dd 52ac125684a003a8da0/$FILE /00075836.PDF
	Enforcing contracts – number of procedures	The World Bank, Doing Business	http://rru.worldbank.org/ DoingBusiness/ExploreTopics/ EnforcingContracts/ CompareAll.aspx
	Enforcing contracts – time	Same	Same
	Enforcing contracts – procedure complexity	Same	Same
	Starting a business – minimum of capital required	Same	http://rru.worldbank.org/Doing Business/Explore Topics/StartingBusiness/ CompareAll.aspx
	Enforcing contracts – cost (% of debts)	Same	http://rru.worldbank.org/Doing Business/ExploreTopics/ EnforcingContracts/Compare All.aspx
Labour market regulation			
	Flexibility of hiring	The World Bank, Doing Business	http://rru.worldbank.org/Doing Business/ExploreTopics/Hiring FiringWorkers/Compare All.aspx
	Flexibility of firing	Same	Same
	Rigidity of hours	Same	Same

Table 8A.1   (continued)

Policy area	Indicator	Source	Internet link
	Number of administrative procedures when recruiting first employee	EU (2002), Benchmarking enterprise policy – Results from the 2002 scoreboard, p. 32	http://europa.eu.int/comm/ enterprise/enterprise_policy/ better_environment/doc/ enterprise_policy_scoreboard_ 2002_en.pdf
	Number of administrative procedures when recruiting additional employee	Same	Same
	Firing costs	The World Bank, Doing Business	http://rru.worldbank.org/Doing Business/Explore Topics/Hiring FiringWorkers/Compare All.aspx
Entrepreneurial motivation			
	Cultural and social norms	Global Entrepreneurship Monitor	Schøtt, Thomas (2005), 'Iværksætterkulturen i Danmark og andre lande', http://www.sam.sdu.dk/~tsc/ CESFOkultur1.doc
	Entrepreneurial motivation	Same	Same
	Self-employment preferences	Eurobarometer	http://europa.eu.int/comm/ public_opinion/flash/f l160_en.pdf
	The wish to own one's own business	Same	Same
	Desirability of becoming self-employed	Same	Same
	Risk	Same	Same

Appendix 8.2: Description of the 24 policy areas

Policy areas affecting opportunities

Entry barriers/deregulation   Minimizing government activities and regulation in existing markets creates new business opportunities within established markets, thereby creating a larger demand for potential entrepreneurs while at the same time improving market dynamics. Rolling back government activities (such as the liberalization of the telecommunication sector in several European countries in the 1990s) or by deregulating the legal barriers (such as relaxing the educational requirements for starting a business in certain sectors) are two ways to improve access to existing markets.

Access to foreign markets   Globalization has opened up increased international opportunities for entrepreneurs. The disappearance of trade barriers and the integration of world markets have made it possible for all types of companies – including new ones – to exploit global opportunities. Even though trade barriers are decreasing as a result of efforts from international organizations and as such are out of the hands of national governments to some extent, national governments can still initiate globalization programmes helping or motivating entrepreneurs to look abroad from the very birth of new firms.

Technology transfer   Effective technology or knowledge transfer regulation opens up and speeds up the process of transferring public research into business, thereby effectively creating new opportunities for potential entrepreneurs. Technology and knowledge transfer regulation can be enhanced by policies encouraging universities (and other institutions engaged in research and development activities) to facilitate the development of ventures based on public funded research. Most important legislation needs to develop the legal infrastructure that gives universities the ownership of intellectual property developed from public funded research as well as the establishment of technology transfer offices that facilitate joint ventures between companies and universities.

Private demand conditions   The willingness of established firms to use new firms as suppliers or partners plays a crucial role in the development of entrepreneurship. For example, the success of Silicon Valley compared to the Boston Route 128 area in the early 1990s has been explained by a much more open attitude to cooperation in Silicon Valley. Policies have only a limited impact on private demand but the public can be a role model in their procurement.

Procurement regulation   Entrepreneurship-friendly procurement regulation increases the number of government contracts for goods and services awarded to new companies, thereby effectively creating better opportunities for potential entrepreneurs. Procurement regulation in the widest sense – including competitive tendering schemes focusing on the purchase of goods, services or science with a potential commercial value – can be made entrepreneurship-friendly by policies encouraging governmental bodies to allocate a specific share of their purchasing to new companies.

Policy areas affecting capital

Loans   Supply of debt capital via more traditional credit markets is vital to entrepreneurial activity. Without a large and efficient credit market to supply firms with efficient debt capital, some entrepreneurs will face a financial barrier making it impossible to seize opportunities. Governments can improve domestic credit markets through initiatives to improve access to debt capital in general or to entrepreneurs specifically. The former includes regulation improving the efficiency and competitiveness in credit markets by making debt capital cheaper and more accessible. The latter includes fiscal guarantees for entrepreneurial loans, making banks more motivated to help entrepreneurs.

Wealth and bequest taxation   Wealth and bequest taxes impact the supply of early stage investment capital directly. High taxation levels negatively affect the potential supply of liquidity among individuals, which then limits the number and size of investments made by business angels, friends or family. Policy initiatives reducing the wealth and bequest tax rates would enlarge the potential amount of seed and early-stage capital.

Business angels   Business angels are typically wealthy individuals who make direct equity investments in the seed stage of companies, and they tend to provide more managerial and business advice through their greater personal involvement than institutional investors do. Although data are scarce, it is believed that total funding by business angels is several times greater than all other forms of private equity finance. Governments in many countries try to cultivate business angels by organizing networks and giving special investment tax incentives. Several countries have also tried to improve information flows between angels and potential entrepreneurs, which otherwise tend to be informal.

Venture capital   Venture capital is an important source of funding for potential high-growth ventures in need of significant capital for development, growth and expansion. In order to enlarge the domestic supply of venture capital, governments can either take initiatives to develop national venture funds or improve venture market regulation to grow existing venture markets. The former includes direct investments and the latter includes relaxing legislation, making it more attractive (or simply possible) for entities, such as pension and insurance funds, to make venture investments.

Capital taxes   Capital taxes also have a direct impact on the supply of capital. High taxation levels reduce potential investment rewards thereby discouraging investments in companies whether new or old. Policy initiatives reducing capital taxation thus increase financial sources. Some countries also offer special tax incentives for investments in new firms intended to improve the number of business angels.

Stock markets and buyouts   An efficient stock market, secondary stock market or efficient markets for buyouts are important in order to gather the necessary capital for expansion of firms. Most countries face the problem of obtaining a critical mass of new firms for a secondary stock market. Development of critical mass must balance two interests.

On one hand listing requirements and regulations must be simple enough to encourage small businesses to make their initial public offerings through a secondary market. On the other hand there must be sufficient disclosure, supervision and enforcement to protect and attract investors.

Policies affecting abilities

Traditional business education   Traditional business education, including basic accounting, marketing and finance, are – needless to say – important abilities not only to run a company, but also to start a company. Differences in the magnitude of business education among developed countries are significant. Some countries include basic business education in the core curriculum in both primary and secondary schools, whereas in other countries it is available only through electives or dedicated business schools. The former approach obviously ensures that a greater share of the population possess the basic business skills needed to run a company. Policy initiatives could ensure that basic business skills are acquired over a broad range of education levels.

Entrepreneurship education   In order to strengthen entrepreneurial abilities through education, teaching methods must be refined from primary schools through universities. Activities that go beyond traditional teaching, such as dedicated entrepreneurship centres, internships, teacher and advisor education, and research, are necessary for success. Policy initiatives should ensure the supply and quality of entrepreneurship education.

Restart possibilities   Serial entrepreneurs are important as they have already proven their ability to establish a business. Yet failed entrepreneurs are not always able to restart because of legislative barriers. The learning experience from the failure itself is debatable. The possible lessons from failure versus the lessons from success are more a philosophical question, but it is unquestionable that barriers to restarters reduce the potential number of entrepreneurs. The policy focus is consequently on reducing the legislative barriers for serial entrepreneurship. Bankruptcy legislation is particularly important but also time and price barriers for restarting a company exist in some countries.

Entrepreneurship infrastructure (public and private)   A strong entrepreneurship infrastructure consists of tightly interlinked regional networks of skilled and specialized advisors that assist entrepreneurs with relevant skills and knowledge, thereby effectively increasing the abilities available to potential entrepreneurs. Advisors can range from lawyers and accountants to experienced entrepreneurs to domain experts at universities. As such, non-governmental involvement is vital in sustaining entrepreneurial networks. However, governments can take an important role by initiating and developing the infrastructure.

Policies affecting incentives

Personal income taxes   High levels of personal income tax reduce the potential financial benefits of starting a business, making it more difficult to reach the cost/benefit equilibrium at which the opportunity becomes worthwhile pursuing. Policy initiatives lowering income taxes are therefore likely to induce a greater number of potential entrepreneurs to engage in entrepreneurial activities.

Business taxes and fiscal incentives   While corporate taxes do not play a central role for new firms with little or no profit subject to taxation, they will eventually have a significant impact on profits for high-growth firms. Furthermore, as globalization continues to develop, corporate taxation will become a central factor for companies choosing the extent to which they will locate operations abroad. Fiscal incentives can lower entry barriers through financial incentives or support, and tax exemptions or rebates, making more potential entrepreneurs willing to engage in entrepreneurial activity. They are, however, a delicate political issue in some countries, and their long-term benefits continue to be questioned.

Social security discrimination   Social security benefits, including health care, pensions and unemployment benefits, can serve as entry barriers if either reduced or eliminated as a result of becoming an entrepreneur. Social security policies that put entrepreneurs and wage-labourers on an equal footing in terms of qualifying for benefits, can neutralize any discrimination that otherwise could have a negative effect on the number of potential entrepreneurs pursuing opportunities.

Administrative burdens   Administrative burdens comprise the amount of time spent collectively to understand and fulfil requirements imposed by governments or other authorities, such as new business registration, filing taxes and financial statements, and understanding which rules and regulations the business is subject to. They can discourage potential entrepreneurs by being overwhelming and difficult to understand as well as being beyond their own abilities to fulfil. In countries with substantial administrative burdens, studies show that both job creation and employment settle at lower levels as a result. Policy initiatives to relieve administrative burdens include relaxing the legal demands required to start and run a company.

Labour market regulation   The negative impacts of strict labour market regulation, such as high minimum wages and rigid firing regulations, are manifold. First, wage employment becomes attractive, thereby increasing the opportunity cost to become an entrepreneur. Second, limitations such as hiring and firing inflexibility can have severe impacts on a corporation trying to develop a culture – often through trial and error – that fits with the overall vision and strategy. Finally, high minimum wages means expensive labour and possibly a limiting barrier for a start-up. Thus the end result of strict labour legislation is constrained levels of entrepreneurship activity. Policy initiatives relaxing labour market regulation include initiatives making it easier to hire and fire personnel as well as lowering the minimum wage level.

Bankruptcy legislation   Bankruptcy legislation needs to balance the conflicting risk propensities of creditors and entrepreneurs. Creditors will not provide as much money to entrepreneurial activities if they do not have significant claims on a bankrupt's assets. On the other hand potential entrepreneurs are less apt to engage in entrepreneurial activity if significant claims are inevitable. The equilibrium at which the maximum number of potential entrepreneurs obtains debt capital to engage in entrepreneurial activities is difficult to both identify and measure, but it is clear that bankruptcy legislation has a strong influence. Governments have a variety of means to relieve the costs of bankruptcy, including debt-relief schemes, restructuring and postponement of debt possibilities. Debt-relief schemes can regulate the length, uncertainty and cost of going bankrupt, thereby altering both direct and indirect costs arising as a result of bankruptcy. Reorganization and postponement of debt typically take place prior to bankruptcy, making it possible to alter the business model and as such the risk of going bankrupt.

Policies affecting culture/motivation

Entrepreneurial motivation   Understanding the motivation behind the few entrepreneurs with visions for creating high-growth and global enterprises is difficult. It is furthermore a very challenging and slow process trying to fuel interest in entrepreneurship. Governments can try to enhance a preference for entrepreneurship by implementing entrepreneurship awards and opinion campaigns.

Group-specific initiatives   Awards and opinion campaigns can be targeted towards specific groups such as women or minority groups in order to boost the number of entrepreneurs specifically in those groups.

Communication about heroes   Elaborating on entrepreneurship history, and communication about and by 'heroes' and others, help to create a sense of history. A sense of history is important for the evolution of a cohesive entrepreneurship culture. Policy initiatives could ensure there is communication about entrepreneurship history and 'heroes' in public schools. Policy initiatives could reward 'heroes' for communicating their stories in public. These heroes will act as role models and affect other people's motivation for becoming entrepreneurs.

9 Government programs to encourage innovation by start-ups and SMEs: the role of US innovation awards
Charles W. Wessner[1]

Policy makers in the United States recognize that innovation remains the key to international competitiveness in the twenty-first century. Moreover, policy makers increasingly recognize that equity-financed small firms are an effective means of capitalizing on new ideas and bringing them to the market. Small firms, however, face a variety of obstacles as they seek to bring new products and processes to the market.[2] In this context, public policies that reduce the structural and financial hurdles facing such innovative small firms can play a useful role in enhancing a nation's innovative capacity. In the United States, innovation awards, such as the Small Business Innovation Research program and the Advanced Technology Program, have proven effective in helping small innovative firms overcome these hurdles while also enhancing networking among US universities, large firms, and small innovative companies.

Success in innovation has helped the United States become the world's leading economy. Remaining innovative requires, as Dr Mary Good notes, 'a *strategy* that provides resources to talented people in an atmosphere that promotes creativity – focused on outcomes ranging from new products to customer satisfaction to new scientific insights to improved social programs – to create wealth and/or improve the human condition'.[3] In this information age, continuing economic leadership requires new strategies that adapt to the new realities of globalized research, development and manufacturing.

US assets and challenges in innovation
Competitive advantages enjoyed by the United States include a large and integrated domestic market, and an economic and institutional infrastructure able to quickly redeploy resources to their efficient use. These are buttressed by a strong higher educational infrastructure, deep and flexible capital and labor markets, and strong science and technology institutions. Flexible managerial and organizational structures and a willingness to adopt innovative management practices and products are distinguishing features of the US economy. A major asset is the entrepreneurial culture that accepts failure as a byproduct of new entrepreneurial initiatives and a willingness of investors to provide second opportunities to experienced, if initially unsuccessful, managers. This cultural and business perspective on failure of a startup is buttressed by bankruptcy laws that limit the liability entrepreneurs face during bankruptcy. The combination of these features generates an adaptive and rapidly changing innovation ecosystem that creates many successful small companies and enables some to grow into new large firms.

Some of these competitive advantages are the result of substantial and sustained public investments in education and research and development – many of them dating to policies adopted during the Cold War period. While overall economic prospects in the

United States today remain healthy, many business leaders, senior academics and experienced policy makers in the United States believe that the country is now facing major challenges to its technological leadership. They point, for example, to inadequacies in the education system, especially at the secondary level where US students score below their peers abroad in science and mathematics. These concerns have spawned recent studies that highlight troubling trends in publications, foreign student retention, high-technology exports and the production of information technology products. It is also true that fewer American students are pursuing science careers, and that the United States may be losing some of its attraction as a destination for the best students from around the world.[4]

The role of foreign students in the US innovation system is generating growing concern. While the United States remains the major destination for students from around the world to pursue advanced training and high-skill employment, these individuals are increasingly offered new opportunities at home and elsewhere. A recent study by the National Academies found that as countries such as China and India develop their own public and private research infrastructure, and as multinational companies outsource more of their research and development (R&D) abroad, there are more opportunities for talented scientists and engineers to pursue world-class research in their native countries.[5] Post 9/11 reductions in visas for foreign students may have accelerated this dispersal by making it more difficult for many scholars to stay and work in the United States, a trend deplored in the reports noted above.[6]

With regard to the falloff of American students pursuing careers in science and engineering, this shift may be an unanticipated byproduct of a reduction in R&D funding levels following the end of the Cold War as federal agencies adjusted to new mission priorities. The fall off in R&D funding, documented by the Board on Science, Technology, and Economic Policy of the National Academies, shows that funding for physics, chemistry and engineering suffered significant cutbacks.[7] (See Figure 9.1.) These reductions in funding have arguably prompted fewer students to pursue science and engineering degrees.[8] In any case, the lag effects of these reductions will take years to be fully manifest.

Responding to this and other concerns about the nation's innovation capacity, the United States Congress recently requested the National Academies to assess the nation's competitive situation and identify concrete steps to ensure US economic leadership. The resulting National Academies report, *Rising Above the Gathering Storm*, notes that weakening federal commitments to science and technology places the future growth and prosperity of the United States in jeopardy:

> Although many people assume that the United States will always be a world leader in science and technology, this may not continue to be the case, inasmuch as great minds exist throughout the world. We fear the abruptness with which a lead in science and technology can be lost – and the difficulty of recovering a lead once lost, if indeed it can be regained at all.[9]

To overcome this growing vulnerability, the report calls for, among other measures, increasing America's talent pool by providing greater incentives for science and mathematics teachers. The report also calls for increasing federal investments in long-term basic research by 10 percent per annum over the next seven years. In addition, it recommends a variety of steps to make the United States a more attractive place to study and perform research for foreign students, including actions to increase the number of visas that permit

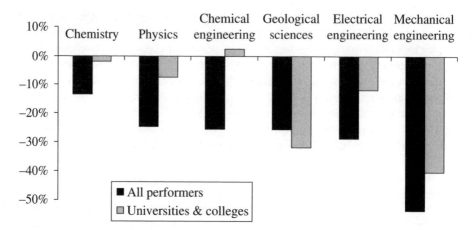

Source: National Research Council (2001), *Trends in Federal Support of Research and Graduate Education*, S. Merrill (ed.), Washington, DC: National Academy Press.

Figure 9.1   Changes in federal research obligations for all performers and university/college performers, FY 1993–FY 1999 (constant 1999 dollars)

US trained foreign students to remain and work in the United States after their studies are completed.[10]

Small innovative businesses are a key source of innovation . . .
Policy makers around the world are increasingly aware that equity-financed small firms are an effective mechanism for capitalizing on new ideas and bringing them to the market.[11] In the United States, small firms are also a leading source of employment growth, generating 60 to 80 percent of net new jobs annually over the past decade. These small businesses also employ nearly 40 percent of the United States' science and engineering workforce.[12] Scientists and engineers working in US small businesses, produce 14 times more patents than their counterparts in comparable large patenting firms – and these patents tend to be of higher quality and are twice as likely to be cited.[13]

In the United States, firms like Microsoft, Intel, AMD, FedEx, Qualcomm and Adobe, all of which grew rapidly in scale from small beginnings, have transformed how people everywhere work, transact and communicate. The resulting growth and social benefits underscore the need to encourage new equity-based high-technology firms in the hope that some may develop into larger, more successful firms that create the technological base for future competitiveness.

. . . Yet small businesses will face major challenges on the road to commercial success
Even so, commonly held myths in the United States about the innovation process pose major obstacles to developing and even maintaining policies that encourage small firms with valuable new ideas to persevere. American policy makers often have strong beliefs in the primacy of the market and a corresponding reluctance to recognize its limitations, despite ample evidence concerning the close interactions between markets and public policy. In the case of early-stage finance, a common American myth, at least among

Washington policy makers, is that 'if it's a good idea, the market will fund it'. In reality there is no such thing as 'The Market'. Unlike the market model found in introductory economics texts, real-world markets always operate within specific rules and conventions that lend unique characteristics to particular markets, and nearly all markets suffer from seriously imperfect information. Indeed, the problem of imperfect capital markets is particularly challenging for fledgling entrepreneurs. The knowledge that an entrepreneur has about his or her product is normally not fully appreciated by potential customers – a phenomenon that economists call *asymmetric information*. This asymmetry can make it hard for small firms to obtain funding for new ideas because, as Michael Spence, a 2001 Nobel Prize winner observed, market noise often obscures the significance of promising new ideas.[14]

Market entry is thus a challenge for new entrepreneurs, especially those with new ideas for a potentially disruptive product. These entrepreneurs tend to be unfamiliar with government regulations and procurement procedures, and academic researchers may be unacquainted with commercial accounting and business practices. Many small firms are therefore at a disadvantage vis-à-vis incumbents in the defense procurement process, and face especially high challenges with regard to market access and finance.[15]

Innovators in large firms also face a similar problem, where multiple options, established hurdle rates for financing new initiatives, and technological and market uncertainties militate against even promising technologies. As Dr Bruce Griffing, the laboratory manager responsible for developing mammography diagnostic technology for General Electric, has noted, 'there is a valley of death for new technologies, even in the largest companies'.[16]

Another hurdle for entrepreneurs is *the leakage of new knowledge* that escapes the boundaries of firms and intellectual property protection. The creator of new knowledge can seldom fully capture the economic value of that knowledge for his or her own firm. This spillover can inhibit investment in promising technologies for large and small firms – though it is especially important for small firms focused on a particularly promising product or process.[17]

The challenge of incomplete and insufficient information for investors and the problem for entrepreneurs of moving quickly enough to capture a sufficient return on 'leaky' investments pose substantial obstacles for new firms seeking private capital. The difficulty of attracting investors to support an imperfectly understood, as yet-to-be-developed innovation is especially daunting. Indeed, the term *Valley of Death* has come to describe the period of transition when a developing technology is deemed promising, but too new to validate its commercial potential and thereby attract the capital necessary for its development.[18] (See Figure 9.2.)

This simple image of the Valley of Death captures two important points. The first is that while there are substantial national R&D investments in the United States and elsewhere, transitioning these investments in research to create valuable products is not self-evident, given the informational and financial constraints noted above. A second, related point is that technological value does not lead inevitably to commercialization. Many good ideas perish on the way to the market. The challenge of policy makers is to help firms create additional, market relevant information by supporting the development of promising ideas through this difficult early phase.

Notwithstanding the reality of these early-stage financing hurdles, many believe that the US venture capital markets are so broad and deep that entrepreneurs can readily

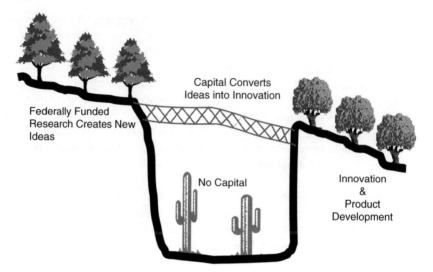

Federally Funded
Research Creates New
Ideas

Capital Converts
Ideas into Innovation

No Capital

Innovation
&
Product
Development

Source: National Research Council (2007), *SBIR and the Phase III Challenge of Commercialization*, Charles W. Wessner (ed.), Washington, DC: The National Academies Press.

Figure 9.2   The Valley of Death

access the capital needed to cross the Valley of Death. In fact, venture capitalists not only have limited information on new firms but are also prone to herding tendencies, as witnessed in the recent dot.com boom and bust.[19] Venture capitalists are also, quite naturally, risk averse. Their primary goal, after all, is not to develop the nation's economy but to earn significant returns for their investors.[20] Accordingly, most funds tend to focus on later stages of technology development because there is more information at this stage in the process about the commercial prospects of the innovation (and hence less risk to their investment). The result is that the US venture capital market, although large, is not focused on early-stage firms: in 2004, startups in the United States received only $346 million or 1.65 percent of the $20.9 billion of available venture capital.

What's more, the amount of venture capital made available varies enormously according to the vigor of the stock market, the normal outlet for Initial Public Offerings – that is, the primary means by which venture capitalists recoup their fund's investments. The collapse of venture capital investment beginning in the second quarter of 2000, for example, followed the dramatic stock market declines of March 2000.[21] Venture funding fell from an unsustainable $94.6 billion in 2000 to $18.9 billion in 2003. Since then, there has been a modest up-tick in funding commitments, with $20.9 billion in funding in 2004, and the figure for 2005 expected to remain in the same neighborhood. First-round funding for new companies remains limited as venture firms continue to invest further downstream where risks are more manageable.

Filling the funding gap
The limitations of the market for venture capital require that small innovative firms seek funding from a variety of sources.[22] In addition to business angels and venture capital firms, early-stage technology firms also seek development funding from industry, federal

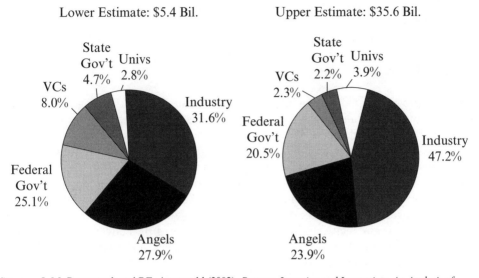

Lower Estimate: $5.4 Bil.   Upper Estimate: $35.6 Bil.

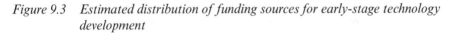

Source: L.M. Branscomb and P.E. Auerswald (2002), *Between Invention and Innovation: An Analysis of Funding for Early-stage Technology Development*, Gaithersburg, MD: National Institute for Standards and Technology.

Figure 9.3   Estimated distribution of funding sources for early-stage technology development

and state governments, and universities. Indeed the diversity of these sources for early-stage funding represents one of the strengths of the US system. There are longstanding state programs such as the Ben Franklin program in Pennsylvania and more recent innovation efforts such as TEDCO in Maryland. Both provide early-stage loans on a limited scale. Surprisingly, among these funding sources the role of the federal government is significant for its size and importance. Research by Branscomb and Auerswald estimates that the federal government provides between 20 and 25 percent of all funding for early-stage technology development – a substantial role by any measure and one often surprising to Americans in its dimensions.[23] (See Figure 9.3.) This federal contribution is rendered more significant in that competitive government awards address segments of the innovation cycle that private institutional investors often (quite rightly) find too risky.

The availability of early-stage financing and its interaction with other elements of the US innovation process are the focus of growing analytical efforts.[24] As we examine below, the Small Business Innovation Research program (SBIR) is the largest example of the government's public–private partnership efforts to draw on the inventiveness of small, high-technology firms though competitive innovation awards. The potential of SBIR in this regard underscores the need to understand how it strengthens the nation's innovation capacity.

The Small Business Innovation Research program (SBIR)

The Small Business Innovation Research program was created in 1982 through the Small Business Innovation Development Act. SBIR was designed to stimulate technological innovation among small private-sector businesses while providing the government with new, cost-effective, technical and scientific solutions to challenging mission problems. SBIR was also designed to provide a role for small businesses in federal R&D and facilitate the development of innovative technologies in the private sector, helping to stimulate the US economy.[25]

The SBIR concept has several significant advantages:

- The program is focused on helping small companies bring their ingenuity to focus on government and societal needs in domains as diverse as health, security, the environment, and energy efficiency and alternative energy sources.
- The needs are articulated by government agencies; the proposals are initiated by individual companies, often new to government R&D programs.
- A two-phase filter is employed with less than 15 percent of applicants being accepted in the first phase and approximately half or less in the second phase.
- The program has no budget line, requires no new funds, and is therefore both politically viable and relatively impervious to the whims of the budget process. This provides the continuity and predictability that encourages small firm participation and, over time, allows for portfolio effects.
- The program is decentralized across the government. Program ownership rests with many agencies quite different in size and with dramatically different missions. The program is not the responsibility of a single 'innovation agency'.

Since its establishment in 1982, the SBIR program has grown to some $2 billion per year and now includes 11 federal agencies that are currently required to set aside 2.5 percent of their extramural research and development budget exclusively for SBIR contracts for small companies with fewer than 500 employees.[26] Each year these agencies identify various R&D topics for pursuit by small businesses under the SBIR program, representing scientific and technical problems requiring innovative solutions. These topics are published as individual agency 'solicitations' that are now normally made available through web postings. A small business can identify an appropriate topic it wants to pursue from these solicitations and, in response, offer a proposal for an SBIR grant. The required format for submitting a proposal is different for each agency. The proposals are reviewed and evaluated on a competitive basis by technical experts, sometimes drawn from the federal laboratories or research centers. Since 1992 more emphasis has been given in the evaluation process to commercialization potential. Each agency then selects the best proposals, as noted, usually less than 15 percent for the first phase. Given the different agency missions, the instruments vary, with the Department of Defense and NASA awarding contracts, and agencies such as the NIH and NSF awarding grants to the most highly qualified small businesses with the most innovative solutions.

SBIR program structure
As conceived in the 1982 Act, SBIR's grant-making process is structured in three phases:

- Phase I grants essentially fund a feasibility study in which award winners undertake a limited amount of research aimed at establishing an idea's scientific and commercial promise. The 1992 legislation prescribed Phase I grants to be no larger than $100 000.[27]

- Phase II grants are larger – typically about $750 000 – and fund more extensive R&D to develop the scientific and technical merit and the feasibility of research ideas.[28]
- Phase III does not involve SBIR funds, but is the stage at which grant recipients should be obtaining additional funds either from a procurement program at the agency that made the award, from private investors, or from the capital markets. The objective of this phase is to move the technology on from the prototype stage and into the marketplace.

Phase III of the program is often fraught with difficulty for small firms. In practice, agencies have developed different approaches to facilitating this transition to commercial viability; not least among them are additional SBIR awards. While some firms with more experience with the program have become skilled in obtaining additional SBIR awards, a wide variety of firms interact with the program. Nearly a third of the recipients of SBIR awards are new to the program each year. Other program participants are successful in obtaining multiple awards – sometimes many awards – over a sustained period. Normally this reflects agency satisfaction with the quality of the research and/or product being provided. It is important to keep in mind that not all proposals call for commercialization, and not all successful SBIR products can be commercialized.[29]

Motivation among firms varies. Previous National Academy of Sciences research has shown that different firms have quite different objectives in applying to the program. Some seek to demonstrate the potential of promising research. Others seek to fulfill agency research requirements on a cost-effective basis. Still others seek a certification of quality (and the investments that can come from such recognition) as they push science-based products towards commercialization.[30]

Features that make SBIR grants attractive from the firm's perspective, aside from the funding itself, include the fact that there is no dilution of ownership or repayment required. Importantly, grant recipients retain rights to intellectual property developed using the SBIR award, with no royalties owed to the government. The government retains royalty free use for a period, but this is very rarely exercised. Selection to receive SBIR grants also tends to confer a certification effect – a signal to private investors of the technical and commercial promise of the technology.[31]

From the perspective of the government, the SBIR program helps officials draw on private sector ingenuity to achieve their respective agency missions.[32] By providing a bridge between small companies and the federal agencies, especially for procurement, SBIR serves as a catalyst for the development of new ideas and new technologies to meet federal missions in health, transport, the environment and defense. In the case of defense procurement, the program offers a valuable bypass to the heavily encumbered defense procurement process with its 'mil-spec' requirements that often impede the adoption of new performance-enhancing technologies. In short, if effectively managed and above all integrated closely with current mission requirements, SBIR can be a win–win opportunity for both the entrepreneur and the government agency – with further benefits to society from the efficiencies and innovations that the program can introduce.

SBIR and the university connection
SBIR also provides a bridge between universities and the marketplace. A significant proportion (nearly 30 percent) of SBIR awards involve university researchers either as firm

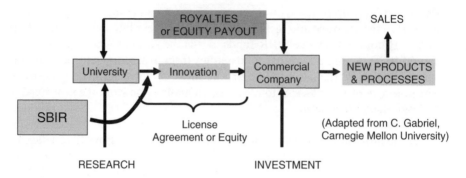

Source: National Research Council (2007), *SBIR and the Phase III Challenge of Commercialization*, Charles W. Wessner (ed.), Washington, DC: The National Academies Press.

Figure 9.4   SBIR and the commercialization of university technology

founders or as participants in the research, in the latter case as principal investigators or subcontractors. This substantial university involvement is somewhat ironic. When the SBIR program was created in the early 1980s, universities strongly objected to the program, seeing it as a source of competition for federal R&D funds. In the course of the 1990s, the perception of the program evolved significantly. Because of the commercialization-sensitive environment created by the Bayh–Dole Act, SBIR awards are increasingly seen by researchers and university administrators as a source of early-stage financial support for university researchers with promising ideas.[33] Today, SBIR is credited with causing the formation of many university-based companies, although the extent of this SBIR effect remains to be documented.[34] The catalytic role of SBIR awards is illustrated in Figure 9.4.

Indeed, SBIR encourages professors to start companies based on their research. Importantly, the availability of the awards and the fact that a professor can apply for an SBIR award without founding a company or quitting his or her university post, encourages applications from academics who might not otherwise undertake the commercialization of their own discoveries. Initial National Academy of Sciences research showed that SBIR awards directly cause the creation of new firms, with positive benefits in employment and growth for local economies.[35] Of course, not all universities in the United States have a strong commercialization culture, and there is variation in the level of success among those that do.[36]

Contrary to what one might expect, the awards generally do not seem to detract from the teaching role of the university professor. On the contrary, the real-life application of research with the attendant recognition in academic, technical, and financial terms can serve as a source of inspiration for students to pursue the real-world applications of their studies to societal needs in health, the environment or national security. Similarly, well-constructed agreements can provide access to otherwise cost-prohibitive technological resources, thus enhancing the relevance of the students' educational experience.[37] University innovation along with early-stage funding by the government has spurred the growth of many successful technology companies, promoting a positive symbiotic relationship between the university and the regional economy.[38]

BOX 9.1   THE NATIONAL ACADEMIES' ASSESSMENT OF SBIR

As the Small Business Innovation Research program approached its twentieth year of operation in 2002, the US Congress requested the National Academies to conduct a 'comprehensive study of how the SBIR program has stimulated technological innovation and used small businesses to meet Federal research and development needs', and to make assessment-based recommendations on improvements to the program.[39] The National Academies is currently assessing the SBIR program as administered at the Department of Defense, the National Institutes of Health, NASA, the Department of Energy, and the National Science Foundation. These five federal agencies together make up 96 percent of SBIR program expenditures.

The Advanced Technology Program – the next phase?
Along with the SBIR program, the Advanced Technology Program (ATP) is an important example of programs designed to help bring high-risk, enabling and innovative civilian technologies to market. Founded in 1989, the ATP mission is to provide funds for the development of generic technologies that are often too risky for individual firms but, if successful, can offer high payoffs for society as a whole.

Proposals for ATP funding are first reviewed by both technical and business experts – one of the distinguishing features of the program. Another key feature is the requirement for matching funds from the firms themselves. This serves as a constant reality check and ensures public funds are effectively used. Moreover, the requirement for significant risk and broad-based economic benefits means that ATP awards complement private capital, since venture capitalists normally search for projects with lower risks that will provide an exit strategy in a relatively short timeframe.

One of the strongest features of the ATP approach is its support for joint ventures. ATP encourages cooperation between large and small companies to develop technologies with broad applications that would be beyond the resources or interest of any individual firm. Small firms find benefit in ATP because it provides them access to the skills, management expertise and marketing reach of larger firms. It also helps them shift from being suppliers to larger firms to a fuller partnership in an ongoing relationship. Large firms also like ATP because the cooperation it facilitates helps them stay agile by providing access to niche expertise and unique talents often found in small firms.

Over the last 15 years, ATP has developed an impressive record of accomplishment. Its awards have helped foster new commercial technologies from fuel cells to proteomics to medical diagnostics to new lithography technologies.[40] In a National Academies study led by Intel's Gordon Moore, the program received high marks for its conception and operation.[41] This includes a highly competitive application process (only 12 percent of applicants are winners), the 50 percent cost share between industry and the government – more for larger companies – and its encouragement of joint ventures to disseminate technologies among small companies, universities and large companies. Internationally it is often seen as a best practice model from the United States.

The ATP and SBIR programs complement each other. The larger award sums offered by ATP, its focus on next-stage commercialization, as well as the synergies it creates between small and large firms make ATP, in effect, the third phase of SBIR – helping to commercialize successful prototypes initially funded by the SBIR program.

Key features of US programs

Both the SBIR and ATP innovation award programs illustrate numerous 'best practice' principles behind successful public–private partnerships:

- First and foremost the programs are intensely competitive, with multiple-stage reviews and a limited number of successful applicants. Although quite different in absolute scale – SBIR at $2 billion and ATP at $160 million – both programs make awards to approximately 12–15 percent of applicants. They are perhaps aptly compared to leading scholarship programs for outstanding students, not only in terms of the success rate but more profoundly in terms of the social investment in private individuals based on the rationale of long-term public gain.
- A distinguishing feature of the American innovation awards is that they are limited in time and amount.
- More formally with ATP, but equally with SBIR, the programs require industry to take ownership through risk and cost sharing. An explicit and distinctive feature of ATP is the focus on collaboration among small companies, large companies and (increasingly) universities. SBIR provides an avenue to cooperative contracts and has a major *de facto* cooperative feature with university-based founders, consultants and principal investigators.

The broader competitive benefits are not insignificant. The dissemination of enabling technologies made possible by these programs makes both small and large firms more competitive. Indeed, large firms increasingly must rely on the niche technological strengths of small companies.[42] Small companies are, of course, the source of tomorrow's large companies. One of the distinguishing features of the US economy is its ability not only to create large numbers of small high-tech companies but also to provide the conditions that enable an exceedingly small number of these new firms to grow into the Intels, Microsofts and Googles of tomorrow.

Even without the growth of these exceptional firms, a vibrant and regularly renewed stock of innovative small and medium-sized companies can play a critical role in helping the government to accomplish its many missions at lower costs and with improved efficiency, thereby contributing to the nation's productivity and, more fundamentally, enabling all citizens to enjoy the fruits of technological advances and economic growth.

Conclusions: learning from each other

While national innovation systems differ in scale and flexibility, the United States faces its own challenges in innovation. We have to address the new competition from low-wage, high-skill countries by becoming more innovative and productive and we have to justify R&D expenditures by creating new jobs and new wealth. To do this, countries have to reform existing institutions and create new ones. Rather than merely announce the need for change, we have to craft new mechanisms that shift incentives in a positive way. As the

SBIR and ATP cases reveal, effective partnerships require entrepreneurs, firms, government agencies and other organizations to be able to each work towards a common goal. For this cooperation to occur successfully, effective industry-led leadership, shared costs and stakes in a positive outcome, as well as regular evaluation and learning, are necessary.

Notes

1. Charles Wessner directs the National Academies' Board on Science, Technology, and Economic Policy's study on Comparative Innovation Policies, in addition to directing a portfolio of research on innovation award programs and technology and entrepreneurship policies. The author would like to express his recognition to the many substantive contributions of his colleague, Dr Sujai Shivakumar.
2. Zoltan J. Acs and David B. Audretsch (1990), *Innovation and Small Firms*, Cambridge, MA: MIT Press.
3. Dr Mary Good, Presentation of 19 October 2005 at the National Academies conference on Accelerating Innovation, held in Washington, DC.
4. See, for example, recent reports by the President's Council of Advisors on Science and Technology, 'Sustaining the nation's innovation ecosystems', January 2004; the Council on Competitiveness, *Innovate America: Thriving in a World of Challenge and Change*, Washington, DC, 2005; and the National Academy of Sciences, National Academy of Engineering, and Institute of Medicine, *Rising Above the Gathering Storm: Energizing and Employing America for a Brighter Economic Future*, Washington, DC: The National Academies Press, 2007.
5. National Research Council (2005), *Policy Implications of International Graduate Students and Postdoctoral Scholars in the United States*, Washington, DC: National Academies Press.
6. See, for example, National Academy of Sciences, National Academy of Engineering, and Institute of Medicine, *Rising Above the Gathering Storm*, op. cit.
7. National Research Council (2001), *Trends in Federal Support of Research and Graduate Education*, S. Merrill (ed.), Washington, DC: National Academy Press.
8. Ibid.
9. National Academy of Sciences, National Academy of Engineering, and Institute of Medicine, *Rising Above the Gathering Storm*, op. cit.
10. Ibid., p. ES-2.
11. Zoltan J. Acs and David B. Audretsch, *Innovation and Small Firms*, op. cit.
12. Small Business Administration, Office of Advocacy, 'Small business by the numbers', June 2004.
13. Ibid.
14. The Nobel Committee cited Spence's contribution in highlighting the importance of market signals in the presence of information asymmetries. For his seminal paper on this topic, see Michael Spence (1974), *Market Signaling: Informational Transfer in Hiring and Related Processes*, Cambridge, MA: Harvard University Press.
15. With regard to the challenges small firms face in obtaining funding, see Lewis M. Branscomb and Philip E. Auerswald (2001), *Taking Technical Risks: How Innovators, Executives and Investors Manage High-tech Risks*, Cambridge, MA: MIT Press. See also Josh Lerner (1999), 'Public venture capital', in National Research Council, *The Small Business Innovation Research Program: Challenges and Opportunities*, C. Wessner (ed.), Washington, DC: National Academy Press.
16. Bruce Griffing, 'Between invention and innovation, mapping the funding for early stage technologies', Carnegie Conference Center, 25 January 2001, Washington, DC.
17. Edwin Mansfield, 'How fast does new industrial technology leak out?', *Journal of Industrial Economics*, **34** (2), 217–24.
18. See Vernon J. Ehlers (1998), *Unlocking Our Future: Toward a New National Science Policy: A Report to Congress by the House Committee on Science*, Washington, DC: GPO. Accessed at http://www.access.gpo.gov/congress/house/science/cp105-b/science105b.pdf.
19. See Tom Jacobs (2002), 'Biotech follows dot.com boom and bust', *Nature*, **20** (10), 973.
20. 'The goal of venture capitalists is to make money for our fund investors – not to develop the economy.' Personal communication with David Morgenthaler, founder of Morgenthaler Ventures and past President of the National Venture Capital Association.
21. William L. Megginson (2004), 'Towards a global model of venture capital?', *Journal of Applied and Corporate Finance*, **16** (1).
22. Lewis M. Branscomb and Philip E. Auerswald (2002), *Between Invention and Innovation: An Analysis of Funding for Early-stage Technology Development*, Gaithersburg, MD: National Institute of Standards and Technology, NIST GCR 02-841, November.
23. It is important to remember that these are estimates. The authors stress the 'limitations inherent in the data and the magnitude of the extrapolations' and urge that the findings be interpreted with caution.

They note further that while the funding range presented for each category is large, these approximate estimates, nonetheless, provide 'valuable insight into the overall scale and composition of early-stage technology development funding patterns and allow at least a preliminary comparison of the relative level of federal, state, and private investments'. For further discussion of the approach and its limitations, see Lewis M. Branscomb and Philip E. Auerswald, *Between Invention and Innovation: An Analysis of Funding for Early-stage Technology Development*, op. cit., pp. 20–24.

24. The growth and subsequent contribution of venture capital have begun to attract the serious study needed to illuminate the dynamics of high-technology firm evolution. See for example, the work of Jeffrey Sohl and colleagues and the University of New Hampshire's Center for Venture Research, described at http://www.unh.edu/cvr

25. The SBIR legislation drew from a growing body of evidence, starting in the late 1970s and accelerating in the 1980s, which indicated that small businesses were assuming an increasingly important role in both innovation and job creation. This evidence gained new credibility with the empirical analysis by Zoltan Acs and David Audretsch of the US Small Business Innovation Data Base, which confirmed the increased importance of small firms in generating technological innovations and their growing contribution to the US economy. See Zoltan J. Acs and David B. Audretsch, *Innovation and Small Firms*, op. cit.

26. These include the Department of Defense, the Department of Health and Human Services, the National Aeronautics and Space Administration, the Department of Energy, the National Science Foundation, the Department of Agriculture, the Department of Commerce, the Department of Education, the Department of Transportation, the Environmental Protection Agency, and, most recently, the Department of Homeland Security.

27. With the agreement of the Small Business Administration, which plays an oversight role for the program, this amount can be higher in certain circumstances (e.g. drug development at NIH), and is often lower with smaller SBIR programs (e.g. the Environmental Protection Agency or the Department of Agriculture).

28. NSF, for example, makes Phase II awards at the $500 000 level. In its Phase II-B plus program, NSF provides up to an additional $250 000 in matching funding for firms that attract private funding – providing an incentive for firms to actively commercialize their product.

29. For example, a logarithm developed under a NASA award to improve air traffic flow within the United States is dependent on adoption by a risk-averse Federal Aviation Administration. Some research answers questions relevant to the agency but does not necessarily generate a product.

30. See Reid Cramer (2000), 'Patterns of firm participation in the Small Business Innovation Research program in southwestern and mountain states', in National Research Council, *The Small Business Innovation Research Program: An Assessment of the Department of Defense Fast Track Initiative*, C. Wessner (ed.), Washington, DC: National Academy Press.

31. This certification effect was initially identified by Josh Lerner (1999), 'Public venture capital', in National Research Council, *The Small Business Innovation Research Program: Challenges and Opportunities*, C. Wessner (ed.), Washington, DC: National Academy Press. For a similar concept from the Advanced Technology Program, see Maryann Feldman and Maryellen Kelly (2001), 'Leveraging research and development: the impact of the Advanced Technology Program', in National Research Council, *The Advanced Technology Program: Assessing Outcomes*, C. Wessner (ed.), Washington, DC: National Academy Press.

32. See National Research Council (2004), *The Small Business Innovation Research Program: Program Diversity and Assessment Challenges*, Washington, DC: The National Academies Press.

33. The Bayh–Dole Act of 1980 is designed to encourage the utilization of inventions produced under federal funding by permitting universities and small businesses to elect to retain title to inventions made in performance of the federally funded program.

34. There is substantial anecdotal evidence supporting this trend. For an illustrative case, see David Audretsch et al. (2000), 'Does the Small Business Innovation Research program foster entrepreneurial behavior? evidence from Indiana', in National Research Council, *The Small Business Innovation Research Program: An Assessment of the Department of Defense Fast Track Initiative*, C. Wessner (ed.), Washington, DC: National Academy Press.

35. National Research Council, *The Small Business Innovation Research Program: An Assessment of the Department of Defense Fast Track Initiative*, op. cit., p. 35.

36. Donald Siegel, David Waldman and Albert Link (2004), 'Toward a model of the effective transfer of scientific knowledge from academicians to practitioners: qualitative evidence from the commercialization of university technologies', *Journal of Engineering and Technology Management*, **21** (1–2), 115–42.

37. Cooperation with private companies is not without risk and requires careful management; yet even controversial agreements like the 1998 Berkeley agreement with Novartis seemed to have provided significant benefits to the university with no loss to academic freedom. See Gordon C. Rausser, Letter to the Editor of *Atlantic Monthly*, 19 May 2000. Accessed at www.cnr.berkeley.edu/pdf/dean_rausser/Atl_ltr_edt_5_2000.pdf.

38. Jennifer A. Henderson and John J. Smith (2002), 'Academia, industry, and the Bayh–Dole Act: an implied

duty to commercialize', White Paper, Center for the Integration of Medicine and Innovative Technology, Harvard University, October.

39. The SBIR assessment was mandated by Congress as a part of SBIR's renewal in 2000. See Public Law 106–554, Appendix I – H.R. 5667, Section 108.
40. Yet despite a growing record of success and positive outside reviews, the House of Representatives has called for its elimination every year since 1996, and the Bush Administration has joined in recommending the program's termination.
41. See National Research Council (2001), *The Advanced Technology Program: Assessing Outcomes*, C. Wessner (ed.), Washington, DC: National Academy Press.
42. As Audretsch and Acs have argued in their seminal study of small companies, small firms show unparalleled capacity to focus on and develop new innovative products and processes. Zoltan J. Acs and David B. Audretsch, *Innovation and Small Firms*, op. cit.

10 Quantitative and qualitative studies of university technology transfer: synthesis and policy recommendations
Donald S. Siegel

Introduction

In the late 1970s, US universities were often criticized for being more adept at developing new technologies than facilitating their commercial use in the private sector (General Accounting Office, 1998). More specifically, some policy makers asserted that the long lag between the discovery of new knowledge at the university and its use by domestic firms had significantly weakened the global competitiveness of American firms (Marshall, 1985).

In 1980, the US Congress attempted to remove potential obstacles to university technology transfer by passing the Bayh–Dole Act. Bayh–Dole instituted a uniform patent policy across federal agencies, removed many restrictions on licensing, and allowed universities to own patents arising from federal research grants. The framers of this legislation asserted that university ownership and management of intellectual property would accelerate the commercialization of new technologies and promote economic development and entrepreneurial activity.

It appears that the legacy of Bayh–Dole is quite dramatic. In the aftermath of this legislation, research universities in the US established technology transfer offices (TTOs) to manage and protect their intellectual property. TTOs facilitate commercial knowledge transfers through the licensing to industry of inventions or other forms of intellectual property resulting from university research. The rate of technology commercialization has increased substantially. The Association of University Technology Managers (AUTM), which represents licensing officers at universities and other research institutions, reported in 2004 that annual measures of university patenting, licensing activity, and startup formation have all increased more than tenfold since the enactment of Bayh–Dole.

In the US and other advanced industrial nations, policy makers view university technology transfer as a potential source of regional economic growth and revenue enhancement for financially strapped institutions of higher learning. The end result is that there is great interest in understanding 'best practices' in university technology transfer.

Academics in various nations have responded to this concern by conducting numerous quantitative and qualitative studies of the effectiveness of university technology transfer. The purpose of this chapter is to review this burgeoning literature. These studies indicate that incentives and organizational practices play an important role in enhancing the effectiveness of technology transfer. Academics have assessed institutions (e.g. universities, science parks, and incubators) and agents (e.g. academic and industry scientists) who are engaged in this activity.

The remainder of this article is organized as follows. In the following section, we present an extensive review of the literature on university technology licensing. The third section discusses studies of startup formation at universities. The final section considers lessons learned from these papers for policy makers and university administrators.

Review of empirical studies on the effectiveness of university technology licensing

Table 10.1 summarizes some recent quantitative and qualitative studies of the effectiveness of university technology transfer licensing. In this context, effectiveness usually refers to a measure of 'productivity', which is constructed from indicators of 'outputs' and 'inputs' of university technology transfer (e.g. Siegel et al., 2003; Thursby and Thursby, 2002; Friedman and Silberman, 2003; and Chapple et al., 2005). Some of these productivity studies are based on non-parametric methods, such as data envelopment analysis (henceforth, DEA), a linear programming method. Others employ parametric estimation procedures, such as stochastic frontier estimation (henceforth, SFE).

Siegel et al. (2003) employ SFE to assess and 'explain' the relative productivity of 113 US university TTOs. In their model, licensing activity is treated as the output, and invention disclosures, full-time equivalent employees in the TTO, and legal expenditures are considered to be inputs. They find that the production function model yields a good fit. Based on estimates of their 'marginal product', it appears that technology licensing officers add significant value to the commercialization process. The findings also imply that spending more on lawyers reduces the number of licensing agreements but increases licensing revenue. Licensing revenue is subject to increasing returns, while licensing agreements are characterized by constant returns to scale. An implication of increasing returns for licensing revenue is that a university wishing to maximize revenue should spend more on lawyers. Perhaps this would enable university licensing officers to devote more time to eliciting additional invention disclosures and less time to negotiating with firms.

The authors supplemented their econometric analysis with qualitative evidence, derived from 55 structured, in-person interviews of 100 university technology transfer stakeholders (i.e. academic and industry scientists, university technology managers, and corporate managers and entrepreneurs) at five research universities in Arizona and North Carolina. The field research allowed them to identify intellectual property policies and organizational practices that could potentially enhance technology transfer performance.

The qualitative analysis identified three key impediments to effective university technology transfer. The first was informational and cultural barriers between universities and firms, especially for small firms. Another impediment was insufficient rewards for faculty involvement in university technology transfer. This includes both pecuniary and nonpecuniary rewards, such as credit towards tenure and promotion. Some respondents even suggested that involvement in technology transfer might be detrimental to their careers. Finally, there appear to be problems with staffing and compensation practices in the TTO. One such problem is a high rate of turnover among licensing officers, which is detrimental to the establishment of long-term relationships with firms and entrepreneurs. Other concerns are insufficient business and marketing experience in the TTO and the possible need for incentive compensation.

Contrary to conventional economic models, they found that variation in relative TTO performance cannot be completely explained by environmental and institutional factors. The implication of this finding is that organizational practices are likely to be an important determinant of relative performance. In a subsequent paper, Link and Siegel (2005)

Table 10.1   Quantitative and qualitative research on the effectiveness of licensing of university-based inventions

Author(s)	Datasets	Methodology	Key results
Jensen and Thursby (2001)	N/A	Theoretical analysis	Faculty involvement in the licensing of a university-based technology increases the probability of success
Thursby et al. (2001)	AUTM, authors' survey	Descriptive analysis of authors' survey/regression analysis	Inventions tend to be disclosed at an early stage of development; elasticities of licenses and royalties with respect to invention disclosures are both less than one; faculty members are increasingly likely to disclose inventions
Bercovitz et al. (2001)	AUTM and case studies, interviews	Qualitative and quantitative analysis	Analysis of different organization structures for technology transfer at Duke, Johns Hopkins, and Penn State; differences in structure may be related to effectiveness
Thursby and Kemp (2002)	AUTM	Data envelopment analysis and logit regressions on efficiency scores	Faculty quality and number of TTO staff have a positive impact on licensing; private universities appear to be more efficient than public universities; universities with medical schools less efficient
Friedman and Silberman (2003)	AUTM, NSF, NRC, Milken Institute 'Tech-Pole' data	Regression analysis – systems equations estimation	Higher royalty shares for faculty members are associated with greater licensing income
Carlsson and Fridh (2002)	AUTM	Linear regression	Research expenditure, invention disclosures, and age of TTO have a positive impact on university licensing
Siegel et al. (2003)	AUTM, NSF and US Census data, interviews	Productivity of university licensing – stochastic frontier analysis and field interviews	TTOs exhibit constant returns to scale with respect to the number of licenses; increasing returns to scale with respect to licensing revenue; organizational and environmental factors have considerable explanatory power
Lach and Schankerman (2004)	AUTM, NSF, NRC	Regression analysis	Higher royalty shares for faculty members are associated with greater licensing income
Chapple et al. (2005)	UK–NUBS/ UNICO survey – ONS	Data envelopment analysis and stochastic frontier analysis	UK TTOs exhibit decreasing returns to scale and low levels of effectiveness; organizational and environmental factors have considerable explanatory power
Link and Siegel (2005)	AUTM, NSF and US Census data, interviews	TFP of university licensing – stochastic frontier analysis	Land grant universities are more efficient in university technology licensing; higher royalty shares for faculty members and higher levels of effectiveness in university technology licensing

find that a particular organizational practice can potentially enhance technology licensing: the 'royalty distribution formula', which determines the fraction of revenue from a licensing transaction that is allocated to a faculty member who develops the new technology. Using data on 113 US TTOs, the authors find that universities allocating a higher percentage of royalty payments to faculty members tend to be more efficient in technology transfer activities (closer to the 'frontier', in the parlance of SFE). Organizational incentives for university technology transfer appear to be important. This finding was independently confirmed in Friedman and Silberman (2003) and Lach and Schankerman (2004), using slightly different methods and data.

Other authors have explored the role of organizational incentives in university technology transfer. Jensen et al. (2003) model the process of faculty disclosure and university licensing through a TTO as a game, in which the principal is the university administration and the faculty and TTO are agents who maximize expected utility. The authors treat the TTO as a dual agent – that is, an agent of both the faculty and the university. Faculty members must decide whether to disclose the invention to the TTO and at what stage – that is, whether to disclose at the most embryonic stage or wait until it is a lab-scale prototype. The university administration influences the incentives of the TTO and faculty members by establishing university-wide policies for the shares of licensing income and/or sponsored research. If an invention is disclosed, the TTO decides whether to search for a firm to license the technology and then negotiates the terms of the licensing agreement with the licensee. Quality is incorporated in their model as a determinant of the probability of successful commercialization. According to the authors, the TTO engages in a 'balancing act', in the sense that it can influence the rate of invention disclosures, must evaluate the inventions once they are disclosed, and negotiate licensing agreements with firms as the agent of the administration.

The Jensen et al. (2003) theoretical analysis generates some interesting empirical predictions. For instance, in equilibrium, the probability that a university scientist discloses an invention and the stage at which he or she discloses the invention are related to the pecuniary reward from licensing, as well as faculty quality. The authors test the empirical implications of the dual agency model based on an extensive survey of the objectives, characteristics, and outcomes of licensing activity at 62 US universities. (See Thursby et al., 2001 for an extensive description of this survey.) Their survey results provide empirical support for the hypothesis that the TTO is a dual agent. They also find that faculty quality is positively associated with the rate of invention disclosure at the earliest stage, and negatively associated with the share of licensing income allocated to inventors.

Bercovitz et al. (2001) examine what could be a critical implementation issue in university management of technology transfer: the *organizational structure* of the TTO and its relationship to the overall university research administration. Based on the theoretical work of Alfred Chandler and Oliver Williamson, they analyze the performance implications of four organizational forms: the functional or unitary form (U-form), the multidivisional form (M-form), the holding company form (H-form), and the matrix form (MX-form). The authors note that these structures have different implications for the ability of a university to coordinate activities, facilitate internal and external information flows, and align incentives in a manner that is consistent with its strategic goals with respect to technology transfer.

To test these assertions, they examine TTOs at Duke, Johns Hopkins and Penn State and find evidence of alternative organizational forms at these three institutions. They attempt to link these differences in structure to variation in technology transfer performance along three dimensions: transaction output, the ability to coordinate licensing and sponsored research activities, and incentive alignment capability. While further research is needed to make conclusive statements regarding organizational structure and performance, their findings imply that organizational form does matter.

In sum, the extant literature on TTOs suggests that the key impediments to effective university technology transfer tend to be organizational in nature (Siegel et al., 2003, 2004). These include problems with differences in organizational cultures between universities and (small) firms, incentive structures, including both pecuniary and non-pecuniary rewards, such as credit towards tenure and promotion, and staffing and compensation practices of the TTO itself.

Review of studies of startup formation at universities

While licensing has traditionally been the most popular mechanism for commercialization of university-based technologies, universities are increasingly emphasizing the entrepreneurial dimension of technology transfer. The Association of University Technology Managers (AUTM, 2004) reports that the number of startup firms at US universities rose from 35 in 1980 to 374 in 2003. This rapid increase in startup activity has attracted considerable attention in the academic literature. Some researchers have focused on the university as the unit of analysis, while others analyze entrepreneurial agents (either academic or non-academic entrepreneurs) (see Table 10.2).

Studies using the university as the unit of analysis typically focus on the role of university policies in stimulating entrepreneurial activity. Roberts and Malone (1996) conjecture that Stanford generated fewer startups than comparable institutions in the early 1990s because the institution refused to sign exclusive licenses to inventor-founders.

Degroof and Roberts (2004) examine the importance of university policies relating to startups in regions where environmental factors (e.g. technology transfer and infrastructure for entrepreneurship) are not particularly conducive to entrepreneurial activity. The authors derive a taxonomy of four types of startup policies: an absence of startup policies, minimal selectivity/support, intermediate selectivity/support, and comprehensive selectivity/support. Consistent with Roberts and Malone (1996), they find that comprehensive selectivity/support is the optimal policy for generating startups that can exploit venture with high growth potential. However, such a policy is an ideal that may not be feasible, given resource constraints. The authors conclude that while spinout policies do matter in the sense that they affect the growth potential of ventures, it may be more desirable to formulate such policies at a higher level of aggregation than the university.

Di Gregorio and Shane (2003) directly assess the determinants of startup formation using AUTM data from 101 universities and 530 startups. Based on estimates of count regressions of the number of university-based startups, they conclude that the two key determinants of startups are faculty quality and the ability of the university and inventor(s) to assume equity in a start up in lieu of licensing royalty fees. Interestingly, the availability of venture capital in the region where the university is located and the commercial orientation of the university (proxied by the percentage of the university's research budget that is derived from industry) are found to have an insignificant impact on the rate of startup formation. The authors also find that a royalty distribution formula that is more favorable to faculty members reduces startup formation, a finding that is confirmed by Markman et al. (2005a). Di Gregorio and Shane (2003) attribute this result to the higher opportunity cost associated with launching a new firm, relative to licensing the technology to an existing firm.

Table 10.2   Quantitative and qualitative research on university-based entrepreneurial activity

Author(s)	Unit of analysis	Data/ methodology	Key results
Louis et al. (1989)	Faculty members in the life sciences	778 faculty members from 40 universities/ regression analysis	Key determinant of faculty-based entrepreneurship: local group norms; university policies and structures have little effect
Zucker et al. (1998b)	Relationships involving 'star' scientists and US biotech firms	Scientific papers reporting genetic-sequence discoveries, data on biotech firms from the North Carolina Biotechnology Center (1992) & Bioscan (1993)/count regressions	Location of star scientists predicts firm entry in biotechnology
Zucker et al. (2000)	Relationships involving 'star' scientists and US biotech firms	Scientific papers reporting genetic-sequence discoveries, data on biotech firms from the North Carolina Biotechnology Center (1992) & Bioscan (1993)/count regressions	Collaboration between star scientists and firm scientists enhances research performance of US biotech firms, as measured using three proxies: number of patents granted, number of products in development, and number of products on the market
Audretsch (2000)	Entrepreneurs in the life sciences	101 founders of 52 biotech firms/hazard function regression analysis	University entrepreneurs tend to be older, more scientifically experienced
Zucker and Darby (2001)	Relationships involving 'star' scientists and Japanese biotech firms	Data on biotechnology firms and the Nikkei Biotechnology Directory	Collaboration between star scientists and firm scientists enhances research performance of Japanese biotech firms, as measured using three proxies: number of patents granted, number of products in development, and number of products on the market
Franklin et al. (2001)	TTOs and university-based startups	Authors' quantitative survey of UK TTOs	Universities that wish to launch successful technology transfer startups should employ a combination of academic and surrogate entrepreneurship
Lockett et al. (2003)	TTOs and university-based startups	Authors' quantitative and qualitative surveys of UK TTOs	Universities that generate the most startups have clear, well-defined spinout strategies, strong expertise in entrepreneurship, and vast social networks

Table 10.2   (continued)

Author(s)	Unit of analysis	Data/ methodology	Key results
Di Gregorio and Shane (2003)	University-based startups	AUTM survey/count regressions of the determinants of the number of startups	Two key determinants of startup formation: faculty quality and the ability of the university and inventor(s) to take equity in a startup, in lieu of licensing royalty fees; a royalty distribution formula that is more favorable to faculty members reduces startup formation
O'Shea et al. (2005)	University-based startups	AUTM survey/count regressions of the determinants of the number of startups	A university's previous success in technology transfer is a key determinant of its rate of startup formation
Lockett and Wright (2005)	TTOs and university-based startups	Authors' quantitative survey of UK TTOs/ count regressions of the determinants of the number of startups	A university's rate of startup formation is positively associated with its expenditure on intellectual property protection, the business development capabilities of TTOs, and the extent to which its royalty distribution formula favors faculty members
Nerkar and Shane (2003)	University-based startups	Longitudinal data from MIT startups/ hazard function analysis	'Radicalness' of the new technology and patent scope increase the probability of survival more in fragmented industries than in concentrated sectors; effectiveness of technology strategies of new firms appears to depend on industry conditions
Meseri and Maital (2001)	TTOs and university-based startups	Authors' qualitative survey of Israeli TTOs	Criteria used by Israeli TTOs to appraise entrepreneurial startups are similar to those employed by venture capitalists
Markman et al. (2004)	TTOs and university-based startups	AUTM survey, authors' survey/linear regression analysis	Equity licensing and startup formation are positively correlated with TTO wages; uncorrelated or even negatively correlated with royalty payments to faculty members
Markman et al. (2005b)	TTOs and university-based startups	AUTM survey, authors' survey/linear regression analysis	There are three key determinants of time to market (speed): TTO resources, competency in identifying licensees, and participation of faculty inventors in the licensing process
Markman et al. (2005a)	TTOs and university startups	AUTM survey, authors' survey/linear regression analysis	The most attractive combinations of technology stage and licensing strategy for new venture creation – early stage technology and licensing for equity – are *least* likely to be favored by the university (due to risk aversion and a focus on short-run revenue maximization)

Table 10.2 (continued)

Author(s)	Unit of analysis	Data/ methodology	Key results
O'Shea et al. (2005)	University-based startups	AUTM survey/count regressions of the determinants of the number of startups	A university's previous success in technology transfer is a key determinant of its rate of startup formation

O'Shea et al. (2005) extend these findings in several ways. First, they use a more sophisticated econometric technique employed by Blundell et al. (1995) on innovation counts, which accounts for unobserved heterogeneity across universities due to 'history and tradition'. This type of 'path dependence' would seem to be quite important in the university context. Indeed, the authors find that a university's previous success in technology transfer is a key explanatory factor of startup formation. Consistent with Di Gregorio and Shane (2003), they also find that faculty quality, commercial capability, and the extent of federal science and engineering funding are also significant determinants of higher rates of university startup formation.

Franklin et al. (2001) analyze perceptions at UK universities regarding entrepreneurial startups that emerge from university technology transfer. The authors distinguish between academic and surrogate (external) entrepreneurs and 'old' and 'new' universities in the UK. Old universities have well-established research reputations and world-class scientists, and are typically receptive to entrepreneurial startups. New universities, on the other hand, tend to be weaker in academic research and less flexible with regard to entrepreneurial ventures. They find that the most significant barriers to the adoption of entrepreneurial-friendly policies are cultural and informational and that the universities generating the most startups (i.e. old universities) are those that have the most favorable policies regarding *surrogate* (external) entrepreneurs. The authors conclude that the best approach for universities that wish to launch successful technology transfer startups is a combination of academic and surrogate entrepreneurship. This would enable universities to simultaneously exploit the technical benefits of inventor involvement *and* the commercial know-how of surrogate entrepreneurs.

In a subsequent paper, Lockett et al. (2003) find that universities that generate the most startups have clear, well-defined strategies regarding the formation and management of spinouts. These schools tend to use surrogate (external) entrepreneurs, rather than academic entrepreneurs, to manage this process. It also appears as though the more successful universities have greater expertise and vast social networks that help them generate more startups. However, the role of the academic inventor was not found to differ between the more and less successful universities. Finally, equity ownership was found to be more widely distributed among the members of the spinout company in the case of the more successful universities.

Using an extended version of the same database, Lockett and Wright (2005) assess the relationship between the resources and capabilities of UK TTOs and the rate of startup formation at their respective universities. In doing so, the authors apply the resource-based view (RBV) of the firm to the university. RBV asserts that an organization's superior performance (in the parlance of strategic management, its 'competitive advantage') is related to its internal resources and capabilities. They are able to distinguish empirically between a university's resource inputs and its routines and capabilities. Based on estimation of count regressions (Poisson and Negative Binomial), the authors conclude that there is a positive correlation between startup formation and the university's expenditure on intellectual property protection, the business development capabilities of TTOs, and the extent to which its royalty distribution formula favors faculty members. These findings imply that universities wishing to spawn numerous startups should devote greater attention to recruitment, training, and development of technology transfer officers with broad-based commercial skills. We will refer back to these results in the following section of the chapter.

Markman et al. (2005b) develop a model linking university patents to new-firm creation in university-based incubators, with university TTOs acting as the intermediaries. They focus on universities because such institutions are responsible for a substantial fraction of technology-oriented incubators in the US. While there have been some qualitative studies of university TTO licensing (e.g. Bercovitz et al., 2001; Siegel et al., 2003; Mowery et al., 2001), they have been based on data from elite research universities only (e.g. Stanford, UC Berkeley, and MIT) or from a small sample of more representative institutions. These results may not be generalizable to the larger population of institutions that do not enjoy the same favorable environmental conditions. To build a theoretically saturated model of TTOs' entrepreneurial development strategies, the authors collected qualitative and quantitative data from virtually the entire population of university TTOs.

A surprising conclusion of Markman et al. (2005b) is that the most 'attractive' combinations of technology stage and licensing strategy for new venture creation, (i.e. early stage technology, combined with licensing for equity) are *least* likely to be favored by the university and thus not likely to be used. That is because universities and TTOs are typically focused on short-term cash maximization, and extremely risk-averse with respect to financial and legal risks. Their findings are consistent with evidence presented in Siegel et al. (2004), who found that TTOs appear to do a better job of serving the needs of large firms than small, entrepreneurial companies. The results of these studies imply that universities should modify their technology transfer strategies if they are serious about promoting entrepreneurial development.

In additional studies (Markman et al., 2004, 2005a), the authors use the same database to assess the role of incentive systems in stimulating academic entrepreneurship and the determinants of innovation speed, or time to market. An interesting result of Markman et al. (2004) is that there is a positive association between compensation to TTO personnel and both equity licensing and startup formation. On the other hand, royalty payments to faculty members and their departments are uncorrelated or even negatively correlated with entrepreneurial activity. This finding is consistent with Di Gregorio and Shane (2003).

In Markman et al. (2005b), the authors find that speed matters, in the sense that the 'faster' TTOs can commercialize technologies that are protected by patents, the greater the returns to the university and the higher the rate of startup formation. They also report that there are three key determinants of speed: TTO resources, competency in identifying licensees, and participation of faculty inventors in the licensing process.

Nerkar and Shane (2003) analyze the entrepreneurial dimension of university technology transfer, based on an empirical analysis of 128 firms that were founded between 1980 and 1996 to commercialize inventions owned by MIT. They begin by noting that there is an extensive literature in management that suggests that new technology firms are more likely to survive if they exploit radical technologies (e.g. Tushman and Anderson, 1986) and if they possess patents with a broad scope (e.g. Merges and Nelson, 1990). The authors conjecture that the relationships between radicalness and survival and scope and survival are moderated by both the market structure or level of concentration in the firm's industry. Specifically, they assert that radicalness and patent scope increase the probability of survival more in fragmented industries than in concentrated sectors. They estimate a hazard function model using the MIT database and find empirical support for these hypotheses. Thus the effectiveness of the technology strategies of new firms may be dependent on industry conditions.

Several studies focus on *individual* scientists and entrepreneurs in the context of university technology transfer. Audretsch (2000) examines the extent to which entrepreneurs at universities are different than other entrepreneurs. He analyzes a dataset on university life scientists in order to estimate the determinants of the probability that they will establish a new biotechnology firm. Based on a hazard function analysis, including controls for the quality of the scientist's research, measures of regional activity in biotechnology, and a dummy for the career trajectory of the scientist, the author finds that university entrepreneurs tend to be older and more scientifically experienced.

There is also evidence on the importance of norms, standards and culture in this context. Based on a qualitative analysis of five European universities that had outstanding performance in technology transfer, Clarke (1998) concluded that the existence of an entrepreneurial culture at those institutions was a critical factor in their success. Roberts (1991) found that social norms and MIT's tacit approval of entrepreneurs were critical determinants of successful academic entrepreneurship at MIT.

Louis et al. (1989) analyze the propensity of life science faculty to engage in various aspects of technology transfer, including commercialization. Their statistical sample consists of life scientists at the 50 research universities that received the most funding from the National Institutes of Health. The authors found that the most important determinant of involvement in technology commercialization was local group norms. They report that university policies and structures had little effect on this activity.

The unit of analysis in Bercovitz and Feldman (2004) is also the individual faculty member. They analyze the propensity of medical school researchers at Johns Hopkins and Duke to file invention disclosures, a potential precursor to technology commercialization. The authors find that three factors influence the decision to disclose inventions: norms at the institutions where the researchers were trained and the disclosure behaviors of their department chairs and peers, respectively.

The seminal papers by Lynne Zucker and Michael Darby and various collaborators explore the role of 'star' scientists in the life sciences on the creation and location of new biotechnology firms in the US and Japan. In Zucker et al. (2000), the authors assessed the impact of these university scientists on the research productivity of US firms. Some of these scientists resigned from the university to establish a new firm, or kept their faculty position but worked very closely with industry scientists. A star scientist is defined as a researcher who has discovered over 40 genetic sequences, and affiliations with firms are defined through co-authoring between the star scientist and industry scientists. Research productivity is measured using three proxies: number of patents granted, number of products in development, and number of products on the market. They find that ties between star scientists and firm scientists have a positive effect on these three dimensions of research productivity, as well as other aspects of firm performance and rates of entry in the US biotechnology industry (Zucker et al., 1998a, 1998b).

In Zucker and Darby (2001), the authors examine detailed data on the outcomes of collaborations between 'star' university scientists and biotechnology firms in Japan. Similar patterns emerge in the sense that they find that such interactions substantially enhance the research productivity of Japanese firms, as measured by the rate of firm patenting, product innovation, and market introductions of new products. However, they also report an absence of geographically localized knowledge spillovers resulting from university technology transfer in Japan, in contrast to the US, where they found that such effects were strong. The authors attribute this result to the following interesting institutional difference between Japan and the US in university technology transfer. In the US, it is common for academic scientists to work with firm scientists at the firm's laboratories. In Japan, firm scientists typically work in the academic scientist's laboratory. Thus, according to the authors, it is not surprising that the local economic development impact of university technology transfer appears to be lower in Japan than in the US.

Lessons learned
The literature review reveals that it is critical for university administrators to think strategically about technology transfer. This means that they must address numerous formulation and implementation issues, which I now consider in turn.

A key formulation issue is the establishment of institutional goals and priorities, which must be transparent, forthright, and reflected in resource allocation patterns. Establishing priorities also relates to strategic choices regarding technological emphasis (e.g. life sciences vs. engineering and the physical sciences) for the generation of licensing and startup opportunities. Opportunities for technology commercialization and the propensity of faculty members to engage in technology transfer vary substantially across fields both between and within the life sciences and physical sciences. Universities must also be mindful of competition from other institutions when confronting these choices. For example, many universities have recently launched initiatives in the life sciences and biotechnology, with high expectations regarding enhanced revenue and job creation through technology transfer. It is conceivable that any potential financial gains from these fields may be limited.

Resource allocation decisions must also be driven by strategic choices the university makes regarding various modes of technology transfer. As noted previously, these modes are licensing, startups, sponsored research and other mechanisms of technology transfer that are focused more directly on stimulating economic and regional development, such as incubators and science parks. Licensing and sponsored research generate a stream of revenue, while equity from startups could yield a payoff in the long term. Universities that stress economic development outcomes are advised to focus on startups since these companies can potentially create jobs in the local region or state. Note also that while a startup strategy entails higher risk, since the failure rate of new firms is quite high, it also can potentially generate high returns if the startup is taken public. It is also important to note that a startup strategy entails additional resources, if the university chooses to assist the academic entrepreneurs in launching and developing their startup.

The extant research also clearly demonstrates the importance of effective implementation of technology transfer strategies. Examples of implementation issues include choices regarding information flows, organizational design/structure, human resource management practices in the TTO, and reward systems for faculty involvement in technology transfer. There are also a set of implementation issues relating to different modes of technology transfer, licensing, start-ups, sponsored research, and other modes that are focused more directly on stimulating economic development, such as incubators and science parks. We now consider each of these in turn, in the context of the quantitative and qualitative analyses cited in previous sections of the chapter.

Human resource management practices appear to be quite important. Several qualitative studies (e.g. Siegel et al., 2004) indicate that there are deficiencies in the TTO with respect to marketing skills and entrepreneurial experience. Unfortunately, field research (Markman et al., 2005a) has also revealed TTOs are not actively recruiting individuals with such skills and experience.

Instead, representative institutions appear to be focusing on expertise in patent law and licensing or technical expertise. Training and development programs for TTO personnel are advised, along with additional administrative support for this activity, since many TTOs lack sufficient resources and competencies to identify the most commercially viable inventions. Training in portfolio management techniques would be extremely useful in this context. Selection, training and development of TTO personnel with such portfolio management skills are recommended. Research has shown that career opportunities for university technology licensing officers are limited and often of short duration (Siegel et al., 2004; Markman et al., 2004), which implies that incentives should be directed towards creating immediate feedback and rewards (i.e. cash) to elicit the desired behaviors.

Organizational incentives are also important. The evidence implies that shifting the royalty distribution formula in favor of faculty members (e.g. allowing faculty members to retain 75 per cent of the revenue, instead of 33 per cent) would elicit more invention disclosures and greater efficiency in technology transfer. A more controversial recommendation is to modify promotion and tenure guidelines to place a more positive weight on technology transfer activities in such decisions. I believe that such changes are warranted at institutions that wish to place a high priority on technology commercialization, although I do not underestimate the difficulty of changing norms, standards and values among entrenched tenured faculty. Finally, a switch from standard compensation to incentive compensation for technology licensing officers could also result in more licensing agreements.

Another key recommendation relating to implementation is improving information flows between academics and the university administration. Technology licensing officers and university administrators with an interest in promoting technology commercialization (perhaps sympathetic department chairs and deans) should devote more effort to eliciting invention disclosures. It is also important to provide information and support for faculty members who express an interest in forming a startup. Given that startup formation requires skills that academic scientists typically do not possess and actions that are somewhat alien to their culture (for example, assessing market demand for their invention), universities should employ business school faculty to train and mentor potential academic entrepreneurs.

Bibliography

Association of University Technology Managers (AUTM) (2004), *The AUTM Licensing Survey, Fiscal Year 2003*, AUTM, Inc: Norwalk, CT.

Audretsch, D. (2000), 'Is university entrepreneurship different?', mimeo, Indiana University.

Bercovitz, J. and M. Feldman (2004), *Academic Entrepreneurs: Social Learning and Participation in University Technology Transfer*, Mimeo, University of Toronto.

Bercovitz, J., M. Feldman, I. Feller and R. Burton (2001), 'Organizational structure as determinants of academic patent and licensing behavior: an exploratory study of Duke, Johns Hopkins, and Pennsylvania State Universities', *Journal of Technology Transfer*, **26**, 21–35.

Blumenthal, D., E.G. Campbell, N. Causino and K.S. Louis (1996), 'Participation of life-science faculty in research relationships with industry', *New England Journal of Medicine*, **335** (23), 1734–9.

Blumenthal, D., E.G. Campbell, M. Anderson, N. Causino and K.S. Louis (1997), 'Withholding research results in academic life science: evidence from a national survey of faculty', *Journal of the American Medical Association*, **277** (15), 1224–8.

Blundell, R., R. Griffith and J. Van Reenen (1995), 'Dynamic count data models of technological innovation', *Economic Journal*, **105**, 333–44.

Carlsson, B. and A. Fridh (2002), 'Technology transfer in United States universities: a survey and statistical analysis', *Journal of Evolutionary Economics*, **12**, 199–232.

Chapple, W., A. Lockett, D.S. Siegel and M. Wright (2005), 'Assessing the relative performance of university technology transfer offices in the UK: parametric and non-parametric evidence', *Research Policy*, **34** (3), 369–84.

Clarke, B.R. (1998), *Creating Entrepreneurial Universities; Organizational Pathways of Transformation*, New York: IAU Press.

Degroof, J.J. and E.B. Roberts (2004), 'Overcoming weak entrepreneurial infrastructure for academic spin-off ventures', *Journal of Technology Transfer*, **29** (3–4), 327–57.

Di Gregorio, D. and S. Shane (2003), 'Why do some universities generate more start-ups than others?', *Research Policy*, **32**, 209–27.

Franklin, S., M. Wright and A. Lockett (2001), 'Academic and surrogate entrepreneurs in university spin-out companies', *Journal of Technology Transfer*, **26** (1–2), 127–41.

Friedman, J. and J. Silberman (2003), 'University technology transfer: do incentives, management, and location matter?', *Journal of Technology Transfer*, **28** (1), 81–5.

General Accounting Office (GAO) (1998), *Technology Transfer: Administration of the Bayh–Dole Act by Research Universities*, Washington, DC: General Accounting Office.

Jensen, R. and M. Thursby (2001), 'Proofs and prototypes for sale: the licensing of university inventions', *American Economic Review*, **91** (1), 240–59.

Jensen, R., J.G. Thursby and M.C. Thursby (2003), 'The disclosure and licensing of university inventions: the best we can do with the s**t we get to work with', *International Journal of Industrial Organization*, **21** (9), 1271–300.

Lach, S. and M. Schankerman (2004), 'Royalty sharing and technology licensing in universities', *Journal of the European Economic Association*, **2** (2–3), 252–64.

Link, A.N. and J.T. Scott (2005), 'Opening the ivory tower's door: an analysis of the determinants of the formation of U.S. university spin-off companies', *Research Policy*, **34** (3), 1106–12.

Link, A.N. and D.S. Siegel (2005), 'Generating science-based growth: an econometric analysis of the impact of organizational incentives on university-industry technology transfer', *European Journal of Finance*, **11** (3), 169–82.

Lockett, A. and M. Wright (2005), 'Resources, capabilities, risk capital and the creation of university spin-out companies', *Research Policy*, **34** (7), 1043–57.

Lockett, A., M. Wright and S. Franklin (2003), 'Technology transfer and universities' spin-out strategies', *Small Business Economics*, **20**, 185–201.

Louis, K.S., D. Blumenthal, M.E. Gluck and M.A. Stoto (1989), 'Entrepreneurs in academe: an exploration of behaviors among life scientists', *Administrative Science Quarterly*, **34**, 110–31.

Louis, K., L.M. Jones, M.S. Anderson, D. Blumenthal and E.G. Campbell (2001), 'Entrepreneurship, secrecy, and productivity: a comparison of clinical and non-clinical life sciences faculty', *Journal of Technology Transfer*, **26** (3), 233–45.

Markman, G., P. Phan, D. Balkin and P. Gianiodis (2004), 'Entrepreneurship from the ivory tower: do incentive systems matter?', *Journal of Technology Transfer*, **29** (3–4), 353–64.

Markman, G., P. Phan, D. Balkin and P. Gianiodis (2005a), 'Entrepreneurship and university-based technology transfer', *Journal of Business Venturing*, **20** (2), 241–63.

Markman, G., P. Phan, D. Balkin and P. Gianiodis (2005b), 'Innovation speed: transferring university technology to market', *Research Policy*, **34** (7), 1058–75.

Marshall, E. (1985), 'Japan and the economics of invention', *Science*, 12 April, 157–8.

Merges, R. and R.R. Nelson (1990), 'On the complex economics of patent scope', *Columbia Law Review*, **90** (4), 839–916.

Meseri, O. and S. Maital (2001), 'A survey analysis of university-technology transfer in Israel: evaluation of projects and determinants of success', *Journal of Technology Transfer*, *26* (1–2), 115–26.

Mowery, D.C., R.R. Nelson, B. Sampat and A.A. Ziedonis (2001), 'The growth of patenting and licensing by U.S. universities: an assessment of the effects of the Bayh–Dole Act of 1980', *Research Policy*, **30**, 99–119.

Nerkar, A. and S. Shane (2003), 'When do startups that exploit academic knowledge survive?', *International Journal of Industrial Organizatio*, **21** (9), 1391–410.

O'Shea, R., T. Allen and A. Chevalier (2005), 'Entrepreneurial orientation, technology transfer, and spin-off performance of U.S. universities', *Research Policy*, **34** (7), 994–1009.

Poyago-Theotoky, J., J. Beath and D.S. Siegel (2002), 'Universities and fundamental research: reflections on the growth of university-industry partnerships', *Oxford Review of Economic Policy*, **18** (1), 10–21.

Roberts, E. (1991), *Entrepreneurs in High Technology, Lessons from MIT and Beyond*, Oxford: Oxford University Press.

Roberts, E. and D.E. Malone (1996), 'Policies and structures for spinning off new companies from research and development organizations', *R&D Management*, **26**, 17–48.

Rogers, E.M., Y. Yin and J. Hoffmann (2000), 'Assessing the effectiveness of technology transfer offices at U.S. research universities', *The Journal of the Association of University Technology Managers*, **12**, 47–80.

Shane, S. (2002), 'Selling university technology: patterns from MIT', *Management Science*, **48** (1), 122–38.

Shane, S. and T. Stuart (2002), 'Organizational endowments and the performance of university start-ups', *Management Science*, **48** (1), 154–71.

Siegel, D.S., D. Waldman and A.N. Link (2003), 'Assessing the impact of organizational practices on the productivity of university technology transfer offices: an exploratory study', *Research Policy*, **32** (1), 27–48.

Siegel, D.S., P. Westhead and M. Wright (2003), 'Assessing the impact of science parks on the research productivity of firms: exploratory evidence from the United Kingdom', *International Journal of Industrial Organization*, **21** (9), 1357–69.

Siegel, D.S., D. Waldman, L. Atwater and A.N. Link (2004), 'Toward a model of the effective transfer of scientific knowledge from academicians to practitioners: qualitative evidence from the commercialization of university technologies', *Journal of Engineering and Technology Management*, **21** (1–2), 115–42.

Thursby, J.G. and S. Kemp (2002), 'Growth and productive efficiency of university intellectual property licensing', *Research Policy*, **31**, 109–24.

Thursby, J.G. and M.C. Thursby (2002), 'Who is selling the ivory tower? Sources of growth in university licensing', *Management Science*, **48**, 90–104.

Thursby, J.G. and M.C. Thursby (2004), 'Are faculty critical? Their role in university licensing', *Contemporary Economic Policy*, **22** (2), 162–78.

Thursby, J.G., R. Jensen and M.C. Thursby (2001), 'Objectives, characteristics and outcomes of university licensing: a survey of major U.S. universities', *Journal of Technology Transfer*, **26**, 59–72.

Tushman, M. and P. Anderson (1986), 'Technological discontinuities and organizational environments', *Administrative Science Quarterly*, **31**, 439–65.

Wright, M., A. Lockett, N. Tiratsoo, C. Alferoff and S. Mosey (2004), 'Academic entrepreneurship, knowledge gaps and the role of business schools', mimeo, University of Nottingham.

Zucker, L.G. and M.R. Darby (2001), 'Capturing technological opportunity via Japan's star scientists: evidence from Japanese firms' biotech patents and products', *Journal of Technology Transfer*, **26** (1–2), 37–58.

Zucker, L.G., M.R. Darby and J. Armstrong (1998a), 'Geographically localized knowledge: spillovers or markets?', *Economic Inquiry*, **36** (1), 65–86.

Zucker, L.G., M.R. Darby and J. Armstrong (2000), 'University science, venture capital, and the performance of U.S. biotechnology firms', mimeo, UCLA.

Zucker, L.G., M.R. Darby and M.B. Brewer (1998b), 'Intellectual human capital and the birth of U.S. biotechnology enterprises', *American Economic Review*, **88** (1), 290–306.

11 Entrepreneurship policy in Bavaria: between laptop and lederhosen*
Marcel Hülsbeck and Erik E. Lehmann

Introduction

As described by Audretsch and Thurik (2001), globalization is shifting the comparative advantage in the OECD countries away from being based on traditional inputs of production towards being based on knowledge. As the comparative advantage is increasingly based on new knowledge, policy makers have responded by enabling its creation and commercialization. Furthermore, new policy approaches are emerging, shifting the focus from national and international aspects toward regions and regional clusters. Examples of these policies mentioned above include for instance encouraging research and development (R&D) spillovers, venture capital and new firm startups (Audretsch et al., 2006). In this new entrepreneurship-based policy, universities play a key role in providing spillovers by means of academic research and human capital in the form of well-trained and educated students (see Siegel and Phan, 2005 for an analytical framework and an excellent summary of the empirical work). The success of a number of different technology clusters is the direct result of enabling policies, such as the provision of research support by universities.

Much attention has recently been focused on the so-called European Paradox. On the one hand, Europe has consistently made some of the largest investments in new knowledge, in the form of research and development, university research and human capital. On the other hand, commercialization, innovation and ultimately economic growth, emanating from those knowledge investments, have been relatively low, and in any case disappointing. Germany, in total, has not yet escaped the European Paradox. Investments in German universities are among the highest in Europe, yet the ensuing commercialization has been disappointing. One exception is the Bavarian state and, in particular, the region around its capital Munich.

From the beginning of the early 1990s, Bavaria has closely followed an entrepreneurship policy that is termed 'between laptop and lederhosen'. This tradeoff describes an entrepreneurship policy that is between the deep-rooted, and often conservative regional traditions versus the emergence of a new entrepreneurship policy that fosters highly innovative firms and thus lowers unemployment and increases welfare. As a consequence, Bavaria has one of the lowest unemployment rates in Europe and is, furthermore, one of the leading regions in biotechnology as well as in other high-technology industries.

The purpose of this chapter is to show how Bavarian policy makers used the advantages – and disadvantages – in the past to formulate a new entrepreneurship policy. The combination of deep-rooted traditions – expressed by 'lederhosen' – and the emergence of highly innovative startups – 'laptops' – was consequently fostered by policy makers. Especially the spillover effects of the universities in Munich are pivotal in the process to promote and foster the foundation and growth of new firms in high-technology industries.

As pointed out by Fritsch (2005) in his introduction to a special issue of *Research Policy* focusing on the regionalization of innovation policy, there are several reasons that provide a strong rationale for the regionalizing of innovation policy instead of an innovation policy on a national scale. One of them is that innovation processes are not spread evenly across space but are concentrated in certain areas. The co-existence of excellent universities and large innovative firms is undoubtly important to generate regional clusters (see also Frischmann, 2005; Romanelli and Khessina, 2005). Left to themselves, the scientific research community and the market are likely to achieve less in terms of economic value and new jobs.

Thus university policy matters. However, studies evaluating university policies are rare (see Link and Scott, 2005 for public sector R&D programs; Hall et al., 2003 for universities as research partners; and Link and Scott, 2003 for research parks; or Feldman and Desroche, 2003 for Johns Hopkins University; and Audretsch and Lehmann, 2005a for technically oriented universities in Germany), and only a few papers directly address entrepreneurship and innovation policy in a German context (like Eickelpasch and Fritsch, 2005 or Eickelpasch et al., 2002; Audretsch et al., 2005a, 2006).

This chapter contributes to this literature by analyzing entrepreneurial policy in a regional context. Starting as an agricultural region without large and innovative firms, Bavaria developed several programs to foster and promote new innovative firms.

The chapter is organized as follows. In the next section we provide a short overview of the 'Free State of Bavaria' and its historical development. The third section describes the new entrepreneurship policy in Bavaria. The regional clusters and thus the success of Bavaria are discussed in the fourth section, and the chapter concludes in the final section.

The entrepreneurial state of Bavaria: past and present
The 'Free State of Bavaria' is the biggest of Germany's 16 federal states (Lander). Covering an area of 70 549 km^2, with roughly 12 million inhabitants (15 percent of all Germans), the population density of 173 inhabitants per km^2 is very low compared to the federal state (Land) of Baden-Wuerttemberg (300 inhabitants/km^2), which is often termed Germany's 'model economy', or the heavily industrialized North Rhine Westfalia with its Ruhr Valley (530 inhabitants/km^2). About 16 percent of Bavarians live in one of only three major cities (population greater than 250 000: Munich, Nuremberg and Augsburg).[1] Bavaria is a rural region, internationally renowned for its traditions and tourist attractions such as Bavarian beer, lederhosen, the Oktoberfest in Munich, Castle Neuschwanstein and the Alps.

Until the 1960s, Bavaria was an economically backward agrarian state, dependent on monetary transfers from other German Lander, with unemployment rates well above the German average. Since then, the Free State of Bavaria has evolved into one of the economically best performing federal states.

The success story started in post-war Germany. Bavaria had always been one of Germany's granaries and had been largely unaffected by the industrial revolution that transformed Lander like North Rhine Westphalia (NRW), Baden-Wuerttemberg (BW) or Saarland (S) into industry clusters for heavy industry (NRW, S) or mechanical engineering (BW). This lack of industrial infrastructure turned out to be an advantage for Bavaria after World War II. Instead of investing in the rebuilding of old and existing industries, Bavaria had to invest in the settlement of new industries.

At the same time, various firms from former Middle- and Eastern-German provinces were looking for new headquarters. In order to attract these possible investors and to level out the locational disadvantages, Bavarian politicians put their talents to work and used their personal networks to convince those industrial leaders to relocate their companies to Bavaria. This kind of personal networking has ever since become a tradition among Bavarian politicians, entrepreneurs and researchers, and has resulted in economical growth as well as corruption scandals (e.g. the 'Amigo Affairs' of 1993 and 2004). By the critics of this entanglement, the Land is often called 'the Amigo State'.

The second strategy to overcome the infrastructural drawbacks was to advance contentious new technologies.[2] In 1957 Germany's first nuclear reactor (named 'FRM I') was put into operation by the Technical University Munich (TUM). This reactor was replaced in 2004 by its successor FRM II. Within the perimeter of these reactors a research and technology cluster – attracting IT, material science and radio-pharmaceutics – emerged. Similarly, the defense industry, which was very unpopular in post-war Germany, was brought to the 'Greater Munich' area, being followed by aerospace and astronautics companies. Nowadays, more than 100 firms in the Munich region produce radio and radar systems, tanks and jet fighters. One of the many outcomes of this policy is the European Aeronautic Defence and Space Company (EADS) in Munich and Augsburg, developing and producing, for example, Airbus, Eurocopter and the European GPS 'Galileo'. Current examples of Bavaria's fondness for disputed technologies are the political and financial endeavors undertaken to create research infrastructure and incubator units in biotechnology close to Munich and Regensburg, as well as the building of a monorail system using magnetic levitation (Transrapid).

Although the measures stated above proved to be successful, Bavaria faced spatial challenges. Unlike its direct neighbor Baden-Wuerttemberg – described as an 'industrial district with intensive intra-regional linkages between suppliers and customers and between small and large firms with a dominant engineering base' (Sternberg, 1999) – the wide territory, the lack of urbanized and industrialized areas and the low population density led to geographically and sectorally dispersed industries. In 1990 the average company size in Bavaria was 70.2 workers compared to a (West) German average of 153.7 workers (Jones and Wild, 1994).

This dispersion and the relative importance of small and medium-sized enterprises (SMEs) caused special problems for regional politics, especially for innovation and know-how transfer. The Bavarian government recognized these problems a long time ago and has never attempted to solve them by allocating technology subsidies into the weaker regions. This kind of regional policy is gratefully left to the Regional Policy Directorate-General of the EU (e.g. Land of Bavaria Objective 2 Program). Opposed to this kind of egalitarian policy measure, Bavaria encouraged the agglomeration of industry and innovation clusters by providing a regionalized research infrastructure of 26 universities and institutes of higher education, three major research establishments, 12 Max Planck Institutes (basic research) and 13 Fraunhofer Gesellschaft establishments (applied research).

Today Bavaria has reaped the rewards of its long-standing entrepreneurial policy. In the period of 1994–2004 real GDP grew about 21.3 percent (BW: 17.2 percent), resulting in Bavaria (2004) being the sixth largest economic power in the EU15 behind France, the UK, Italy, Spain and the Netherlands. Regarding entrepreneurial activity, Bavaria has the highest entrepreneurship rate in Germany (11.9 per cent). The overall export rate is 44.9 percent (1994: 31.9 percent); export activities into the new EU member states have grown 279 percent since 1994. The unemployment rate (6.9 percent) is the second lowest in Germany (BW: 6.5 percent), and youth unemployment (7.3 percent) is the lowest in all the EU25 countries.

Table 11.1 shows the differences between Bavaria and the other Lander. The 16 Lander include three city-states (Berlin, Bremen and Hamburg), and the five new Lander, which were part of East Germany prior to 1990. With a GDP per capita (2004) of €31 000, Bavaria holds second place in Germany, right behind Hessen (€32 100) with its financial center Frankfurt/Main. The fact that about 5.8 percent of all employees are working in the R&D sector expresses the innovative character of Bavarian firms.

Reviewing all the figures, it can be said that Bavaria is Germany's economic engine with regard to jobs, economic growth and innovation. Moreover this dynamic growth has not been financed by public spending, as public spending in R&D is far lower than the German average, with the lowest public spending rate of all German Lander (9.3 percent of GDP); or, only about 30 percent of spending in R&D stems from public sources. In contrast, Bavaria shows the highest investment rate of all West-German territorial states

Table 11.1   The 16 German Bundesländer

State	GDP/ capita[a]	Revenue per employee[b]	R&D/ employee[c]	Public R&D spending[d]	Patents[e]	Unemploy- ment rate
Bavaria	31.0	241.2	5.82	19.8	109	6.9
Baden-Wurttemberg	29.8	207.5	5.12	21.0	121	6.2
Brandenburg[f]	17.5	209.8	2.13	63.3	13	18.7
Hessen	32.1	202.7	5.51	19.0	62	8.2
Mecklenburg-Vorpommern[f]	17.3	181.4	0.88	84.9	12	20.5
Lower Saxony	23.1	278.1	3.99	27.0	35	9.6
North Rhine Westphalia	26.6	237.5	2.65	37.6	43	10.2
Rhineland Pfalz	23.5	235.1	3.69	24.6	53	7.7
Saarland	24.6	207.2	0.62	62.8	33	9.2
Saxony[f]	18.5	178.0	3.32	49.9	19	17.8
Saxony-Anhalt[f]	18.2	234.2	1.42	73.5	16	20.3
Schleswig-Holstein	23.5	236.7	2.21	54.1	22	9.8
Thuringia[f]	17.9	159.7	2.99	46.3	31	16.7
Berlin[g]	23.0	299.3	10.49	45.4	27	17.6
Bremen[g]	35.6	344.8	3.00	51.0	26	13.3
Hamburg[g]	45.4	678.4	4.60	48.4	57	9.7
Germany	26.4	236.6	4.24	30.0	59	10.5

Notes: [a] 31 March 2005, [b] in €1000, [c] per 100 employed people, [d] as % of total R&D spending, [e] patents per 100 000 inhabitants, [f] formerly GDR, [g] city state.

Source: Institut der Deutschen Wirtschaft (2005) (www.iwkoeln.de).

(14.5 percent of the federal states budget) and the lowest per capita public debt (€1861), which is nearly 74 percent lower than the German average.

As the basis for this, Bavaria's entrepreneurial development since the end of World War II has evolved around three key aspects:

- The lack of locational advantages to attract industry settlement in Bavaria and the need for relocating former Middle- and East-German companies led to the use and fortification of personal networks between politicians and entrepreneurs/managers that were complemented by researchers in the later stages.
- These networks fostered political niches for socially unpopular key technologies, enabling further establishment of high-tech industries.
- The economic geography of the state made it inefficient to deploy a territory-wide investment policy, and thus supported the early adoption of cluster concepts. In this synopsis it is quite evident that Bavaria faced the challenges of an entrepreneurial economy earlier than most economies in Europe. Moreover Bavaria has developed an efficient set of policy measures to meet these challenges.

But still the question remains: is Bavaria's success mere luck, historical coincidence, or has it managed to develop a tradition of entrepreneurial policy?

Entrepreneurship policy

Institutionalizing entrepreneurship policy
27 May 1993 provided the necessary exogenous shock to shift Bavarian entrepreneurial policy from informal, personal networks towards institutional measures. On this day, the Prime Minister of Bavaria, Max Streibl – successor to Franz Josef Strauss – resigned from all political duties because of alleged bribery.[3] He was accused of having lobbied a personal friend and aerospace entrepreneur by contracting with the national Ministry of Defense, as well as having helped this friend to get sponsored by the national Ministry of Research and Technology and the regional development assistance institutions (LfA – Foerderbank Bayern). Considering Bavaria's post-war history, this collusion of politics and economy was the Free State's main element of entrepreneurial policy. In the public's view it was political suicide. The new Prime Minister, Edmund Stoiber, had learned his lesson from Streibl's fate and institutionalized entrepreneurial policy. The starting point was the privatization of state owned companies and the disposition of major and minor shares of private companies held by the state. On the one hand, this served as a signal to the public that the web between politics and business was unwoven. On the other hand, this privatization equipped the state with the necessary funds to establish institutional measures of entrepreneurial policy.

The proceeds of the privatization accounted for over €5 billion (1994–2004), and were invested into two frameworks supporting five goals in four key technologies in Bavarian entrepreneurship. The first framework 'Future Bavaria Campaign' (started in 1994, funding so far has been about €5 billion) aims at five relevant strategic goals:[4]

1. The promotion of groundbreaking research and technology in the fields of transportation technologies, material sciences, environmental technologies, genetics/biotechnology and medicine, and medical technology.

2. The creation of effective technology transfer between science and industry.
3. The facilitation of new ventures and business startups.
4. The assistance for SMEs in addressing new international markets.
5. The strengthening of the position of practical orientation in education.

The second framework 'High-tech Bavaria Campaign' (started in 2000 with nearly €1.5 billion in funding so far) aims at the same goals as the first campaign, but is meant to emphasize the importance of key technologies: life sciences (genetics, biotechnology, medicine, medical technology), energy and environment (including transportation), material sciences and microsystems (including mechatronics).

These campaigns are organized and coordinated by the State Ministry of Economic Affairs in cooperation with the State Ministries of Science (goal 1) and Education (goal 5), which have created three public limited companies to execute projects within the frameworks: 'Bayern Innovativ' promotes technology transfer between science and industry (goal 2). 'Bayern Kapital' supplies venture capital and financial aid for startup companies and SMEs (goal 3) and 'Bayern International' assists SMEs in addressing new international markets (goal 4). Additional regional help comes from the Bavarian Chambers of Commerce (goal 2) and regional development assistance institutions (goal 3).

Bavarian entrepreneurial policy measures
According to Nam (2000), Bavaria's entrepreneurial policy measures can be classified into a policy of dialogue between all partners concerned, higher education and professional training, SME establishment support and research, and a technology transfer policy. These measures are illustrated below, with special regard to the frameworks and institutions discussed earlier.

The roots of the dialogue policy within the frameworks are the 'Bayern Innovativ' public limited company. Having received initial financing of more than €50 million, it aims to enhance regional and international networking among Bavarian research associations, industry partners and business services in targeted innovative technologies. The company operates throughout the state, designing and providing a wide range of promotional platforms, such as managed networks for key technologies, round tables, congresses, shared booths at international exhibitions and internet collaboration platforms. Additionally, freely accessible database systems provide information and facilitate personal contacts being established by various institutions: 'Key technologies in Bavaria' contains contact information for 12 000 innovative firms in Bavaria; BAYDAT offers information about 1000 scientists interested in cooperating with industrial partners; and SISBY helps to select the optimal location for startup companies and international investors.

Furthermore 14 user application centers at Bavarian universities have been established to facilitate contacts between science and industry by providing assistance with actual technical problems. Also, 25 not-for-profit information centers (mainly in cooperation with local chambers of commerce) in Bavaria offer help with regional, national and international contacts, round tables, local congresses, workshops, patents and consulting services.

Last but not least 'Bayern International' and the 'Invest in Bavaria' programs provide similar services for international contacts, including site selection services, shared booths at international high-tech exhibitions, international trade visits for entrepreneurs, and joint delegations of entrepreneurs and politicians.

These policies make use of the Bavarian tradition of personal networks while substituting the old 'amigo' networks with new innovation networks. This measure is obviously closely connected to the idea of technology transfer by personal and institutional networks, and must be seen as a precondition to technology transfer.

The availability and quality of regional human capital is one of the most important factors regarding the regional competitiveness of innovative industries (Nam, 2000). To meet the resulting demand for higher education and professional training, the Bavarian government integrated the following steps in its entrepreneurial policy. The higher education development plan was adjusted to the goals established in the entrepreneurial policy frameworks. This new plan emphasizes regional educational foci for universities, and universities of applied sciences, reflecting local research and industrial activities. In addition to the regionalization of education, internationalization is promoted to stimulate the international exchange of young scientists. For instance, international university centers have been funded to conduct exchange and research projects that total more than 200 up to now. Since August 1998 approximately 200 bachelor and master degree programs have been introduced and supplemented by subject-specific language training to enhance the international competitiveness of scientists trained in Bavaria.

To prepare exceedingly gifted students and scientists for scientific or science-related careers, the 'Elite Network of Bavaria' program was launched as a coordinated effort for the promotion of particular young scientists. Via this program, a total of 20 elite degree courses and about ten international graduate research training groups have been established. The courses feature specialized and interdisciplinary coursework, an international orientation, emphasis on holistic personal growth as well as intensive counseling and support.

Beyond this, remarkable efforts were made to establish facilities for vocational professional training. In order to support SMEs mainly depending on external human resources development, the chambers of commerce, universities and universities of applied sciences created regional training networks and facilities (partly financed by the Ministry of Economic Affairs). 'Bayern Innovativ' set up a special branch to guarantee state-wide professional training facilities (including its own MBA program). These educational measures aspire to further enhance the attractiveness of the location of particular Bavarian regions for certain technologies, and to establish SMEs within these technology fields.

Like in most other models of entrepreneurial policy, a lot of SME establishment support is achieved through financial aid in form of loans, grants and guarantees. Within the general entrepreneurial policy framework two programs have been launched. The BAYTOU Program funds the development and conceptualization of new products, processes and services carrying severe technological and business risks. In the Bavarian Technology Promotion Program (BAYTP) loans, grants and guarantees are granted for developing and implementing new technologies in products and processes. Further guarantees are offered for innovation and cooperation projects of and between research institutions and firms.

In addition to EU and nationwide funding for SMEs, the Bavarian policy has established special seed and venture capital for innovation oriented firms by 'Bayern Kapital', a venture capital company. Using a co-investment model for leverage, 'Bayern Kapital' has – in cooperation with private lead investors and the national technology venture capital company (tbg) – generated venture capital investments of approximately €300 million. To date, affiliated companies have created about 2000 highly skilled jobs in Bavaria.

Further funds from the 'High-tech Bavaria Campaign' were used to create three topic and region oriented seed funds (each €4.5 million) as well as innovation and R&D programs. The seed funds comprise the fields of information technology in the Nuremberg area, medical technology and pharmaceuticals (Nuremberg/Erlangen) and environmental technology in the region of Augsburg. The tbg has invested a supplementary €7.5 million in the seed funds so far. The ERP Innovation Program offers loans for innovations in products, processes and services in life sciences, microsystems, new materials, and energy and environmental technologies. R&D efforts in these key technologies are supported by grants for companies, interfirm cooperative projects or research institutes. Financial instruments can be seen as the second building block to exert a pull on new technology firms to settle or be founded in Bavarian regions.

The research and technology transfer policy is the most ambitious of Bavaria's entrepreneurial policy measures. It extends from building the necessary research infrastructure and long-term basic research to ad hoc consulting of industry–science collaborations. By funding research infrastructure, Bavaria has managed to attract three major research institutions (German Aeronautics and Space Centre, MPI of Plasma Physics, National Research Centre for Environment and Health), and 12 Max Planck Institutes conducting basic research in physics, biology, life sciences and intellectual property and law. Moreover 13 Fraunhofer Gesellschaft institutes and research groups directing applied research in microsystems, IT and new materials have been attracted by the Free State. Moreover the establishment of the headquarters of these organizations in Bavaria has partly been financed by the 'Future Bavaria Campaign'. To form a comparable research infrastructure in Bavarian universities, research clusters in the key technology fields defined by the 'High-tech Bavaria Campaign' have been institutionalized at Bavarian universities and universities of applied science. In order to put an emphasis on this development, specialized research profiles have been assigned to universities by the legal framework act of higher education. Within this legal framework, bonus programs for research publications and third-party funding are incentivized to stimulate research. Local technology transfer centers assist scientists in obtaining third-party funding. To press ahead with interdisciplinary research, 45 collaborative research centers in Bavarian institutions of higher education as well as over 40 inter-university research networks are promoted.

Bavarian technology transfer can be described by all actions that implement the results of scientific research into the relevant technology markets. Two programs ('Hochsprung' and 'Fluegge') facilitate business startups by scientists, providing counseling, networking (Hochsprung) and financial backing (Fluegge). Scientists and non-scientific entrepreneurs can test their ideas by participating in regional business plan contests. Besides that, scientists get assistance on how to patent their inventions. On the one hand the Bavarian university patent initiative ('Bayern Patent') is meant to stimulate the transfer of scientific developments via professional commercialization by developing the necessary local patenting infrastructure at universities, and on the other hand the Fraunhofer patent initiative offers legal and commercial consulting services for scientists who are planning on patenting their work. Most transfer activities are coordinated and organized by

28 technology transfer centers, located in Bavarian universities (12) and universities of applied science (16).

The second pillar of the technology transfer policy is the 23 technology oriented incubators, providing affordable business spaces and facilitating collaboration between scientists, technicians and business executives. Herein firms benefit from the proximity to renowned research institutions, vocational training, consulting services and management assistance. Additional sponsoring is provided by the Bavarian Research Foundation for cooperation projects between industrial and scientific partners in order to enhance rapid transfer of scientific findings into industrial implementation.

In contrast to the two aforementioned aspects, the research and technology transfer policy aims not only to attract key technology industries but also to promote regional innovation clusters, consisting of research, industry and business services.

Drawing the parallels between Bavaria's traditional and current entrepreneurial policy, one can argue that Bavaria has managed to combine its traditional virtues with the necessary institutionalization of entrepreneurial policy.

- The successful informal personal networks have been transformed, by the use of dialogue policy, into more formalized collaboration and innovation networks.
- Key technologies have been elicited from their societal niches and have been financially supported as well as promoted by policies of higher education. As a result industrial innovators find ample sources of human and monetary capital in Bavaria.
- Research and technology transfer policies amplify the existing locational advantages of natively grown industry clusters, by extending them into innovation clusters of knowledge generating, applying and intermediating organizations.

The particular advantage of this policy bundle lies in the interlocking effects of highly skilled and networked entrepreneurs operating in innovative environments, providing easy access to required resources. The proven winning concept of the past, which has been adopted today still, has to be challenged to be a winning concept for future technologies.

Key technologies and innovation clusters – preliminary observations
After a decade of heavy investment, most of the privatization proceeds have been spent, and therefore not much state equity is left to be sold, resulting in the fact that the state has already started programs to cut down costs in higher education. The investments into entrepreneurial policy have, so far, led to impressive short-term growth and innovation rates of the Bavarian economy. Whether these achievements will persist in the future or will decline proportional to possible investments largely depends on the infrastructures of the technologies addressed. As one decade of policy is a rather short period of time to evaluate the success of the measures taken, we do not intend to judge these policies but will try to raise some open topics by discussing three institutionalized innovation networks: Life Sciences Bavaria, BAIKEM (microsystems) and BAIKUM (environmental technology). They are chosen because they reflect key technologies addressed by the 'High-tech Bavaria Campaign', employ discriminative knowledge bases, and for the pragmatic reason of data availability.

Life sciences rest on an 'analytic knowledge base' founded on deductive processes, codified knowledge in patents, documentations and research publications, and radical

Table 11.2 List of the top 20 universities in Germany (as measured by the firms located around this university)

University	Firms[a]	km[b]	Staff[c]	Grants[d]	SSCI students[e]	SCI students[f]
LMU München	51	17.9	412 633	83 681	43 633	8 119
Uni Frankfurt	26	19.5	265 845	50 976	26 324	5 715
Uni Hamburg	24	13.25	87 924	8 870	1 361	329
Uni Stuttgart	16	16.2	403 180	203 489	4 779	12 104
HU Berlin	14	7.78	352 676	55 167	20 769	4 936
Uni Köln	12	5.9	299 294	51 409	47 112	9 395
TU München	10	8.8	462 522	205 463	1 619	14 976
TU Karlsruhe	9	36.7	322 389	120 261	4 102	11 818
Uni Düsseldorf	7	18.57	145 912	19 382	14 697	4 762
Uni Erlangen-Nürnberg	6	14	290 793	103 212	12 861	7 144
Uni Freiburg	6	40.33	212 177	40 121	12 334	4 942
FU Berlin	5	5.5	435 784	73 023	30 290	6 260
TU Aachen (RWTH)	5	3.4	473 740	205 389	7 884	20 570
Uni Jena	5	15.8	198 905	34 142	7 615	2 864
U-GH Paderborn	4	17	161 200	40 386	6 993	8 676
Uni Bielefeld	4	15.5	190 698	39 114	15 831	4 400
Uni Bremen	4	25.5	224 573	82 507	11 749	4 800
UdB München	4	14.25	131 395	7 858	1 054	1 104
Uni Kiel	4	40.75	238 427	63 196	13 000	6 513
Uni Regensburg	4	40	153 090	26 069	11 192	3 696

Notes:
TU indicates technical oriented university, UdB indicates a university of the Armed Forces.
[a] Measured by the number of firms located closest to this university, [b] φ km is the average distance of the firms located near this university, [c] 'Staff' is expenditure on personnel (in thousand DM), [d] 'Grants' are research grants, [e] number of students in the social sciences, [f] number of students in the natural sciences.

Source: Audretsch and Lehmann (2005a).

innovation by the creation of new knowledge. New products are being created by research collaboration between firms and research organizations (Asheim and Coenen, 2005). Audretsch and Lehmann (2005a, 2005b) showed that a short distance to a research intense university fosters both the foundation of new innovative firms and the growth rates of those firms. The analysis of a sample of 272 German IPO firms between 1997 and 2002 provided evidence that most of those firms were clustered around universities in Bavaria (see Table 11.2). Of the included 272 firms, 65, or close to 25 percent, are located around the Bavarian capital, Munich, and nearly one third of those IPOs are located in Bavaria.

Life Sciences Bavaria is the shining example of Bavaria's regionalized entrepreneurial policy. It consists of two biotechnology clusters in the Munich area and in the city of Regensburg. The Munich cluster consists of 24 biotech companies, three basic research institutes (MPIs for biochemistry, neurobiology and psychiatry), both Munich universities (LMU, TUM), which have been ranked as Germany's leading research universities in natural sciences (2005), the National Research Centre for Environment and Health, the Institute of Agronomy and Plant Breeding, the university of applied sciences

Weihenstephan (food technology) and two biotechnological research networks (immunology, prions). There are 13 specialized business services mainly offering venture capital, legal and business advice. Regarding this comprehensive structure, the Munich biotech cluster seems to be very well positioned for the future and it seems that the Bavarian government's plan to create Europe's leading biotech region has worked out quite well. Meanwhile the other Bavarian biotech cluster (BioPark Regensburg) consists of 20 biotech companies, the University of Regensburg and two business service companies (venture capital, medical technology consulting). Compared to the Munich cluster the long-term success of this cluster might be contended. But still both examples show that regional entrepreneurial policy in Bavaria has been able to create high-tech clusters of new scientific and analytic technologies virtually out of nowhere.

The case of microsystems and environmental technology networks is different. They do not only differ from biotechnology with regard to the knowledge base applied but also concerning the industries' age and the diversity of their applications. Both industries are founded on synthetic knowledge bases, wherein innovations are achieved by combining existing knowledge through inductive processes. Therefore, applied problem-oriented (tacit) 'engineering' knowledge is needed, often embedded in craft and practical skills. New products are created by interactive learning in supplier–purchaser networks (Asheim and Coenen, 2005).

The *Microsystems innovation network* (BAIKEM), consisting of 60 firms, developed two smaller clusters in the Nuremberg area (27 percent of all firms) and Munich (25 percent), and the other 48 per cent are spatially dispersed all over Bavaria. Obviously BAIKEM is more dispersed than the Life Sciences Bavaria network (36 per cent in the Munich cluster, 30 percent in BioPark Regensburg). This could be caused by the necessary synthetic knowledge deriving from electronic/electrical and mechanical engineering. Therefore microsystems are mainly developed by long-established engineering firms that do not get incentives to (re-)locate their plants according to entrepreneurial policy measures. The observable clustering effects in the Nuremberg area derive from the region's strong industrial tradition in electrical/electronic and mechanical engineering (35 percent of the regional industrial workforce is employed in this industry), which has led to dense supplier–purchaser networks. The interactive learning within this industry is supported by specialized business services of industrial relations and sales agencies, serving as knowledge mediators along the supply chain. Two Fraunhofer institutes for applied research (integrated circuits, integrated systems and device technology) – including the one that developed MP3 technology – are located near Nuremberg. Moreover Nuremberg has strong research and industrial competence in medical technology, which is one of the major fields of application for microsystems. In contrast to the Nuremberg area, Munich does not have a strong industrial tradition in the relevant fields of engineering. The clustering of 15 microsystems firms could be explained by the sheer size of Munich's industrial districts, which makes it very probable to find relevant engineering firms in the area.

The firms within the *BAIKUM innovation network* for environmental technology derived from a multiplicity of industries, using analytic and synthetic knowledge. It is an eclectic industry in relation to technologies and knowledge bases, with the only common factor being that the field of application is environmental technology. Concerning these appliances, it is a very young sector, which is not profiting from well-established intra-industry networking along supply chains. The highest spatial concentration of the 35 companies in the network can be found around Augsburg (seven firms, i.e. 20 percent), and all other firms are widely spread across Bavaria (13 locations with one to three firms).

Most of the relevant research institutions are in Augsburg and Munich. Many specialized business services provide engineering consulting services, which could be developed as a means to bring together the necessary knowledge bases. There is only a little observable spatial clustering within this industry, as far as we can see in this superficial examination. This could be due to its newness, the variety of established root industries, or differing knowledge bases. It seems that the entrepreneurial policy measures undertaken have not yet led to the desired effect of creating a spatially and socially dense web of knowledge and technology transfer. The future development of these aspects will show whether the managed networking activity can substitute for the lacking proximity.

Concluding remarks
As we have seen in this case study, Bavaria is indeed a land of contrasts between laptops and lederhosen. On the one hand it is still the agrarian state renowned for its tourist attractions and strong traditions. On the other hand it has managed to establish a new tradition of progress: the intuitional attempts of the post-war era to attract different industries have been translated into institutionalized entrepreneurial policy yielding its fruits today. The 'Bavarian model' has even been exported to other countries facing similar challenges and could prove to be useful for other economies as well (e.g. Eastern European countries).

Recapitulating, there are four lessons to be learned from Bavarian entrepreneurial policy:

1.   The policy must consider the industrial history of the region concerned and must use the existing resources instead of using an egalitarian approach of spreading investments evenly across industrial sectors.
2.   Similarly the spatial and infrastructural aspects (networks) should be used (and implemented) to guide investment decisions.
3.   The kind of technology transfer and networking needed depends on the knowledge base characteristics of the targeted industries.
4.   'Not how much but how' public financial resources are spent is important.

Any attempts to facilitate innovations, intra- and interindustry cooperation should be tailored to these characteristics. However, entrepreneurship policy also depends on policy specific variables. One key factor – regarding Bavaria and Baden-Wurttemberg – is political stability. Both states differ significantly from the other 14 Lander. In both cases the conservative Christian Democratic Union (CDU, in Bavaria called CSU) has run the states for more than half a century. This, however, gives an incentive for a long-term policy instead of a myopic view fixated on the next election.

Notes
*   We are grateful to two anonymous referees for helpful comments and suggestions.
1.   Another 5 percent live in cities with 100 000 to 250 000 inhabitants.
2.   This trend was especially promoted by the notorious Bavarian politician Franz Josef Strauss (1915–88), who was German national minister of nuclear policy until 1956, national minister of defence (1956–62), national minister of finance (1966–69) and Prime Minister of Bavaria (1978–88).

3. This is the so called 'Amigo Affair'. The expression has become the term used in Germany for all kinds of entanglement between politics and economy.
4. The sixth goal 'Realization of social innovation (e.g. museums, kindergartens, housing projects)' cannot be seen as means to promote entrepreneurship.

Bibliography

Asheim, B.T. and L. Coenen (2005), 'Knowledge bases and regional innovation systems: comparing Nordic clusters', *Research Policy*, **34** (8), 1173–90.

Audretsch, D.B. and E.E. Lehmann (2005a), 'Do university policies make a difference?', *Research Policy*, **34** (3), 343–47.

Audretsch, D.B. and E.E. Lehmann (2005b), 'Does the knowledge spillover theory of entrepreneurship hold for regions?', *Research Policy*, **34** (8), 1191–202.

Audretsch, D.B. and E.E. Lehmann (2005c), 'Do locational spillovers pay? Empirical evidence from German IPO data', *Economics of Information and New Technology*, **15**, 71–81.

Audretsch, D.B. and R. Thurik (2001), 'What is new about the new economy: sources of growth in the managed and entrepreneurial economies', *Industrial and Corporate Change*, **10**, 267–315.

Audretsch, D.B., M. Keilbach and E.E. Lehmann (2005a), 'The knowledge spillover theory of entrepreneurship and technological diffusion', in G. Libecap (ed.), *Advances in the Study of Entrepreneurship, Innovation and Economic Growth: University Entrepreneurship and Technology Transfers: Process, Design, and Property Rights*, Amsterdam: Elsevier, pp. 69–91.

Audretsch, D.B., M. Keilbach and E.E. Lehmann (2006), *Entrepreneurship and Growth*, Oxford and New York: Oxford University Press.

Audretsch, D.B., E.E. Lehmann and S. Warning (2005b), 'University spillovers and new firm location', *Research Policy*, **34**, 1113–22.

Berhoff, S., G. Federkeil, P. Giebisch, C.D. Hachmeister, D. Müller-Böling and M. Siekermann (2005), 'Das CHE-Forschungsranking deutscher Universitäten 2004', Arbeitspapier Nr. 62.

Eickelpasch, A. and M. Fritsch (2005), 'Contests for cooperation – a new approach in German innovation policy', *Research Policy*, **34** (8), 1269–82.

Eickelpasch, A., I. Pfeiffer and O. Pfirrmann (2002), 'The InnoRegio Program: implementing the promotion and developing the networks', *Economic Bulletin*, **39**, 281–9.

Federal Ministry of Education and Research (2004), *Facts and Figures 2002*, available at http://www.bmbf.de.

Feldman, M. and P. Desroche (2003), 'Research universities and local economic development: lessons from the history of the Johns Hopkins University', *Industry and Innovation*, **10**, 5–24.

Frischmann, B.M. (2005), 'Commercializing university research systems in economic perspective: a view from the demand side', in G. Libecap (ed.), *Advances in the Study of Entrepreneurship. Innovation and Economic Growth: University Entrepreneurship and Technology Transfer: Process, Design, and Property Rights*, **16**, Amsterdam: Elsevier, pp. 155–86.

Fritsch, M. (2005), 'Editorial: regionalization of innovation policy – introduction to the Special Issue', *Research Policy*, **34** (8), 1123–7.

Hall, B., A. Link and J. Scott (2003), 'Universities as research partners', *Review of Economics and Statistics*, **85**, 485–91.

Jones, P.N. and T. Wild (1994), 'Opening the frontier: recent spatial impacts in the former inner-German border zone', *Regional Studies*, **28** (3), 259–73.

Link, A. and J. Scott (2003), 'The growth of research triangle parks', *Small Business Economics*, **20**, 167–75.

Link, A. and J. Scott (2005), 'Evaluating public sector R&D programs: the advanced technology program's investment in wavelength references for optical fiber communications', *Journal of Technology Transfer*, **30**, 241–51.

Nam, C.W. (2000), 'Decentralized industrial policy in Germany. Case study: Bavaria', *European Planning Studies*, **8** (2), 201–9.

Romanelli, E. and O.M. Khessina (2005), 'Regional industrial identity: cluster configurations and economic development', *Organization Science*, **16** (4), 344–58.

Siegel, D.S. and Ph.H. Phan (2005), 'Analyzing the effectiveness of university technology transfer: implications for entrepreneurship education', in G. Libecap (ed.), *Advances in the Study of Entrepreneurship. Innovation and Economic Growth: University Entrepreneurship and Technology Transfer: Process, Design, and Property Rights*, **16**, Amsterdam: Elseviers, pp. 1–38.

Sternberg, R. (1999), 'Innovative linkages and proximity: empirical results from recent surveys of small and medium sized firms in German regions', *Regional Studies*, **33** (6), 529–40.

12 Issues in evaluation: the case of Shell Livewire
Francis J. Greene and David J. Storey

Introduction

Enterprise policy is predicated on the basis that it is possible to alter the behaviour of people. Prior to such interventions, some people may be unaware of their entrepreneurial potential, shy of their entrepreneurial capability or feel intimidated by their inability to fund their entrepreneurial ambitions. Enterprise policy, if successful, should resolve some or all of these limitations.

Unfortunately, while enterprise policy is widespread across developed economies there is little evaluation of impact. Even where there has been evaluation (e.g. Lerner, 1999 and Wallsten, 2000 (US's SBIR programme); and del Monte and Scalera, 2001 (Italy's Law 44 programme); Riding and Haines, 2001 (loan guarantee schemes); Wren and Storey, 2002 (consultancy support); and Chrisman, 1989, 1999; Chrisman and Katrishen, 1994; and Chrisman and McMullan, 2000, 2004 (US Small Business Development Centers)), we still often don't know what does work and what does not (Lundström and Stevenson, 2001).

This chapter begins by discussing some of the issues faced in evaluating enterprise programmes. It suggests that the optimal evaluation techniques, if we wish to accurately specify the additionality of programmes, is to use matched samples of the 'treated' and the 'unwashed' and then subsequently use econometric techniques to account for their observable and unobservable characteristics (e.g. Heckman, 1979; Heckman and Smith, 1996), so as to accurately measure policy impact.

The discussion then moves on to suggesting that besides the comfort of knowing that our hard-earned euros, dollars or pounds are well accounted for, programme stakeholders often want to know if the programme is well-managed (Chelimsky, 1997). Evaluations are also problematic (Weiss, 1999). One such problem, as we shall show, is that the objectives of evaluations are often opaque (Smithson, 1981). Second, econometric analyses are expensive, which may prove onerous for resource-constrained enterprise programmes (Picciotto, 1999). Third, evaluations only tend to come at particular points in a programme's development. Typically, this is in terms of some *ex post* requirement to ensure that costs outweigh benefits (Papaconstantinou and Polt, 1997; Martin and Sanderson, 1999). However, enterprise programme evaluators may be involved *ex ante* by assessing the nature of any market failure that the programme designers seek to solve. Alternatively, management issues also intrude *in vivo* because particular programmes have choices about their implementation.

This chapter seeks to provide guidance, particularly to managers and evaluators in tightly cost-constrained contexts, on how they can use particular methods to aid developments in their particular programme. To illustrate this we make use of an evaluation conducted on Shell Livewire, which is one of the largest and best known youth enterprise development programmes in the UK. Our discussion of this enterprise programme first traces our earlier involvement with a sister programme, Shell Technology Enterprise Programme (STEP). We then introduce the features of the Shell Livewire programme and, thereafter, discuss the difficulties of arriving at a clear understanding of its objectives. One central contribution of this chapter is to take the programme's fuzzy objectives and conceptually and empirically derive a model to help guide the process of converting stated targets into identifiable measures. Subsequently, we discuss the methodology of the evaluation and then provide our empirical findings. We conclude with a discussion of how the funders and managers received our findings and the main lessons we derived from this case study.

Issues in evaluation

Storey's (2003) general complaint about evaluations of enterprise programmes is that many of them fail to accurately delineate the characteristics of programme participants. His view is that there is a hierarchy of evaluation methodologies from simple monitoring exercises that count the number of participants (step I); assess client satisfaction (step II); or test their feel for the efficacy of the programme (step III). Beyond these simple steps are evaluation exercises proper that are attempts to match with some 'average' participant (step IV); attempts that seek to match assisted and non-assisted participants on observable differences (step V); or that make use of sample selection effects which control for observable and unobservable differences between the two samples (step VI). In effect, then, the outcomes suggested by very many monitoring and simple evaluations are questionable because they have failed to take account of observable and non-observable differences between programme participants.

A more generic complaint about most evaluations of enterprise programmes is that they treat these as simple 'black boxes' in which the inputs (e.g. the firm or individual) are compared to outputs (e.g. number of start-ups, survival, growth) to ascertain the additionality that may be attributed to the particular programme (Schmid et al., 1996; Chen, 1990). This ignores the contextual nature of evaluation. Evaluators often bring a set of expectations that diverge from those being evaluated. They may be seeking to objectively appraise the net economic benefits of the programme, or seeking to use the evaluation to extend their relationship with those being evaluated. In turn, the evaluated may fear the evaluation because they regard it as a threat to the existence of the programme. The objectives of the evaluation funders may also be opaque: funders may say that they are interested in outcomes, but may neglect to indicate that their motive was to improve the managerial process used by the programme. They may, alternatively, choose to completely ignore any findings, as is often the case with evaluations, by complaining that these are obtuse, irrelevant or have failed to come up with the 'correct' messages (van der Meer, 1999; Weiss, 1999).

This brings us to a second point. Full-blown econometric evaluations are expensive. For example, Roper and Hewitt-Dundas' (2001) study of grant funding to Irish firms sampled 1853 firms, while Meager et al.'s (2003) evaluation of the Prince's Trust made use of a treatment and a control group of 2000 and 1600, respectively. For smaller programmes, it may prove more difficult to appropriately fund such evaluations, especially if they believe that resources should be spent on the ground on 'client facing' activities rather than 'administrative' functions.

A third issue is that there is often a presumption that the design of the programme is optimal. The usual logic here is that there is evidence of some market failure in particular environments. In terms of US youth enterprise programmes, there is a tendency to target those in the education system (e.g. Mini Society, YESS!, and the plethora of tertiary level entrepreneurship programmes (Katz, 2004)). The belief here is that the education system can create awareness of the entrepreneurial option and improve the entrepreneurial capacity of younger people, which, in turn, will ultimately increase the supply of potential entrepreneurs (Walstad and Kourilsky, 1998, 1999).

In Europe, the focus is much more on converting existing latent entrepreneurship into actual entrepreneurship. Social outcomes still persist but European programmes tend to take as their starting point that there exist persistent and identifiable market failures in terms of either information or finance. Hence, there are programmes such as the Austrian Senior Expert Pool, Entrepreneurship for the Youth (Greece) or the Genesis Enterprise Programme (Ireland) that provide soft support. Others like Business Incubators (Portugal) or DtA-Micro-Loan (Germany) provide hard support. More usually, though, programmes provide a mixture of the two (e.g. Law 44 (Italy), WIFI (Austria), ADIE (France) or the Prince's Trust (UK)).

For these programmes to be appropriate, it is often necessary for them to demonstrate that there is an identifiable market failure that they are seeking to address. In terms of youth entrepreneurship, empirical studies (Blanchflower and Oswald, 1998; Greene, 2005) have demonstrated that there are high levels of latent entrepreneurship among young people but that this does not translate into actual entrepreneurship because the individuals have either low levels of 'credible' human capital, limited networks (Birley, 1985) or poor access to funding (Blanchflower and Oswald, 1998).

Designing enterprise programmes, however, does not end with the identification of market failures. Enterprise support is a congested and keenly contested industry. SMIE (2003) estimates, for instance, that there were 68 youth enterprise programmes in Europe out of a bewildering 2517 enterprise programmes. These, though, are only the most visible (OECD, 2001): Salles (1999) estimates that France had 1830 youth enterprise programmes even prior to the recent changes in French enterprise policy.

Such levels of actual and potential 'competition' between programme providers have a number of consequences for programme stakeholders. For potential participants, there is the obvious problem of negotiating their way through the multitude of programmes (Turok and Raco, 2000). Programmes also have to show that they do not 'displace' or 'crowd out' existing provision. Equally, evaluators also have to show that a particular programme is not only better than the counterfactual but is in some way 'superior' to the existing provision in that it alone addresses its perceived market failure. This is rarely done, which is perhaps a little ironic given that one of the justifications for evaluation is that it seeks to judge, *inter alia*, the potential impact of displacement, deadweight and crowding out.

Instead, what evaluators and programme designers often focus on is testing individual identifiable mission statements such as the Ewing Kauffman Foundation's aim to 'strive to foster an environment nationwide in which entrepreneurs have the information and tools they need to succeed', or the Prince's Trust, which began with the aim 'To help young people who would not otherwise have the opportunity, to develop their self-confidence, achieve economic independence, fulfill their ambitions and contribute to the community through the medium of self-employment' (Dalgleish, 1993, p. 662). This, of course, avoids the tricky problem of how such objectives are to be assessed.

A final difficulty with 'black box' evaluations is that they are normally *ex post* rationalizations of the average treatment effects of particular programmes. This neglects *ex ante* design issues or, if evaluators come too late to this stage, the *in vivo* processes adopted by programmes. This may be judged important because there are a number of implementation choices that programmes can make to establish their competitive advantage in the enterprise support sector. Mole (2005) suggests these range from rationing choices (e.g. geographic focus, sectoral orientation, specific groups such as women or ethnic minorities), administration choices (e.g. delivered by host organization or partners), through to the type of soft or hard support provided. These, in turn, present other choices: some programmes may seek to mediate through continued bespoke face-to-face support delivered by professionals, while others may provide *ad hoc* or generic advice delivered by volunteers or electronically. The effectiveness of such bundles of implementation choices can often be missed by *ex post* evaluations, which may be particularly important to resource-constrained programmes that are seeking to improve their management (Sefton, 2003).

STEP and Shell Livewire
The previous section of this chapter identified that although step VI evaluations are generally preferable, there are instances where they are inappropriate because of resource constraints, opaque objectives, or a need to consider how resource-constrained programmes can improve their own management. In this section, we introduce our case study of Shell Livewire. We begin, however, by tracing our initial involvement with its sister programme (STEP) because this explains how we ended up conducting the evaluation of Shell Livewire.

The STEP programme
STEP was, and is, a programme sponsored by Shell UK Ltd. Administered through a project team contracted by the Shell Enterprise Unit and delivered at the local level by a national network of support providers, it seeks to place second year undergraduates in a small firm for eight weeks during their summer vacation. Its aim is to encourage undergraduates to become familiar with a small firm and, thereby, change any negative attitudes that they may have about a career in such an environment (Belfield, 1999). A second aim is to encourage a wide range of small firms to be more open to employing graduates and to see graduates as a valuable resource.

An evaluation was conducted of STEP participants matched against comparable non-STEP participants over the period 1994–97 by staff from our research centre. The findings of the research were, *inter alia*, that STEP students, compared with non-participants, were no more employable but were more likely to use the experience as a mechanism for developing their careers with larger firms rather than with smaller firms (Westhead, 1998; Westhead et al., 2001; and Fraser et al., 2006).

Conducting this study had two main benefits: it raised important policy questions about the impact of student work placements; and it brought us the prestige of working with a major corporate sponsor.

Shell UK's motives for funding the evaluation could only be guessed at. This is a stylized feature of evaluation (Weiss, 1999). What was clear, however, was that they were not greatly troubled by the positive or negative impacts of the programme. Indeed, what pleased them about the evaluation was that it revealed an important managerial insight: the evaluation demonstrated that the local support agencies managing the programme were sending STEP participants to the same small firms year in, year out. This came as a surprise to Shell UK who had, implicitly, an objective that STEP should be focused on firms with no experience of undergraduates, with the objective of changing small firms' attitudes towards graduate employment.

The Shell Livewire programme
This brings us to Shell Livewire. Based on our earlier STEP evaluation, we anticipated that we could also conduct an econometric evaluation of Shell Livewire, to estimate the average treatment effect of the programme. Our initial consultations, however, were not particularly favourable. Shell Livewire is administered for Shell UK by a project team who subsequently manage the programme through a range of local service suppliers similar to those used in the STEP evaluation. As with any organization faced with external evaluators, they were somewhat suspicious of what the evaluation could achieve.

Moreover, besides the (implicit) urge from the funders to look at management practices, there were other issues at play preventing a full econometric analysis. First, the design of the Shell Livewire programme is complex. It consists of two separate programmes of activity. The first consists of an enquiry and outreach service, which provides young enquirers (aged 16–30), interested in learning more about starting a business, with four (different) business publications. These are a self-assessment tool/explanation of the start up process (*Could This Be You/Start Your Own Business*); a *Business Opportunity Profile*; a *Market Research Booklet*; and a *Business Plan Booklet*. The booklets also guide individuals to other sources of advice and support. Alternatively, either following receipt of these booklets, or independently, individuals may make use of the outreach service, which consists of one-to-one counselling with a Shell Livewire advisor or another designated advisor.

The second programme run under the Shell Livewire umbrella is a national competition – with local and regional heats – to find successful young entrepreneurs. To enter this competition, individuals need to be aged between 16 and 30; to have completed a business plan; and to be currently running a new business (not necessarily set up with Shell Livewire support). Cash prizes are provided to the winner, together with considerable publicity through coverage in newspapers, specialist magazines, radio and television.

While robust evaluation methodologies exist for treating programmes with multiple aims (Lechner, 2002; Frolich, 2004), we were only asked to evaluate the enquiry and outreach service. In seeking to evaluate this service, however, there is a particular problem. Unlike other youth enterprise programmes, this one does not seek to ration its services to particular groups (e.g. the unemployed). It is open to everyone, including those who are already self-employed, and anyone can hear of it through its promotional literature or via its website. This made it difficult to construct an appropriate control group because we could not be sure that the control group members could be easily identified as being independent (Frolich, 2004). For example, programme 'participants' may have simply heard of Shell Livewire or briefly visited its website. The same is true of 'non-participants'. Such problems may make it difficult to appropriately match the treatment and control groups (Heckman and Smith, 1996). Brown et al. (1995), for example, argue that 'nonexistent or problematic control groups is recognized by many to be a major weakness' (p. 671).

A second difficulty was that programme targets were somewhat opaque. Hence, while its mission statement is fairly typical of youth enterprise programmes – 'to develop, manage and share quality programmes which improve opportunities for young people to realise their potential through the creation and development of their own business. Such programmes will contribute towards a more buoyant economy and a community of more fulfilled individuals' – its specific targets are almost equally vague:

Target 1:   'to distribute materials on youth enterprise';
Target 2:   'to promote awareness of enterprise amongst young people (16–30) and those who work with them';
Target 3:   'to assist young people interested in starting a business';
Target 4:   'to generally promote the importance of young people starting and growing businesses'; and
Target 5:   'to help young people established in business to expand'.

Such targets are unhelpful when trying to succinctly capture the net outcomes of particular programmes. For instance, Target 1 is unhelpful since it does not provide criteria against which to judge the success or otherwise of the target. Target 2 is little better since it does not distinguish between support providers and potential clients. Similar doubts persist about the other targets since it is not altogether clear if these are directed towards people interested in entrepreneurship or those who are already running their own business.

Our suspicion, therefore, was that the design of the enquiry and outreach programme was poorly specified. We saw a role for our evaluation in providing managerial guidance on improving the specification of these objectives as well as giving some tentative indications of its likely impact on the behaviour of its participants.

An assessment framework
Designers need to ensure that their enterprise programme is justified by addressing a market failure evident in the environment that is not currently resolved by another programme. Such investigations are rare: evaluators, instead, are usually presented with a vision or mission statement (the objective) and a series of targets. Evaluators clearly need to translate these objectives and targets into specific measures. Hence, for an evaluation of a police force, the objective may be 'to ensure the locality is a law-abiding and safe community'. Its targets may be to cut burglaries and the specific measure here might be 'to reduce burglaries by 10%' within a given time-scale.

But this is not the end of the process (Figure 12.1). There is a need for data to be collected before any measure of 'success' can be estimated. These findings then have to be presented to the relevant stakeholders. This helps stakeholders review the nature of the targets and measures, and, less frequently, it may lead to new objectives being specified. Even so, the procedure can have important 'externality' benefits. By this we mean that not-for-profit organizations frequently find certain services, which are not thought to be mainstream to the objectives of the organization and which rarely appear as explicit targets, are highly valued (Hanberger, 2001). The assessment process can highlight this and, in some cases, lead to the service being developed and the organization being re-focused.

Evaluation, then, is not the end of the management accountability trail (Pitcher, 2002). Instead, it is a circular process in which the assessment findings are used to clarify

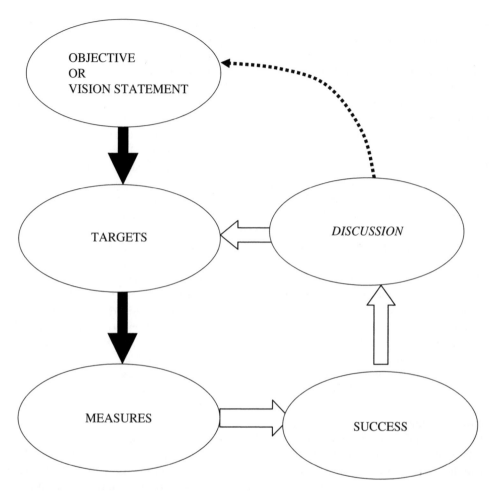

Figure 12.1   The assessment cycle

the objectives of the organization and are then used by the management to assess performance.

Constructing measures

Because of the opaque nature of Shell Livewire's targets, considerable interpretation was needed before we could arrive at identifiable measures. We also recognized that we could not fully account for all of the targets in our evaluation and, therefore, derived four measures to capture their heterogeneity.

Measure 1: The total number of enquiries to Livewire

Our first, albeit simple, measure is the absolute number of enquiries received by Livewire, and whether these increase over a given period of time. The limitation of such a measure is that it may partially reflect Targets 1, 2 and 4, but it also reflects entrepreneurial awareness in general.

Measure 2: The proportion of enquirers making the transition to self-employment, taking account of their human capital

Our second measure is the number of enquirers to Livewire that are in business (self-employment) at some later date. This has two limitations. First, enquirers may have been intending to start a business prior to contacting Livewire, and contact may not have influenced that decision. Second, Livewire receives enquiries from some young people already in self-employment.

A more robust measure is the number of enquirers in any given time period making the *transition* into business. To estimate this three issues have to be addressed. First, data on the employment status of enquirers at the time of their first contact with Livewire, are needed. Second, as Reynolds and Miller (1992) show, venture creation is often neither a sequential nor a short process. Third, transition by young people into self-employment is strongly influenced by human capital, reflected in age (Johansson, 2000), gender (Blanchflower and Meyer, 1994) and education (Dolton and Makepeace, 1990). The differences in human capital among enquirers, therefore, need to be held constant.

Measure 3: The current enterprise disposition measure, taking account of human capital

The limitation of Measure 2 is that it only includes those actually starting a business. This ignores the possibility that youth enterprise support could be judged to be successful if enquirers become *more likely* to start a business, without necessarily having actually started. A measure of whether former enquirers were, in some sense, subsequently more 'enterprising' following their contact with Livewire is needed. To formulate such a measure we made three assumptions. First, enquirers contact Livewire because they wish to create a new venture or because they are interested in developing their existing business. Second, at some point in time *after* their initial contact with Livewire, it is possible to make contact with former enquirers. Third, a snapshot can be provided of their *current* entrepreneurial aspirations or achievements *following* prior contact with Shell Livewire.

To achieve this, we drew on the categorization provided by Kouriloff (2000). He identified four groups in the Australian population: actual, intending, potential and no wish to start. To reflect the objectives of Livewire we also distinguish between those business owners who employ only themselves and those who employ others, whereas Kouriloff combined them into a single group. From this we distinguished five groups of participants on the programme:

- The former enquirer has entered self-employment and is now an employer of others. These constitute Group 5 individuals and are called 'employers';
- The former enquirer has entered self-employment but does not employ others. These constitute Group 4 individuals and are called the 'self-employed';
- The former enquirer has not entered self-employment but is currently taking steps to enter self-employment in the near future. Reynolds and Miller call such individuals 'nascents', whereas Kouriloff refers to them as 'intending'. They constitute Group 3;
- The former enquirer has not entered self-employment, and currently has no plans to do so, but reports that starting a business is possible in the future. These individuals constitute Group 2. Kouriloff calls these individuals 'potentials' but we prefer the more objective term 'possibles'; and

● The former enquirer has not entered self-employment and has no plans in the fore-
seeable future to do so. These individuals constitute Group 1 and are called the
'non-movers', but 'no wish to start' by Kouriloff.

To operationalize this measure, success is assumed to range from former enquirers that
are currently 'employers' (Group 5) to 'non-movers' (Group 1).

Measure 4: Satisfaction with advice received from Livewire (EVALUATE), taking
account of human capital
Our final measure of the programme was to make use of the reported participant views
of how valuable the programme was – the so-called 'happy sheets'. The limitations of this
approach are well known: first, happiness with a service does not necessarily convert into
action. So, in this case, while enquirers may be happy with the way information was delivered by Livewire, this may not have influenced their decision to enter self-employment.[1]
Second, results from 'happy sheets' are particularly susceptible to who asks the questions
and how they are asked.[2] While acknowledging these distinct limitations, we judged that
it might offer insights into programme design, particularly if we asked participants to
compare Livewire with its 'competitors'. Participants were then asked to score their
assessment of Livewire and other programmes on a scale between 1 and 7, where 1 was
of no value and 7 was vital.

Data
As Reynolds and Miller (1992) suggest, one central feature of venture creation is that it
is not an instantaneous process. The period of gestation between an idea and actually
starting to trade can, in some instances, be longer than three years. Hence, an examination of changes in attitude or employment status, a few months after contacting Livewire,
would risk underestimating any contribution made by the advice and assistance offered.
This, however, has to be balanced against the period between advice and follow-up being
overly long. For this highly mobile client group there is a high risk of contact details being
out of date very quickly, and biased samples being drawn. There is also the risk that accuracy of recall falls with time.

To resolve this issue it was decided in late 1999 to draw a sample of Livewire enquirers
that had first contacted the organization in 1996, 1997 and 1998. This meant that the first
enquiry was made, in some cases, only a few months previously, but could be up to just
over three years. This provided a range of durations that later could be used to test for
differences in employment status and attitudes over time.

Three types of data were used in the evaluation. The first was Livewire's enquiry records
for 1996–98 of which 9303 (27.17 per cent) were in 1996, 8687 (25.37 per cent) in 1997 and
16 242 (47.43 per cent) in 1998. The data consisted of their name, age, gender, educational
qualifications, address and employment status.[3] Such information was used to formulate
Measure 1.

The second was data collected on the outcome of these enquirers. First, representatives
of Livewire conducted a telephone survey in the autumn of 1999. Of the 9878 enquirers
contacted 20 per cent were from 1996, 46.5 per cent from 1997 and 33.5 per cent from
1998. This produced 1031 responses – a rate of 10.4 per cent. Two postal surveys, this time
by the researchers (one of 5000, the other of 1000), were also conducted in late 1999 to

early 2000. Both the telephone and the postal surveys used an identical questionnaire. In total, 1405 responses were generated – a response rate of 8.8 per cent. The temporal distribution of respondents reflected that of enquirers with, for example, 27 per cent of both enquirers and respondents making their first contact with Livewire in 1996. The 1405 respondents, however, differed so cases were dropped to ensure that the sample and population means did not differ significantly in terms of age of enquirer, gender, educational qualifications, or employment state. In total, 1164 cases are used in the analysis, with these closely reflecting the population of enquirers.[4]

Data description
Table 12.1 provides a brief description of the variables used and some descriptive statistics of both the dependent and independent variables (mean and standard deviation). Drawing on prior research the expected influence of these independent variables on the entrepreneurial propensity of an individual (ENTSTATE) is also hypothesized.

The table shows respondents were generally satisfied (mean score 4.58) with the services they received from Shell Livewire (EVALUATE). Following contact with Shell Livewire, 36 per cent decided the entrepreneurial option was not for them (NONMOVERS). The next most common groups were those currently pursuing, but not yet implementing, the creation of a new venture (NASCENTS) (21 per cent), and those with some future expectation of entrepreneurship (POSSIBLES) (21 per cent). In total, just over one in five entered some form of self-employment: the self-employed with no employees (SELF) made up 18 per cent and the self-employed with employees (SELF&EMP) 4 per cent.

Table 12.1   Description of variables

Variable name	Definition	Expected sign	Mean	Std dev.	N
Dependent variables					
ENTSTATE	4 = self-employed with employees, 3 = self-employed, 2 = nascent entrepreneur, 1 = possible, 0 = non-mover		1.36	1.27	1121
SWITCHEM	1 = currently self employed, 0 = not in self-employment when first contacting Livewire				
EVALUATE	Evaluation of Shell Livewire start-up services: 7 vital, 1 no value by all respondents		4.58	1.51	1074
Independent variables					
Background factors					
RESPONSE	1 postal respondent, 0 otherwise	n.s.	0.26	0.44	1164
YEAR1996	1 contacted Livewire in 1996, 0 otherwise	?	0.27	0.44	1164
YEAR1997	1 contacted Livewire in 1997, 0 otherwise	?	0.26	0.44	1164
YEAR1998	1 contacted Livewire in 1998, 0 otherwise (control variable)	?	0.47	0.50	1164
Personal factors					
GENDER	1 = male, 0 = female	+	0.60	0.49	1164
AGE	Age of respondent	+	22.73	2.83	993
AGE2	Age of respondent squared	−	524.8	130.7	993

Table 12.1   (continued)

Variable name	Definition	Expected sign	Mean	Std dev.	N
Educational attainment level					
POSTGRAD	1 = postgraduate degree, 0 otherwise	+	0.04	0.19	1144
DEGREE	1 = degree, 0 otherwise	+	0.27	0.44	1144
GRAD	POSTGRAD + DEGREE	+	0.31		1144
HNDHNC	1 = HND/HNC, 0 otherwise	−	0.10	0.29	1144
ALEVELS	1 = A Levels, 0 otherwise	−	0.15	0.36	1144
VOCQUAL	1 = vocational qualification, 0 otherwise	−	0.16	0.36	1144
GCSE	1 = GCSEs, 0 otherwise	−	0.17	0.38	1144
NO_QUAL	1 = no qualifications, 0 otherwise	−	0.11	0.25	1144
Employment status when contacted Livewire					
STUDENT	1 = student, 0 otherwise	?	0.18	0.39	770
UNEMPLOY	1 = unemployed, 0 otherwise	+	0.48	0.50	770
SE_EMP	1 = self-employed, 0 otherwise (control variable)	+	0.06	0.23	770
EMPLOYED	1 = employed, 0 otherwise	−	0.28	0.45	770
Current entrepreneurial disposition					
SELF&EMP	1 is self-employed with employees, 0 otherwise	+	0.04	0.20	1164
SELF	1 is self-employed, 0 otherwise	+	0.18	0.39	1164
NASCENTS	1 is in the process of starting a venture, 0 otherwise	+	0.21	0.41	1164
POSSIBLES	1 would consider setting up a venture in the future, 0 otherwise	−	0.21	0.40	1164
NON-MOVERS	1 would not consider setting up a venture, 0 otherwise (control variable)	−	0.36	0.48	1164
Evaluation by self-employed individuals of support services					
LIVEWIRE	7 vital, 1 no value	?	4.04	1.94	138
PRINCE'S TRUST	7 vital, 1 no value	?	4.92	1.92	135
LEA	7 vital, 1 no value	?	4.85	1.97	102
Use of Shell Livewire services					
CTBYBOOK	1 used Could This Be You/Start Your Own Business, 0 otherwise	+	0.52	0.50	1151
BOPBOOK	1 used Business Opportunity Profile, 0 otherwise	+	0.22	0.41	1151
MRBBOOK	1 used Market Research Booklet, 0 otherwise	+	0.28	0.45	1151
BPBBOOK	1 used Business Plan Booklet, 0 otherwise	+	0.35	0.48	1151
CO_ORDIN	1 visited/made contact with Livewire coordinator, 0 otherwise	+	0.13	0.34	1151
COUNSEL	1 visited/made contact with another business counsellor, 0 otherwise	+	0.15	0.35	1151

Table 12.1 also shows that self-employed individuals, when asked to rank their satisfaction with Shell Livewire's (LIVEWIRE) support, alongside support from other agencies, suggested that the Prince's Trust and Enterprise Agencies seemed to provide a more valued service (PRINCE'S TRUST and LEA). It is also interesting to note that the average score of the currently self-employed enquirers (LIVEWIRE = 4.04) is markedly lower than for all enquirers (EVALUATE = 4.58). Both these issues are discussed in more detail later.

The four measures
The purpose of this section is twofold. First, it introduces the findings for each of the four measures and details the ways in which these measures might be constructed. Second, it highlights some of the general issues that resulted from our evaluation. We therefore discuss each of the four measures in turn and intersperse this, where appropriate, with our observations about general issues for evaluations seeking to improve the management of enterprise programmes.

Measure 1: The total number of enquiries to Livewire
Figure 12.2 shows the total number of enquiries received by Shell Livewire since 1982. Enquiry growth has been rapid so that, by 1999, almost 30 000 young people per year were making contact with Livewire. This growth has been fairly continuous, implying this is independent of macroeconomic conditions. Livewire managers viewed this as a key success measure. Our view was that there was a need to distinguish between the casual Livewire enquirer and those who used the programme as a mechanism to enter business. In short, the aggregate data were open to many, and different, interpretations.

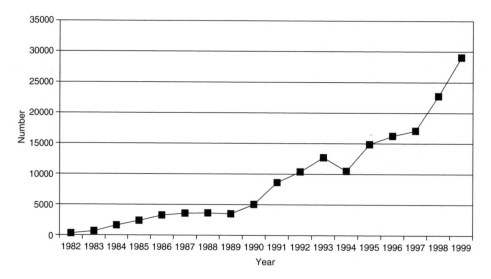

Figure 12.2   Number of enquiries to Livewire by year, 1982–99

Table 12.2   Changes in employment status of respondents

Previous employment status	Current employment status				
	Self-employed	Employed	Student	Unemployed	Total
Self-employed	*0.032*	0.019	0.003	0.004	0.057
Employed	0.057	*0.185*	0.013	0.023	0.278
Student	0.015	0.065	*0.089*	0.017	0.185
Unemployed	0.110	0.240	0.038	*0.091*	0.479
Total	0.213	0.509	0.143	0.135	1.000

Measure 2: The proportion of enquirers making the transition to self-employment (SWITCHEM)

Table 12.2, however, shows that the programme seemingly makes an impressive contribution to the transition into self-employment. The first column (self-employment) shows that 21.3 per cent of Livewire enquirers were self-employed when contacted. Of these, 18.1 per cent made the transition into self-employment (3.2 per cent were previously self-employed) with the vast majority of them being previously unemployed. This, too, is seemingly impressive since, even after normalizing the numbers in each state at the time of the enquiry, the unemployed are subsequently more likely to be in self-employment than those who were formerly students or employees.

To further examine the factors influencing the transition to self-employment, a standard Probit model is used to explain whether former Livewire enquirers, not in self-employment when first contacting Livewire, were in self-employment by 1999/2000. The dependent variable is SWITCHEM, which takes a value of 1 when the enquirer moved into self-employment and zero for all other states.

The results are shown in Table 12.3. Model 1 shows the influence of human capital on switching to self-employment; Model 2 adds the YEAR variables. Finally, Model 3 adds the use of Livewire services.

Model 3 summarizes the position. It shows the AGE and YEAR1996 variables are positive and significant, implying it is the older (young) people who are most likely to make the transition to self-employment. This is expected (Dolton and Makepeace, 1990; Blanchflower and Meyer, 1994; and Williams, 2004). The positive sign on YEAR1996 could reflect the time taken for venture creation. Since some ventures take many months to come to fruition, the more historic enquirers are more likely to have actually started in business. None of the Livewire business booklets are significant, whereas contacting a Shell Livewire coordinator (CO-ORDIN) or another counsellor (COUNSEL) has a significant positive sign.

Measure 3: The current enterprise disposition measure

The evidence, particularly from Tables 12.1 and 12.2, suggests that Livewire makes a sizeable contribution to individuals seeking to make the transition into self-employment. Table 12.1, for example, showed that, in 1999/2000, 36 per cent of former Livewire enquirers were 'non-movers' in the sense of having no plans whatever of starting a

Table 12.3   Probit model on transition to self-employment (dependent variable =
SWITCHEM)

	Model 1		Model 2		Model 3	
	Coeff	Z stat	Coeff	Z stat	Coeff	Z stat
AGE	0.069	3.34***	0.083	3.81***	0.082	3.61***
GENDER	−0.065	−0.56	−0.087	0.74	−0.111	−0.92
GRAD	0.024	0.20	−0.013	−0.11	−0.019	−0.15
YEAR 1997			0.225	1.60	0.143	0.94
YEAR 1996			0.354	2.47**	0.312	1.95*
CTBYBOOK					0.156	−1.29
BOPBOOK					−0.160	−0.98
MRBBOOK					−0.064	−0.34
BPBBOOK					0.117	0.162
CO-ORDIN					0.492	3.14***
COUNSEL					0.672	4.40***
Const	−2.384	−5.00	−2.841	−5.47	−2.866	0.553
N	641		641		636	
R^2	0.02		0.03		0.08	
Log-likelihood	−317.14		313.92		296.21	
Chi^2	12.18		18.63		51.78	
Sig.	0.007		0.002		0.000	

Note: *** statistically significant at the p. 0.01 level; ** statistically significant at the p. 0.05 level; and * statistically significant at the p. 0.1 level.

business, while 22 per cent were in some form of self-employment. This means that more than 40 per cent are considering, with varying degrees of intensity, starting a business. This compares well with Kouriloff's (2000) findings that 64 per cent of his Australian random sample had 'no wish to start a business', and 5 per cent were currently business owners.[5]

To explore further the dimensions of any transitions, Table 12.4 presents three ordered Probit models that are used to explain the ENTSTATE measure (ranging from NON-MOVER = 0 to SELF&EMP = 4). Model 1 shows the human capital variables make a modest contribution to explaining ENTSTATE. AGE is significant with a positive sign.[6] In contrast with Table 12.3, the GENDER variable is also significant, implying that males were currently more likely to have a higher entrepreneurial propensity.[7] In Model 2, the inclusion of the enquiry year is significant, implying that those making their enquiries in 1996 were significantly more likely to be currently in a higher entrepreneurial state than those enquiring in 1998.

It will be recalled that a similar result was obtained for Measure 2, which examined actual transitions to self-employment. There it was argued that the lower rate of entry into self-employment by the 1998 cohort could reflect the length of the gestation period required before starting a business. Obtaining a very similar result with ENSTATE, which does take account of gestation, suggests the 1998 cohort is less likely, even with time, to enter self-employment, than the earlier cohort.

Table 12.4   Ordered Probit models (dependent variable = ENTSTATE) of factors impacting on entrepreneurial disposition

	Model 1		Model 2		Model 3	
	Coeff	Z stat	Coeff	Z stat	Coeff	Z stat
AGE	0.0739	5.81***	0.080	6.17***	0.072	5.40***
GENDER	0.150	2.08**	0.150	2.07**	0.139	1.89*
GRAD	0.030	0.41	0.026	0.34	0.036	0.47
YEAR 1997			−0.011	−0.13	−0.101	1.14
YEAR 1996			0.259	2.95***	0.130	1.37
CTBYBOOK					0.102	1.40
BOPBOOK					−0.094	−0.92
MRBBOOK					−0.259	2.30**
BPBBOOK					0.086	0.88
CO-ORDIN					0.673	6.45**
COUNSEL					0.574	5.75*
Const						
N	944		944		935	
R²		0.015		0.018		0.051
Log-likelihood		−1371.01		−1365.72		1307.3
Chi²		40.51		51.17		140.9
Sig.		0.000		0.000		0.000

Note: *** statistically significant at the p. 0.01 level; ** statistically significant at the p. 0.05 level; and * statistically significant at the p. 0.1 level.

Model 3 examines these factors, together with the services provided by Livewire. As before, AGE and GENDER continue to be significant. The use of counselling services – CO-ORDIN and COUNSEL – is significantly positively associated with ENTSTATE. MRBBOOK – the use of the Livewire Market Research booklet – has a significant negative sign. This may be because use of the booklet enabled the enquirer to realistically assess markets, so providing a valuable service by dissuading unsuitable people from starting in business. However, the negative sign is counter-intuitive and suggests the need to review the contribution of the booklet.

Overall, when we presented these points to Livewire managers, we were wary about classifying the programme as a success. Partly, this was because of a lack of transparency in the process of first identifying, and then translating, targets into suitable metrics. Livewire managers robustly rejected the implication that such a process was opaque, since Livewire is essentially a signposting service that points individuals to other sources of support. Our response was that surely it was possible to move from nebulous targets to targets that could be captured by transparent metrics.

Measure 4: Satisfaction with advice received from Livewire
Besides quantifying the dimensions of any transitions into self-employment, we were also concerned with issues of satisfaction. Table 12.5, therefore, shows satisfaction with Livewire compared with two other support providers (Prince's Trust and Local Enterprise Agencies

Table 12.5   Shell Livewire compared to other sources of support

	Livewire	Prince's Trust	Local Enterprise Agency
Self-employed (SELF)			
Mean	4.01	4.92***	4.88***
Std Dev.	1.98	1.95	1.98
N	112	111	88
Self-employed with employees (SELF & EMP)			
Mean	4.15	4.92**	4.71(n.s.)
Std. Dev.	1.80	1.84	2.02
N	26	24	14
All self-employed			
Mean	4.04	4.92***	4.85***
Std Dev.	1.94	1.92	1.97
N	138	135	102

Note: *** statistically significant at the p. 0.01 level; and ** statistically significant at the p. 0.05 level.

(LEAs)) for those respondents currently in self-employment. Only the views of this group of former enquirers are sought because they are (by far) the most likely to have used the service of an additional source of advice. They can be viewed as better informed customers.

The first section of the table shows the results for the self-employed without employees (SELF), and the second section for the self-employed with employees (SELF&EMP). The third section combines the two. Section 1 shows respondents score Livewire significantly below the Prince's Trust and Local Enterprise Agencies (LEAs). Section 2 shows the scores reported by the much smaller number of enquirers that, in 1999/2000, were SELF&EMP. The scores reported by this group for the three main support providers are slightly, but consistently, below those reported by the SELF group in Section 1, implying this group is the least likely to value advice. This group also report lower scores for Livewire than for the Prince's Trust or the LEAs, although the small number of cases means the LEA score is not significantly different. Finally, in section 3, SELF and SELF&EMP are combined, confirming the findings for the two groups considered separately.

The low scores for Livewire among those currently self-employed might reflect the different services it provides. In particular, the Prince's Trust provides not only guidance but also funding. If young entrepreneurs value funding highly, then the higher scores of the Prince's Trust are to be expected. While this may explain the difference between the Prince's Trust and Livewire, it does not explain why other organizations providing identical services to Livewire, such as LEAs, also score more highly.

A second explanation is that Livewire is primarily an information and signposting service, taking enquiries from young people considering starting a business. If the enquirer then decides to develop their business idea, then they are 'passed on' to a counsellor who is likely to be from an LEA. If the business then develops, the enquirer may view the major contribution as being made by the LEA rather than by Livewire.

Table 12.6 shows the results of an ordered Probit model to explain satisfaction with Livewire, where the dependent variable is EVALUATE. The format of the table is the same as Tables 12.3 and 12.4, except that on this occasion we also include the RESPOND and

Table 12.6   *Ordered Probit models (dependent variable = EVALUATE) satisfaction with Shell Livewire*

	Model 1		Model 2		Model 3		Model 4	
	Coeff	Z stat	Coeff	Z Stat	Coeff	Z Stat	Coeff	Z Stat
AGE	−0.036	−2.99***	−0.054	−4.30***	−0.049	−3.84**	−0.049	−3.75***
GENDER	−0.153	−2.16*	−0.121	−1.70	−0.164	−2.29**	−0.198	−2.74**
GRAD	−0.273	−3.66***	−0.261	−3.49***	−0.267	−3.56**	−0.287	−3.80***
YEAR 1997			−0.566	−6.29***	−0.133	−1.31	0.004	0.04
YEAR 1996			−0.330	−4.02***	−0.255	−3.09***	−0.173	−2.02*
CTBYBOOK							0.130	1.77
BOPBOOK							0.332	3.38***
MRBBOOK							0.018	0.17
BPBBOOK							0.257	2.69**
CO-ORDIN							0.449	4.37***
COUNSEL							0.047	0.47
RESPOND					−0.863	−9.10**	−0.973	−9.65***
SELF					−0.181	−2.08*	−0.235	−2.63**
N	900		900		900		900	
R²	0.001		0.023		0.05		0.072	
Log-likelihood	−1556.4		−1535.1		−1488.84		−1458.5	
Chi²	31.24		73.72		166.26		226.9	
Sig.	0.000		0.000		0.000		0.000	

Note: *** statistically significant at the p. 0.01 level; ** statistically significant at the p. 0.05 level; and * statistically significant at the p. 0.1 level.

SELF variables in Model 3, before including all variables in Model 4. Model 1 shows that satisfaction scores are strongly influenced by the human capital of the enquirer. Males, older respondents and graduates are all likely to score Livewire less highly than younger, non-graduate females.

All these factors continue to influence satisfaction scores when more variables are added. Model 3 shows that, in addition to the human capital variables, the YEAR1996 variable has a significant negative sign. Satisfaction with Livewire was lower among enquirers in that year than in the base year of 1998 – implying an improvement in satisfaction in more recent times.

It will be recalled from Table 12.1 that satisfaction scores with Livewire are low among those former enquirers that are currently self-employed. Since more of the 1996 enquiry cohort has had time to enter self-employment, this suggests the need for the SELF variable to be included in the equation. Model 3 shows SELF has the expected negative sign but, even so, YEAR1996 continues to be significant, implying improved reported satisfaction among more recent enquirers, even taking account of their current employment status.

Model 3 also exhibits a strong negative sign on the RESPOND variable. This suggests that satisfaction with Livewire was significantly lower among former enquirers that were surveyed by post, as opposed to those surveyed by telephone. It will be recalled that the postal survey was returned anonymously to the researchers. The telephone survey, however, was not as clearly anonymous since Livewire nominees conducted it. One interpretation of this finding is that respondents felt able to offer more strongly negative opinions to 'external' researchers than to the organization itself.[8]

Finally, in Model 4, the use of the individual Livewire services is included, together with all the earlier variables. All variables found to be significant in the earlier models continue to be significant, but three Livewire variables also appear. Model 4 shows that use of the *Business Opportunities Profile Booklet* (BOPBOOK) and use of the *Business Planning Booklet* (BPBBOOK) are positive influences on satisfaction. Making contact with a Livewire coordinator (CO-ORDIN) also enhanced satisfaction.

Overall, Livewire emerges with some credit from Measure 4. It suggests that more recent enquirers to Livewire are more satisfied with the service they received than were enquirers from 1996. It also suggests that the Livewire literature, and the opportunity to meet a coordinator, enhanced satisfaction.

Nonetheless, it is clear that, among the self-employed, satisfaction with 'competitor' organizations was higher than with Livewire. Equally, Livewire satisfaction rates were lower among those who were self-employed when compared with those who had not entered self-employment. The third issue is that enquirers in 1998 were not only less likely to have entered self-employment, but reported they were less likely to enter self-employment in the future than enquirers from earlier years. This might imply that the increase in the number of Livewire enquirers in 1998 led to a fall in 'quality'.

The prime response of Livewire management to these findings was to question the extent to which enquirers were aware of the roles played by Livewire and these other organizations. Livewire, it was argued, primarily acts as a signposting service, but does work closely with other agencies. When enquirers to Livewire were passed on to a business counsellor, this was often to an Enterprise Agency. Where that counsellor provided valuable advice, as they frequently did, the enquirer when asked about external assistance spoke positively about the Enterprise Agency who provided the advice, rather than about Livewire who had effected the introduction. This realization encouraged the management of Livewire to consider a stronger 'branding' of its activities among enquirers.

Essentially, therefore, our main acknowledged managerial recommendation was that Livewire managers needed to work more closely with Enterprise Agencies to ensure that Livewire's contribution was more identifiable. Our other findings – the lack of satisfaction with Livewire and the seeming insubstantial nature of its market research booklet – were unenthusiastically received. We felt that these issues questioned the validity of a signposting and consciousness raising service but this view was rejected by Livewire. The measures that we suggested were also rejected. Our 'rules of thumb' were not seen as appropriate 'messages' for a signposting organization such as Livewire. For Livewire managers, the programme was a valuable 'stepping stone' in supporting the entrepreneurial intentions of young people and, while there was a need to ensure that Livewire worked harder with Enterprise Agencies, there was largely little wrong with a service of this type and certainly no need for prescriptive measures.

Conclusions

This chapter has focused on the contextual nature of evaluation. It has used the case study of Shell Livewire to explore some of the issues faced by evaluators wishing to be responsive to resource constraints and the *in vivo* managerial concerns of enterprise support programmes. In opening up the 'black box', however, our case study of Shell Livewire identified that one of the major issues facing evaluators of such programmes is the opaque nature of targets and the difficulty of translating these into identifiable measures. This chapter developed a framework for assessing this process. It then formulated specific measures that approximated to some (but not all) of the publicly stated targets of Livewire. Our main operational conclusion is that Livewire may seem to be altering the behaviour of young people, but that this is not necessarily wholly attributable to the programme.

Equally, satisfaction with Livewire seemingly declines with higher levels of exposure to self-employment. This produced some managerial insights into how the Livewire programme could better brand its signposting services. It is, therefore, possible for evaluations of this type to provide important managerial information. However, two important caveats remain. First, it is not altogether clear if the low valuation of Livewire among the self-employed is due to a lack of awareness of Livewire services; an inherent reluctance of entrepreneurs to recognize the role of others (de Meza, 2002); or that the contribution of Livewire is genuinely marginal. Second, the fieldwork for this research relied on two differing modes of data collection. The externally generated results produced lower satisfaction levels with Livewire than the internal results. Our interpretation, therefore, is that researchers, programme managers and funders not only have to be responsive to the managerial context within which evaluations operate, but also sensitive to the way data are collected.

Overall, the managers of Livewire were unenthusiastic about the key findings of this evaluation, viewing them, implicitly, as reflecting a failure on the part of the evaluators to understand the nature of a signposting service. In contrast, the evaluators remain wedded to the view that enterprise policies that seek to induce 'attitudinal change' seem to have a cavalier view of targets, measures and objectives.

Notes

1. An example of this in the UK is the evaluation of the Golden Key training package. This showed that while business owners very much liked the programme, as did bank managers, there was no statistically significant difference in the performance of participants and otherwise comparable non-participants (British Bankers Association, 2001).
2. An example of this is presented later.
3. In practice, the information collected at the time of enquiry was not complete in all cases.
4. See Greene and Storey (2004) for further details.
5. The Global Entrepreneurship Monitor (2002) may also be considered for comparison. It reports Total Entrepreneurship Activity across all countries for 18–24 year olds to be 17.2 per 100, and that for 25–34 year olds to be 18.9. While the comparison is imperfect, the fact that the UK is close to the middle of the country distribution, does suggest that Livewire enquirers were atypical of UK 18–30 year olds.
6. The squared term of AGE was also included but was not significant, implying that, at least up to the age of 30, entrepreneurial propensity increases linearly with age. All combinations of the education variables were also included, but none were individually significant, so only the GRAD variable is included in the table.
7. The GRAD variable is included – despite being non-significant. All combinations of the education variables from Table 12.1 were included, but none were found to be significant.
8. Further analysis of EVALUATE showed that the broad findings from Table 12.6 did not differ between the survey methods, but merely that those replying by post scored Livewire much lower than those contacted via telephone.

Bibliography

Belfield, C.R. (1999), 'The behaviour of graduates in the SME labour market: evidence and perceptions', *Small Business Economics*, **12** (3), 249–59.
Birley, S. (1985), 'The role of networks in the entrepreneurial process', *Journal of Business Venturing*, **1**, 107–17.

Blanchflower, D.G. and B. Meyer (1994), 'A longitudinal analysis of the young self-employed in Australia and the United States', *Small Business Economics*, **6**, 1–20.

Blanchflower, D. and A.J. Oswald (1998), *Entrepreneurship and the Youth Labour Market Problem: A Report for the OECD*, OECD: Paris.

British Bankers Association (2001), *The Evaluation of the Golden Key Package Component of the Small Business Initiative*, London: BBA.

Brown, M.A., T. Randall Curlee and S.R. Elliott (1995), 'Evaluating technology innovation programs: the use of comparison groups to identify impacts', *Research Policy*, **24**, 669–84.

Chelimsky, E. (1997), 'Thoughts for a new evaluation society', *Evaluation*, **3** (1), 97–118.

Chen, H.T. (1990), *Theory-driven Evaluations*, London: Sage.

Chrisman, J.J. and F. Katrishen (1994), 'The economic-impact of small business development center counseling activities in the United States – 1990–1991', *Journal of Business Venturing*, **9** (4), 271–80.

Chrisman, J.J. (1989), 'Strategic administrative and operating assistance: the value of outside consulting to pre-venture entrepreneurs', *Journal of Business Venturing*, **4**, 401–18.

Chrisman, J.J. (1999), 'The influence of outsider-generated knowledge resources on venture creation', *Journal of Small Business Management*, **37** (4), 42–58.

Chrisman, J.J. and W.E. McMullan (2004), 'Outsider assistance as a knowledge resource for new venture survival', *Journal of small Business Management*, **42** (3), 229–44.

Chrisman, J.J. and W.E. McMullan (2000), 'A preliminary assessment of outsider assistance as a knowledge resource: the longer term impact of new venture counseling', *Entrepreneurship Theory and Practice*, **24** (3), 37–53.

Cooper, A.C., T.B. Folta and C. Woo (1995), 'Entrepreneurial information search', *Journal of Business Venturing*, **10** (2), 107–20.

Dalgleish, M. (1993), 'An evaluation of the Prince's Youth Business Trust', *Employment Gazette*, January, 661–6.

Daly, M. (1987), 'Lifespan of businesses registered for VAT', *British Business*, 3 April, 28–9.

de Meza, D. (2002), 'Overlending', *Economic Journal*, **112** (477), February, F17–F31.

del Monte, A. and D. Scalera (2001), 'The life duration of small firms born within a start-up programme: evidence from Italy', *Regional Studies*, **35** (1), 11–22.

Dolton, P.J. and G.H. Makepeace (1990), 'Self-employment among graduates', *Bulletin of Economic Research*, **42** (1), 35–53.

Evans, D. and L.S. Leighton (1989), 'Some empirical aspects of entrepreneurship', *American Economic Review*, **79**, 519–35.

Fraser, S., D.J. Storey and P. Westhead (2006), 'Student work placements: do they pay-off or shift tastes?', *Small Business Economics*, **26** (2), 125–44.

Frolich, M. (2004), 'Program evaluation with multiple treatments', *Journal of Economic Surveys*, **18** (2), 181–224.

Gimeno, J., T.B. Folta, A.C. Cooper and C.C. Woo (1997), 'Survival of the fittest? Entrepreneurial human capital and the persistence of under-performing firms', *Administrative Science Quarterly*, **42**, 750–83.

Global Entrepreneurship Monitor (GEM) (2002), *GEM Global Report*, Babson College: Babson Park.

Greene, F.J. (2005), 'Youth entrepreneurship: latent entrepreneurship, market failure and enterprise support', NCGE Discussion Paper, NCGE, Birmingham.

Greene, F.J. and D.J. Storey (2004), 'The value of outsider assistance in supporting new venture creation by young people', *Entrepreneurship and Regional Development*, **16** (2), 145–59.

Hanberger, A. (2001), 'What is the policy problem', *Evaluation*, **7** (1), 45–62.

Heckman, J. (1979), 'Sample selection bias as a specification error', *Econometrica*, **47**, 153–61.

Heckman, J.J. and J.A. Smith (1996), 'Experimental and nonexperimental evaluation', in G. Schmid, J. O'Reilly and K. Schomann (eds), *International Handbook of Labour Market Policy and Evaluation*, Cheltenham, UK and Brookfield, USA: Edward Elgar, pp. 37–88.

Holtz-Eakin, D., D. Joulfaian and H.S. Rosen (1994), 'Sticking it out: entrepreneurial survival and liquidity constraints', *Journal of Political Economy*, **102** (1), 53–75.

Johansson, E. (2000), 'Self-employment and liquidity constraints', *Scandinavian Journal of Economics*, **103** (1), 123–34.

Katz, J.A. (2004), *Survey of Endowed Positions in Entrepreneurship and Related Fields in the United States*, Kansas City, MO: Kauffman Foundation.

Kouriloff, M. (2000), 'Exploring perceptions of a priori barriers to entrepreneurship: a multidisciplinary approach', *Entrepreneurship Theory and Practice*, **25** (2), 59–79.

Larsson, L. (2003), 'Evaluation of Swedish youth labor market programs', *Journal of Human Resources*, **37** (4), 891–927.

Lechner, M. (2002), 'Some practical issues in the evaluation of heterogeneous labour market programs by matching methods', *Journal of the Royal Statistical Society A*, **165**, 59–82.

Lerner, J. (1999), 'The government as venture capitalist: the long run impact of the SBIR Programme', *Journal of Business*, **72** (3), 285–318.

Lundström, A. and L. Stevenson (2001), *Entrepreneurship Policy for the Future*, Stockholm: Swedish Foundation for Small Business Research.

Martin, S. and I. Sanderson (1999), 'Evaluating public policy experiments', *Evaluation*, **5** (3), 245–58.

Meager, N. (1996), 'From unemployment to self-employment: labour market policies for business start-up', in G. Schmid, J. O'Reilly and K. Schomann (eds), *International Handbook of Labour Market Policy and Evaluation*, Cheltenham, UK and Brookfield, USA: Edward Elgar, pp. 489–519.

Meager, N., P. Bates and M. Cowling (2003), *Business Start-up Support for Young People, Delivered by The Prince's Trust: A Comparative Study of Labour Market Outcomes*, Brighton: IES.

Mole, K.F. (2005), *International Review of Business Support and Brokerage*, London: Small Business Service.

OECD (1998), *Fostering Entrepreneurship*, Paris: OECD.

OECD (2001), *Putting the Young in Business: Policy Challenges for Youth Entrepreneurship*, Paris: OECD.

Papaconstantinou, G. and W. Polt (1997), 'Policy evaluation in innovation and technology: an overview', in *Policy Evaluation in Innovation and Technology: Towards Best Practices*, Paris: OECD, pp. 9–14.

Picciotto, R. (1999), 'Towards an economics of evaluation', *Evaluation*, **5** (1), 7–22.

Pineda, R.C., L.D. Lerner, M.C. Miller and S.J. Phillips (1998), 'An investigation of factors affecting the information-search activities of small business managers', *Journal of Small Business Management*, **36** (1), 60–71.

Pitcher, J. (2002), 'Policies and programs to address disadvantage among young people: issues for evaluation', *Evaluation*, **8** (4), 474–95.

Reynolds, P.D. and B. Miller (1992), 'New firm gestation: conception, birth and implications for research', *Journal of Business Venturing*, **7**, 405–17.

Reynolds, P.D., D.J. Storey and P. Westhead (1994), 'Cross-national comparisons of the variation in new firm formation rates', *Regional Studies*, **28**, 443–56.

Riding, A.L. and G. Haines (2001), 'Loan guarantees: costs of default and benefits to small firms', *Journal of Business Venturing*, **16** (6), 595–612.

Roper, S. and N. Hewitt-Dundas (2001), 'Grant assistance and small firm development in Northern Ireland and the Republic of Ireland', *Scottish Journal of Political Economy*, **48** (1), 99–117.

Salles, P. (1999), 'L' Entreprenariat des Jevnes en France', Paris, DEFi Jevnes, November, paper prepared for the Rome Conference, available at LEED programme, Territorial Development Service, OECD, Paris.

Schmid, G., J. O'Reilly and K. Schomann (1996), 'Theory and methodology of labour market Policy and evaluation', in G. Schmid, J. O'Reilly and K. Schomann (eds), *International Handbook of Labour Market Policy and Evaluation*, Cheltenham, UK and Brookfield, USA: Edward Elgar.

Sefton, T.A.J. (2003), 'Economic evaluation in the social welfare field', *Evaluation*, **9** (1), 73–91.

Small Business Service (2000), *Small Business Statistics*, London: Department of Trade and Industry.

SMIE (2003), 'The support measures and initiatives for enterprises', available at http://europa.ell.int/comm/enterprise/smie/.

Smithson, M. (1981), 'A method for evaluating and improving goal consensus for social action programs', *Evaluation and Program Planning*, **4**, 261–71.

Storey, D.J. (2003), 'Entrepreneurship, small and medium sized enterprises and public policies', in D. Audretsch and Z. Acs (eds), *The Handbook of Entrepreneurship*, London: Kluwer, pp. 473–511.

Storey, D.J., K. Keasey, R. Watson and P. Wynarczyk (1987), *The Performance of Small Firms: Profits, Jobs and Failures*, London: Croom Helm.

Taylor, M.P. (1999), 'Survival of the fittest? An analysis of self-employment duration in Britain', *Economic Journal*, **109** (454), C140–C155.

Turok, I. and M. Raco (2000), 'Developing expertise in small and medium-sized enterprises: an evaluation of consultancy support', *Environment and Planning C*, **18** (4), 409–27.

van der Meer, F.B. (1999), 'Evaluation and the social construction of impacts', *Evaluation*, **5** (4), 387–406.

Wallsten, S.J. (2000), 'The effects of government-industry R & D programs on private R & D: the case of the Small Business Innovation Program', *RAND Journal of Economics*, **31** (1), Spring, 82–100.

Walstad, W.B. and M.L. Kourilsky (1998), 'Entrepreneurial attitudes and knowledge of black youth', *Entrepreneurship Theory and Practice*, **23** (2), 5–18.

Walstad, W.B. and M.L. Kourilsky (1999), *Seeds of Success: Entrepreneurship and Youth*, Dubuque, IA: Kendall/Hunt.

Weiss, C.H. (1999), 'The interface between evaluation and public policy', *Evaluation*, **5** (4), 468–86.

Westhead, P. (1998), 'Benefits associated with the 1994 Shell Technology Enterprise Program', *Journal of Small Business and Enterprise Development*, **5**, 60–78.

Westhead, P., D.J. Storey and F. Martin (2001), 'Outcomes reported by students who participated in the 1994 Shell Technology Enterprise Program', *Entrepreneurship and Regional Development*, **13**, 163–85.

Williams, D.R. (2004), 'Youth self-employment: its nature and consequences', *Small Business Economics*, **23**, 323–36.

Wren, C. and D.J. Storey (2002), 'Evaluating the effect of soft business support upon small firm performance', *Oxford Economic Papers – New Series*, **54** (2), 334–65.

Index

Titles of publications are in *italics*.

excludable goods 20
Exist program, Germany 48
Exist Seed program, Germany 48–9

Feldman, M. 195
finance, *see* funding
firm turnover, and economic growth 67
fiscal incentives 170; *see also* tax incentives
Flanders, R. 25
foreign markets access 167
foreign students, role in US innovation system
    173–4
framework of entrepreneurship policy
    measures 3–7, 107–8
Franklin, S. 193
Friedman, J. 189
Fritsch, M. 102, 201
Frosch, R. 32
funding
    access to 8
    early stage technology development 24–5,
        26–7, 174–7
    entrepreneurship, Bavaria 206–7
Future Bavaria Campaign 204–5

Gabr, H. 150
Galbraith, J.K. 65, 66
Gale, W.G. 55
Gartner, W.B. 96
GDP and business ownership rate 100
Germany
    entrepreneurship policy 47–50
    policy framework analysis 158
    see also Bavaria
Gerschenkron, A. 71
Global Entrepreneurship Monitor (GEM)
    81–2, 145–6
Gompers, P.A. 25–6
Good, M. 25–6
government agencies, small business and
    entrepreneurship 45
government intervention
    channels 9–11
    dangers of 60–61
    see also entrepreneurship policy; policies;
        policy areas
government production of income-elastic
    services 75
Griffing, B. 175
Grilo, I. 98
group-specific initiatives 171
growth, *see* economic growth

Hart, D.M. 101, 103, 126
health insurance deductibility 57

Hébert, R.F. 130
Henderson, R. 20
Henrekson, M. 76, 84
heroes, communication about 171
Hewitt-Dundas, N. 214
high-growth firms, data 146–7
High-tech Bavaria Campaign 205, 207
Hoffmann, A. 146, 150
holistic entrepreneurship policy 113–14
Holtz-Eakin, D. 74
household-related services and
    entrepreneurship, Sweden 75–7
Howitt, P. 67
Hsu, D.H. 28, 33
human capital and entrepreneurship policy,
    Bavaria 206
human resources and university technology
    transfer 197

imperfect appropriability 20–23
In Search of Excellence (Peters and Waterman)
    43
incentives
    disincentives of government policies 55–6
    and entrepreneurship 87, 150
    for necessity entrepreneurship 77–9
    policies affecting 169–71
    for savings in welfare state 73–5
    for university technology transfer 189, 197
income-elastic services, Sweden 75
income sources, Sweden 81
income tax, effect on entrepreneurship 56
individual entrepreneurs, support, Germany
    48–9
individual wealth formation, incentives 73–5
industry level entrepreneurship study 4
information, contracting for 23–5
information asymmetries
    and funding problems 58, 175
    and market failures 30–31
infrastructure
    for entrepreneurship 169
    lack of as challenge to entrepreneurs 25
innovation
    obstacles to 174–6
    and student trends, US 173–4
innovation gap, role of policy 25–9
innovation networks, Bavaria 208–11
innovation policy
    negative effects 56–7
    US 172–83
    see also entrepreneurship policy
innovation support as public/private
    partnership 134–5
innovation systems, Germany 49–50